Third Edition

Elementary & Middle School Social Studies

An Interdisciplinary Instructional Approach

Pamela J. Farris

Distinguished Teaching Professor
Northern Illinois University

Boston   Burr Ridge, IL   Dubuque, IA   Madison, WI   New York   San Francisco   St. Louis
Bangkok   Bogotá   Caracas   Lisbon   London   Madrid
Mexico City   Milan   New Delhi   Seoul   Singapore   Sydney   Taipei   Toronto

McGraw-Hill Higher Education

*A Division of The **McGraw-Hill** Companies*

ELEMENTARY & MIDDLE SCHOOL SOCIAL STUDIES: AN INTERDISCIPLINARY
INSTRUCTIONAL APPROACH, THIRD EDITION

Published by McGraw-Hill, an imprint of The McGraw-Hill Companies, Inc., 1221 Avenue of the Americas,
New York, NY 10020. Copyright © 2001, 1997 by The McGraw-Hill Companies, Inc. All rights reserved.
No part of this publication may be reproduced or distributed in any form or by any means, or stored in a
database or retrieval system, without the prior written consent of The McGraw-Hill Companies, Inc.,
including, but not limited to, in any network or other electronic storage or transmission, or broadcast
for distance learning.

Some ancillaries, including electronic and print components, may not be available to customers outside
the United States.

This book is printed on acid-free paper.

2 3 4 5 6 7 8 9 0 QPF/QPF 0 9 8 7 6 5 4 3 2 1

ISBN 0–07–232224–1

Vice president and editor-in-chief: *Thalia Dorwick*
Editorial director: *Jane E. Vaicunas*
Sponsoring editor: *Beth Kaufman*
Developmental editor: *Cara Harvey*
Marketing manager: *Daniel M. Loch*
Project manager: *Jill R. Peter/Jayne Klein*
Production supervisor: *Sandy Ludovissy*
Coordinator of freelance design: *Rick D. Noel*
Cover designer: *Annis Wai-Yi Leung*
Cover images: *©Charles Thatcher/Tony Stone Images; crayons,*
Photodisc: The Object Series, Moments in Life
Photo research coordinator: *John C. Leland*
Photo research: *Connie Gardner Picture Research*
Senior supplement coordinator: *David A. Welsh*
Compositor: *Shepherd, Inc.*
Typeface: *10/12 Times Roman*
Printer: *Quebecor Printing Book Group/Fairfield, PA*

Library of Congress Cataloging-in-Publication Data

Farris, Pamela J.
    Elementary and middle school social studies : an interdisciplinary instructional approach /
Pamela J. Farris.—3rd ed.
        p.   cm.
    Includes bibliographical references and indexes.
    ISBN 0–07–232224–1
    1. Social sciences—Study and teaching (Elementary)—United States. 2. Social
sciences—Study and teaching (Middle school)—United States. 3. Language experience
approach in education—United States. I. Title.

LB1584 .F37   2001
372.83'044—dc21
                                                        00–036158
                                                        CIP

www.mhhe.com

To my son, Kurtis,
who shares a love
of social studies

Brief Contents

Contents

"Let us put our minds together and see what life we can make for our children." These words of wisdom were shared by Sitting Bull with members of the U.S. Congress in the late 1800s. As elementary and middle school teachers, we have the same goal for our students, to make a better life for them. As teachers, we try to present social studies in meaningful, relevant ways.

Social studies has six basic tenets:

- Children should be actively involved in their learning.
- Children should be given opportunities to make decisions and become decision makers.
- Children need to use their previously gained knowledge and experiences as a learning scaffold.
- Children need to develop a positive self-concept in which they feel secure, effective, competent, and capable.
- Children need to develop an appreciation for the aesthetics of a subject.
- Children need to be productive, contributing citizens.

The third edition of *Elementary & Middle School Social Studies: An Interdisciplinary Instuctional Approach* was developed on the basis of these tenets.

Approach

Based on interdisciplinary instruction as its pedagogical focus, *Elementary & Middle School Social Studies: An Interdisciplinary Instructional Approach,* Third Edition, provides the "theory into practice" that preservice and inservice teachers can both understand and appreciate. Oftentimes this entails combining social studies concepts and objectives with those of other content areas; that is, geography and science, economics and math, history and language arts. The arts help students develop an appreciation for their own heritage and others.

The chapters are written by experts from their respective social science as well as elementary and middle school fields. Within the chapters are social studies activities that can be linked with other content areas for effective and efficient interdisciplinary instruction.

Organization

Chapter objectives are listed at the beginning of each chapter followed by the theoretical background in social studies and interdisciplinary instruction. National social studies standards are stressed throughout. In addition, several examples of activities for developing social studies concepts, particularly in the areas of history, geography, and civics, with lower and upper elementary as well as middle school students are included in this textbook along with several Web site addresses.

The opening chapter of the book is "Social Studies and Interdisciplinary Instruction: A Look at Social Studies." This chapter provides an overview of the social studies: anthropology, economics, geography, history, political science (civic education), and sociology. It includes current national standards and recommendations on how social studies is best taught.

Chapter 2, "Social Studies and Interdisciplinary Instruction: A Look at Interdisciplinary Instruction," provides the reader with insights into the philosophy, rationale, and goals of interdisciplinary instruction. The latter part of the chapter describes how social studies can be integrated in the elementary and middle school classroom. The end of the chapter presents an example of an interdisciplinary thematic social studies unit.

Chapter 3, "Classroom Assessment in Social Studies," presents ways of including authentic assessment in terms of rubrics, checklists, and portfolios. In addition, objectives and benchmarks for social studies instruction are discussed.

Chapter 4, "Early Childhood Social Studies," focuses on the young child's (K–2) widening awareness of the social studies environment. The chapter elaborates on how the child moves from viewing self to family to neighborhood to community to state to nation to world and finally to the universe itself. There are numerous examples of how interdisciplinary curricular activities can be used to teach basic social studies concepts.

Linking social studies and the language arts is the focus of Chapter 5, "Reading, Writing, and Discussing: Communicating in Social Studies." This chapter further elaborates on and extends the ideas presented in Chapter 4 in the grade 2–8 curriculum. The inclusion of children's literature as supportive and enriched reading material for social studies instruction is examined. Stages of the writing process and different types of writing in the social studies, such as narrative, expository (descriptive and explanatory), and persuasive, are discussed. In addition, the importance of discussion is considered along with cooperative learning.

Personalizing instruction in social studies is significant, as is activating students' prior knowledge of related concepts. Chapter 6, "Facilitating Learning through Strategic Instruction in Social Studies," examines brain research findings and other learning research as it presents a variety of ways that teachers can assist students in acquiring and extending their knowledge of social studies.

Chapter 7, "Another Time, Another Place: Bringing Social Studies to Life through Literature," explores in further depth the use of children's literature to teach history and geography. This chapter weaves the social studies curriculum with a cloth of quality children's books on geographic and historical themes. Ways of using thematic units of study in social studies instruction are shared as a means of providing choices for students so they can select areas of study in which they have a personal interest.

Chapter 8, "Geography: Exploring the Whole World through Interdisciplinary Instruction," includes the geography for life standards and provides numerous examples of literature-based instruction of geography skills and strategies.

Active participation is essential in political science and civic education. Chapter 9, "Civic Education in a Democratic Society," discusses democratic ideals and core values of a democratic society. Character education is also examined in this chapter.

"Economics Education: Ways and Means" is the title of Chapter 10. This portion of the textbook includes an overview of economic concepts and two thematic units of study.

Personalizing instruction is further examined in Chapter 11, "Drama in the Social Studies: Gateway to the Past, Pathway to the Future." Ways teachers can use drama as "living history" lessons are presented as the chapter points out how social studies develops children's attitudes, values, and perspectives. By combining drama and social studies, the aesthetic is awakened in students and becomes part of their vision of social studies.

Interdisciplinary instruction must include the arts. Chapter 12, "Social Studies and the Arts: From Inner Journeys to Faraway Lands," shares ways music and the visual arts can be incorporated as a part of social studies instruction. In addition, social studies instruction is tied to the Multiple Intelligences.

Students with attention deficit disorder (ADD) and learning disabilities (LD) typically have difficulty acquiring many social studies concepts. Chapter 13, "Social Studies for All Learners," explains how an interdisciplinary approach to teaching social studies instruction can be used successfully with all children.

Our students live in a technological world. Certainly technology has become important in the teaching of social studies. This is examined in Chapter 14, "Automation, Innovation, Participation: Infusing Technology into the Social Studies."

Community is the focus of Chapter 15, "It All Depends on Your Point of View: Multicultural Education in the Social Studies." This chapter describes how children develop prejudices and the role of the classroom teacher in helping students to accept other cultures and beliefs.

The last chapter is entitled "Social Studies, Bilingualism, Respect, and Understanding: Making the Connections." This chapter discusses cultural awareness including specifically Hispanic children as well as the complex diversity within Asian and Pacific American communities. The chapter provides a vast array of integrated social studies activities for bilingual students whose first language is not English.

Features

Elementary & Middle School Social Studies: An Interdisciplinary Instructional Approach, Third Edition, offers several practical aspects for the preservice and inservice teacher including:

- *Focus Boxes* that take a closer look at important topics
- *In the Classroom Mini Lesson* boxes that present lesson ideas that can be used in the classroom
- Annotated, comprehensive lists of children's literature
- Developmentally appropriate activities featuring the six primary social sciences
- Actual children's work demonstrates instructional outcomes
- An emphasis on social studies standards throughout the text
- Teacher resources at the end of each chapter
- An Instructor's Manual with suggested class activities, discussion questions, resources, Web sites, and test items

Such features make this a book that serves as both an instructional tool and a teaching resource.

New to This Edition

This edition focuses on teaching the social studies via an interdisciplinary approach—a pedagogical change from the last edition. Other changes and additions include the following:

- *New Chapter* featuring the arts and social studies—coverage requested by the reviewers of the text
- Activities based on brain research as well as the Multiple Intelligences
- Web sites for student and teacher use
- Instructor resources to supplement instruction

The third edition offers the shared belief of seventeen elementary and middle school educators that social studies instruction can be enriched by interdisciplinary instruction. Through such instruction students will develop and maintain a lifelong interest in social studies that will result in their making positive contributions as responsible citizens in our democratic society. This edition has been expanded to include numerous examples of interdisciplinary instruction. More lessons and unit plans for middle school instruction have been included.

Acknowledgments

At this point I would like to thank the various authors, all of whom who were selected on the basis of their expertise:

Martha Brady, Northern Arizona University
Richard A. Fluck, Northern Illinois University
Carol J. Fuhler, Iowa State University
Mary Louise Ginejko, Samuel Gompers Junior High, Joliet, IL
Marjorie R. Hancock, Kansas State University
Kenneth King, Northern Illinois University
Bonnie L. Kuhrt, Carl Sandburg Middle School, Rolling Meadows, IL
Steven L. Layne, Butler Junior High School, Oak Brook, IL
Lisa M. Mehlig, Northern Illinois University
Pamela A. Nelson, Dominican University
Jill Scott-Cole, Henry-Senachwine Elementary School, Henry, IL
Carla Cooper Shaw, Northern Illinois University
L. Ruth Stryuk, Northern Illinois University
Billie Jo Thomas, Northern Illinois University
Maria P. Walther, Gwendolyn Brooks Elementary School, Aurora, IL
Terry Whealon, Northern Illinois University

On behalf of all the chapter authors, we would like to gratefully acknowledge the significant assistance and encouragement we received from preservice and inservice teachers. Many of the ideas presented in this book either came from their suggestions or were field tested in their classrooms. For this, we are indebted to them.

I am greatly appreciative of the assistance and encouragement offered by my editors, Beth Kaufman and Cara Harvey. In addition, I'd like to thank Jill Peter and Jayne Klein, project managers. I'd also like to thank Dawn and Greg Farris who assisted in the word processing of this edition.

Having a large number of authors requires substantial assistance and review. I would like to thank the following individuals who served as reviewers of the manuscript. Their insights, suggestions, and honest critical comments have greatly improved this edition of the book.

Sarah Caldwell, Fort Valley State University
Sharon Y. Cowan, East Central University
Helen L. Felber, University of Massachusetts, Dartmouth
Duane M. Giannangelo, The University of Memphis
Robert E. Kirschmann, University of Bridgeport
Timothy Lewis Heaton, Cedarville College
Judith Ann Mitchell, Kennesaw State University
Tonja L. Root, Valdosta State University
Kenneth C. Schmidt, University of Wisconsin, Eau Claire
Jerry Weiner, Kean University
Dan A. White, Abilene Christian University

Certainly it takes lots of effort and encouragement from the home front for a book to come to fruition. To my husband and son goes my deepest gratitude for their support.

The social studies have always been a true love of mine. Reading historical fiction as a child opened my eyes to the lives and times of other people and cultures as I read of the Middle Ages, the Civil War, and Westward Expansion. Biographies enabled me to learn of heroes and heroines of our past. For instance, I learned of the deeds of Crispus Attucks, Paul Revere, George Washington, and Abigail Adams during the Revolutionary War.

As an adult I can remember well those teachers who went beyond the realm of social studies to put things in what is now referred to as *interdisciplinary instruction*. They made social studies come alive for me. The field trip to the canal that was once part of the Erie Canal system. The seventh-grade teacher who ran across the room wielding a yardstick, jumping on a chair and then his desk, shouting, "Charge!" as we envisioned Teddy Roosevelt leading his men up San Juan Hill. The music teacher who shared the background of such songs as "America, the Beautiful" and "Red River Valley" as well as pointing out that as history changes, so does music. The construction of relief maps. The oral reports on political leaders and then having a U.S. senator come to our school. The sharing of current events and how they affected our lives in our small midwestern town. All of these events and much more have made me love social studies.

By weaving a web of social studies and other content areas, teachers can pique the interests of students and motivate them to better understand and accept their world and other cultures. It is by linking social studies and interdisciplinary instruction that this can best be accomplished.

Pamela J. Farris
Distinguished Teaching Professor
Northern Illinois University

Elementary & Middle School Social Studies

Chapter 1

Social Studies and Interdisciplinary Instruction

A Look at Social Studies

Pamela J. Farris and Terry Whealon
Northern Illinois University

Social studies should be the study of how citizens in a society make personal and public decisions on issues that affect their destiny.

—*Jeffrey Linn*
"Whole Language in Social Studies"

Objectives

———————————————————◦∿◦———————————————————

Readers will

- be aware of the six social sciences that make up social studies (anthropology, economics, history, geography, political science/civics, and sociology);
- be aware of the skills of a citizen actor;
- discover how the social sciences can be integrated for instruction;
- be aware of the steps in teaching social studies as a decision making process; and
- be aware of the national curriculum standards for social studies instruction.

Introduction

The fresh smells of a new school year permeate the air—newly waxed floors, freshly painted rooms, chalk on the chalkrail. Marty Hammond's first graders are already engaged in learning an economic lesson about corn. On the first day of school Marty, a teacher in rural Illinois, asked her students several questions about their interests, what they liked, and what they didn't like. When she asked what their favorite food was, most of the children responded, "Sweet corn." She wasn't surprised because sweet corn is a common favorite; it is locally grown and very plentiful during August and September. Marty decided that since her students liked to eat sweet corn, she would take the opportunity to use corn as a social studies lesson.

Marty found several picture books about corn and maize that she read to her students. They talked about the importance of corn. Afterward, they drew pictures about corn: planting, tending, and harvesting. During the first week of school, the class went to a nearby grocery store and purchased sweet corn. They cooked the corn in a big pot on a portable electric burner in their classroom and ate it for lunch. The next day, a farmer who grows sweet corn visited the class and brought some cornstalks with him. He told the students about how he tills the soil and plants the corn and explained the measures he takes to prevent soil erosion. He showed pictures of the harvesting equipment used to pick sweet corn. The farmer also talked about how the corn must be harvested at just the right time so that the kernels don't get too hard for people to eat. He told the students that corn must be eaten soon after it is picked or it will spoil. If the corn doesn't quickly reach the people who buy it or the factories that can it, the farmer loses money. The following day the first graders toured a local factory that cans corn and peas. Later, the class will visit a farm that is harvesting corn for livestock feed. In the spring, Marty's class will plant corn in a small garden plot on the school playground.

Another teacher, John Salter, and his fourth-grade teaching partner, Sue Kissinger, devoted several weeks of their summer vacation to putting together their social studies units for the year. In addition to covering the exploration and development of the United States, they plan to focus on four major cultural studies during the year: African Americans, Asians, Jewish people, and Native Americans.

Beginning the year, John shares children's literature about Native Americans with his students. His students read and discuss Lynne Cherry's (1992) *A River Ran Wild,* a picture book about how the Nashua Indians respected nature and the environment. Through reading and talking about the book, students gain a better understanding of the anthropological and ecological history of the Nashua River Valley in what is now lower New Hampshire and upper Massachusetts. Other picture books are also available for the students to read; for instance, Rafe Martin's (1992) *The Rough-Face Girl,* which is the Algonquin Indian version of Cinderella, or *The First Strawberry: A Cherokee Story* (Bruchac 1993), the creation story of how the first woman became angry with her husband but forgave him upon discovering strawberries. In addition, each student selects one of three historical novels about Native Americans: Jean Fritz's (1983) *The Double Life of Pocahontas,* Paul Goble's (1990) *Dream Wolf,* or Scott O'Dell's (1988) *Black Star, Bright Dawn.* Each student reads the chosen book and writes about his or her reaction in a literature response journal. Every day, the students give their journals to John, who reads the journals and writes comments and questions for the students to read and react to. In addition, students discuss the books with peers who are reading the same selection.

One of the activities students engage in is making their own buffalo robe stories. This project gets students to think about the importance of their own lives and interests. The students cut brown paper grocery bags into ten-inch strips, soak the strips a few minutes in water before wadding them into balls to give them a leathery look, then stretch them out on the table to dry. The next day, each student uses crayons or felt-tipped markers to draw four major events, one from each of the last four years of his or her life. While the students work, a CD of Native American songs plays in the background. After all the stories are finished, the students sit Indian fashion around an unlit campfire made of sticks found on the playground during recess. The students then share the stories behind each picture on their buffalo robes. This enables the students and John to get to know one another better.

In addition to the picture books and novel studies, John has selected Gary Paulsen's (1988) *Dogsong* to read aloud to his students, while Sue has chosen Ken Kesey's (1991) *The Sea Lion* to read aloud to her students. Both teachers have elected to use Virginia Sneve's (1989) *Dancing Teepees: Poems of American Indian Youth* to incorporate poetry and dance into their unit.

Sue teaches in the classroom next to John's. Since the school has a limited number of books for each unit, their classes will take turns studying the different cultures. While John's class starts with Native Americans, Sue's begins with Asian culture. Sue opens her unit by reading to her class a Korean folktale, *The Sun Girl and the Moon Boy* (Choi 1997), which is similar to Little Red Riding Hood. Her students will read Momoko Ishii's (1987) *The Tongue-Cut Sparrow* (translated by Katherine Paterson), a Japanese folktale about a kind old man and his greedy wife, as a class discussion book. They will also read *El Chino* (Say 1990), a true story of a Chinese boy who became a famous bullfighter, and *The Land I Lost* (Nhuong 1982), which depicts daily life in Vietnam prior to the Vietnam War. Students with limited reading skills read *Water Buffalo Days: Growing Up in Vietnam* (Nhuong 1997), a true story of adventure and excitement of growing up in a rural Vietnamese village. Sue has chosen *How the Ox Star Fell from Heaven* (Hong 1991) to read aloud because it is one of her favorite stories. Members of the Asian community come to speak to her class about their countries' customs and traditions.

In another state, Patricia Johnson's fifth graders incorporate technology and literature with their study of World War II. Using social studies textbooks as a reference, Patricia branches out, requiring all students to read *Snow Treasure* (McSwigan 1942), a story of how courageous Norwegian children hid gold bars from the German army during the occupation of Norway. For most of her students, this is a quick read. As they read, they write their reactions to the book in journals, which they then share in a grand conversation at the beginning of social studies class. Upon the conclusion of *Snow Treasure,* about five days of reading homework, Patricia lets her students select another novel to read as part of a literature circle group. The choices include *Lily's Crossing* by Patricia Reilly Giff (1997), a story about a British girl and a Hungarian boy who live through the bombing of England; *Number the Stars,* the Newbery Medal book by Lois Lowry (1989) that depicts how a family hides a Jewish girl and smuggles her family out of Denmark to Sweden; *Under the Blood Red Sun* by Graham Sailsbury (1995), a book for above-average readers about Tomi, a Japanese boy who witnesses Pearl Harbor and must help his family when his fisherman father is sent to an internment camp in Texas; and *Stones in Water* by Donna Jo Napoli (1998), about a group of Italian boys who attend a movie in Italy during World War II only to be kidnapped by the Nazis and used for forced labor. Students get into small groups to discuss the books as well as to identify historical events and concepts.

Patricia is fortunate as her classroom is equipped with four computers wired for the Internet. As a reference, students can get an overview of World War II from the Eyewitness CD-ROM *History of the World 2.0* (Dorling Kindersley 1998). The literature groups also seek out information on their respective geographical settings (i.e., Great Britain, Denmark, Sweden, and Hawaii).

Students may then check the World Wide Web for sites. Patricia gives the students a list with which they must start.

Web Sites for World War II
Holocaust Sites

http://www.altavista.digital.com/cgbin/query?pg=q&what=web&fmtz&q=RESCUERS
   This site gives information on individuals who helped save Jews from the Holocaust.
http://yvs.shani.net/
   This is the location for the United States Holocaust Museum.
http://www.channels.no/AnneFran.html
   This is the location of the Anne Frank House in Amsterdam.

Japanese Internment Sites

http://www.geocities.com/Athens/8420/camps.html
   Students can discover locations of various sites where Japanese were taken during World War II at this site.
http://www.he.net/-sparker/cranes.html
   This is the Cranes for Peace Site, a good accompaniment for the book *Sadako and a Thousand Paper Cranes* (Coerr 1979). Sadako is the young girl who died of leukemia as a result of the atomic bombing of her city.

Patricia has each literature circle group make a class presentation at the end of the unit. Each student contributes to a written report and the group project. Group projects may be a drama, diorama, or collage depicting an important scene in the book, a character chart comparing the attributes of the primary characters, an illustration of the sequence of the story, a museum exhibit, or other creative endeavor that the students propose and Patricia approves in advance. As a culminating activity, the students do origami and make paper cranes.

Tim Lamphere, a middle school teacher, also likes to use an interdisciplinary approach with units. Like those teachers depicted previously, Tim believes that through reading historical novels and nonfiction children's literature, students develop empathy for and a better understanding of the people, places, and events they study. In addition, Tim has discovered that students maintain a higher degree of interest in social studies when he uses children's literature to teach social studies. This allows students to become more personally involved with social studies because they can discuss or write about their own reactions to different events or aspects of social studies. He tries to incorporate the arts and science whenever possible. This is an interdisciplinary approach to the elementary curriculum as the instruction is integrated with different content area concepts being presented. Interdisciplinary instruction necessitates that the teacher plan well, be organized, and rely on meaningful, relevant materials for instruction.

Tim Lamphere's seventh graders never quite know what to expect. The one thing they do know is that social studies class will be interesting. During the spring semester, Tim brought in firewood and made a campfire (unlit, of course), in the center of the classroom. With the desks pushed back and students seated on the floor around him, Tim beat on a drum as he shared the following:

The Spring

Behold, my brothers (and sisters), the spring has come; the earth has received the embrace of the sun and we shall soon see the results of that love!

Every seed is awakened and so has all animal life. It is through this mysterious power that we too have our being and therefore yield to our neighbors, even our animal neighbors, the same right as ourselves, to inhabit this land.

–Sitting Bull, Tatanka Yotanka,
Hunkpapa Sioux, Lakota
(From Neil Philip [Ed.]. 1997. In a Sacred Manner I Live:
Native American Wisdom. *New York: Clarion Books.)*

Next, Tim read a Native American tale, *The Rough-Face Girl,* an Algonquin tale retold by Rafe Martin (1992). The students discussed how this story was similar to the traditional Cinderella. Then Tim had his students take turns reading *Many Nations: An Alphabet of Native America* by Joseph Bruchac (1997), which gives a brief description about one aspect of the culture of various American Indian tribes. This was followed by having the students listen to Chief Lelooska narrate Kwakiutl tales courtesy of the CD to the accompanying picture book, *Echoes of the Elders: The Stories and Paintings of Chief Lelooska* (Chief Lelooska 1997). Next Tim shared poetry and short stories from *The Serpent's Tongue* (Wood 1997) and *Lasting Echoes: An Oral History of Native American People* (Bruchac 1997). To change the pace and still keep his students interested, Tim had the students sit in a circle and hand each student a large handkerchief to use as a blindfold. One student was selected to be the "eagle" to silently capture the prey and escape; in other words, to retrieve a set of keys (placed in the center of the circle) and leave the circle. The barefooted "eagle" deftly grasped the keys and noiselessly escaped from the circle. The next student chosen to be the "eagle" wasn't so successful; the keys jingled as he picked them up and the blindfolded students quickly pointed him out. This Sioux game proved to be an excellent listening activity for the middle schoolers.

After putting the students in groups of three, Tim took his class to the library to research tribes. During their time in the computer lab, the students searched for Web sites to locate additional information. For a reading activity, the class read two books. The first was *Trouble's Daughter: The Story of Susanna Hutchinson, Indian Captive* (Kirkpatrick 1998), a novel based on the true story. In 1643, Susanna's family lived in the wilderness near Long Island Sound during a period when the Dutch settlers and the native tribes were at war. Lenape warriors, an Algonquin-speaking tribe that later became known as the Delaware Indians, attacked the farm, massacring Susanna's family and taking nine-year-old Susanna captive. The Lenape tribe adopts her. Susanna learns the tribe's ways but never forgets her family. A few years later, Susanna is traded back to Dutch family members as part of a treaty agreement. Patricia McKissack's (1997) *Run Away Home,* the story of an Apache boy named Sky who escapes from a train taking him to the reservation. Sarah, a black girl, and her mother nurse Sky back to health after he contracts swamp fever. When the White Supremacist Knights of the Southern Order try to force Sarah's family off their farm, Sky helps fight them off.

The class was assigned to read four chapters each night. The following day, the students engaged in a lively conversation about the portion of the book they had read.

Children get a better understanding of what life is like for other people by studying different cultures from throughout the world.

© Lawrence Migdale

Tim noted the comments made by various students on a legal pad on his clipboard. Tim gave the students in his class who had reading difficulties audiotapes of the book that had been recorded earlier by a volunteer parent. Following the twenty minutes of discussion, the students worked in their groups on their reports and projects. Three weeks after the unit begun, the students shared their reports and projects with the class.

ᐧᐧ Teaching Social Studies

When children enter school they bring with them a wealth of knowledge that they have gleaned through informal schooling. They have likes and dislikes, opinions, and beliefs. Research about learning suggests that the "kinds and amounts of knowledge one has before encountering a given topic (i.e., the state of Michigan) in a discipline (i.e., social studies) affect how one component skills, or exhaustiveness; it is an issue of depth, interconnectedness, and access" (Leinhardt 1992, 21).

Learning is largely social in nature. Children learn from others: parents, siblings, relatives, friends, and other significant individuals in their lives. Thus, social studies instruction naturally lends itself to an integrated curriculum based on the personal and social aspects of learning. Social studies is more than a collection of facts for children to memorize; it is an understanding of how people, places, and events came about and how people can relate and respond to each other's needs and desires, as well as how to develop respect for different viewpoints and cultural beliefs. In short, social studies is the study of cultural, economic, geographic, and political aspects of past, current, and future societies. In 1994, the National Council for the Social Studies (NCSS) developed new standards for teaching the social studies. Through ten themes, social studies are taught in an integrated approach (see Focus Box 1.1).

1.1   *Focus Box*

Ten Themes for Social Studies, K–12

The National Council for the Social Studies (1994) has adopted the following ten themes of study for social studies instruction in kindergarten through grade 12. The themes are interrelated and draw from all the social sciences and related fields of scholarly study.

1. **Culture.** Human beings create, learn, and adapt culture. Human cultures are dynamic systems of beliefs, values, and traditions that exhibit both commonalities and differences. Understanding culture helps us understand ourselves and others.

2. **Time, Continuity, and Change.** Human beings seek to understand our historic roots and to locate ourselves in time. Such understanding involves knowing what things were like in the past and how things change and develop—allowing us to develop historical perspective and answer important questions about our current condition.

3. **People, Places, and Environments.** Technological advancement has ensured that students are aware of the world beyond their personal locations. As students study content related to this theme, they create their spatial views and geographic perspectives of the world; social, cultural, economic, and civic demands mean that students will need such knowledge, skill, and understanding to make informed and critical decisions about the relationships between humans and our environment.

4. **Individual Development and Identity.** Personal identity is shaped by one's culture, by groups, and by institutional influences. Examination of various forms of human behavior enhances understanding of the relationships between social norms and emerging personal identities, the social processes that influence identity formation, and the ethical principles underlying individual action.

5. **Individuals, Groups, and Institutions.** Institutions exert enormous influence over us. Institutions are organizational embodiments to further the core social values of those who comprise them. It is important for students to know how institutions are formed, what controls and influences them, how they control and influence individuals and culture, and how institutions can be maintained or changed.

6. **Power, Authority, and Governance.** Understanding of the historical development of structures of power, authority, and governance and their evolving functions in contemporary society is essential for the emergence of civic competence.

7. **Production, Distribution, and Consumption.** Decisions about exchange, trade, and economic policy and well-being are global in scope, and the role of government in policy making varies over time and from place to place. The systematic study of an interdependent world economy and the role of technology in economic decision making is essential.

8. **Science, Technology, and Society.** Technology is as old as the first crude tool invented by prehistoric humans, and modern life as we know it would be impossible without technology and the science that supports it. Today's technology forms the basis for some of our most difficult social choices.

9. **Global Connections.** The realities of global interdependence require understanding of the increasingly important and diverse global connections among world societies before there can be analysis leading to the development of possible solutions to persisting and emerging global issues.

10. **Civic Ideals and Practices.** All people have a stake in examining civic ideals and practices across time and in diverse societies, and a stake in determining how to close the gap between present practices and the ideals on which our democratic republic is based. An understanding of civic ideals and practices of citizenship is critical to full participation in society.

From: National Council for the Social Studies. 1994. *Curriculum Standards for Social Studies: Expectations of Excellence.* Washington, DC: National Council for the Social Studies. © National Council for the Social Studies. Reprinted by permission.

Social studies at the elementary and middle school levels is usually taught by means of an integrated approach that combines two or more of the social sciences for instructional purpose. The instructional emphasis for elementary and middle school students is on teaching history, geography, and civics as the three core pillars of social studies instruction in elementary and middle school. This chapter focuses on social studies instruction and the introduction of the six social sciences.

The Social Sciences

To integrate the social sciences fully, it is important that the teacher understand each of the six social sciences (anthropology, economics, history, geography, political science/civics, and sociology), which constitute social studies at the elementary and middle school levels. Each of these is described in this section.

Anthropology

Anthropology is the field of study concerned with the discovery of what people were like from earliest existence. Considered as part of this study are the how, what, and why people change over the years. Typically, an anthropologist conducts an on-site study. That is, an anthropologist actually visits and investigates the locale where the people lived or continue to live. This kind of research enables the anthropologist to better understand and appreciate the people and their culture by living with them and recording their actions and comments.

The two primary branches of anthropology are physical and cultural. *Physical anthropology* is the study of the physical aspects of humankind. Archaeology deals with the gathering of information about human cultures by "excavation of sites of former human habitations—ancient dwellings, monuments, objects of art, tools, weapons, and other human works covered over by the soil of time" (Pelto and Muessig 1980, 2). *Cultural anthropology* is concerned with the different types of human behavior, past, and present, found throughout the world (Allen and Stevens 1998).

Some basic premises of anthropology are as follows:

1. Culture is a total way of life, not just a superficial set of customs. It largely shapes how we feel, behave, and perceive as we adapt to our world.
2. Every cultural system is an interconnected series of ideas and patterns for behavior in which changes in one aspect generally lead to changes in other segments of the system.
3. Every human cultural system is logical and coherent in its own terms, given the basic assumption and knowledge available to the given community.
4. Study of almost any behavior and beliefs among nonmodern peoples, no matter how unusual, is of direct relevance to understanding our own culture. Humans everywhere shape their beliefs and behaviors in response to the same fundamental human problems.
5. Many traditional cultural practices and beliefs that once seemed quaint and outmoded have been found to have a pragmatic basis.

6. Individuals differ from one another in attitudes, information, skills, culturally values resources, and other attributes.
7. Although the people of the world may be roughly and arbitrarily categorized into major population groups, based on a very limited number of physical characteristics, there are no "pure races" and there never have been (Pelto and Muessig 1980).

Culture is a significant factor in anthropology. Thus anthropologists study a people's contributions in terms of language, music, art, literature, religion, law, and so on. Artifacts, such as cooking utensils and weapons, also provide insight into a people's culture. Anthropologists analyze the data, then compare and contrast the culture with other cultures either of the same time period or throughout the ages.

Economics

Economics is the field of study concerned with the production, distribution, exchange, and consumption of products. An economist analyzes these four concepts and suggests ways to improve the distribution or production of various products or the economy in general. These basic concepts can be readily taught to elementary and middle school students. For instance, first or second graders can analyze *production* as they compare the goods and services provided by businesses in their community. They might visit a local manufacturer of mattresses, hot dogs, or yarn. The product doesn't matter; it needs to be some type of goods. Students could observe a service business by visiting a fast-food restaurant or a pizza parlor and watching how hamburgers or pizzas are made or by going to a local print shop and observing brochures being printed to promote sales of an upcoming event.

In a unit on the *distribution* of products third and fourth graders can study how goods and services are made available to consumers through advertising, selling, and shipping. For instance, they might visit a local shoe store to learn how the manager selects and orders sneakers and how the sneakers are shipped. By looking through newspapers and magazines and watching television advertisements, the students can compare how sneakers are promoted.

The third topic of economics, *exchange,* involves the study of money. Although this topic is introduced in kindergarten, it is typically studied in depth in the first through fourth grades. A visit to a local bank after a class discussion about currency and how checks and credit cards are used for exchange is an appropriate activity for this topic.

It is important for children to understand that *consumption* is determined by the needs and wants of the buyer. In addition, older children need to become familiar with federal and state agencies that protect the buyer from fraud or other illegal acts. For instance, most children are familiar with the FBI warning on videotapes that prohibits the duplication of copyrighted movies.

History

History is the study of how people lived in the past. This may include how people lived in the local community, the United States, or the world. The National Center

Firsthand experiences with elements from different historical periods enable children to better understand and appreciate other cultures and other times.

© Lawrence Migdale

for History in the Schools (1994, 29–30) suggests the following eight topics for study based on the National Standards:

1. Family life now and in the the recent past; family life in various places long ago.
2. History of students' local community and how communities in North America varied long ago.
3. The people, events, problems, and ideas that created the history of their state.
4. How democratic values came to be, and how they have been exemplified by people, events, and symbols.
5. The causes and nature of various movements of large groups of people into and within the United States, now and long ago.
6. Regional folklore and cultural contributions that helped to form our national heritage.
7. Selected attributes and historical developments of various societies in Africa, the Americas, Asia, and Europe.
8. Major discoveries in science and technology, their social and economic effects, and the scientists and inventors from many groups and religions responsible for them.

According to the National Assessment of Educational Progress (NAEP) (U.S. Department of Education, 1994, 18), students in grades 4 to 8 are to study the following four major historical themes across eight chronological periods of time:

1. *Change and continuity in American democracy.* This includes the basic premises on which the Declaration of Independence is founded, the U.S. Constitution, the Bill of Rights, slavery, the reasons for major wars (i.e., Civil War, World War I, and World War II), and civil rights.

2. *The gathering and interactions of peoples, cultures, and ideas.* How contributions of many peoples and cultures from different countries, races, and religious customs and beliefs have resulted in the heritage and development of society in America.

3. *Economic and technological changes and their relation to society, ideas, and the environment.* This considers the major changes in America that transformed it from an agrarian society to an industrial leader to the bellwether nation in technological innovations and how those changes impacted society, ideas, and the environment.

4. *The changing role of America in the world.* This theme considers how America was initially an isolated country that was primarily self-sufficient to how today it depends on resources and goods from other nations. The relationship of geography, interests, and ideals as they pertain to foreign policy are examined.

The preceding themes are to be studied by fourth through eight graders in the context of eight periods of U.S. history:

Years	Period Addressed
Beginnings to 1607	Three Worlds and Their Meeting in the Americas
1607–1763	Colonization, Settlement, and Communities
1763–1815	The Revolution and the New Nation
1801–1861	Expansion and Reform
1850–1877	Crisis of the Union: Civil War and Reconstruction
1865–1920	The Development of Modern America
1914–1945	Modern America and the World Wars
1945–present day	Contemporary America

Teachers encourage fourth- through eighth-grade students to be aware of the *chronology of historical events* as well as to dig through historical facts and information to discover why events took place. This is known as *historical inquiry.* Understanding why things happen helps students to develop critical thinking skills as they create hypotheses for the reasons behind social movements, wars, and so on. Often students must weigh the evidence on its own merits. For example, the Potato Famine in the mid-1800s in Ireland resulted in millions of deaths among the lower-class citizens and the immigration of masses of Irish to the United States. Potatoes were the staple food of the lower classes and when a blight caused the potatoes to rot, millions of Irish starved. Yet, there was an ample amount of food in the country to meet the needs of all of its people. Why did Ireland's neighbor, Great Britain, fail to send aid to help the Irish? By reading and uncovering the facts, students gain insights on the plight of the Irish during the late 1840s and early 1850s. Many wealthy Irish were large landowners who were afraid to give food to their starving tenant farmers for fear that other landowners would disapprove or that the large number of lower classes would cause a rebellion. Since Ireland was predominately Catholic, British politicians virtually ignored the situation, as they were members of the Church of England and were Protestants. Only one ship with aid was ever sent from Great Britain to Ireland during the Potato Famine; that was organized by a British charity group.

Through social interaction, children learn not only about their immediate world, but about the global society as well.

© Lawrence Migdale

There are other aspects of historical inquiry that upper-elementary and middle school students could investigate rather than the result of wars, famines, and natural disasters. For instance, students could compare major breakthroughs or inventions in medical science that have taken place as a result of wars (examples: triage from the Vietnam War, plasma during World War II, nurses at battlefield sites from the Civil War). Or perhaps they might consider the development of specific weaponry (examples: aircraft carriers during World War II, targeted missiles during the Persian Gulf War, minefields in the Kosovo War).

Geography

Geography is the study of the earth, including its features and the distribution of its human inhabitants and other life. Children should become familiar with five geography themes: location, place, relationships within places, movement, and regions (Joint Committee on Geographic Education 1984). Children are first introduced to these topics in terms of their own homes and neighborhoods.

The first geography theme, that of *location,* describes where specific places or points are on a map or on the earth's surface. It also describes the relationship between places—for example, the number of miles between San Diego and Phoenix.

The second theme, that of *place,* describes the unique or distinct characteristics of a place. This includes both physical and human characteristics. For instance, the flat land and fertile soil of the prairies of Illinois and Iowa allow for the production of large corn and soybean crops. On the other hand, the cool summers and acid soil of Maine provide the perfect combination for growing blueberries.

The third geography theme, *relationships within places,* describes how people react to their environment and the changes they may make. Examples include preserving the wood owl by not cutting down a forest of trees for lumber and not allowing a company to build a plant on a river that would pollute the water and kill the fish.

Movement is the fourth geography theme. In a highly mobile society such as ours, movement is a very important topic in that it characterizes how people travel from place to place, how they communicate with each other, and how they depend on products (such as oil from the Middle East and auto parts made in Mexico) and information from other areas.

The last geographic theme, that of *regions,* involves categorizing areas according to their features: climate, landform, land use, natural vegetation, culture, and so forth. For instance, the Midwest is the biggest beef-producing region in the United States, and the South is the largest producer of tobacco in the world.

A geographic activity for third graders might be to have them visit a state park and make a map of the park. They could indicate where the people stay (in the park lodge) and eat (in the park restaurant) as well as illustrate the hills and meadows. Major hiking trails could be depicted along with paved roads.

Political Science—Civics Education

Political science, also referred to as civics, is the study of how people govern themselves. It includes the analysis of governing institutions, processes, and laws. The structure of government and the responsibilities and duties of elected and appointed government officials are all part of political science.

In elementary schools, the examination of the political system is important so that children gain an understanding of how government works. By creating a democratic classroom that allows for open discussion of issues and voting on those issues, the teacher can begin to set the stage for the students to become active participants in the democratic process. Later, such involvement will lead to active and concerned citizenship.

Upper-elementary and middle school students need to develop a coherent and consistent set of values, particularly those contained in the political documents (e.g., U.S. Constitution, Declaration of Independence, and the Bill of Rights) that frame the values, beliefs, and ethical principles to which this nation adheres. Some educators are opposed to any overt involvement of students with value-related issues. "Efforts to protect students from serious value-related issues are counterproductive, as this forces them to look elsewhere for answers to serious questions" (Allen and Stevens 1998, 32).

A good yearlong political science activity is to create a self-governing board of the class. Members of the class should be elected to the governing board. Whenever disciplinary or other problems arise, the board can hold a hearing on the case and make a judgment. This may be as simple as a decision to request pizza be served more frequently in the cafeteria or that measures be taken to recycle used paper in the classroom.

Sociology

Sociology is the study of humans and their interactions in groups. Groups may be as small as a nuclear family or as large as the AFL-CIO union or the Catholic Church. Sociologists look for common values and beliefs. Unlike the *field study* of anthropologists, sociologists tend to conduct *case studies* of either individuals or a group over a period of time. A case study usually consists of information pertaining to the daily routine of the individuals or the group.

For children, the study of sociology may begin with the study of families, followed by the study of neighborhoods and communities, and on to the study of larger groups. Sociology also involves the study of people from different cultures.

❧ Integrating the Social Sciences

At the elementary and middle school level, the six social sciences can be integrated as a unit of study. The social sciences are listed in Table 1.1 along with the examples of questions social scientists from each of these six areas of study would ask about the Civil War. Particular consideration during instruction should be devoted to historical, geographical, and political/civic events prior to, during, and after the Civil War.

The classroom teacher should incorporate all the social sciences in social studies instruction because all are important in a democratic society. "Schools are a microcosm of global society. Within a country like the U.S. that is so culturally and linguistically diverse, the need for intergroup knowledge, understanding, and respect is critical" (Bieger 1996, 308). In addition, it is crucial that the teacher create a classroom environment that will help students become good citizens.

Students need to realize that the social studies are often intertwined with other content areas such as science. Consider the evolution of transportation and the technology to move goods and people. When explorer Louis Joliet and missionary priest Pierre Marquette were sent by the Governor of New France (now Canada) to verify that the Mississippi River did indeed flow south, they made an observation that changed the course of history. Joliet and Marquette believed if the Illinois and DesPlaines Rivers could be connected by a canal, it would make a continuous route between the Mississippi River and the Great Lakes. One hundred fifty years later, the canal was built. It would impact all the social sciences—anthropology, economics, geography, history, political science, and sociology. A young politician named Abraham Lincoln supported the idea because anyone with a boat and toll money would gain from the canal's construction. In a political move, Congress moved the border between Illinois and Wisconsin north in 1818 so that the canal wouldn't be bogged down in political differences. The Illinois and Michigan (I&M) Canal opened in 1848 at a cost of $6.4 million—an expense that nearly bankrupted the State of Illinois. But in the five years following its opening, Chicago's population increased by over 400 percent. Towns sprung up along the 97 miles of banks of the I&M canal, each adding to the culture of the Midwest.

Similarly, it is important for students to become familiar with the world through global education. Increasingly, what happens in another part of the world has an impact on the United States. For instance, in 1998, the economic decline in Asia and Brazil caused the U.S. and European stock markets to falter.

Students need to learn about other continents, nations, and cultures. Consider that many elementary students believe that Africa is a country like France or Mexico. It is difficult for some students to fathom that Africa has fifty-three countries, each of which is quite unique. From a geographical standpoint, the immense size of Africa is difficult to comprehend. The area of China, Europe, and the United States could all fit at the same time within the African continent (Johnston, Smith and Brown 1998). Such understandings are essential for students to become responsible citizens.

TABLE 1.1

The Social Sciences That Constitute Elementary Social Studies

Social Science	Definition	Type of Question Asked About the Civil War
Anthropology *Culture*	The study of human beings in terms of race, culture, physical characteristics, and environmental and social relations	What type of medical care was provided to wounded soldiers? How did the ratio of whites to African Americans differ between the North and the South? How did the two armies use African Americans during the war?
Economics	The study of the production, distribution, exchange, and consumption of goods and services	What were the primary products of the North? Of the South? Why was it important to the South to sell goods to England? What kind of bartering occurred between the soldiers?
Geography	The study of land, sea, and air and the distribution of animal and plant life, including human beings and their industries	Compare the types of agriculture used on Southern plantations with those of the western states of the Union. How did the type of land influence the crops that were raised by each? Why was it important for the North to control the Mississippi River?
History	The study and recording of important events that may include an explanation of their causes	What was the significance of John Brown's raid and his later hanging? Why did the Union Army under Sherman try to destroy everything they encountered on their way to Atlanta? Why did President Lincoln appoint U.S. Grant to command the Union Army?
Political Science (Civics)	The study of governmental institutions and processes	What was the significance of having Richmond, Virginia, the capital of the South rather than New Orleans or some other city? How was the government of the Confederate States similar in structure to that of the United States?
Sociology	The study of people and their institutions and processes	In both armies, men joined regiments named for the state in which they lived. Why was this important? Compare the lifestyle of a freed slave living in the North with that of a slave in the South. Compare the culture of the agrarian South with that of the industrialized North.

✍ Skills Needed to Become a Good Citizen Actor

One goal of social studies is to produce "citizen actors." That is, students must learn "how citizens in a society make personal and public decisions on issues that affect their destiny" (Linn 1990, 49–50). Children need to learn how to make good decisions. Unfortunately, too often children are not given the opportunity to demonstrate or even practice decision making. Parents, other adults, or even peers often make decisions for children that the children themselves should make. That is not to say that children should be permitted to make adult decisions. For example, an eight-year-old should not be asked whether her mother or father should take job A or job B. However, children should be allowed to have some options; this is essential in creating a learning environment that offers relevant and meaningful study material. For instance, in an integrated instruction classroom in which students are studying the topic of pioneer life, the students may work in small groups on projects. The grouping may be based entirely on the students' own selection of which project they would like to work on. In addition, the students can be given the option of selecting which of five or six books about pioneer life they would like to read and discuss in another small group. Students may individually prepare oral or written reports or write poems, or they may work with others to create a drama about a specific aspect of pioneer life and present it to the class.

In the field of social studies, one of the most basic documents for guiding curriculum development was presented by the National Council for the Social Studies (NCSS) in 1989. In its position statement, the NCSS reiterates the point that one major goal of social studies is to produce citizen actors through civic participation.

The NCSS statement further expands this concept: "Social studies programs have a responsibility to prepare our people to identify, understand, and work to solve the problems that face our increasingly diverse nation and interdependent world. . . . [P]rograms that combine the acquisition of knowledge and skills with the application of democratic values to life through social participation present an ideal balance in social studies" (NCSS 1989, 377).

The NCSS states (1989, 378) that "skills essential to citizen participation in civic affairs can be grouped in a problem-solving/decision-making sequence in the following categories":

Skills Related to Acquiring Information

Reading skills
Study skills
Reference and information search skills
Technical skills unique to the use of electronic devices

Skills Related to Organizing and Using Information

Thinking skills
Decision-making skills
Metacognitive skills

Skills Related to Interpersonal Relationships and Social Participation

Personal skills
Group interaction skills
Social and political participation skills

Teachers need to consider these skills when creating an integrated social studies curriculum for elementary and middle school students.

In 1994, the NCSS adopted curriculum standards for social studies. Performance expectations are described in Focus Box 1.2 at the end of this chapter.

❧ Building Curriculum for Integrated Instruction and Social Studies Integration

The National Commission on the Social Studies (1990), in its highly publicized document *Charting a Course: Social Studies for the 21st Century,* identifies a set of characteristics for the social studies curriculum that establishes exemplary guidelines for integration. Social studies provide the obvious connection between the humanities and the natural and physical sciences. To assist students to see the interrelationships among branches of "knowledge, integration of other subject matter with social studies should be encouraged whenever possible" (p. 3).

Central to social studies instruction should be observing, role playing, reading, and writing. Students must use creative and critical thinking skills for problem solving, decision making, and resolving differences. Students must also develop and use strategies that help them to be independent learners and responsible citizens. They must learn to work together with their peers through cooperative and collaborative efforts.

The study of social studies should avail itself of a wide variety of learning materials, not only textbooks but also children's literature (picture books, historical fiction, nonfiction, poetry, contemporary fiction) that can be incorporated into the curriculum. For instance, Tomasino (1993, 7) believes that "good cultural literature and relevant social studies activities reveal people's similarities as well as differences and develop cultural literacy in young students." In addition, children should be able to examine original materials or sources whenever possible. For example, artifacts, documents, and maps available from local libraries and historical museums add relevance and meaning to children's discovery of social studies. Working with U.S. Census Bureau statistics can provide children with insights into demographic data and help them understand the role of mathematics in the study of social studies. Examining the effects of industrialization on the environment brings science into social studies. Media in the form of films, videotapes, interactive video, overhead transparencies, paintings, sculptures, quilts, and so on offer enrichment for social studies topics at all grade levels.

Hennings (2000, 8) adds to the rationale for integrating social studies instruction in the following statement: "Communication is central to learning. . . . Today's

Displaying their work encourages these students to speak up in class.

Courtesy of Kurtis R. Fluck. Used by permission

teachers are unleashing the power of communications by introducing learning strategies that rely on *social interaction*. Oral modeling of reading and writing, collaborative reading and writing, dialogue, and peer journals are just a few of these strategies."

Social interaction is essential if children are to become responsible and literate citizen actors. Thus, a literate person does not become literate (acquire literacy skills) or use literacy in isolation. In fact, all literate people must use their literacy in a *social context* in which they interact with others in groups. Concurrently, people do not learn to become good citizens actors unless they engage in purposeful activities in which they *interact and communicate* with others in group situations. When asked why people need to be able to read and communicate, most pragmatists would say, so that people can solve the everyday problems they encounter as members of society. Good citizens encounter problems that require the use of literacy skills to make wise decisions in consort with others for the good of society. In the next section we develop a curricular context for integrating social studies in the curriculum.

A model for curriculum integration was developed by Banks, Banks, and Clegg (1998) that is based on the decision-making process. This process can be integrated into the curriculum at all levels and provides an ideal opportunity for integrated instruction activities in social studies. The following section breaks down the various parts of the process and gives examples of the kinds of integrated instruction activities that can occur during each step.

Through discussion groups, new understandings and concepts are acquired by students.
© Lawrence Migdale

✍ The Decision-Making Process

Before describing the decision-making process, it is important to note that issues should be at the heart of the social studies curriculum. Banks, Banks, and Clegg (1998, 179) support this notion this way: "[M]aking decisions can be one of the most interesting and important components of the social studies curriculum. It adds vitality to the curriculum and helps make it significant to both students and the teachers. The study of social issues gives students an opportunity to get a better understanding of the dynamic and changing nature of our society, their responsibilities as citizens in a democracy, and the importance of concepts such as equality and human dignity in maintaining a democracy." Shirley Engle (1985, 265) states the case even more strongly: "The failure to deal in a rigorous and uncluttered way with current social problems is one of the most unconscionable defects of the social studies today. . . . The direct study of social problems has been proposed as a cornerstone of our specialty by social studies reformers over and over again, beginning as early as the recommendations of the Committee on the Social Studies in 1916."

✍ Defining the Process

Step 1: Deriving an Issue

Students read and discuss ideas presented in myriad sources. This provides them with sufficient background information to see the issue, the dilemma it poses to society, and its relevance to them as members of society.

In this step students might read basic documents such as the Constitution, bills, laws, and so forth. They might also read journal, magazine, and newspaper articles, as well as literature in the form of biographies, other nonfiction, and fiction. They then might be asked to interpret and discuss in group situations both the implications and interconnectiveness of what they have read.

Step 2: Expressing Tentative Choices Based on Tentative Values

Students engage in group interaction activities in which they communicate alternate choices and explain and test the values that are driving their choices as they relate to the issues. This might include collaborative writing and analytical and synthesis writing, among other integrated instruction activities.

Step 3: Gathering Information to Test Choices

Students acquire research techniques that enable them to interact with primary documents such as bills, laws, the Constitution, personal journals, primary and secondary sources, and so on. They develop skills of oral inquiry through interviewing authoritative people on their topic. Students engage in analytical and synthesis writing as they organize the data presented. They also interpret data presented and use maps and graphs to find answers to their questions. As members of the groups, they use collaborative reading and writing as they write drafts of positions based on their research.

Step 4: Evaluating Data and Identifying Tested Choices

Students master communication skills through debates and persuasive speaking and writing as they move toward group and individual choices on the issue. They evaluate their choices and values expressed earlier on light of their newly acquired knowledge. They arrive at choices on which they will act.

Step 5: Acting on Choices in Society

Students act on the choices agreed on by the group. They engage in purposeful and meaningful communications, both written and oral, as they become civic actors in trying to resolve the issue. They evaluate the impact of their decisions as they interpret the ramifications of their civic participation and realize the importance of their roles as citizen actors. They might conduct surveys, write letters to politicians proposing legislation, make posters, deliver talks and speeches, canvass people, and write journals.

It should be apparent that the process just outlined lends itself beautifully to the acquisition of literacy skills and citizen actors skills in an integrated fashion. Next we turn to more concrete examples of activities at various elementary levels that follow the steps of the decision-making process.

Illustrative Examples of Integrated Social Studies Activities

The National Commission on the Social Studies (1990) and *Curriculum Standards for Social Studies* (NCSS 1994) provide examples of integrating activities that can serve as a stimulating springboard to more in-depth units of instruction. At the kindergarten level, children explore their own immediate environment as well as environments far distant in time and space. Meaningful understandings can be achieved through the use of songs, stories (including children's own pictures), artifacts, overhead transparencies, mapmaking, model building, and slide-tape or videotape presentations of a drama.

In the remaining grades of early childhood education, grades 1 through 3, children can readily understand the concepts of communities past and present and how laws and individual behavior have an impact on the nature of communities. A literature-based reading program affords students the opportunity to explore these concepts by reading stories about and descriptions of different kinds of people living under different conditions—for example, hunters in tropical rain forests, farmers of European villages, pioneers and immigrant settlers in the United States, Native Americans, urban and rural dwellers. Such a program gives children an opportunity to expand their awareness. At this level, literature should be selected to provide children with insights into the diversity of people and social divisions that make up the multicultural community we call Earth. At this level, children's understanding should not come solely from printed material; drawing, building, quilt making, singing, and acting out parts can also be used to expand their consciousness of the variety of human social experience.

In middle childhood education, grades 4 through 6, the content should focus on U.S. history, world history, and geography, both physical and cultural. In the reading program, teachers should draw from literature that provides stories about Native Americans, early European explorers and settlers, the nation's founders, populists, suffragists, inventors, activists, business and labor leaders, and other political, economic, and cultural figures to demonstrate the diversity and historical complexity of American society. In addition, children should study in depth the basic documents that provide the foundation of our democratic society. This same approach can be used to engage children in learning about world history as well.

At the early adolescent level or middle school level, students should study local and national social, political, and economic relationships and patterns of behavior in depth. When exploring local history, children might study old buildings and successive architectural styles to discover how people in the area have made their living, displayed their idealism, and organized and lived within their private spaces. Conducting oral interviews with older neighborhood residents and different cultural groups, analyzing historical census data, studying old photographs, and consulting newspaper files can introduce students to active historical and geographic research.

The ability to look carefully and productively at the worlds we have created in our neighborhoods, towns, cities, and countryside is a major goal of effective social studies education *at all levels*. This requires that related issues be critically examined throughout the elementary years. In fact, such noted authorities on social studies as Shirley Engle (1985) suggest that each school should devote part of its academic year to the exploration of an identified issue at all grade levels.

By now it should be clear that social studies can be integrated into the curriculum to achieve one of the primary goals of education, that of producing good citizens. Other chapters expand on the broad examples of how social studies fit into the integrated curriculum.

Chapter Summary

Social studies is the study of the cultural, economic, geographic, and political aspects of past, current, and future societies. When social studies is incorporated into an integrated curriculum, children are allowed to make decisions about what they want to learn and how they will learn it. Through the use of children's literature, writing, and discussion, students discover concepts in anthropology, economics, geography, history, political science, and sociology. Because self-selection of reading materials in children's literature and activities allows for personalization of learning, children become more fully engaged and interested in social studies learning than they would with teacher-assigned textbook readings. Students also learn to become decision makers.

The decision-making process consists of five steps: (1) deriving an issue, (2) expressing tentative choices based on tentative values, (3) gathering information to test choices, (4) evaluating data and identifying tested choices, and (5) acting on choices in society. Through active participation, children learn to become decision makers and responsible citizen actors. They also learn to be independent learners and thinkers.

By examining the development of their immediate and surrounding worlds, children gain insight into each of the social sciences that make up social studies. In so doing, they better understand the interdependency of people both locally and in the global society.

Children's Books

Bruchac, J. 1993. *The first strawberry: A Cherokee story.* A. Vojtech. New York: Dial. The creation story of the Cherokee Indians.

Bruchac, J. 1997. *Lasting echoes: An oral history of Native American people.* San Diego: Silverwhistle/Harcourt Brace. More than a hundred Native Americans stories are shared in this book. Bruchac, himself an American Indian, presents the stories of seven generations.

Bruchac, J. 1997. *Many nations: An alphabet of Native America.* Illus. R.F. Goetzl. Boston: Bridgewater Books. From Anishanabe artists making birch bark bowls to Zuni elders saying prayers for the day that is done, this book is an essential for a Native American unit. Twenty-six tribes are depicted.

Cherry L. 1992. *A river ran wild.* Orlando, FL: Harcourt Brace Jovanovich. In this true story of the Nashua River, the author describes the environmental damage caused by civilization.

Choi, Y. 1997. *The sun girl and the moon boy: A Korean folktale.* New York:Knopf. This story is similar to Little Red Riding Hood. A girl and a boy use their wits and a bit of luck to escape from a hungry tiger and bring the first rays of sunlight and moonlight to the world.

Coerr, E. 1979. *Sadako and a thousand paper cranes.* Illus. R. Himler. New York: Yearling. The story of Sadako is a simple one. After the atomic bomb attack on her city, she develops leukemia. She believes if she makes one thousand paper origami cranes, she will survive. While the book can be read to children in kindergarten, even adults find the story poignant.

Fritz, J. 1983. *The double life of Pocahontas.* New York: Putnam. A historical fiction account of Indian Princess Pocahontas.

Giff, P. R. 1997. *Lily's crossing.* New York: Delacorte. Lily is used to spending the summer at the beach but World War II changes her life. She finds a new friend, Albert, who has escaped from Hungary only to lose most of his family. Together they survive the bombing of England by the Germans.

Goble, P. 1990. *Dream wolf.* New York: Bradbury. A beautifully illustrated book about a Native American legend.

Hong, L. T. 1991. *How the ox star fell from heaven.* New York: Whitman. A novel about an Asian legend.

Ishii, M. 1987. *The tongue-cut sparrow.* Trans. K. Paterson, illus. S. Akabar. New York: Lodestar, Dutton. A Japanese version of the well-known folktale of the fisherman and his wife, who is never satisfied with the gifts she receives.

Kesey, K. 1991. *The sea lion.* Illus. N. Waldman. New York: Viking. One of a few books about the Pacific Northwest Indians, this book depicts the legend of the sea lion.

Kirkpatrick, K. 1998. *Trouble's daughter: The story of Susanna Hutchinson, Indian captive.* New York: Delacorte. Based on the true story of the massacre of Susanna's family by Lenape warriors in 1643 and her being taken captive by members of the tribe. A good book for middle school students.

Lowry, L. 1989. *Number the stars.* Boston: Houghton Mifflin. Ten-year-old Annemarie and her best friend Ellen live in Copenhagen during the German occupation. When Jews are "relocated," Annemarie's family takes Ellen in and pretends she is a family member. Annemarie's courage saves her friends life.

Martin, R. 1992. *The rough-face girl.* Illus. D. Shannon. New York: Putnam. This is the Algonquin Indian version of the Cinderella tale. It is one of the most haunting and beautiful of the more than 1,500 versions of Cinderella.

McKissack, P. C. 1997. *Run away home.* New York: Scholastic Press. During the 1880s, Apaches were taken by train from their home in Arizona to reservations in Florida. This historical novel tells of Sky, an Apache boy, who escapes from the train and is rescued by Sarah, a black girl. When Sarah's family is threatened by a White Supremacist group, Sky helps fight them off and save the family farm. A thought-provoking book for upper-elementary children and middle schoolers.

McSwigan, M. 1942. *Snow Treasure.* New York: Dutton. During the 1940 occupation of Norway by the German army, Norwegian children smuggled gold bars to a cave for hiding. The story keeps students riveted.

Napoli, D. J. 1998. *Stones in water.* New York: Scholastic. During WWII three teenage boys in Italy set out to see a movie. They are taken by soldiers and forced to work in a camp for the Axis powers.

Nhuong, H. Q. 1982. *The land I lost: Adventures of a boy in Vietnam.* New York: Harper & Row. Describes daily life in Vietnam prior to the war, including the duties of parents and children.

Nhuong, H. Q. 1997. *Water buffalo days: Growing up in Vietnam.* New York: HarperCollins. This chapter book makes a good readaloud for primary students. An autobiography, Nhuong tells how he fought off tigers and wild pigs that threatened his Vietnamese village.

O'Dell. S. 1988. *Black star, bright dawn.* Boston: Houghton Mifflin. A compelling Native American story told by master storyteller Scott O'Dell.

Paulsen, G. 1988. *Dogsong.* New York: Bradbury. The story of a Native American boy growing up.

Philip, N. (Ed.). 1997. *In a sacred manner I live: Native American wisdom.* New York: Clarion Books. Ranging from quotes by Chief Powhatan in 1609 to Leonard Crow Dog, a Sioux medicine man quoted from a piece he wrote in 1995, this is an excellent book on Native American wisdom. Others quoted include Blackhawk, Black Elk, Chief Joseph, Geronimo, Sitting Bull, and Tecumseh.

Salisbury, G. 1995. *Under the blood red sun.* New York: Yearling. After Pearl Harbor is attacked, a boy must become the man of the family when his Japanese father is sent to an internment camp on the mainland.

Say, A. 1990. *El chino.* Boston: Houghton Mifflin. The true story of a Chinese boy who grew up to be a bullfighter in Spain.

Sneve, V. 1989. *Dancing teepees: Poems of American Indian youth.* New York: Holiday House. A collection of poetry written by Native American children.

Wood, N. (Ed.). 1997. *The serpent's tongue: Prose, poetry, and art of New Mexico Pueblos.* New York: Dutton. A comprehensive book with lots of examples of Pueblo artwork and poetry as well as stories. Excellent resource book for middle schoolers and teachers.

Teaching Resources

The following resources are available from the African Studies Center at Boston University. Contact: African Outreach Program, Boston University, 270 Bay State Road, Boston, MA 02215.

Web site: http://www.bu.edu/AFR

Africa Inspirer. This is a CD-ROM by Tom Snyder Productions (1997) that is good for grades 4 to 8.

How Big Is Africa? This 17′ by 22′, full-color poster map shows how Europe, the United States and China would all fit in Africa. Also included are lesson plans, reproducible maps, and cutouts (cost $9.95 plus $5.00 for shipping).

Software

Dorling Kindersley. 1998. *History of the World 2.0.* New York: DK Multimedia.

References

Allen, M. G., and R. L. Stevens: 1998. *Middle grades social studies: Teaching and learning for active and responsible citizenship.* Boston: Allyn and Bacon.

Banks, J. A., C. A. M Banks, and A. A. Clegg. 1998. *Teaching strategies for the social studies.* 5th ed. New York: Longman.

Bieger, E. M. 1996. Promoting multicultural education through a literature-based approach. *The Reading Teacher* 49 (4): 308–12.

Engle, S. H. 1985. A social studies imperative. *Social Education* 49: 264–5.

Hennings, D. G. 2000. *Communication, language and literacy learning.* 7th ed. Boston: Houghton Mifflin.

Johnston Smith, D., and B. Brown. 1998. How big is Africa? *Social Education* 62 (5): 278–81.

Joint Committee on Geographic Education. 1984. *Guidelines for geographic education.* Washington, DC: Association of American Geographers.

Leinhardt, G. 1992. What research on learning tells us about teaching. *Educational Leadership* 49 (7): 20–7.

Linn, J. B. 1990. Whole language in social studies. *Social Science Record* 27 (2): 49–55.

National Center for History in the Schools. 1994. *National standards for history (K-4).* Los Angeles: National Center for History in the Schools.

National Commission on the Social Studies. 1990. *Charting a course: Social studies for the 21ˢᵗ century.* Washington, DC: National Council for the Social Studies.

National Council for the Social Studies (NCSS). 1989. In search of a scope and sequence for social studies. *Social Education* 53 (6): 376–9.

National Council for the Social Studies (NCSS). 1994. *Curriculum standards for social studies: Expectations of excellence.* Washington, DC: National Council for the Social Studies.

Pelto, P., and R. Muessig. 1980. *The study and teaching of anthropology.* Columbus, OH: Merrill.

Tomasino, K. 1993. Literature and social studies: A spicy mix for fifth graders. *Social Studies and the Young Learner* 5: 7–10.

U.S. Department of Education. 1994. *U.S. history framework for the 1994 National Assessment of Educational Progress (NAEP).* Washington, DC: U.S. Department of Education.

1.2   Focus Box

Curriculum Standards for the Social Studies–Performance Expectations

I. Culture

Social studies programs should include experiences that provide for the study of *culture and cultural diversity,* so that the learner can:

Early Grades

a. explore and describe similarities and differences in the ways groups, societies, and cultures address similar human needs and concerns;

b. give examples of how experiences may be interpreted differently by people from diverse cultural perspectives and frames of reference;

c. describe ways in which language, stories, folktales, music, and artistic creations serve as expressions of culture and influence behavior of people living in a particular culture;

d. compare ways in which people from different cultures think about and deal with their physical environment and social conditions;

e. give examples and describe the importance of cultural unity and diversity within and across groups.

Middle Grades

a. compare similarities and differences in the ways groups, societies, and cultures meet human needs and concerns;

b. explain how information and experiences may be interpreted by people from diverse cultural perspectives and frames of reference;

c. explain and give examples of how language, literature, the arts, architecture, other artifacts, traditions, beliefs, values, and behaviors contribute to the development and transmission of culture;

d. explain why individuals and groups respond differently to their physical and social environments and/or changes to them on the basis of shared assumptions, values, and beliefs;

e. articulate the implications of cultural diversity, as well as cohesion, within and across groups.

II. Time, Continuity, and Change

Social studies programs should include experiences that provide for the study of *the ways human beings view themselves in and over time,* so that the learner can:

Early Grades

a. demonstrate an understanding that different people may describe the same event or situation in diverse ways, citing reasons for the differences in views;

b. demonstrate an ability to use correctly vocabulary associated with time such as past, present, future, and long ago; read and construct simple timelines; identify examples of change; and recognize examples of cause and effect relationships;

c. compare and contrast different stories or accounts about past events, people, places, or situations, identifying how they contribute to our understanding of the past;

Middle Grades

a. demonstrate an understanding that different scholars may describe the same event or situation in different ways but must provide reasons or evidence for their views;

b. identify and use key concepts such as chronology, causality, change, conflict, and complexity to explain, analyze, and show connections among patterns of historical change and continuity;

c. identify and describe selected historical periods and patterns of change within and across cultures, such as the rise of civilizations, the development of transportation systems, the growth and breakdown of colonial systems, and others;

d. identify and use various sources for reconstructing the past, such as documents, letters, diaries, maps, textbooks, photos, and others;

d. identify and use processes important to reconstructing and reinterpreting the past, such as using a variety of sources, providing, validating, and weighing evidence for claims, checking credibility of sources, and search for causality;

e. demonstrate an understanding that people in different times and places view the world differently;

e. develop critical sensitivities such as empathy and skepticism regarding attitudes, values, and behaviors of people in different historical contexts;

f. use knowledge of facts and concepts drawn from history, along with elements of historical inquiry, to inform decision-making about and action-taking on public issues.

f. use knowledge of facts and concepts drawn from history, along with methods of historical inquiry, to inform decision-making about and action-taking on public issues.

III. People, Places, and Environments

Social studies programs should include experiences that provide for the study of *people, places, and environments,* so that the learner can:

Early Grades

a. construct and use mental maps of locales, regions, and the world that demonstrate understanding of relative location, direction, size, and shape;

b. interpret, use, and distinguish various representations of the earth, such as maps, globes, and photographs;

c. use appropriate resources, data sources, and geographic tools such as atlases, data bases, grid systems, charts, graphs, and maps to generate, manipulate, and interpret information;

d. estimate distance and calculate scale;

e. locate and distinguish among varying landforms and geographic features, such as mountains, plateaus, islands, and oceans;

f. describe and speculate about physical system changes, such as seasons, climate and weather, and the water cycle;

g. describe how people create places that reflect ideas, personality, culture, and wants and needs as they design homes, playgrounds, classrooms, and the like;

Middle Grades

a. elaborate mental maps of locales, regions, and the world that demonstrate understanding of relative location, direction, size, and shape;

b. create, interpret, use, and distinguish various representations of the earth, such as maps, globes, and photographs;

c. use appropriate resources, data sources, and geographic tools such as aerial photographs, satellite images, geographic information systems (GIS), map projections, and cartography to generate, manipulate, and interpret information such as atlases, data bases, grid systems, charts, graphs, and maps;

d. estimate distance, calculate scale, and distinguish other geographic relationships such as population density and spatial distribution patterns;

e. locate and describe varying landforms and geographic features, such as mountains, plateaus, islands, rain forests, deserts, and oceans, and explain their relationships within the ecosystem;

f. describe physical system changes such as seasons, climate and weather, and the water cycle and identify geographic patterns associated with them;

g. describe how people create places that reflect cultural values and ideals as they build neighborhoods, parks, shopping centers, and the like;

Continued

1.2   Focus Box   Continued

Curriculum Standards for the Social Studies–Performance Expectations

h. examine the interaction of human beings and their physical environment, the use of land, building of cities, and ecosystem changes in selected locales and regions;

i. explore ways that the earth's physical features have changed over time in the local region and beyond and how these changes may be connected to one another;

j. observe and speculate about social and economic effects of environmental changes and crises resulting from phenomena such as floods, storms, and drought;

k. consider existing uses and propose and evaluate alternative uses of resources and land in home, school, community, the region, and beyond.

h. examine, interpret, and analyze physical and cultural patterns and their interactions, such as land use, settlement patterns, cultural transmission of customs and ideas, and ecosystem changes;

i. describe ways that historical events have been influenced by, and have influenced, physical and human geographic factors in local, regional, national, and global settings;

j. observe and speculate about social and economic effects of environmental changes and crises resulting from phenomena such as floods, storms, and drought;

k. propose, compare, and evaluate alternative uses of land and resources in communities, regions, nations, and the world.

IV. Individual Development and Identity

Social studies programs should include experiences that provide for the study of *individual development and identity,* so that the learner can:

Early Grades

a. describe personal changes over time, such as those related to physical development and personal interests;

b. describe personal connections to place—especially place as associated with immediate surroundings;

c. describe the unique features of one's nuclear and extended families;

d. show how learning and physical development affect behavior;

e. identify and describe ways family, groups, and community influence the individual's daily life and personal choices;

f. explore factors that contribute to one's personal identity such as interests, capabilities, and perceptions;

g. analyze a particular event to identify reasons individuals might respond to it in different ways;

h. work independently and cooperatively to accomplish goals.

Middle Grades

a. relate personal changes to social, cultural, and historical contexts;

b. describe personal connections to place—as associated with community, nation, and the world;

c. describe the ways family, gender, ethnicity, nationality, and institutional affiliations contribute to personal identity;

d. relate such factors as physical endowment and capabilities, learning, motivation, personality, perception, and behavior to individual development;

e. identify and describe ways regional, ethnic, and national cultures influence individuals' daily lives;

f. identify and describe the influence of perception, attitudes, values, and beliefs on personal identity;

g. identify and interpret examples of stereotyping, conformity, and altruism;

h. work independently and cooperatively to accomplish goals.

V. Individuals, Groups, and Institutions

Social studies programs should include experiences that provide for the study of *interactions among individuals, groups, and institutions,* so that the learner can:

Early Grades

a. identify roles as learned behavior patterns in group situations such as student, family member, peer play group member, or club member;

b. give examples of and explain group and institutional influences such as religious beliefs, laws, and peer pressure, on people, events, and elements of culture;

c. identify examples of institutions and describe the interactions of people with institutions;

d. identify and describe examples of tensions between and among individuals, groups, or institutions, and how belonging to more than one group can cause internal conflicts;

e. identify and describe examples of tension between an individual's beliefs and government policies and laws;

f. give examples of the role of institutions in furthering both continuity and change;

g. show how groups and institutions work to meet individual needs and promote the common good, and identify examples of where they fail to do so.

Middle Grades

a. demonstrate an understanding of concepts such as role, status, and social class in describing the interactions of individuals and social groups;

b. analyze group and institutional influences on people, events, and elements of culture;

c. describe the various forms institutions take and the interactions of people with institutions;

d. identify and analyze examples of tensions between expressions of individuality and group or institutional efforts to promote social conformity;

e. identify and describe examples of tensions between belief systems and government policies and laws;

f. describe the role of institutions in furthering both continuity and change;

g. apply knowledge of how groups and institutions work to meet individual needs and promote the common good.

VI. Power, Authority, and Governance

Social studies programs should include experiences that provide for the study of *how people create and change structures of power, authority, and governance,* so that the learner can:

Early Grades

a. examine the rights and responsibilities of the individual in relation to his or her social group, such as family, peer group, and school class;

b. explain the purpose of government;

c. give examples of how government does or does not provide for needs and wants of people, establish order and security, and manage conflict;

d. recognize how groups and organizations encourage unity and deal with diversity to maintain order and security;

Middle Grades

a. examine persistent issues involving the rights, roles, and status of the individual in relation to the general welfare;

b. describe the purpose of government and how its powers are acquired, used, and justified;

c. analyze and explain ideas and governmental mechanisms to meet needs and wants of citizens, regulate territory, manage conflict, and establish order and security;

d. describe the ways nations and organizations respond to forces of unity and diversity affecting order and security;

Continued

1.2   Focus Box   Continued

Curriculum Standards for the Social Studies–Performance Expectations

e. distinguish among local, state, and national governments and identify representative leaders at these levels such as mayor, governor, and president;

f. identify and describe factors that contribute to cooperation and cause disputes within and among groups and nations;

g. explore the role of technology in communications, transportation, information-processing, weapons development, or other areas as it contributes to or helps resolve conflicts;

h. recognize and give examples of the tensions between the wants and needs of individuals and groups, and concepts such as fairness, equity, and justice.

e. identify and describe the basic features of the political system in the United States, and identify representative leaders from various levels and branches of government;

f. explain conditions, actions, and motivations that contribute to conflict and cooperation within and among nations;

g. describe and analyze the role of technology in communications, transportation, information-processing, weapons development, or other areas as it contributes to or helps resolve conflicts;

h. explain and apply concepts such as power, role, status, justice, and influence to the examination of persistent issues and social problems;

i. give examples and explain how governments attempt to achieve their stated ideals at home and abroad.

VII. Production, Distribution, and Consumption

Social studies programs should include experiences that provide for the study of *how people organize for the production, distribution, and consumption of goods and services,* so that the learner can:

Early Grades

a. give examples that show how scarcity and choice govern our economic decisions;

b. distinguish between needs and wants;

c. identify examples of private and public goods and services;

d. give examples of the various institutions that make up economic systems such as families, workers, banks, labor unions, government agencies, small businesses, and large corporations;

e. describe how we depend upon workers with specialized jobs and the ways in which they contribute to the production and exchange of goods and services;

f. describe the influence of incentives, values, traditions, and habits on economic decisions;

Middle Grades

a. give and explain examples of ways that economic systems structure choices about how goods and services are to be produced and distributed;

b. describe the role that supply and demand, prices, incentives, and profits play in determining what is produced and distributed in a competitive market system;

c. explain the difference between private and public goods and services;

d. describe a range of examples of the various institutions that make up economic systems such as households, business firms, banks, government agencies, labor unions, and corporations;

e. describe the role of specialization and exchange in the economic process;

f. explain and illustrate how values and beliefs influence different economic decisions;

g. explain and demonstrate the role of money in everyday life;

h. describe the relationship of price to supply and demand;

i. use economic concepts such as supply, demand, and price to help explain events in the community and nation;

j. apply knowledge of economic concepts in developing a response to a current local economic issue, such as how to reduce the flow of trash into a rapidly filling landfill.

g. differentiate among various forms of exchange and money;

h. compare basic economic systems according to who determines what is produced, distributed, and consumed;

i. use economic concepts to help explain historical and current developments and issues in local, national, or global contexts;

j. use economic reasoning to compare different proposals for dealing with a contemporary social issue such as unemployment, acid rain, or high quality education.

VIII. Science, Technology, and Society

Social studies programs should include experiences that provide for the study of *relationships among science, technology, and society,* so that the learner can:

Early Grades

a. identify and describe examples in which science and technology have changed the lives of people, such as in homemaking, childcare, work, transportation, and communication;

b. identify and describe examples in which science and technology have led to changes in the physical environment, such as the building of dams and levees, offshore oil drilling, medicine from rain forests, and loss of rain forests due to extraction of resources or alternative uses;

c. describe instances in which changes in values, beliefs, and attitudes have resulted from new scientific and technological knowledge, such as conservation of resources and awareness of chemicals harmful to life and the environment;

d. identify examples of laws and policies that govern scientific and technological applications, such as the Endangered Species Act and environmental protection policies;

e. suggest ways to monitor science and technology in order to protect the physical environment, individual rights, and the common good.

Middle Grades

a. examine and describe the influence of culture on scientific and technological choice and advancement, such as in transportation, medicine, and warfare;

b. show through specific examples how science and technology have changed people's perceptions of the social and natural world, such as in their relationship to the land, animal life, family life, and economic needs, wants, and security;

c. describe examples in which values, beliefs, and attitudes have been influenced by new scientific and technological knowledge, such as the invention of the printing press, conceptions of the universe, applications of atomic energy, and genetic discoveries;

d. explain the need for laws and policies to govern scientific and technological applications, such as in the safety and well-being of workers and consumers and the regulation of utilities, radio, and television;

e. seek reasonable and ethical solutions to problems that arise when scientific advancements and social norms or values come into conflict.

Continued

1.2   *Focus Box*   Continued

Curriculum Standards for the Social Studies–Performance Expectations

IX. Global Connections

Social studies programs should include experiences that provide for the study of *global connections and interdependence,* so that the learner can:

Early Grades	Middle Grades
a. explore ways that language, art, music, belief systems, and other cultural elements may facilitate global understanding or lead to misunderstanding;	a. describe instances in which language, art, music, belief systems, and other cultural elements can facilitate global understanding or cause misunderstanding;
b. give examples of conflict, cooperation, and interdependence among individuals, groups, and nations;	b. analyze examples of conflict, cooperation, and interdependence among groups, societies, and nations;
c. examine the effects of changing technologies on the global community;	c. describe and analyze the effects of changing technologies on the global community;
d. explore causes, consequences, and possible solutions to persistent, contemporary, and emerging global issues, such as pollution and endangered species;	d. explore the causes, consequences, and possible solutions to persistent, contemporary, and emerging global issues, such as health, security, resource allocation, economic development, and environmental quality;
e. examine the relationships and tensions between personal wants and needs and various global concerns, such as use of imported oil, land use, and environmental protection;	e. describe and explain the relationships and tensions between national sovereignty and global interests, in such matters as territory, natural resources, trade, use of technology, and welfare of people;
f. investigate concerns, issues, standards, and conflicts related to universal human rights, such as the treatment of children, religious groups, and effects of war.	f. demonstrate understanding of concerns, standards, issues, and conflicts related to universal human rights;
	g. identify and describe the roles of international and multinational organizations.

X. Civic Ideals and Practices

Social studies programs should include experiences that provide for the study of *the ideals, principles, and practices of citizenship in a democratic republic,* so that the learner can:

Early Grades	Middle Grades
a. identify key ideals of the United States' democratic republican form of government, such as individual human dignity, liberty, justice, equality, and the rule of law, and discuss their application in specific situations;	a. examine the origins and continuing influence of key ideals of the democratic republican form of government, such as individual human dignity, liberty, justice, equality, and the rule of law;

b. identify examples of rights and responsibilities of citizens;

c. locate, access, organize, and apply information about an issue of public concern from multiple points of view;

d. identify and practice selected forms of civic discussion and participation consistent with the ideals of citizens in a democratic republic;

e. explain actions citizens can take to influence public policy decisions;

f. recognize that a variety of formal and informal actors influence and shape public policy;

g. examine the influence of public opinion on personal decision-making and government policy on public issues;

h. explain how public policies and citizen behaviors may or may not reflect the stated ideals of a democratic republican form of government;

i. describe how public policies are used to address issues of public concern;

j. recognize and interpret how the "common good" can be strengthened through various forms of citizen action.

b. identify and interpret sources and examples of the rights and responsibilities of citizens;

c. locate, access, analyze, organize, and apply information about selected public issues—recognizing and explaining multiple points of view;

d. practice forms of civic discussion and participation consistent with the ideals of citizens in a democratic republic;

e. explain and analyze various forms of citizen action that influence public policy decisions;

f. identify and explain the roles of formal and informal political actors in influencing and shaping public policy and decision-making;

g. analyze the influence of diverse forms of public opinion on the development of public policy and decision-making;

h. analyze the effectiveness of selected public policies and citizen behaviors in realizing the stated ideals of a democratic republican form of government;

i. explain the relationship between policy statements and action plans used to address issues of public concern;

j. examine strategies designed to strengthen the "common good," which consider a range of options for citizen action.

Chapter 2

© Jean-Claude LeJeune

Social Studies and Integrated Instruction

A Look at Interdisciplinary Instruction

Pamela J. Farris
Northern Illinois University

Students do not merely passively receive or copy input from teachers, but instead actively mediate it by trying to make sense of it and to relate it to what they already know (or think they know) about the topic.

—**Jere Brophy**
"Probing the Subtleties of Subject-Matter Teaching"

Objectives

—————————————————————— ⟶ ——————————————————————

Readers will

- recognize that critical thinking skills need to be taught as part of social studies and interdisciplinary instruction;
- understand the relationship of language arts and social studies in interdisciplinary instruction; and
- be able to develop ways to promote decision making with students.

Introduction

Social studies serves as an integration of the social sciences: anthropology, economics, geography, history, political science, and sociology. In addition, social studies promotes the development of critical and creative thinking as children learn to assume their role as responsible citizens in a democratic society. According to Brophy (1992, 8):

> In social studies, students are challenged to engage in higher-order thinking by interpreting, analyzing, or manipulating information in response to questions or problems that cannot be resolved through routine application of previously learned knowledge. Students focus on networks of connected content structured around powerful ideas rather than long lists of disconnected facts, and they consider the implications of what they are learning for social and civic decision making.

For this to occur, learning must be both meaningful and relevant to students.

The other content areas such as language arts, math, and science share many of the same basic principles of social studies. These include such basic learning principles as: (1) respect for the learner and the teacher, (2) belief in the role of the teacher as a facilitator of learning, and (3) encouragement of learners to experiment and take risks. Moreover, like the arts, social studies is both personal and social. Social studies is driven from the inside by the need to communicate and shaped from the outside toward the norms of society.

With these shared principles, it is appropriate that interdisciplinary instruction play a major role in the social studies curriculum. This chapter outlines interdisciplinary instruction and its essential elements. Other chapters describe how the integrated instruction approach can be effectively incorporated in the social studies curriculum.

Interdisciplinary Instruction

In the late 1890s and early 1900s, John Dewey and his mentor, Francis Parker, founded the progressive education movement. Their work at the University of Chicago's famous laboratory school encouraged teachers to provide more opportunities for hands-on instruction. Dewey promoted "learning by doing," the belief that children learn best when they are active participants in the learning process.

In the 1950s and 1960s, Hilda Taba pointed out the need for character education. Perhaps her most important contribution to social studies was the *spiral curriculum,* in which social studies concepts are introduced and later continuously elaborated upon throughout elementary and middle school. Jerome Bruner further stressed the idea of the spiral curriculum.

In the 1970s and 1980s, James Banks pointed out the need to create citizens who were decision makers. He also emphasized the need for multicultural education in social studies and throughout the elementary and middle school curriculum. By the twenty-first century, the idea of interdisciplinary instruction—the teaching of more than one content at the same time—had become well entrenched as an instructional technique.

Traditional Versus Interdisciplinary Instruction: Philosophical and Psychological Underpinnings

The traditional instructional approach is the direct instruction, skills-based, behaviorist approach. The interdisciplinary instructional approach has its roots in the progressive education, constructionist approach. These approaches differ in terms of views of knowing, learning, and motivation. Behaviorists believe that knowledge is present outside oneself and that it can be broken down into tiny, discrete units. Constructionists believe that knowledge develops from within as the individual attempts to "construct" meaning out of experience, both firsthand and vicarious (McCarty 1991). Inquiry becomes an essential aspect of learning.

Behaviorists believe that learning takes place *only* within the context of appropriately reinforced responses to events (or stimuli). These may be simple responses (one specific unit of behavior) or complex responses (a series of behaviors) (Weil, Calhoun, and Joyce 2000). On the other hand, constructionists believe that learning takes place in the flow of daily human experiences and is an ongoing process. Thus, all individuals are learners and all are teachers. Children learn from each other as well as from the teacher. Likewise, the teacher learns from students and other teachers.

Behaviorists believe motivation to learn is extrinsic, based on external rewards. Constructionists believe that motivation to learn is based on the individual's own natural curiosity and interests as well as one's tendency to set and achieve self-determined goals. Students are given more choices in the interdisciplinary instructional approach than with direct instruction. In addition, they are expected to serve as active participants in their learning—making decisions, setting goals, and engaging real and relevant learning activities, thereby becoming more responsible for their learning.

✑ Essential Elements of Literacy Learning

Literacy learning requires that the language arts (listening, speaking, reading, writing, viewing, visually representing, and thinking) be integrated in instruction. This section describes the role of listening, speaking, reading, and writing as part of social studies and interdisciplinary instruction.

A teacher should pose interesting questions that require students to use higher-level thinking skills during group discussions.

©Photo by Jean-Claude LeJeune

In the Classroom Mini Lesson

Cooperative/Collaborative Attentive Listening

This listening-speaking activity is appropriate for students in grades 2 through 8. Begin by dividing the students into groups of six, and proceed to give each group member one-sixth of a paper circle that is eight inches in diameter. Next, inform the students that they are to listen carefully to a folktale as it is read aloud because each group of students must decide as a group what the six main events of the folktale are. Once a group has identified the six events, have each group member illustrate one of the events on his or her sixth of the circle. (Note: The number of students per group along with a corresponding number of events may be changed, depending on class size or number of significant events in a particular folktale.)

When a group has completed its illustations, each member describes his or her illustration of one event. Then the events are put in proper order and the story is completely retold. Each group's final product becomes a completed circle of six pie-shaped illustrations that tell the story in clockwise order, starting at the twelve o'clock position. When glued to bright-colored construction paper, the completed circles make an effective bulletin board display.

This activity can be extended into the writing arena by having each student write the first draft of a story and then illustrate each event in the story. By drawing the various scenes and placing them in a desired sequence, students can modify and refine a story before they begin the final writing.

Following are some suggested folktales for cooperative/collaborative attentive listening.

Farris, Pamela J. 1996. *Young Mouse and Elephant: An East African Folktale.* Ilus. Valeri Gorbachev.
  Boston: Houghton Mifflin.
Galdone, Paul. 1968. *The Horse, the Fox, and the Lion.* New York: Clarion.
Galdone, Paul. 1982. *What's in Fox's Sack? An Old English Tale.* New York: Clarion
Kellogg, Steve. 1991. *Jack and the Beanstalk.* New York: Morrow.

Historical picture books that can be used with this activity for grades 3 through 5 include:

Fleming, Candace. 1998. *The Hatmaker's Sign: A Story by Benjamin Franklin.* Illus. by Robert Andrew
  Parker. New York: Orchard.
Fowler, Susi Gregg. 1998. *Circle of Thanks.* Illus. by Peter Catalotto. New York: Scholastic.
Lawson, Julie. 1997. *Emma and the Silk Train.* Illus. by Paul Mombourquette. Toronto, Ontario: Kids
  Can Press.

Shown here is the story of *Young Mouse and Elephant: An East African Folktale* as drawn by a group of six third graders. The story begins as Young Mouse brags that he is the strongest animal. His grandfather tells him that Elephant is the strongest animal. Young Mouse goes off to seek out Elephant and the adventure, and the fun, begins.

From: Farris. P. J. (2001). *Language Arts: Process Product and Assessment.* 3rd ed. McGraw-Hill.

Listening

Listening involves giving attention to others. As such it requires self-discipline. The listener must carefully consider what the other person is saying and, while doing so, think of a response. Thus, the listener must anticipate what the speaker will say and call upon previously gained knowledge to judge what the speaker is saying.

In integrated instruction classrooms, listening is important because students are taught to value each other's contributions. Since students learn from each other, being a

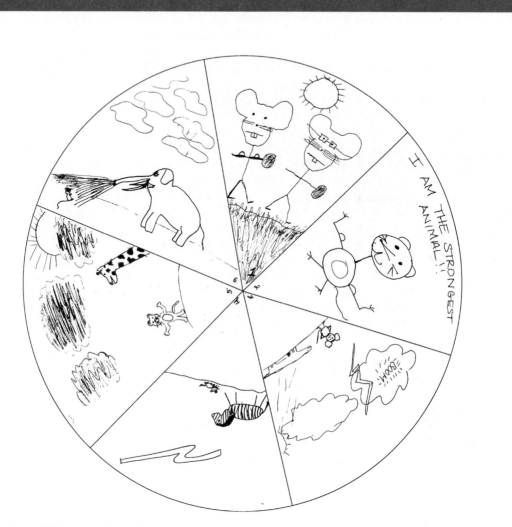

Folktales help children appreciate other cultures and also are good circle stories. After listening to their teacher read *Young Mouse and Elephant: An East African Folktale,* these third graders illustrated the primary events of the story and then retold it as a group.

good listener is paramount to being a good learner. Much knowledge and understanding are gained via listening, which is in turn used in speaking, reading, and writing.

Speaking

Although listening is a vital language art, it accompanies speaking in developing discussion and presentation skills. Children learn from interacting with each other. According to Eliot Wigginton (in Meek 1990, 35), "Learning is basically a social enterprise, and all the great educational philosophers have reiterated that point over and over again." A discussion based on a topic of mutual interest enables children to further their knowledge and to refine their understanding regarding that topic.

Developing discussion skills requires students to become good listeners and good speakers. They must also develop the ability to ask questions in order to probe the thoughts of others. Moreover, discussion skills require timing, patience, and the ability to interpret what has and has not been stated.

In addition to developing discussion skills, students need to develop the ability to speak before groups to share their knowledge and understandings. The more opportunities students have to speak before the class, the more at ease they become. In social studies, this may begin as book talks about children's books with social studies themes. The student tells why the book was selected to read and briefly outlines the important aspects of the book. For instance, second or third graders might engage in reading biographies such as David Adler's picture book series of famous Americans such as *A Picture Book of Rosa Parks* (Adler 1993) and *A Picture Book of Eleanor Roosevelt* (Adler 1991) and present the information orally. Upper-elementary and middle school students might begin the same way, sharing biographies they've read. Leonard Everett Fisher, Jean Fritz, Russell Freedman, and Diane Stanley are noted authors of biographies for children. Students should be encouraged to use appropriate props during their oral presentations. For instance, one fourth grader wore wire rim glasses, a triangular paper hat, and carried a kite to present his overview of Benjamin Franklin.

Other opportunities for speaking in front of the class include reports on specific historical or geographical topics. Students should be encouraged to use note cards or even create charts with markers to serve as low-tech teleprompters so that they will have easy access to the information they want to convey.

Reading

Reading used to be thought of as a sequence of skills that were taught in isolation. Today, reading is taught as strategies, with skills being taught as they arise and are needed.

To become a strategic reader, the students must become familiar with different ways to approach a topic or read textual material. For instance, if the topic is the new independent countries that formerly made up the Soviet Union, the teacher may have students work together in groups to develop a schematic diagram of what they already know about these independent states (see Figure 2.1).

Thus, the students recall previously gained knowledge before reading about the independent states. Newly gained information gleaned through their reading will be assimilated as they continue to read about and further discuss the topic.

Writing

Writing instruction has changed dramatically within the past twenty years. Now reading and writing are both considered to be processes of meaning making. Writing is considered a recursive activity in that the students generate ideas and questions, gather information and organize their ideas, draft their compositions, and revise and

Formerly USSR

Boris Yeltsin president –INDEPENDENT STATES
of Russia

Need foreign aid

Selling nuclear weapons

Now independent countries

–Economic problems

Overthrow of communism

Ethnic fighting

FIGURE 2.1   Schematic diagram of the independent states that were formerly republics of the USSR by a group of sixth-grade students.

edit the drafts before they share the final version of their writings (Farris 2001; Tompkins 1998).

The integrated instruction approach opened up writing instruction in that writing occurs across the curriculum. No longer are students limited to writing social studies reports; instead, new options are available, including writing in literature response journals and writing poetry, letters, plays, and so on.

❧ *Goal of Interdisciplinary Instruction*

The goal of interdisciplinary instruction is to produce lifelong learners. This is done through respecting the learner, the teacher, and the content. The learning process is stressed as well as the final product. In addition, evaluation and assessment involve a variety of methods and techniques, not just paper-and-pencil tests.

Teaching the Way Students Learn

Advocates of integrated instruction focus on the learner, the concepts to be taught, and the environment. By interacting with books, materials, and other children, students expand their own knowledge and understanding. Enjoyable learning experiences are emphasized. Children are challenged but not threatened. They are encouraged to take risks, knowing that they might fail but that in taking the risk they will have gained from the failed experiences as well.

As a facilitator of learning, the teacher attempts to broaden students' interests in both breadth and depth. Refinement of interest is also supported.

Students develop a positive self-concept by being able to engage in activities of their own choosing and being decision makers. Freedom to choose results in students using their leisure time to pursue their interest in a topic.

Encouraging Decision Making

In making decisions of their own choosing, students are able to pinpoint and refine topics that interest them. In doing so, they are often allowed to work with other students who share a similar interest in a topic. Such collaboration and cooperative learning activities require group decision making as questions arise and decisions must be made, just as is true in any democratic society.

Collaborative projects help children develop the skills of cooperation as they become decision makers.
©Photo by Jean-Claude LeJeune

Teachers can establish a variety of social studies themes as part of the social studies curriculum. Students can help determine through the decision-making process how these themes are to be covered. What materials will be read? What activities are appropriate? What kinds of projects lend themselves to a topic? These and other questions can be addressed by the students either individually or as part of a group.

Creating Citizen Actors

Through democratic decision making, children learn to become "citizen actors"; that is, they learn the role of adult citizens by taking part in classroom civic activities. They learn to express their viewpoints without criticism, the first right of the Bill of Rights being freedom of speech. They learn the importance of casting an opinion or ballot on an issue, be it whether the school cafeteria should serve pizza once a week or who should be the class postmaster for the grading period.

Young and Vardell (1993) point out the value of using theater with nonfiction books such as Aliki's (1986) *Feelings* or Russell Freedman's (1992) *An Indian Winter*. Reader's theatre can help develop empathy in children and help them understand other points of view.

If one explores the literature that is being developed on the purposes and goals of social studies and integrated instruction, one can find ample evidence for the logical incorporation of activities from the two to produce citizen actors. Why citizen actors?

As Linn (1990, 49–50) writes:

Social studies should be the study of how citizens in a society make personal and public decisions on issues that affect their destiny. To keep us from becoming a nation of observers instead of participants, students need to be shown early that the point of social studies is not to be found in terminology like ethnocentric, executive branch, and traditional values, but instead in one's own relationship and personal identification with these terms. One goal of social studies must be to assist youth in organizing concepts in line with their personal reality: connecting new concepts and ideas with known factors in their lives.

The role of the citizen actor is a crucial one for students. Without being cast as such, they are less apt to engage fully in the rights and privileges of being a citizen in a democratic society.

❧ Interdisciplinary Instruction and the Social Studies

In the past, social studies instruction largely centered around the social studies textbook, with some hands-on projects added by the classroom teacher. Brophy (Bracey 1993, 654) referred to elementary social studies textbooks as being "remarkably uniform consisting of compendia of facts organized with the expanding communities curriculum structure." According to Routman (1991, 281):

> Typically, we have taught social studies by saying, "Take out your social studies book and open to page ____." Then there follows a whole-class, round-robin reading, with the teacher stopping occasionally to ask questions and lead the discussion. . . . [S]uch exercises are boring and fail to engage many students.

For students to develop and sustain an interest in social studies, they must have a desire to learn more about it and be motivated to do so. At that point, they become engaged learners.

As Wells (1990, 15) so aptly states, "Unlike many other skillful performances, literate behavior cannot be learned simply by observation and practice." The same is true of being a citizen actor. To paraphrase Wells, democratic behavior cannot be learned simply by observation and practice. Students need to engage in democratic processes in the classroom—collaborative projects, discussions, cooperative learning, problem resolution, and so on—if they are to become effective and responsible citizens as adults.

From brain research, we've learned that learning is both personal and social with a major emotional component in each aspect. As social studies teachers we recognize we must engage our students both personally and socially in the learning experience. "To be fully literate is to have the disposition to engage appropriately with the texts of different types in order to empower action, feeling, and thinking in the context of purposeful social activity" (Wells 1990, 14).

The subject matter boundary of social studies needs to be broken down and integrated instruction principles erected. "At the very least, school tasks can be integrated through common reading and writing processes that cross subject matter. Interdisciplinary themes that provide opportunities to grapple with interpretations, understand others' perspectives, and solve problems require the content of social studies, science, and mathematics, not just of literature" (Hiebert and Fisher 1990, 63). Teaching social studies in an interdisciplinary curriculum serves to strengthen the tenets of the social sciences as well as the other content areas. As children listen, discuss, read, and write about social studies content, they develop a deeper understanding and appreciation of social studies and its respective social sciences. Political science and civics become more than voting in an election—they are how our government works. Supply and demand are understood through discussions and activities that demonstrate the need and demand for a product as well as the economic impact on a community. For instance, the protection of the spotted owl as an endangered species prohibited lumbering to occur in a major forest area in the western part of the United States. This action resulted in hundreds of lumberjacks and sawmill workers being forced out of work and in the price of lumber greatly increasing due to lack of supply.

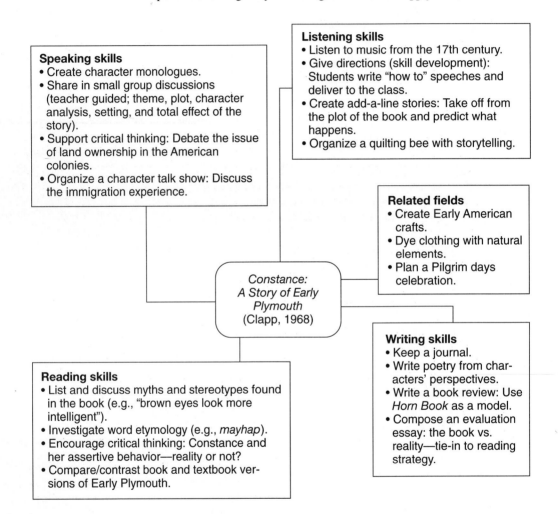

Listening skills
- Listen to music from the 17th century.
- Give directions (skill development): Students write "how to" speeches and deliver to the class.
- Create add-a-line stories: Take off from the plot of the book and predict what happens.
- Organize a quilting bee with storytelling.

Speaking skills
- Create character monologues.
- Share in small group discussions (teacher guided; theme, plot, character analysis, setting, and total effect of the story).
- Support critical thinking: Debate the issue of land ownership in the American colonies.
- Organize a character talk show: Discuss the immigration experience.

Related fields
- Create Early American crafts.
- Dye clothing with natural elements.
- Plan a Pilgrim days celebration.

*Constance:
A Story of Early
Plymouth*
(Clapp, 1968)

Writing skills
- Keep a journal.
- Write poetry from characters' perspectives.
- Write a book review: Use *Horn Book* as a model.
- Compose an evaluation essay: the book vs. reality—tie-in to reading strategy.

Reading skills
- List and discuss myths and stereotypes found in the book (e.g., "brown eyes look more intelligent").
- Investigate word etymology (e.g., *mayhap*).
- Encourage critical thinking: Constance and her assertive behavior—reality or not?
- Compare/contrast book and textbook versions of Early Plymouth.

Idea extensions:

Pilgrim days celebration
Fabricate a Pilgrim village. The different shops will make or sell items that were made in the villages: dried/canned goods, dyes, etc.

Quilting bee with storytelling
Make a quilt from old material brought from home. Tell the stories of the material and stories of family quilts. The history and importance of quilts can be discussed.

Small group discussions
Discuss the myths of settlements of the early colonists vs. the reality of the harsh situations or the myths of stepparents: book vs. media image.

Single-discipline literature unit: Language arts   Theme: Movement in U.S. history

From: Stahl, L., & Johnson, H. 1994. Models for implementing literature in content studies. *The Reading Teacher,* 48 #3, pp. 198–207. Used by permission, International Reading Association.

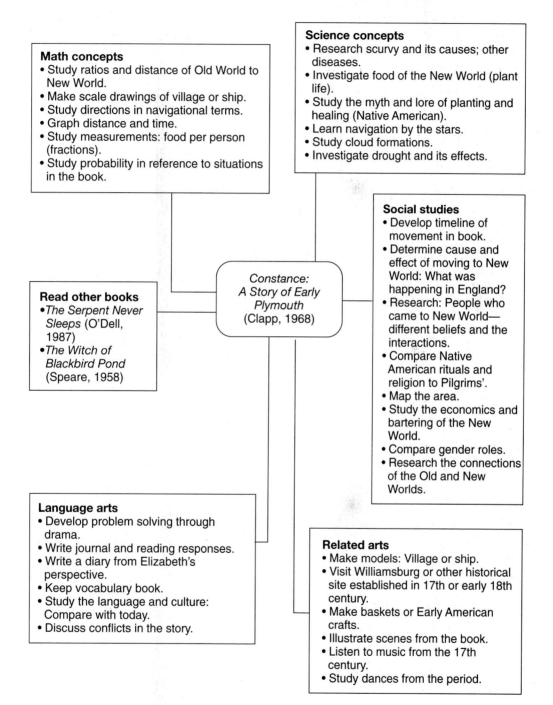

Interdisciplinary literature unit   Theme: Movement in U.S. history

From: Stahl, L., & Johnson, H. 1994. Models for implementing literature in content studies. *The Reading Teacher,* 48 #3, pp. 198–207. Used by permission, International Reading Association.

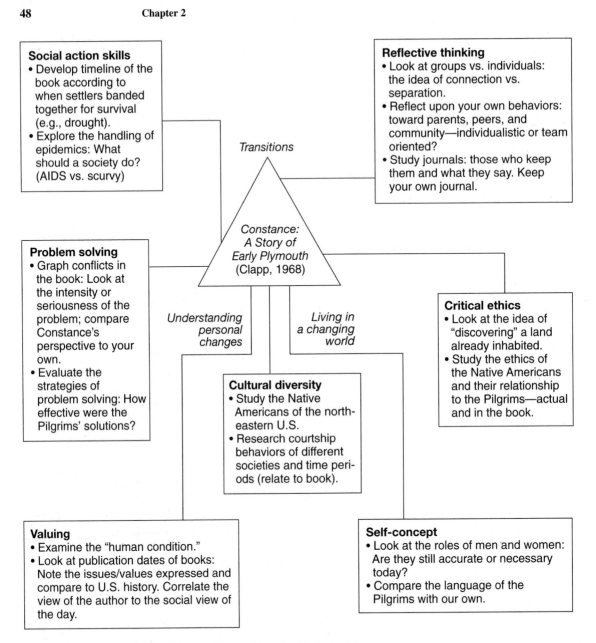

Social action skills
- Develop timeline of the book according to when settlers banded together for survival (e.g., drought).
- Explore the handling of epidemics: What should a society do? (AIDS vs. scurvy)

Transitions

Reflective thinking
- Look at groups vs. individuals: the idea of connection vs. separation.
- Reflect upon your own behaviors: toward parents, peers, and community—individualistic or team oriented?
- Study journals: those who keep them and what they say. Keep your own journal.

Constance: A Story of Early Plymouth (Clapp, 1968)

Problem solving
- Graph conflicts in the book: Look at the intensity or seriousness of the problem; compare Constance's perspective to your own.
- Evaluate the strategies of problem solving: How effective were the Pilgrims' solutions?

Understanding personal changes

Living in a changing world

Critical ethics
- Look at the idea of "discovering" a land already inhabited.
- Study the ethics of the Native Americans and their relationship to the Pilgrims—actual and in the book.

Cultural diversity
- Study the Native Americans of the northeastern U.S.
- Research courtship behaviors of different societies and time periods (relate to book).

Valuing
- Examine the "human condition."
- Look at publication dates of books: Note the issues/values expressed and compare to U.S. history. Correlate the view of the author to the social view of the day.

Self-concept
- Look at the roles of men and women: Are they still accurate or necessary today?
- Compare the language of the Pilgrims with our own.

Integrative literature unit: Transitions   Theme: Movement in U.S. history

From: Stahl, L., & Johnson, H. 1994. Models for implementing literature in content studies. *The Reading Teacher,* 48 #3, pp. 198–207. Used by permission, International Reading Association.

Building a Social Studies Curriculum

In building a social studies curriculum that utilizes interdisciplinary instructional principles, the first step is to identify which social studies concepts should be introduced to students. These should be important concepts that foster both critical and creative thinking and provide an intellectual challenge that students can achieve.

The next step is to outline the type of learning experiences and skills to be taught. The types of student attitudes being developed must also be taken into consideration. Furthermore, it is imperative that the learning climate encourage both inquiry and choice (Routman 1991).

A variety of evaluation and assessment procedures need to be used to gather sufficient information to determine each student's growth and development in the social studies. Checklists, anecdotal records, attitudinal surveys, benchmarks met, lists of books read, journal entries, writing samples, rubrics, and videos of plays or projects are all appropriate measures for this type of curriculum. If there are state or local testing mandates, some provision must be made so that students become used to taking paper-and-pencil tests under a time limitation.

Applying Interdisciplinary Instructional Principles to Classroom Activities

An excellent way to use interdisciplinary instruction as part of the social studies in the elementary/middle school curriculum is through thematic units (Pappas, Kiefer, and Levstik 1998). A thematic unit may be based around a theme such as the Revolutionary War, coming-of-age ceremonies in different cultures around the world (Chinese, African, American Indian, Jewish, etc.), civil rights, economic systems, or any of the social studies standards and substandards. The teacher may provide a variety of books for the students to read in small groups or may select one or two books for the entire class to read. When thematic units are used, the social studies textbook is used as a reference work. (See the interdisciplinary thematic unit on the Middle Ages at the end of this chapter.)

Small groups of students read the same book(s) and then discuss what they have read. In their discussion groups, they formulate questions they want and expect to be answered in the next segment of their reading. After writing down their questions, they write down the answers as they read the material.

Routman (1991) offers informal guidelines for planning an integrated, interdisciplinary social studies unit. She suggests that the process and procedure be considered foremost in integrating a content area such as social studies with the language arts. Here are her specific recommendations (pp. 279–80):

The classroom teacher should integrate social studies throughout the elementary curriculum.

© Lawrence Migdale

1. Develop a semantic web as the class or group brainstorms the topic.
2. Have students select a subtopic by listing their first, second, and third choices of subtopics.

In the Classroom Mini Lesson

Interdisciplinary Social Studies Lesson Plan

*T*he following lesson plan is based on national social studies standards as outlined in Chapter 1 as well as the Illinois Learning Standards for Social Science (Illinois State Board of Education, 1997). Most states have likewise created learning standards and substandards for social studies.

National Social Studies Learning Standard: II. Time, Continuity, and Change: Social studies programs should include experiences that provide for the study of the ways human beings view themselves in and over time, so that the learner can demonstrate an understanding that different people may describe the same event or situation in diverse ways, citing reasons for the differences in views.

Illinois Learning Standard—State Goal 16: Understand events, trends, individuals, and movements shaping the history of Illinois, the United States, and other nations.

Substandard—Goal 16.A.1c. Describe how people in different times and places viewed the world in different ways.

Grade Level: Third

Lesson Plan Objective: Compare and contrast how two different groups of people perceived the geographic area in which they lived.

Time Span: Four days

Materials: Overhead transparencies and markers; overhead projector

Picture books:

Lynn Cherry. 1992. *A River Ran Wild.* Orlando: Harcourt Brace.

Sneed B. Collard. 1999. *1,000 Years Ago on Planet Earth.* Illus. Jonathan Hunt, Boston: Houghton Mifflin. (3 copies)

Florence Perry Heide and Judith Heide Gilliland. 1999. *The House of Wisdom.* Illus. Mary Grandpre. New York: DK Ink. (3 copies)

Ellen B. Jackson. 1998. *Turn of the Century.* Illus. Jan Ellis. New York: Charlesbridge. (3 copies)

Procedures: Read to the class the picture book *A River Ran Wild* by Lynn Cherry. Have the class select three different time periods from the book. For each time period, have students in the class volunteer to offer views of the people who lived near the Nashua River. Make a semantic map on a transparency for

3. Divide the students into small groups of up to four students per subtopic.
4. Have the group develop questions to research for their subtopic of study.
5. Have each group meet with another group to confer over the questions each group generated for their respective subtopics.
6. Have each group establish a format for using resources to discover the answers to the questions they generated about their subtopic.
7. Have all the students take notes on their subtopics.
8. Let students use their notes to write rough drafts.
9. Have each group present the information they gathered to the entire class. (A variety of formats may be used: quiz shows, radio shows, festivals, plays, travelogues, etc.)
10. Have classmates evaluate presentations orally. At least two positive statements must be given by students before a suggestion for improvement can be given.

each of the time periods. Display these on the overhead projector for discussion. Make a T chart listing how the different time periods were alike and how they differed in the ways they used the river.

Have the students get into small groups of three students. Each group selects one of the other three picture books mentioned in the earlier list. The students take turns reading their book aloud. After they read the book, they make a semantic map of two different groups of people and how they viewed the same event or situation. Next have the students list comparisons and differences in a T chart. Finally, each student uses the information from the T chart to write a descriptive, expository piece comparing and contrasting the views and perceptions of the two groups of people.

Day 2: The students proof each other's work for accuracy and writing skills. The students then rewrite to produce their final drafts. They make an illustration to accompany their descriptive writing.

Day 3: The students are regrouped in groups of three so that each member of the group had read and written about a different book. The students each give a brief book talk and then read their descriptive paper and share their illustration.

Follow-up Activity: Have the students find newspaper or magazine articles. The students can compare how the same story (i.e., news, sports, weather) is reported by different reporters. Put the articles on the same news event on construction paper and place on the bulletin board along with T charts of how the stories are similar and how they differ.

Assessment:

Scoring: 5 points—Student must include three similarities and three differences for the two groups of people.

4 points—Student must include total of five similarities/differences.

3 points—Student must include total of four similarities/differences.

2 points—Student must include total of three similarities/differences.

1 point—Student must include total of two similarities/differences.

The writing piece will be graded on a scale of 1–3, with 3 being well developed, 2 average, and 1 as needs work.

11. Evaluate group interactions and content learned. This is done by the teacher and through student self-evaluations. In addition, an essay test given by the teacher may be included at this point.

As part of this interdisciplinary unit, music from the Middle Ages was shared and discussed by the students. *Bartering* was introduced as an economic term as students were given a variety of different items to trade. Art projects included drawing illustrations of major scenes and characters. Students considered home remedies as part of science.

Routman's process/procedure approach allows for efficient classroom organization and structure. Little time is wasted as the students proceed through the eleven steps. All of the students contribute to one another's learning in the area of social studies. Thus, learning becomes a social activity.

Chapter Summary

Social studies instruction can be integrated into the elementary/middle school curriculum to meet common goals. As a result, the learner, the teacher, and the social studies content are respected. Students are encouraged to make choices and take risks in their learning. As citizen actors, they repeatedly engage in the democratic process in their classroom as they develop an interest in and greater understanding of social studies.

Children's Books

Adler, D. 1991. *A picture book of Eleanor Roosevelt.* New York: Holiday House. A biography of former First Lady and humanitarian Eleanor Roosevelt. (Gr. 1–3)

Adler, D. 1993. *A picture book of Rosa Parks.* New York: Holiday House. A biography of civil rights activist Rosa Parks. (Gr. 1–3)

Aliki. 1986. *Feelings.* New York: Morrow Junior Books. This picture book for primary-grade children explores different emotions.

Freedman, R. 1992. *An Indian winter.* New York: Holiday House. Actual photos show the conditions Indians faced during the winter months.

References

Bracey, G. W. 1993. Elementary curriculum materials: Still a way to go. *Phi Delta Kappan* 74 (8): 654, 656.

Brophy, J. 1992. Probing the subtleties of subject-matter teaching. *Educational Leadership* 49 (7): 4–8.

Farris, P. J. 2001. *Language arts: Process, product, and assessment.* 3rd ed. Boston: McGraw-Hill.

Hiebert, E. H., and C. W. Fisher. 1990. Whole language: Three themes for the future. *Educational Leadership* 47 (6): 62–3.

Illinois State Board of Education. 1997. *Illinois Learning Standards for Social Science.* Springfield, IL: Illinois State Board of Education.

Linn, J. B. 1990. Whole language in social studies. *Social Science Record* 27 (2): 49–55.

McCarty, B. J. 1991. Whole language: From philosophy to practice. *The Clearing House* 65 (2): 73–6.

Meek, A. 1990. On 25 years of Foxfire: A conversation with Eliot Wigginton. *Educational Leadership* 47 (6): 30–6.

Pappas, C. C., B. Z. Kiefer, and L. S. Levstik. 1998. *An integrated language perspective in the elementary schools: Theory into action.* 3rd ed. New York: Addison-Wesley.

Routman, R. 1991. *Invitations: Changing as teachers and learners K–12.* Portsmouth, NH: Heinemann.

Tompkins, G. E. 1998. *Language arts: Content and teaching strategies.* 4th ed. New York: Macmillan.

Weil, M., E. Calhoun, and B. Joyce. 2000. *Models of teaching.* 6th ed. Englewood Cliffs, NJ: Prentice-Hall.

Wells, G. 1990. Creating the conditions to encourage literate thinking. *Educational Leadership* 47 (6): 13–7.

Young, T. A., and S. Vardell. 1993. Weaving reader's theatre and nonfiction into the curriculum. *The Reading Teacher* 46 (5): 396–406.

In the Classroom Mini Lesson

Thematic Unit on the Middle Ages

*U*ntil recent years, few trade books about the Middle Ages have been available for children to read. The "age of chivalry" greatly interests children. This unit was designed for students in grades 5 through 8.

The entire class reads E. L. Konigsburg's *A Proud Taste for Scarlet and Miniver* and engages in the integrated activities as outlined in Figure 2.2. At the conclusion of these activities, each student then selects and reads a second novel about the Middle Ages and keeps a literature journal to record reactions and responses. Students are paired with someone who is also reading the same book. They read and write in their response journals, then exchange journals to share their thoughts and reaction on the same material. They meet with their partner each day or every other day to discuss the book. The social studies textbook is used as needed for reference.

Children's Books

Aliki. 1983. *Medieval Feast.* New York: Thomas Crowell. (Gr. 2–7)   J 394.15
    Nobility of the manor house and their serfs prepare for a visit from the king and the queen, complete
    with their royal entourage. The illustrations demonstrate a variety of preparatory activities including
    hunting, fishing, and preparing food.

Bellairs, John. 1989. *The Trolley to Yesterday.* New York: Dial. (Gr. 4–8)
    This time warp story takes Johnny and his friend, Fergie, back to 1453 and the Byzantine Empire. The
    two friends arrive in Constantinople just prior to the Turkish invasion.

Cushman, Karen. 1994. *Catherine, Called Birdy.* New York: Clarion. (Gr. 6–8)   J paperbacks
    Birdy is fourteen and she faithfully keeps a diary of her experiences in England in 1290. The diary spans
    a one-year period during which Birdy's father attempts to marry her off for money or land. This book is
    a Newbery Honor Book.

Cushman, Karen. 1995. *The Midwife's Apprentice.* New York: Clarion. (Gr. 4–8)
    The setting is the Middle Ages where a young orphan must fend for herself until she becomes
    apprenticed to a midwife. Very accurate descriptions of details of the period. This book won the 1995
    Newbery Award.

de Angeli, Marguerite. 1949. *The Door in the Wall.* New York: Doubleday. (Gr. 5–8) Adult F PZ7.D35
    D.1949
    This award-winning book is the story of Robin, the son of a knight, who becomes ill and loses the use of
    his legs. A monk takes him in and teaches him woodcarving. Along the way, Robin also learns patience
    and strength. When the castle of Lindsay is threatened, Robin rescues the townspeople.

Hunt, Jonathan. 1989. *Illuminations.* New York: Bradbury. (Gr. 3–5)
    This alphabet book includes pictures of words that are from the Middle Ages.

Konigsburg, E. L. 1973. *A Proud Taste for Scarlet and Miniver.* (Gr. 4–8) F FG
    Illustrated by the author, this historical fiction novel focuses on Eleanor of Aquitaine. Proud Eleanor is
    waiting for her young husband, King Henry II, to join her in heaven. Henry had died before she had, but
    has not yet been judged favorably by the angels. While she waits, Eleanor reflects on the various events
    of her life. Children will find this book to be both interesting and amusing.

Lasker, Joe. 1976. *Merry Ever After: The Story of Two Medieval Weddings.* New York: Viking. (Gr. 3–8) J 392.5
    Two weddings, one of a couple from nobility and the other of a peasant couple, are described as the
    book looks at the betrothed couples as children and their marriages as teenagers.

Macaulay, David. 1973. *Cathedral: The Story of Its Construction.* Boston: Houghton Mifflin. (Gr. 3–8) Oversize
    This book is a classic picture book that goes into intricate detail, portraying the actual design and Folio
    construction of a magnificent cathedral. FO 72 b

Macaulay, David. 1978. *Castle.* Boston: Houghton Mifflin. (Gr. 3–8)
    This book illustrates the various phases of the construction of a castle. P Mac

Continued

Osband, Gillian, and Andrew, Robert. 1991. *Castles.* New York: Orchard. (Gr. K–8)
 This pop-up picture book is filled with information that will intrigue students. Early designs of castles are depicted, including how they expanded over the years. Castle life is discussed along with the lives of knights. The book portrays and describes ten castles still in existence from a variety of European countries.

Temple, Frances. 1994. *The Ramsay Scallop.* New York: Orchard. (Gr. 7–8)
 In a marriage designed to join their parents' estates, thirteen-year-old Elenor is betrothed to Thomas, who left on a crusade eight years earlier, in 1292. When they are reluctant to wed, Father Gregory sends Elenor and Thomas on a pilgrimage to Ramsey, Spain, where they receive a scallop shell. This book is targeted at the mature reader.

Winthrop, Elizabeth. 1985. *The Castle in the Attic.* New York: Holiday House. (Gr. 4–7)
 William receives an old, realistic model of a castle as a gift from the housekeeper. She warns him that it is very special. This fantasy will appeal to students interested in magic and the wizards of the Middle Ages.

Winthrop, Elizabeth. 1993. *The Battle for the Castle.* New York: Bantam. (Gr. 4–7)
 In this sequel to *The Castle in the Attic,* William is transported back to Sir Simon's castle in the Middle Ages using a magic token sent by his former housekeeper. With the help of his friend Jason, William must destroy the invading rats and save the kingdom.

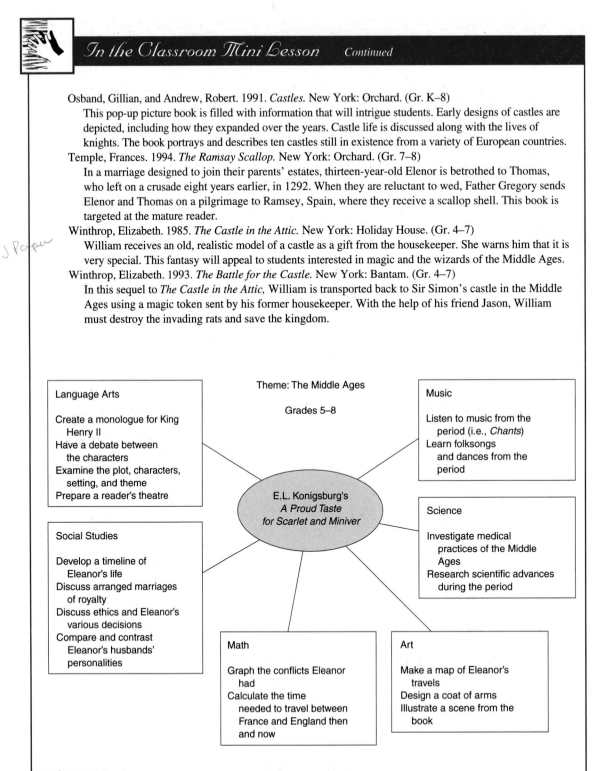

FIGURE 2.2   Integrated Unit. Theme: The Middle Ages, Grades 5–8.

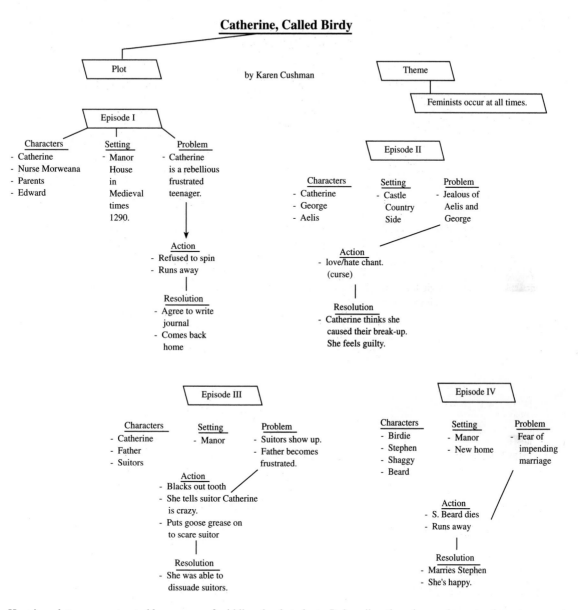

Here is a plot map constructed by a group of middle school students. It describes the primary elements, characters, problems, and settings of *Catherine, Called Birdy*.

This illustration by a student accompanied the group's plot map for *Catherine, Called Birdy*.

Chapter 3

© Elizabeth Crews

Classroom Assessment in Social Studies

L. Ruth Struyk and Lisa M. Mehlig
Northern Illinois University

Assessment helps the teacher gauge each student's strengths and weaknesses, and aids in instructional decision making.

—George W. Maxim
Social Studies and the Elementary School Child (4th Ed.)

Objectives

———————————— ⌇ ————————————

Readers will

- understand the difference between assessment and evaluation in social studies;
- be able to explain different assessment methods; and
- be able to construct a variety of different assessment tools for social studies.

Introduction

Teaching social studies as an interdisciplinary approach has resulted in increased instructional time at the elementary level as teachers integrate social studies into art, language arts, math, music, physical education, and science. Rather than "running out of time" to fit social studies in during the school day, many teachers have viewed social studies as a content area in which the other content areas can be extended and taught.

Over the past several years, social studies has become a more visible school subject, and the conception of learning social studies has evolved from doing and knowing to experiencing and making meaning. The tacit and piecemeal curriculum that has long characterized the social studies classroom seems to be gradually giving way to a more coherent and integrated set of objectives, benchmarks, and performance indicators. This approach is goal oriented with an emphasis on learner outcomes: the knowledge, skills, attitudes, values, and dispositions to action that teachers wish to develop in students (Alleman & Brophy, 1999b, 334).

The National Council for the Social Studies (NCSS) Advisory Committee on Testing and Evaluation (1994, 3–5) recommends the following guidelines for assessment in social studies:

- Evaluation instruments should: focus on the curriculum goals and objectives; be used to improve curriculum and instruction; measure both content and process; be chosen for instructional, diagnostic, and prescriptive purposes; and reflect a high degree of fairness to all people and groups.
- Evaluation of student achievement should: be used solely to and improve teaching and learning; involve a variety of instruments and approaches to measure knowledge, skills, and attitudes; be congruent with the objectives and the classroom experiences of the students examined; and be sequential and cumulative.
- State and local agencies should: secure appropriate funding to implement and support evaluation programs; support the education of teachers in selecting, developing, and using assessment instruments; involve teachers and other social studies professionals in formulating objectives, planning instruction and evaluation, and designing and selecting evaluation instruments; and measure long-term effects of social studies instruction.

Consider questioning as the spokes of a wagon wheel. Convergent questions, that is, questions with only one right answer, are like the spokes going in toward the hub of the wheel. Divergent questions, that is, questions with many possible correct responses, are like the spokes pointing outward with many possibilities. Assessment and evaluation in social studies must be more than true/false or multiple-choice questions that measure low-level thinking skills. This chapter examines how assessment can measure higher-level thinking skills through the use of testing and authentic, alternative measures.

❧ Classroom Assessment in Social Studies

For many years, no one thought about how students learned and how learning styles also affected students' ability to be successful on assessment activities. However, current literature and school reform reflect a growing belief that students do, indeed, learn differently (e.g., visually, auditorily, kinesthetically, spatially). Similarly, in recent years, to reflect the changes in understanding learning styles, teachers have designed classroom assessments that have moved from traditional paper-and-pencil quizzes and tests to a variety of assessment methods. In an attempt to combine classical assessment design factors with emerging assessment trends, teachers are utilizing a variety of assessment methods in conjunction with instructional activities to facilitate their ability to determine how well students understand and act on instructional objectives. It is important to remember that no matter what type of assessment tools teachers use, those assessments must provide information about the instructional objectives.

The first and foremost purpose of assessment should be to inform educators, students, and parents about the level of understanding and ability of the students in relation to the instructional objectives. Without clear and precise information relating to the objectives, the evaluations that teachers make are not going to generate informed instructional decisions. The stronger the information obtained from the assessment tool, the stronger the evaluation, whether the evaluation influences lesson planning or is used as a final indicator of students' understanding of the material (i.e., grades).

✍ *Assessment Versus Evaluation*

Because of the interactive nature of assessment and evaluation, it is often easy to confuse the two concepts. *Assessment* refers to the collection, storage, and retrieval of data (Cangelosi 1990; Popham 1995; Weber 1999). Assessments are merely tools for collecting the data or information about the students' levels of understanding of the instructional objectives. Data may be retained in a grade book, on individual tests stacked on the teacher's desk, or in an electronic grade book using a software program. In the classroom, some of the assessment tools used to collect information regarding students' performance include projects, portfolios, quizzes, homework, presentations, and traditional teacher-made tests. *Evaluations* involve teacher judgments that are made based on the information obtained from the assessment. When instructional objectives and assessments are aligned, then the more information obtained about the objectives through various assessments results in a greater potential to make accurate decisions regarding students' performance.

Although there are many methods of assessing students' performance, all of these methods fall into two basic categories, formal and informal. *Formal assessments* are very structured assessments that are planned in advance, administered under controlled situations, and have detailed scoring schemes. Formal assessment includes traditional teacher-made tests, oral presentations, and group projects. Standardized tests are the most formal tests schools use because the administration of the test, the scoring, and the interpretation of an individual student's score is compared with a grounded, well-defined framework or against predetermined levels of achievement. *Informal assessments* are unplanned, unstructured, and spontaneous. Informal assessments are the questions teachers ask to find out what the students know during class activities, discussions, and other activities. Informal assessments are also those nonverbal cues that teachers use to determine students' level of attentiveness or confusion (i.e., blank stares, daydreaming). More than 80 percent of teachers' daily activities are spent conducting informal assessment activities (Wiggins, 1989).

Formative and Summative Evaluations

Similarly, evaluations can be broken into two categories, formative and summative (Cangelosi 1990; Popham 1995; Weber 1999). *Formative evaluations* are decisions made by teachers that influence their immediate teaching. Asking a series of questions over material and then deciding the students are ready to move on to new material is an example of a formative evaluation. *Summative evaluations* are those that indicate either an end point in a unit or level of student performance.

The teacher determining a grade for a particular grading period after adding all of the assessment scores is an example of a summative evaluation because it represents the final level of the students' performance. As with informal assessments, formative evaluations occur many times during a lesson while summative evaluations are used to communicate individual performance on students' work throughout the year.

To make sound evaluation decisions—both formative and summative—quality assessments, whether formal or informal, that consider ten key factors must be developed. According to Herman, Aschbacher, and Winters (1992, 13), those key factors are:

1. Assessments must measure the instructional goals and objectives.
2. Assessments must involve the examination of the processes as well as the products of learning.
3. Performance-based activities do not constitute assessments per se.
4. Cognitive learning theory and its constructivist approach to knowledge acquisition support the need to integrate assessment methodologies with instructional outcomes and curriculum content.
5. An integrated and active view of student learning requires the assessment of holistic and complex performances.
6. Assessment design is dependent on assessment purpose; grading and monitoring student progress are distinct from diagnosis and improvement.
7. The key to effective assessment is the match between the task and the intended student outcome.
8. The criteria used to evaluate student performance are critical; in the absence of criteria, assessment remains an isolated and episodic activity.
9. Quality assessment provides substantive data for making informed decisions about student learning.
10. Assessment systems that provide the most comprehensive feedback on student growth include multiple measures taken over time.

In relation to the preceding ten key factors, assessment information should further relate to the instructional objectives not only by content but also by behavioral construct. Several models of taxonomies are currently in use (e.g., Bloom, Cangelosi, and Quellmalz). No matter which taxonomy is used, the intent is to have a match between the behavior by which students learned the instructional objective (cognitive, psychomotor, and affective) and the assessment activities. Bloom's taxonomy, the taxonomy with which teachers are most familiar, subdivides cognitive behaviors into six levels. The following six levels of taxonomy are adapted from Bloom et al. (1956):

1. **Knowledge.** Knowledge is defined as the remembering of previously learned material. An example of a knowledge-level item would be "Who was the second president of the United States?" +1 for John Adams.
2. **Comprehension.** Comprehension is defined as the ability to grasp the meaning of material. An example of a comprehension-level item would be "In your own words, paraphrase the second Bill of Rights." +1 for the right of each individual to own firearms.

3. ***Application.*** Application refers to the ability to use learned material in new and concrete situations. An example of an application-level item would be "You and your friend are in the mall after school. As you walk out of one of the stores, the mall security guard stops you and accuses you of shoplifting. He places you in the mall security office and wants to search your bags. What should you do? Please explain why you choose to answer as you did?" +1 for calling a parent or other adult. +1 for indicating that under the law you have the right to make a phone call.

4. ***Analysis.*** Analysis refers to the ability to break down material into its component parts so that its organizational structure may be understood. An example of an analysis-level question would be "Analyze the effects of mass production on economical situations." Answer should include explanation that economic situation was enhanced by the availability of more goods produced cheaply while still maintaining quality. Goods were now available to more individuals at a price they could afford, thus increasing the standard of living.

5. ***Synthesis.*** Synthesis refers to the ability to put parts together to form a new whole. The following is an example of a synthesis-level item. "You are traveling along the Oregon trail in late summer. You are at the base of the Rocky Mountains and are deciding whether to continue along the trail and be on the other side by winter or stay where you are for the winter. Defend your decision. Be sure to include dangers, if any, for continuing, cost of supplies for crossing or staying, and what you will do for housing if you stay."

6. ***Evaluation.*** Evaluation is concerned with the ability to judge the value of a poem, research project, or statement for a given purpose. An example of an evaluation-level item would be "Using the following assessment criteria, evaluate each of four of your peers' research papers and provide comments to them so that may include those revisions when they prepare the next draft."

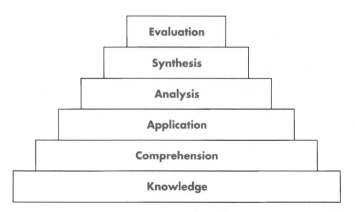

Bloom's taxonomy of educational objectives: cognitive domain.

However, for most teaching activities, a breakdown of the cognitive taxonomy into two major divisions and five categories is appropriate. The two major divisions would be knowledge and intellectual levels. Knowledge-level assessment activities are those that measure simple memory, such as matching a state to its capital, remembering facts about the beginning of the Revolutionary War, and steps for amending the Constitution. Intellectual-level activities measure higher-level thinking skills such as how well students comprehend a particular passage; how well they can identify examples of concepts; whether or not they can determine why a relationship exists; when it is appropriate to use a particular rule, theory, or law; and problem solving that involves a combination of synthesis, evaluation, and analysis. By matching what the student knows about the content of the objective (e.g., history of the Great Salt Lake from 1885 to 2000) and the construct of the objective (e.g., memorization), the assessment will be congruent with the instructional objective.

In many instances, the assessment activities can be incorporated into the learning activity. This can be accomplished by using checklists or rubrics for oral presentations (see Figure 3.1) or by having students using peer evaluations for group work. An example might be a group of students giving a presentation regarding what supplies must be included in a covered wagon in relation to the number of persons, the type of animal pulling the wagon, and the terrain. A group who was presenting what would be needed for a family of five when crossing the plains would have different content in the presentation than a group with the same family preparing to follow the Oregon Trail across the Rockies. During the presentation a teacher can assess the content by following the criteria of the rubric for the oral presentation and the analytical scoring for the content. For the same learning activity, group members could follow their presentation by evaluating each member's contribution to the development and delivery of the project. The different ways that learning activities can be assessed by rubrics or combining rubrics with analytical scoring will be discussed later in the chapter.

It is extremely important that no matter what assessment tool is used or the type of activity, the assessment results should be made available to the student in a timely manner. The longer an assessment activity is not returned to students, the less important and relevant it becomes. Traditionally, assessments are used to assign grades, yet the purpose of the assessment is to provide feedback to the teacher, for instructional purposes. In other words, assessment enables the teacher to know what to teach next or reteach. If the assessment results are returned two weeks later, the assessment is for summative evaluation purposes only (i.e., assigning a grade). If assessment results are returned immediately and assessment components are reviewed with students, then the assessment activity truly becomes a learning activity. By incorporating learning activities with assessment activities, it is possible to create positive learning environments in relation to assessment as well as learning activities. By creating a nonthreatening learning environment that includes assessment, it may be possible that such activities may also help reduce the stigma of tests and assessment activities as threatening or punitive.

Undeniably, a primary function of assessments in the classroom is to provide educators with data upon which they can determine and report levels of achievement, ability, and competency. Therefore, to make accurate and appropriate decisions based on assessment information, teachers must use a variety of instruments that are closely aligned to instructional objectives. Instructional objectives identify the focus of the instruction and notify students of skills that must be acquired through the course of instruction and demonstrated at times of assessment. In addition to the importance of matching delivery and assessment methods to instructional objectives in terms of content and construct, however, teachers must also be sure to gather sufficient data upon which they make their decisions. Therefore, to increase the accuracy of decisions, teachers should assess each objective with more than one tool. Furthermore, teachers should assess each object with variant tools to ensure that they are measuring the students' skill ability rather than the students' ability to complete the assessment task itself. Finally, teachers can increase the accuracy of their decisions, not only through multiple measures of a given unit, but also through multiple measures over time.

Benchmarks

Increasingly states are setting learning benchmarks for social studies instruction. In other words, students are expected to understand specific social studies concepts by certain grade levels. An example of a benchmark is the following: *By the end of fourth grade the student is able to state and describe the three branches of government.* Teachers need to make certain their social studies curriculum objectives and goals include their respective state's benchmarks.

Methods of Assessments

Students can be assessed in a variety of ways. Different techniques are used for informal assessments (i.e., those that are less structured, spontaneous) than are used for formal assessments (i.e., those that are structured, planned) (Cangelosi 1990; Miller 1995; Popham 1998, Weber 1999). Teachers can collect information in several different ways using informal assessments techniques.

The most common method of informal assessment is that of questions the teacher directs to the students during class discussions and group activities. By asking students questions that address the learning activities, teachers can get a general understanding of how well the students are understanding the material. It is important to remember that a teacher using questions directed to the students during the learning activities must be sure that all students are actively participating in responding to the question. In this way, the teacher gets a realistic picture of the class's level of understanding of the material rather than probing the understanding of just a few students. An accurate measure can be accomplished by asking students by name to respond directly to questions. It is important, however, to remember that if a student does not know the answer, the student should not be made to feel ignorant or less able. When the class as a whole doesn't know the answer to a series of questions, teachers clearly recognize the need to reteach or review the given information. In many instances, the teacher may need to prompt the students to facilitate the students in formulating, articulating, or clarifying responses. It is also appropriate to encourage students to pass

Children need to critique and to evaluate their own work if they are to grow as learners.
©Mary Kate Denny/PhotoEdit

the question on to a classmate as long as the student is not always allowed to demonstrate avoidance behavior.

During group activities, the teacher may not be able to pose questions to the class as a whole to get a measure of the students' understanding. Instead, the teacher may walk around the room and gather information about students' understanding by listening to the groups and documenting common understandings and misunderstandings. In addition, to get feedback about group understanding or to assist the group in moving forward or considering different methods of approaching the activity, the teacher could ask questions of the individual groups and group members. By asking questions of the individual groups and the class as a whole, the teacher keeps the students focused on the instructional objectives and, therefore, the purpose of the activity. It is important for teachers to continually monitor the students' progress in the activity so that when the activity is finished the teacher can determine whether the students need to spend more time refining their knowledge or whether the teacher can begin to present new material.

☜ Assessment Tools

If the purpose of assessment were just to provide the teacher with information about students' understanding of the classroom activities and there were no need to be accountable to students, other teachers, parents, school personnel, and the com-

Computer software aids teachers in recording student performance. Here a teacher works at home recording student test grades.

©Frank Siteman/Stock Boston

munity, formal assessments would not be necessary. That is unrealistic. Teachers must have detailed information that indicates how well students are achieving the instructional objectives in order to inform parents, students, school personnel, and the community of the students' achievement, ability, and competency. To better accomplish this, teachers must give formal assessment activities. In addition to providing the accountability needed within the educational community, formal assessment activities help determine how well each student understands the instructional objectives. Such information is extremely important if the goal of the teaching is for the teacher to help the student achieve the learning objectives. Without the formal assessment activities, teachers' perceptions of what a student understands may be misleading. If, during informal assessment activities, the teacher only asks the student questions that the student cannot answer, then the teacher's perception of the student's ability will be that the student has not achieved the instructional objectives. If the teacher asks only questions that the student can answer, then the teacher's perception is that the student has achieved the instructional objectives. Formal assessments (i.e., those that are structured, planned, have detailed scoring schemes) are a means by which teachers can gather further data to determine an overall picture of how well students have achieved the learning objectives. Formal assessments include paper-and-paper tests, performance assessments, formal observations, and portfolios. All assessments, whether formal or informal, are based on instructional objectives. An instructional objective is the cognitive (i.e., thinking), psychomotor (i.e., physical), and affective (i.e., valuing) behavior that the teacher expects students to use when learning. Objectives should be listed in student outcome form (e.g., the student will be able to define the vocabulary words for the lesson). In addition, the objective should always be written so that the student's achievement of the objective is observable (e.g., define, remember, recall, analyze, paraphrase). The following is an example of an objective taken from the Illinois Learning Standards in Social Science (Illinois Board of Education, 1997): "Students will identify concepts of responsible citizenship including respect for the law, patriotism, civility and working with others" (p. 44).

Paper-and-Pencil Tests

Traditionally, instructional objectives have been assessed using the paper-and-pencil tests. These tests rely on multiple-choice, true-false, matching, fill-in-the-blank, short answer, and essay questions. While every teacher is familiar with these tests, these tests do not necessarily provide information regarding the instructional objectives. The number one factor when designing the assessment activity as indicated by Herman, Aschbacher, and Winters (1992) is that the assessment items measure the instructional goals and objectives. If the assessment items do not match the content and the behavioral construct of the objective, then the assessment is of little value (Cangelosi 1990; Popham 1995). When writing items, teachers should ask, "When answering this assessment item, do students have to think about the content and use the construct of the instructional objective in order to be successful?"

☙ *Alternative Assessment*

According to Alleman and Brophy (1999a), the purpose of the learning situation determines the different forms and times for assessment. In addition, the purpose also determines how the assessment will be used to carry out social studies goals for the ten thematic strands. Alleman and Brophy (1999a) suggest developing alternative assessment tools to quizzes and teacher-made tests. They have created six guiding principles for such alternative assessment tools:

- Assessment is considered an integral part of the curriculum and instruction process;
- Assessment is viewed as a thread that is woven into the curriculum, beginning before instruction and occurring at junctures throughout in an effort to monitor, assess, revise, and expand what is being taught and learned;
- A comprehensive assessment plan should be goal oriented, appropriate in level of difficulty, feasible, and cost effective;
- Assessment should benefit the learner (promote self-reflection and self-regulation) and inform teaching practices; and
- Assessment results should be documented to "track" resources and develop learning profiles. (Alleman and Brophy 1999a, 16)

Assessment needs to be considered as an integral part of the curriculum and not as an additional task or afterthought.

Rubrics

Assessment activities other than the traditional paper-pencil test can be measured and evaluated using assessment instruments such as rubrics or checklists. Rubrics attempt to combine information that is assessed holistically (i.e., the assessment activity has a range of points but the points cannot be broken down specifically) and information that is assessed analytically (i.e., the assessment activity has a range of points and the points are clearly identified so that student knows exactly where points were lost). Furthermore, rubrics, like traditional paper-pencil tests, may not assess one instructional objective but may focus on several. The following are examples of rubrics. The rubric in Figure 3.1 was created to provide information to students doing oral presentations. It assesses not only the students' oral presentation skills but also their understanding of the content. This type of rubric may be one that is used to assess students in two content areas, language arts and social studies. To create the rubric, teachers must have an understanding of their instructional objectives and what behaviors students must demonstrate to indicate their level of ability or understanding of the content and construct of those objectives. If the rubric in Figure 3.1 only measured speaking skills, then a student who has excellent presentation skills will receive a higher score in social studies than will a student who has poor speaking skills but who has achieved the instructional objectives in social studies. The second rubric (Figure 3.2) incorporates elements of report writing on a 0 to 4 scale.

When creating a scoring rubric, it is important that teachers remember two important factors contributing to the creation of the rubric. First, the rubric should be easy to use and, second, should use an even set of numbers for the criteria. The first factor is that the rubric should be kept simple. The more complex the rubric, the harder it is for teachers to score and to score consistently. Therefore, the number of scoring criteria should be kept manageable given the assessment

Name:_____ Date:_____

Content	4	3	2	1	0
Oral Presentation	Excellent voice & diction	Good voice & diction	Trouble hearing voice & understanding some words	Rarely could hear or understand words	No attempt
Historical Content	No errors	Only minor errors	Several major errors	Many errors	No attempt
Organization of Historical Content	No organizational errors	Only minor errors	Several major errors	Many errors	No attempt

FIGURE 3.1 An example of a scoring rubric for an oral presentation in social studies.

Evaluating Writing: Reports

	References (5)	Organization (5)	Presentation (5)	Sentence Structure (5)	Mechanics (5)

4	4+ references
	magazines
	encyclopedia
	books
	internet
	video
	newspaper
	interview
		Strong content
		Strong beginning,
		  middle, and end
		Flow
		All ideas
		  sequenced
		All ideas logical
		Neat
			Fresh, original
			Focuses on topic
			Many supporting
			  details
			4+ visual aids
				Clearly written
				Complete sentences
				Compound/
				  complex sentences
				Variety of sentence
				  length
				Good content
				  vocabulary
					Few or no errors:
					Capitalization
					Ending
					  punctuation
					Commas
					Paragraphs
					  indented
					Spelling

3	3+ references
	magazines
	encyclopedia
	books
	internet
	video
	newspaper
	interview
		Most ideas
		  connected
		Good beginning,
		  middle, and end
		Most ideas
		  sequenced
		Most ideas logical
			Some original ideas
			General focus
			  on topic
			Some supporting
			  details included
			3+ visual aids
				Most sentences
				  clearly written
				Most sentences
				  complete
				Simple sentences
				Some variety
				  of length
				Some content
				  vocabulary
					Some errors:
					Capitalization
					Ending
					  punctuation
					Commas
					Paragraphs
					  indented
					Spelling

2	2+ references
	magazines
	encyclopedia
	books
	internet
	video
	newspaper
	interview
		Some ideas
		  connected
		Attempts
		  beginning, middle,
		  and end
		Not always
		  sequenced
		Not always logical
			Few original ideas
			Moves away
			  from focus
			Few supporting
			  details
			2+ visual aids
				Some unclear
				  sentences
				Some run-on,
				  fragmented
				  sentences
				Little variety
				  of length
				Little content
				  vocabulary
					Many errors:
					Capitalization
					Ending
					  punctuation
					Commas
					Paragraphs
					  indented
					Spelling

1	1+ references
	magazines
	encyclopedia
	books
	internet
	video
	newspaper
	interview
		Few ideas
		  connected
		Lacks beginning,
		  middle, and end
		Little sequence
		Little logic
			Incomplete ideas
			Unfocused
			Lacks details
			1+ visual aids
				Sentences
				  not clear
				Frequent
				  fragmented
				  sentences
				No variety
				No content
				  vocabulary
					Serious errors:
					Capitalization
					Ending
					  punctuation
					Commas
					Paragraphs
					  indented
					Spelling

0	No attempt	No attempt	No attempt	No attempt	No attempt

FIGURE 3.2   An example of a scoring rubric for a written social studies report.

Written by: McWilliams, S., Vance, H., & Newsome, P. (1998). Tifton, GA: Omega Elementary School, Tift County School System. Used by permission.

activity. For example, rubrics for written assessment activities would be different from those designed to assess oral activities. Written assessments allow the teacher to reread the information. Oral presentations, however far are more difficult to assess. If it is possible, teachers should videotape the oral presentation and then review it later to double-check scoring. However, limiting the number of scoring criteria for an oral activity as opposed to a written one makes immediate scoring more manageable.

The second critical factor in designing rubrics (as well as rating scales) is to consider the range of numeric or descriptive values that can be placed on a particular component of the activity. Teachers want to be sure to provide a range of points or descriptors that give the students and other members of the educational community appropriate levels of feedback. Teachers want to avoid designing rubrics that provide only holistic measures or provide meaningless and vague feedback. For example, the rubric in Figure 3.1 does not allow the teacher or other evaluator to choose an insignificant, middle-of-the-road rating that would fail to provide the teacher and student with meaningful information about the student's achievement of the objective.

Also, teachers who use rubrics should be sure to provide students with a copy of the rubric at the time that the activity is introduced. Such practice enables students to evaluate their own work before it is evaluated by either another student or the teacher. This helps students to engage in self-teaching, self-reflection, and self-evaluation (Batzle 1992; Farr and Tone 1994; Miller 1995).

Portfolio Assessment

Portfolio assessment is one method of many to collect information about what the students know in relation to the instructional objectives. Portfolio assessment is a way for teachers, students, and parents to see an overall picture of each student's growth. Perhaps more significantly, portfolio assessment enables students to see their progress in relation to themselves, not in relation to how they perform against their classmates.

When considering the use and design of a portfolio, the teacher needs to take into account the purpose of the portfolio. Portfolios basically have two purposes. One type of portfolio is the instructional portfolio (Batzle 1992; Farr and Tone 1994; Miller 1995). The purpose of the instructional portfolio is as a tool used by the teacher and the student to direct the instruction for the student. The other form of portfolios is the assessment portfolio (Batzle 1992; Farr and Tone 1994; Miller 1995). An assessment portfolio is considered a high-stakes portfolio. It is a portfolio that is used for evaluating how well a student has done in relation to a set of standards and is used in the promotion of students from one grade to another.

For either type of portfolio to be successful, there needs to be a well-defined structure for developing and evaluating the portfolio. One such structure is the R-ICE method (Cole et al. 1997). R-ICE stands for Rationale, Intent, Content, and Evaluation. Before any portfolio assessment can be undertaken, there should be a sound rationale for the portfolio. Is the portfolio being used as an instructional portfolio or an assessment portfolio? The rationale must be clearly stated and understood by the teacher, students, and parents. The intent of the portfolio should also be clearly stated and understood. Is the intent of the portfolio to indicate how well the

Projects are an excellent alternative to tests. Here a student explains her social studies project to her teacher.

©Photo by Jean-Claude LeJeune

student has learned the instructional objectives of social studies or is the intent of the portfolio to show how well the student can articulate the social studies content using writing skills or oral presentation skills? Such a portfolio can be used to assess not only social studies content but also oral and writing skills for language arts classes.

Determining the content of the portfolio is a process that can include both the student and the teacher. It is important at this point to note that a portfolio is not just a random collection of student works or a file for all homework papers. The content is defined by the intent of the portfolio. If the portfolio is to be used to show a student's growth, then the collection should show early works of the student, including work that was not always the student's best work. If the portfolio is an assessment portfolio, then it should include only the student's best work since the student will be evaluated on that work.

The last part of any portfolio assessment is evaluation. How will the students' work be evaluated? This is where a clear statement of the purpose or the intent of the portfolio is important. Without clear evaluation processes, the evaluation of the portfolios will probably not be consistent. Portfolios can be assessed using checklists, student-teacher conference, peer evaluation, and rubrics. Batzle (1992) suggests the following steps for involving students and parents in the evaluation process. First, the student chooses a sample and reviews it with a peer. Next the student shares the sample with the class. After the student has shared the sample with the class, he/she then reflects and writes about why he/she has chosen the sample and explains its value. The student takes the same home for the parents' comments and reflections. Finally, the student puts the work in the portfolio so that the teacher

NAME: _____

WHY I INCLUDED THIS WORK

Why I believe this piece should be included _____

_____

_____

_____

_____

This piece shows my progress _____

_____

_____

_____

_____

Parent's Comments:

I think my child's work shows _____

_____

_____

_____

_____

Teacher's Comments:

I think this student's work shows _____

_____

_____

_____

_____

FIGURE 3.3   Example of a student's, parent's, and teacher's criticism of a piece of student work.

can write a formal evaluation. Figure 3.3 indicates how a summary sheet can include comments from the student, parents, and teacher about the student's work and progress in the portfolio.

Portfolio assessment has several advantages. One is that the students can see their improvement over time. In this respect, portfolios are also a great motivational resource for students. Throughout the educational process, students are always being compared with their peers. With portfolio assessments, students can look at how much they have grown in relation to themselves. This can be done by keeping progressive works in the portfolio, a growth chart, or any other type of communication works for showing the learning that has taken place. By examining portfolios, the students get a sense of the efforts they have put forth. Portfolios let students have ownership of their work and the direction they want to take in learning. The student and the teacher together decide what the focus of the portfolio will be. Because this process gives students ownership in their own work, it therefore tends to provide more motivation for students (Batzle 1992). As the students and teacher work together to create the goals of the portfolio, the student also becomes involved in the learning process.

One of the primary limitations of portfolios is the space required for collection and storage. If a classroom has twenty-five students, a place to store twenty-five portfolios will need to be created. If the content of the portfolio fits nicely into a file folder or an accordion folder, space may not be a problem. But many portfolios contain more information than can be maintained in a folder. If the portfolio is an assessment portfolio, there needs to be a working portfolio where students keep a variety of their materials so that when they get ready to pull together the final portfolio, all of their materials are readily accessible. The responsibility of maintaining portfolios is also problematic, especially if portfolios are moved through the school system along with the students. If the portfolios are assessment portfolios, they can become very bulky over time. Storage for an entire school becomes problematic. Even with the use of technology, portfolios that have been copied to disks or to videotapes still require storage space. Digital systems of the future will help resolve this problem.

Projects

Projects are popular social studies activities designed to be engaging and open-ended. As such they pose a challenge for evaluating the work. Projects tend to be done over a period of time and can be fairly complex in nature. A third-grade class may build a model community with each student contributing a building (hospital, school, grocery store, shoe store, gas station, auto dealership, etc.). Sixth graders may be encouraged to select a country and present a small-group project that reflects the culture, economy, geography, and history of that nation. Rubrics can be designed to meet the assessment demands of the projects, For small groups, the rubric must consider both individual contributions and group tasks accomplished.

A sixth-grade class did individual projects on the Roman Empire. Some of the topics selected for the projects included Roman Influences in Great Britain, Roman Architecture, Julius Caesar, Cleopatra, Roman Generals, Life as a Roman Citizen, and the Punic Wars. Over a six-week period, students developed and wrote a report on their topic along with a project for presentation for parents. The time line was as follows:

Week One: Choose a topic; check resources (library and Web sites); gather written material on topic.
Week Two: Begin project notebook; outline/display.
Week Three: Complete research; write the first draft of report, start building display.
Week Four: Continue to collect items for display.
Week Five: Write a second draft of report; design graphs or charts for display; use PowerPoint to label display.

+---+
| Rubric for Roman Empire Project |
| |
| Name of Student: _____ Room: _____ |
| |
| Title of Report: _____ |
| |
| WRITTEN REPORT   (10 PTS.) _____ |
| |
| DISPLAY   (10 PTS.) _____ |
| |
| CREATIVITY OF PROJECT   (10 PTS.) _____ |
| |
| THOROUGHNESS OF PROJECT   (10 PTS.) _____ |
| |
| TOTAL POINTS: _____ |
+---+

FIGURE 3.4   An example of a rubric for a project.

Week Six: Write and word process final report; set up display at home and do self-evaluation of project; make final adjustments/revisions; transport display and report to school for display.

Figure 3.4 shows an example of a rubric that can be used for the Roman Empire project.

An oral history project works well with the middle school–aged students. Grant Wiggins (1989, 42–43) suggests the following project:

> You must complete an oral history project based on interviews and written sources and present your findings orally in class. The choice of subject matter will be up to you. Some of the examples of possible topics include: your family, running a small business, substance abuse, a labor union, teenage parents or recent immigrants. You are to create three workable hypotheses based on your preliminary investigations and come up with four questions you will use to test each hypothesis.
>
> To meet the criteria, [you] must:

- investigate three hypotheses;
- describe at least one change over time;
- demonstrate that you have done your homework research;
- interview four appropriate people as resources;
- prepare at least four questions related to each hypothesis;
- ask questions that are not leading or biased;
- ask follow-up questions when appropriate;
- note important differences between fact and answers you receive;
- use evidence to support your choice of the best hypothesis; and
- organize your writing and your class presentation.

Projects, as with presentations, can be scored using a rubric or a checklist. The most important factors are clearly indicating to the student what they are to do, and then having a scoring scheme that clearly indicates those students who have met the project's criteria.

Project boards can be effective means for students to share their work on a unit of study. This display accompanies a research paper on the Roman Empire.

©Courtesy of Kurtis R. Fluck. Used by permission.

Manipulatives

Manipulatives can make excellent alternative assessment tools, provided that content is stressed and the materials provide a good match with the social studies learning goals. For example, primary-grade students may be asked to draw the most important thing they learned. Learning stations with manipulatives such as maps, globes, artifacts, and photographs can be used. When such learning stations are used with primary students, upper-grade students can be used as peer assistants to record the younger students' responses (Alleman and Brophy 1997).

Chapter Summary

In summary, assessing students is a complicated and complex process. If assessment were easy, teachers would never question the results of their tests, the results of standardized tests, or their evaluation of portfolios. To create assessments that more accurately measure instruction, teachers need to plan learning and assessment activities based on predetermined instructional objectives. If the teachers create a strong link between the two, then the assessment will provide a solid basis for evaluating and reporting students' performance. It is important to remember that assessment of student learning should include a variety of assessment activities, not just traditional paper-and-pencil tests. When the teacher uses a variety of assessment tools to assess the student, the teacher will have a more complete picture of the students' level of understanding of instructional objectives. As information from assessment activities is collected during the grading periods, teachers have many pieces of information to use to communicate students' achievement to parents. As the year continues, more information is added throughout the use of various assessment activities so that by the end of the school year, teachers have a clear, more thorough understanding of students' level of achievement. Because the multitude of assessment activities provide many pieces of information from which the teacher can make decisions, the final summative evaluation for the student will be far more accurate.

References

Alleman, J., and J. Brophy. 1997. Elementary social studies instruments, activities, and standards. In *Handbook of classroom assessment,* ed. G. Phye, 321–57. San Diego, CA: Academic Press.

Alleman, J., and J. Brophy. 1999a. Current trends and practices in social studies assessment for the early grades. *Social Studies and the Young Learner* 11 (4): 15–17.

Alleman, J., and J. Brophy. 1999b. The changing nature and purpose of assessment in the social studies classroom. *Social Education* 65 (6): 334–7.

Batzle, J. 1992. *Portfolio assessment and evaluation: Developing and using portfolios in the classroom.* Cypress, CA: Creative Teaching Press.

Bloom, B. S. (ed.), M. D. Englehart, E. J. Furst, W. H. Hill, and D. R. Krathwohl. 1956. *Taxonomy of educational objectives: Handbook I, Cognitive Domain.* New York: David McKay.

Cangelosi, J. S. 1990. *Designing tests for evaluating student achievement.* New York: Longman.

Cole, K. B., L. R. Struyk, D. Kinder, J. K. Sheehan, and C. K. Kish. 1997. Portfolio assessment: Challenges in secondary education. *The High School Journal* 80 (4): 261–272.

Farr, R., and B. Tone. 1994. *Portfolio and performance assessment: Helping students evaluate their progress as readers and writers.* Fort Worth, TX: Harcourt Brace College.

Herman, J. L., P. R. Aschbacher, and L. Winters. 1992. *A practical guide to alternative assessment.* Arlington, VA: Association for Supervision and Curriculum Development.

Miller, W. H. 1995. *Alternative assessment techniques for reading & writing.* West Nyack, NY: The Center for Applied Research in Education.

National Council for the Social Studies. 1994. *Expectations of excellence: Curriculum standards for social studies.* Washington, DC: National Council for the Social Studies.

Popham, W. J. 1998. *Classroom assessment: What teachers need to know.* Boston, MA: Allyn and Bacon.

Weber, E. 1999. *Student assessment that works: A practical approach.* Boston, MA: Allyn and Bacon.

Wiggins, G. 1989. Teaching to the authentic test. *Educational Leadership* 70: 703–13.

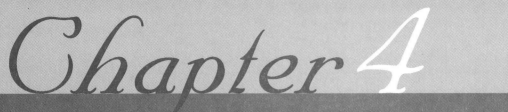

Chapter 4

© Jean-Claude LeJeune

Early Childhood Social Studies

Billie Jo Thomas
Northern Illinois University

A child's world is one that supports questioning minds by offering a variety of "doings" designed to satisfy and extend a child's natural sense of wonder.

—George W. Maxim,
Social Studies and the Elementary School Child. 6th Ed.

Objectives

Readers will

- become familiar with early childhood social studies curriculum content;
- understand the eight circles of awareness;
- be able to demonstrate techniques of interdisciplinary instruction in teaching preschool through second grade students; and
- understand the role of interdisciplinary instruction in early childhood social studies.

Introduction

Integrating social studies instruction enables children to be active participants in their learning. At the early childhood level, this translates into many opportunities for firsthand social studies experiences. These experiences should be accompanied by the students' language questioning to discover more information, probing ideas, making connections with previously gained knowledge, and making predictions about what to expect next.

Literacy and language are part of everything the teacher does in the classroom. There is no need to set aside a special time for language or literacy development when instruction is integrated. Regardless of the discipline, students will be using spoken language, listening skills, nonverbal communication, music, pictures, books, writing instruments, and field trips. This approach is successful from early childhood through postdoctoral education. Young children, in their desire to learn about the world around them, practice oral and written language skills, nonverbal communication, and print awareness that create later literacy (Seefeldt 1997). "Learning to deal with the words in reading and writing is part of developing literacy, but it is not the ultimate goal, which is meaning construction" (Cooper 1997, 167). Hence, for the young child, integrating social studies and reading and writing is a natural combination.

If equal instructional time is devoted to physical, cognitive, social, and emotional development, teachers should spend 25 percent of their instructional time on the social studies knowledge base. They cannot wait until children are in fourth grade to begin teaching social studies for the same reasons they would not wait until then to teach mathematics or literacy. Fourth grade is too late; children's basic attitudes and concepts are formed by then. Lessons in which 25 percent of the curriculum content comes from social studies will help shape the citizens of tomorrow.

Early Childhood

Early childhood is the period of development from conception to eight years of age. It includes the unborn, infants, toddlers, and children in nursery school, kindergarten, and grades one through three. This chapter focuses on methods, materials, and activities for preschool through grade 2 students. The traditional early childhood curriculum areas are language arts, science, mathematics, physical development, social studies, fine arts, and creativity.

Curriculum Content and Social Studies

Each curriculum area contains a body of knowledge that includes vocabulary, facts, and concepts defining the discipline. This body of knowledge is what educators call curriculum content. Information is the content of the lesson being taught about the discipline (Brown and Brown 1985; Smith 1982). Computer programs also lend themselves to social studies instruction for the young child (Haugland 1995).

This chapter addresses the matter of how to teach the curriculum content for social studies in preschool through second grade through an interdisciplinary approach. Social studies content is taken from the knowledge base concerning human groups and how they behave. Emotional studies and social studies are often confused in classrooms. A simple way to differentiate them is to think of emotional as internal and social as external. The subject of emotional studies involves learning about what takes place within the individual. Feelings such as love, hate, fear, anxiety, hope, and so forth are part of the emotional knowledge base. Social studies, on

Having a special day for grandparents to visit the classroom can set the stage for a history discussion, particularly if the grandparents share stories of their youth.

© Lawrence Migdale

the other hand, always involves at least two people. The social studies knowledge base thus refers to groups, whether large or small in number.

Sometimes there is confusion about the difference between the social studies knowledge base and the social process of being in groups in the classroom. Preschool teachers sometimes say, "I teach social studies during recess and lunch." However, this is incorrect because these teachers are not transmitting information from the social studies knowledge base to the child. The child is in a social situation, but we are often in social situations. This does not mean we are learning anything from a knowledge base. Being in a social group does not mean we are learning social studies; we may even be in a social group learning about another knowledge base, such as science or music (Charlesworth and Lund 1990).

The traditional social studies curriculum at the preschool and lower grade levels focuses on content that teaches about groups of people in terms of the following: current topics, economics, geography, history, and international and global education. A brief description of each area follows with a few samples of content.

The content of *current topics* varies, depending on current topics of interest in the newspaper, on television, in the family, and in the community. Common topic content includes political concepts, environment, peace and war, safety, news, and career education.

The content of *economics* in preschool and kindergarten includes information about *wants and needs* (there is a big difference between the two, as well as between supply and demand), *doing without* (to paraphrase a popular rock song, when you request something, you may not get what you want but you may get something you need), and *money,* such as types of paper and coins, different countries' currency, and what money represents.

The content of *geography* in preschool and kindergarten includes information about the *earth,* such as roundness, movement, earth, sky, and water; *direction,* such as east, west, north, south, up, and down; *location,* such as poles, equator, beside, between, through, and on top of; *regions,* such as awareness of oceans, continents, halves, and so on; *maps* as print experiences and a beginning awareness of maps representing something else in the real world.

The content of *history* in preschool and kindergarten includes information about developmentally appropriate approaches to *time,* such as yesterday, today and tomorrow; *change,* such as growth, beginnings, and endings; *continuity of human life,* such as child, parents, grandparents, great-grandparents; *the past,* such as Daddy's pet, Daddy's baby picture, and so forth; and *holidays,* such as the Fourth of July, Thanksgiving, and birthdays.

The content of *international and global education* taps a wide range of a child's previously gained knowledge. Developmentally appropriate content would include *children* in different nations, *families* around the world, *similarities* in people (for example, all people eat and have or had mothers, *conflict* between nations, and the *interdependence* of people (Why does it matter to us what happens in Somalia or Kuwait?).

✍ *Egocentrism and Eight Circles of Awareness*

In early childhood, in all five of the social studies curriculum areas, the child learns first about himself or herself. The three main areas of interest for young children are *me, myself,* and *I.* Egocentrism is the starting point for *all* curriculum areas in early childhood; then learning broadens into wider and wider circles of awareness, each directly linked to the children's *me, myself,* and *I.* The eight circles shown in Figure 4.1 represent the levels of awareness about self, family, neighborhood, community, state, nation, world, and universe.

Teachers should be familiar with the eight circles of awareness because children learn the values, beliefs, and stereotypes of the community in which they live (Banks 1992). By being introduced to the contributions of other cultures, children can learn to celebrate the diversity of humankind.

To understand how a child's awareness of the social studies environment moves from the egocentrism of self through the other seven encompassing circles, one could consider a specific topic, for instance, food preferences, means of transportation to school, or ways of celebrating certain family events. Let's take the specific topic of hair color as an example. First, the child learns about his or her own hair color, then about the hair color of family members and close friends, then about the hair color of neighbors and community acquaintances. Next, the child be-

FIGURE 4.1   The child's widening awareness of the social studies environment.

gins to form an impressionistic awareness of people (usually somehow related to him or her) in other states and their hair color, say, Grandpa's and Uncle Joe's; then the child begins to gain an awareness that people everywhere have hair and it has color. First, however, the child must learn about his or her hair; then the child relates further knowledge to himself or herself. The child must be exposed through whole language experiences to the vocabulary, facts, and concepts so that she or he can formulate mental ideas about hair color and acquire sufficient vocabulary to learn more.

   Figure 4.1 illustrates how the child builds one concept of hair color from the inner, self dimension through the other seven levels to the universe dimension. The five areas of the social studies curriculum all build on these eight levels of awareness. Each level builds on the foundation of the previous narrower one. Figure 4.2 provides examples of activities for the self dimension for each of the five curriculum areas.

   Figure 4.3 gives examples of activities for the family dimension and shows how this dimension builds around self. Figure 4.4 gives examples of how neighborhood builds around family, which has built around self.

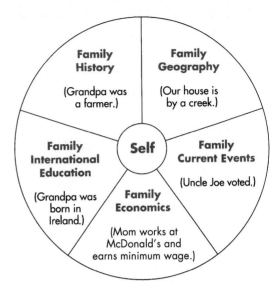

FIGURE 4.2   Examples of concepts of self in the five social studies curriculum areas.

FIGURE 4.3   Examples of family building on self in the five social studies curriculum areas.

FIGURE 4.4   Examples of neighborhood building on self and family in the five social studies curriculum areas.

Thematic Unit: Getting Along with Others, Grades 1–3

Carlson, Nancy. 1989. *I Like Me.* New York: Viking Penguin. (Gr. K–2) This is an upbeat book about the importance of liking yourself.

Crosby, Bill. 1998. *The Meanest Thing to Say.* Illus. V. P. Honeywood. New York: Cartwheel. Part of the Little Bill series, two friends have a disagreement.

Cutler, Jane. 1993. *Darcy and Grams Don't Like Babies.* Illus. Susannah Ryan. New York: Scholastic. (Gr. K–2) A little girl adjusts to having a new sibling.

Duffey, Betsy. 1990. *The Math Whiz.* Illus. Janet Wilson. New York: Viking Penguin. (Gr. 2–3) Marty can solve any math problem but he hates P.E. He resolves it with some help from his teacher.

Golenbock, Peter. 1990. *Teammates.* Illus. Paul Bacon. San Diego: Harcourt Brace. (Gr. 2–3) The true story of the friendship between Pee Wee Reese, an all-star shortstop, and Jackie Robinson, the first African American to play major league baseball. They were teammates on the Brooklyn Dodgers.

Heine, Helme. 1986. *Friends.* New York: Aladdin. (Gr. K–3) Imagine a rooster, a mouse, and a pig as best friends. As they go through the day they each make a contribution to the various games they play. And in the end they learn to accept each other's uniqueness.

Kellogg, Steven. 1986. *Best Friends.* New York: Dial. (Gr. K–3) Kathy is jealous of Louise, who gets to go away to summer camp. When Louise returns and gets a new puppy, Kathy feels sorry for herself. In the end, the two girls share the puppy.

Leverich, Kathleen. 1991. *Best Enemies, AGAIN.* New York: Morrow. (Gr. 2–3) Priscilla and Felicity find it difficult to get along. Felicity always picks on Priscilla until one day Felicity gets her due reward.

Moore, Inga. 1991. *Little Dog Lost.* New York: Macmillan. (Gr. K–3) The importance of making new friends and of cooperating with others are the themes of this book. Two lonely children who have recently moved to the country make friends who help them find their lost dog.

Raschka, Chris. 1993. *Yo? Yes!* New York: Orchard. (Gr. K–4) Two young boys from different cultures strike up a friendship.

Rylant, Cynthia. 1998. *Poppleton and Friends.* Illus. Michael Teague. Poppleton the Pig learns the value of having friends.

Steig, William. 1971. *Amos and Boris.* New York: Farrar, Straus, and Giroux. (Gr. K–3) This is the classic picture book that has friendship as a major theme. It also points out that size is not really important.

Zamorano, Ana. 1997. *Let's Eat!* Illus. Julie Vivas. New York: Scholastic. (Gr. K–3) Set in Spain, this is a delightful story of a family preparing for the birth of a new baby.

Primary Focus Book

For this thematic unit, *Amos and Boris* is read aloud with the class. As the teacher reads the book, questions can be posed.

How did Amos become friends with Boris?

Why would Amos want to be Boris's friend? Why would Boris want to be Amos's friend?

How can Amos save Boris?

Why didn't Amos go out during low tide?

Have you ever had a good friend move away? How did it make you feel?

What makes someone a best friend?

Suggested Activities

- Have students draw pictures of themselves playing or working with a friend.
- Have students write about a time they had a disagreement with a friend or a brother or sister. How did they resolve it?
- Discuss ways to get along with a bully.
- Have students list three things they like about themselves.
- Bring in an assortment of poetry about friends and read a poem each day to the class. Write the poem on chart paper and read it through with the class three or four times during the day. Give each student a copy to put in a ring binder as part of their own poetry collection.
- Invite the students to help create a bulletin board on friends. What would they like included? Who will be responsible for each part?
- The students may draw pictures of something they like to do with a friend.
- The children can write a poem about a friend with the help of the teacher, a teacher's aide, or an older student.
- The students can make a collage of things that friends do together.
- If a student has moved away, the class can write letters and mail them to the student's new address.

✒ *Methods and Developmental Limitations*

To be successful in early childhood classrooms, interdisciplinary instruction must operate within certain limitations that apply to all early childhood learning. Activities must be concrete, real, and relevant to the child and his or her world; they must be child directed (this implies choices by the child). Detailed guidelines provided by the National Association for the Education of Young Children (NAEYC) appear in Bredekamp (1987).

Simply put, *concrete* means that the materials can be perceived by the senses of touch, sight, hearing, smell, and taste (Gilbert 1989). *Real* means that the actual object should be there. For example, use a real orange rather than a plastic one or a picture of one or a story of one. Young children engage in optimal learning when they use their senses to explore something real. While doing this, they acquire vocabulary about the real thing. In the case of an orange, words such as *round, soft, color, orange, peel, sweet,* and *juicy* might constitute acquired vocabulary. *Relevant* means that what the child is learning about should be present in the child's natural environment. Therefore, the child would be expected to use this material or behavior in his or her home or community. For example, we teach young children about cars, buses, and trains (always remember the egocentrism and start with their family's main mode of transportation, be it bicycle, bus, or car) before we teach them about rickshaws. We teach first about what is concrete, real, and relevant.

Returning to the orange example, we teach about oranges, bananas, and familiar fruits because we can make sure the child has them for a class snack or eats them at home. Later, in the intermediate grades, teachers can help children build on these early concrete, hand-on experiences and, after physical brain development is complete, relate them to kumquats and other exotic fruits.

There are limits to the type of abstract language and abstract thinking that children under eight years of age can engage in because of their normal but incomplete physical brain and nerve development. What concerns us here is that children in preschool and kindergarten need to choose from developmentally appropriate hands-on activities that are concrete, real, and relevant to their world (Bredekamp 1987; Hamilton and Flemming 1990; Hunt and Renfro, 1982).

The NAEYC defines what is developmentally appropriate in terms of age and the individual (Bredekamp 1987, 2):

> Age appropriateness. Human development research indicates that there are universal, predictable sequences of growth and change that occur in children during the first 9 years of life. These predictable changes occur in all domains of development—physical, emotional, social, and cognitive. Knowledge of typical development of children within the age span served by the program provides a framework from which teachers prepare the learning environment and plan appropriate experiences . . .
>
> Individual appropriateness. Each child is a unique person with an individual pattern and timing of growth, as well as individual personality, learning style, and family background. Both the curriculum and adults' interactions with children should be responsive to individual differences. Learning in young children is the result of interaction between the child's thoughts and experiences with materials, ideas, and people. These experiences should match the child's developing abilities while also challenging the child's interest and understanding.

Computers can be helpful social studies aids. This third grader is attempting to travel across the United States using the software program *Oregon Trail III*.

©Photo by Elizabeth Crews

✺ Techniques of Interdisciplinary Instruction

With a knowledge of the limitations on how young children learn, teachers can use developmentally appropriate, child-directed, hands-on activities with concrete, real, and relevant materials. They need to use the child's egocentrism and ever-widening social perspective (Piaget 1952), represented by the eight circles of awareness, as the foundation for their social studies curriculum plans. Building on this foundation, teachers are able to use an interdisciplinary approach in teaching the social studies curriculum content. Appropriate techniques include teaching vocabulary, facts, and concepts through speaking and listening vocabulary; dictated and written stories; books, magazines, and other printed materials; the child's drawn pictures and written print; nonverbal communication; field trips and print in the environment; and music.

Speaking and Listening Vocabulary

Speaking and listening vocabulary is built into everything teachers do in the classroom. The one-on-one "Good morning" greeting between teacher and child is an example of social development while language and literacy skills are also being expanded. Films and videotapes also aid vocabulary development. Other sample activities follow. The primary curriculum content area for each is given in parentheses.

Engaging in dramatic play helps children develop social skills. Through experimentation, children learn what is and is not acceptable behavior without being unduly penalized for their actions.

© Lawrence Migdale

- Informal small group discussion about the aquarium during free playtime (science)
- Large-group discussion with a classroom visitor, such as a Puerto Rican mother with her new baby (social studies)
- Experimentation with the five types of magnets in the science corner (science)
- Listening for higher or lower (or louder or softer) sounds on the new instruments on the music table (music)
- Talking about and looking for the mile markers on a field trip (mathematics)
- Playing in the sociodramatic play area while dressing, talking, and listening like a chosen character would (social development)
- Describing facial expressions in pictures held by the teacher, and discussing when they are appropriate and when they are not (emotional development)
- Telephoning ill classmates from the principal's office to say the class misses them and hopes they are well soon (social development)
- Making pancakes: measuring, stirring, baking, and following the rebus-picture recipe (physical development and mathematics)

In all the foregoing activities, the main content knowledge base being taught is language or literacy. However, all the activities will directly develop skills necessary for early literacy.

Dictated and Written Stories and Letters

Along with dictated and written stories, teachers can use letters, songs, and lists across the curriculum. Social studies content activities, such as the aforementioned one involving the Puerto Rican mother and baby, often lend themselves to dictated written communications such as invitations, time schedules, maps of how to find the classroom and where to park, thank-you notes, an order for a thank-you flower, and so on. Because of their developmental level, most kindergartners and preschoolers verbally dictate these to the teacher, who then prints them for the children. The teacher should print each communication exactly as dictated, errors included, because it is the children's creation.

Although a child may write an entire message alone, this does not always happen at the kindergarten level. Most five-year-olds will sign their name and, using invented spelling, print a few letters or words. It should be noted that it is harmful to force young children to copy words and phrases over and over. By first grade, children are using invented spelling as they move toward conventional spelling.

"Picture storybooks provide many sources for expressive and imaginative writing" (Norton 1999, 259). Norton believes that by having children write letters to friends, family members, teachers, and librarians will encourage them to write expressively. She suggests such books as *The Jolly Postman* (Ahlberg and Ahlberg 1986), a book in which a postman delivers letters to fairy-tale characters such as the Three Bears, the Big Bad Wolf, and Cinderella, and *Stringbean's Trip to the Shining Sea* (Williams 1988), in which a boy sends postcards back home during a camping trip across the United States.

Here are some examples of other social studies content activities that involve writing:

- Writing to the local mass transit authority for information about the system
- Writing a history of the child's life or a family history
- Writing a shopping list for purchases at the grocery store
- Writing to a kindergarten class in a foreign country
- Writing to a local politician
- Writing to the President of the United States
- Writing to someone the child has seen on the television news or in the newspaper

Having children write about their own life after hearing a story about another child lets children understand that there are similarities among children and their families. For instance, *My Father's Boat* (Garland 1998), is the story of a Vietnamese boy who learns how to fish from his father. The story tells of how the grandfather taught the boy's father to fish. The book is based on the Vietnamese proverb, "When you are young, you need your father; when you are old, you need your son." After hearing the story, children can write and illustrate about something they were taught by a parent or grandparent.

Books, Magazines, and Other Printed Materials

As discussed earlier, all printed materials used in the classroom should be concrete, real, and relevant to the lives of young children. This means that they should not be specially published just for education. They should exist outside of schools or home classsrooms. They should be found instead in such environments as the home, workplace, grocery store, church, gas station, and so forth. Books written for young

Picture books are an excellent resource in social studies.

©Photo by Elizabeth Crews

children's enjoyment, such as fairy tales, nursery rhymes, and popular tales such as *The Very Hungry Caterpillar* (Carle 1986), *Lilly's Purple Plastic Purse* (Henkes 1996) and *Koala Lou* (Fox 1989) are also good choices because they were not created just to meet language or literacy goals such as learning five new vocabulary words per day. Printed materials are considered real and relevant if they would still exist even without a formal classroom.

A well-stocked book corner is an asset to any early childhood classroom. It should include a wide variety of books, including mail order catalogs, a first encyclopedia, phone books, nursery rhymes, fairy tales, big books (both commercially published and those made in class), modern books, traditional fables, poetry, children's magazines (such as *Ladybug, Spider,* and *Our Big Outdoors*), brochures, music, and maps. A common rule of thumb is to have six books for each child in the class and to change books every three weeks. This allows the children to make choices. It is also important for teachers to allow children time on a daily basis to browse through the books.

The books and other printed materials should include content from all curriculum areas, including social studies. Examples of books that contain information from the social studies knowledge base are listed in the Children's Books section at the end of this chapter.

Suggestions for antibias criteria for the selection of books for young children are given in Derman-Sparks & A.B.C. Task Force (1989) and Bredekamp (1987). Labbo and Field (1996), and Huck, Hepler, Hickman, and Kiefer (2001) provide lists of books celebrating culturally diverse families.

Drawing Pictures and Writing Print

Drawing and writing require eye-hand coordination, visual discrimination, and fine muscle development, all of which are necessary for literacy. Regardless of what children are drawing or writing, these skills develop anyway. For example, drawing a flower is of as much benefit as printing a capital *P* over and over. If a child chooses to print the *P* over and over again, that is fine; otherwise, the skills will develop as the child uses instruments to draw or write whatever she or he wants to draw or write.

Drawing and writing also develop literacy skills regardless of the curriculum content area. For example, the following subjects drawn by young children all have whole language value but none have language or reading as the main knowledge base (curriculum areas are shown in parentheses):

Children need ample opportunities to illustrate their feelings and desires.

© Lawrence Migdale

- My family (social studies)
- Ways we travel (social studies)
- Shoes people wore in Ancient Rome (social studies)
- Chinese paper money (social studies)
- My piano (music)
- Babies (social studies, science)
- Water (science)

Five-year-olds practice using pencils, pens, markers, and crayons. They also need paper that is at least eleven inches by fourteen inches. A variety of writing instruments and kinds of paper are desirable so that children can learn about the physical limitations of each kind. While acquiring literacy skills, they also learn about the physical world (science).

Nonverbal Communication

Gestures, dress, and facial expressions are types of nonverbal communication. Young children need to learn to visually discriminate similarities and differences in order to communicate verbally and read. For example, someone yelling, "Stop!" with a smile on her face is communicating something very different from someone yelling, "Stop!" with a fist held up. Following are some other examples of activities involving nonverbal communication; again, curriculum content areas are given in parentheses. All these activities contribute to literacy and language development.

- The look on the bus driver's face when all thirty of us board the city bus (social development)
- A class discussion about what we and others do with our mouths when we are angry, happy, sad, and so on (social development)
- Reading a story about a girl who is afraid of flying and how her body expresses fear (emotional development)

Field Trips and Print in the Environment

Field trips and print in the environment stimulate so much spoken language and discussion, trigger so much new vocabulary, and provide so many concrete, real, and relevant materials and activities that almost everything about them contributes directly to language and literacy development. Written communication is stimulated through invitations, thank-you notes, maps, and so forth. Print is available everywhere in the environment, and children are motivated to read or pay attention to signs and then later to follow up with books and stories. Some field trips with content in various curriculum areas, but still developing literacy, are trips to the following places:

- Science museum (science)
- Bakery (social studies)
- Grocery store (social studies, mathematics)
- Mathematics academy (mathematics)
- Music store (music)
- Circus (physical education, social studies)
- Garden (science, social studies)

Programs for young children should include as many field trips as time allows. One transported trip per month and another as a walking field trip per week are a minimum.

Field trips are useful in all areas of social studies as indicated in the following:

- History: visit our old park, our old school, our old classroom
- Economics: visit stores, banks, factories
- Current events: visit a newspaper office, television station
- International education: visit homes of people from other nations, ethnic museums
- Geography: visit hills, lakes, mountains, islands, whatever is in the local environment

Music

Music involves auditory communication, written communication through notes, visual memory, pattern repetition, visual discrimination, and so on. It is an important component of any integrated approach, and the skills developed through music are directly applicable to literacy and language skills. The following music activities for the social studies content area would be desirable for literacy development:

- Writing to a kindergarten class in Honduras and asking what their favorite songs are
- Playing tone bells or the xylophone by color coded musical notes (The C tone bell, xylophone C bar, and the C note on the music sheet are all red; B is blue on all; C is yellow, and so on.)
- Listening to different kinds of recorded music and identifying what country the music is from, such as jig, polka, cancan

Some Web sites can be shared by the teacher with the entire class during a social studies unit of study.
©Photo by Elizabeth Crews

- Listening to musical selections such as a funeral dirge, the "Wedding March," and Sousa marches and deciding when it is appropriate to play each and when it is not

🔊 Sample Lesson Plan Outline

Examples of general plans for vocabulary, materials, and content are shown in the following outline. The outline includes all five social studies curriculum areas for the self dimension of awareness shown in Figure 4.1 and the examples of concepts of self presented in Figure 4.2. Child-directed, developmentally appropriate, hands-on, concrete, real, and relevant materials and activities are used.

Lesson Plan Outline
Circle of Awareness: SELF

I. Social studies area: HISTORY
    A. Possible vocabulary
        Birth, death, generations, grandfather, grandmother, aunt, uncle, cousin, brother, sister, old, new, antique, was, is, will be, past, present, future, growth
    B. Concrete materials
        1. Photographs of the child at birth, of birthdays, of parent at birth, of parents on birthdays, of relatives
        2. Baby clothing worn by the child, by other family members; the child's old and new toys

3. Child's old and new Valentines, birthday cards, or other greeting cards; family's cards
4. Graphs charting child's height during the year, showing growth
5. Puppets available in classroom showing the progression of development from birth through 6 years of age
6. Books, films, and tapes available in the classroom that depict children in the first 6 years of life; that depict families with older, middle-aged, and young adults and teenagers, young children and infants; that depict pioneer families, Depression-era families, gay nineties families, future families, and so forth
7. Short-lived animals (gerbils, caterpillars, and so on) in the classroom so that children have the opportunity to experience life and death
8. A short video showing how a person walks during different stages of life

C. Activities
1. Have class, large-group, and small-group discussions about the foregoing materials and make sure each child has a concrete article to relate to, such as a photograph of himself or herself at birth, at each discussion.
2. Have children paint or draw a picture of the historical family they liked most in the film they just saw.
3. Have each child dictate a short letter to some older person in his or her family.
4. Have children sing songs with you about the special occasions shown on the cards they have brought to school. Make up songs or rhymes.
5. Have several books about families, babies, birth, and death available in the book corner for children to choose from.
6. Take a field trip to a busy place and watch how different people walk differently at different ages.

II.   Social studies area: ECONOMICS
A. Possible vocabulary
Money, coins, nickels, dimes, quarters, dollars, allowance, gift, presents, want, need, purchase, buy, receipt, sell, trade, honesty, cheat, greed, sharing, charity
B. Concrete materials
1. Nickels, dimes, quarters, dollars, sample checks
2. Mail order catalogs
3. Wooden puzzles about coins
4. Paper puzzles about different paper money for each child to cut up
5. Classroom dramatic play area set up as a grocery store or a flower store or a clothing store, and so on
6. Examples of good chairs, cheap chairs, good shirts, cheap shirts, sturdy materials and easily broken materials, such as drinking glasses
7. Books about money, honesty, greed, sharing, and charity available in the book corner for children to choose from

C. Activities
1. Have the class choose something in the room or make something that they would be willing to give to another class or group. Then have them dictate a letter about it, and deliver the letter and gift to the other group.
2. Have class members draw a picture of something they would never give away.
3. Make a large wall graph with pictures of items the children feel they must have and another with pictures of items they would like to have but could do without. They can draw them or cut them out of catalogs, or you can draw them.
4. Discuss and show pictures of nonverbal communication. Can you tell whether someone wants to get into the movie theater but has no money? Can you tell whether someone is hungry but cannot eat? Can you tell when someone has money to spend?
5. Sing songs about money, wishes, and hopes.
6. Use flash cards of pictures of children being honest and dishonest. Each time a picture shows honesty, have the children play their rhythm instrument triangles. Every time a picture shows greed, have the children blow on kazoos.

III. Social studies area: GEOGRAPHY
A. Possible vocabulary
Land, water, air, hill, mountain, rock, sand, mud, valley, sky, waterfall, cornfield, island, cliff, on, under, inside, between
B. Concrete materials
1. Sand and water table
2. Dirt and water table
3. Boxes of different kinds of rocks and dirt
4. Puppets and a box to use with prepositions such as *on, in, through,* and *above*
5. Slides, films, and tapes of mountains or other geographical features not present in the immediate locale
6. Musical recordings about the earth—for example, "This Land Is Your Land, This Land Is My Land" and "Garden Song"
7. Travel posters depicting geographical forms such as lakes and islands
8. Modeling clay to form earth features such as hills and valleys
C. Activities
1. Take a walking field trip and have a picnic. Discuss the land forms in the immediate environment.
2. Have children dictate letters to people who live in different places asking them for photographs and information about local landforms.
3. Make a collage from travel magazines of lakes, mountains, valleys, and so on.
4. Have children draw pictures with felt-tipped markers showing where they would like to live.

        5. Have a picture-sorting activity using magazine pictures of environmentally healthy or unhealthy mountains, islands, lakes, and so forth.

        6. Have the children match calendar pictures (or other scenic outdoor pictures) to different musical compositions and explain why they matched each picture to each musical composition.

IV. Social studies area: CURRENT EVENTS

    A. Possible vocabulary

    Newspaper, television news, tabloid, community, state, nation, catastrophe, human interest story, weather, hurricane, accident, celebration, Hollywood, movies

    B. Concrete materials

        1. Newspaper articles brought by the children from home

        2. Videotapes of television news programs

        3. Bulletin board on which to display stories and reports

        4. Weather maps

    C. Activities

        1. Discuss each article or picture the children bring in and put it on the bulletin board.

        2. Show videotapes of television news and discuss which stories are about disasters, which are about the weather, which are about celebrations, and so on.

        3. At the end of the day, have the children vote on what they would consider the "current event of the day" in the classroom.

        4. Take a field trip to a local newspaper.

        5. Have a local newspaper or television reporter visit the classroom.

        6. Have the children forecast the weather for the next day. Make a picture record of the forecast, and check it the next day.

        7. Keep a record of new art and music releases.

V. Social studies area: INTERNATIONAL AND GLOBAL EDUCATION

    A. Possible vocabulary

    Country, world, sharing, foreign languages, Spain, France, Third World, food, toys, homes, clothing, flag, stamps, military, war

    B. Concrete materials

        1. Snack foods from different countries

        2. Clothing from different countries

        3. Pictures of homes in different countries

        4. Toys from different cultures and countries

        5. Books about other countries in other languages and about war

        6. Recordings of music from other countries, such as the cancan, Irish jig, polka, and so on; and recordings of various national anthems

        7. Recordings of the same story being read in different languages

        8. Films and pictures of modes of transportation in different countries

        9. A picture chart showing how children can help one another

    C. Activities

        1. Discuss similarities in pictures showing where people live or find shelter in different countries.

        2. Show films and posters from embassies of different countries.

3. Begin a resource file of children's games from around the world, and teach one game to a small group of children.
4. Have children dictate letters to children or schools in other countries asking about the similarities and differences in their schools and ours.
5. Sort pictures that depict war and those that depict peace, and make a two-part bulletin board display.
6. Have children draw pictures showing the places they would most like to visit.
7. Have the children demonstrate dances from other nations.
8. Have people from other nations visit the classroom and bring samples of baby clothes, food, toys, and music.
9. Take a field trip to homes of people who have lived in other countries.

This lesson plan outline is only one of many that could be developed for the dimension of self. Moreover, many similar lesson plans could also be developed for each of the other seven dimensions of social awareness. (Figures 4.3 and 4.4 present examples of the family and neighborhood dimensions.) The possibilities are limitless.

Chapter Summary

While mindful of the limitations on how young children learn, teachers can use child-directed, hands-on activities with concrete, real, and relevant materials for teaching social studies via an integrated approach. These activities should be based on the child's egocentrism and ever-widening social perspective represented by eight circles of awareness as the foundation for social studies curriculum plans. Building on this foundation, teachers can use different whole language activities (speaking and listening vocabulary; dictated and written stories; books, magazines, and printed materials; the child's own drawn pictures and written print; nonverbal communication; field trips; and music) to teach the five social studies curriculum areas (history, economics, geography, international and global education, and current events).

Children's Books

Ahlberg, J., and A. Ahlberg. 1986. *The jolly postman.* Boston: Little, Brown. A postman makes his rounds delivering letters to nursery rhyme and fairy-tale characters.

Barger, T. 1980. *Special friends.* New York: Julian Messner. A girl tells of her rewarding and enjoyable visits with her elderly neighbor. This book reveals the differences that occur as one becomes older.

Bauer, C. 1981. *My mom travels a lot.* New York: Frederic Warne. A little girl points out the good and bad things about a mother's job that takes her away from home a great deal.

Breinburg, P. 1973. *Shawn goes to school.* New York: Crowell. Shawn always wanted to go to school, but when the first day of nursery school came along, he didn't like it very much. He wouldn't play and started to cry. This book lets youngsters know that many children have a hard time when they first go to school. Pictures of an African American family and multicultural students enhance the text.

Brown, M. 1998. *D.W.'s lost blankie.* Boston: Little, Brown. When Arthur's little sister D.W. loses her blankie, she doesn't think she'll ever be able to sleep again.

Carle, E. 1986. *The very hungry caterpillar.* New York: Philomel. Colorful illustrations and fluid text explain the many ways the caterpillar satisfies its hunger and grows.

Caseley, J. 1998. *Mickey's class play.* New York: Greenwillow. When Mickey's costume is destroyed before the play, the entire family pitches in to make another duck suit. Children will focus on the thrill of being the center of attention.

Clifton, L. 1983. *Everett Anderson's goodbye.* New York: Holt, Rinehart and Winston. Everett Anderson comes to terms with his grief after his father dies.

Cosby, B. 1998. *The meanest thing to say.* Illus. V. P. Honeywood. New York: Cartwheel. Part of the Little Bill series by Bill Cosby, this story tells of two friends and how they interact with each other.

Cosby, B. 1998. *Shipwreck Saturday.* Illus. V. P. Honeywood. New York: Cartwheel. Two friends spend Saturday sailing the boy's new sailboat. Unfortunately the boat accidentally gets broken.

Everitt, B. 1992. *Mean soup.* San Diego, CA: Harcourt Brace Jovanovich. Horace has a bad day. His mother boils a pot of water and then screams into it. Horace joins her, and together they make "mean soup." The book shares a way to let out emotions without hurting others.

Feiffer, J. 1998. *I lost my bear.* New York: Morrow, Jr. When a little girl loses her teddy bear, no one will help her find it. She ventures out on her own and discovers more than anyone ever expected.

Fisher, I. 1987. *Katie-Bo.* New York: Adama Books. At first Jim and his brother, Teddy, are confused and nervous when they learn their family is going to adopt a Korean baby. However, both come to agree that adoption is a very special way to have a sister, and Katie-Bo becomes a very special sister.

Fox, M. 1989. *Koala Lou.* Illus. P. Lofts. San Diego, CA: Harcourt Brace Jovanovich. Koala Lou is the oldest child in a large family. Because her mother is busy with the younger children, Koala Lou believes her mother no longer loves her. But when Koala Lou finishes second in a tree climbing race, her mother gives her a big hug and tells her that she loves her, always has, and always will.

Garland, S. 1998. *My father's boat.* Illus. T. Rand. New York: Scholastic. A Vietnamese boy learns to fish on his father's shrimp boat.

Greenfield, E. 1974. *She comes bringing me that little baby girl.* Philadelphia: Lippincott. A black family helps a new brother deal with a new baby sister when he really wanted a brother. This story deals with gender roles and sibling rivalry and is told in a lighthearted manner with a hint of black dialect.

Greenspun, A. A. 1992. *Daddies.* New York: Philomel. The author tells how she lost her own father at an early age. She then presents a collection of pictures of fathers and their young children.

Hazen, B. 1985. *Why are people different?* Racine, WI: Western. This story helps children understand the differences in people so that they will not be frightened of others but instead will develop relationships with children who are different.

Henkes, K. 1996. *Lilly's purple plastic purse.* New York: Greenwillow. Lilly brings her treasures to school in her purse only to humorous results.

Howe, J. 1987. *I wish I were a butterfly.* San Diego, CA: Harcourt Brace Jovanovich. The little cricket will not sing because he thinks he is ugly. He wants to be beautiful like a butterfly. However, the cricket finds out that everyone is special in some way, and he starts to sing. The butterfly hears him and wishes he were a cricket. This book lets each child know that he or she is special. The artwork is beautiful.

Johnson, A. 1992. *The leaving morning.* Illus. D. Soman. New York: Orchard. This book describes the emotions of leaving one home and learning to love another home.

Krauss, R. 1998. *You're just what I need.* Illus. J. Noonan. New York: Trophy. A mother plays hide-and-seek with her young child.

Marino, B. 1979. *Eric needs stitches.* Reading, MA: Addison-Wesley. Through a series of photographs Eric is shown going to the emergency room to get stitches in his knee after a bad fall. Although this story is too long for preschoolers, it does show the father as the nurturing parent.

McBratney, S. 1997. *Guess how much I love you.* Illus. I. Bates Boston: Candlewick. The sharing of love between parent and child is conveyed in this delightful picture book.

McBratney, S. 1998. *Just you and me.* Illus. I. Bates. Boston: Candlewick. When a storm approaches, shy Little Goosey doesn't want to share shelter with anyone but her dad. He understands how Little Goosey feels.

McDermott, G. 1972. *Anansi the spider.* New York: Holt, Rinehart and Winston. This folktale from the Ashanti in Ghana tells the story of Anansi, an animal with human qualities who gets into trouble.

Morris, W. 1987. *The magic leaf.* New York: Atheneum. Long ago in China, Lee Foo, a smart man, seeks and finds the magic leaf. He also finds a lot of trouble.

Norac, C. 1998. *I love you so much.* Illus. C. K. Dubois. New York: Doubleday. Lola the hamster wakes up each morning with some important words to say. But she doesn't know who to say them to. Her cheeks puff out with the words but she still doesn't say them. At the end of the day, her magical message bursts forth!

Polacco, P. 1998. *Thank you, Mr. Falker.* New York: Philomel. Little Trisha has problems learning to read. To her the letters get all jumbled up until her fifth-grade teacher helps her learn to read. This is the autobiographical story of Patricia Polacco's struggle with dyslexia and her tribute to the teacher who helped her deal with it.

Politi, L. 1973. *The nicest gift.* New York: Scribner. This is the story of a Mexican boy who loses his dog, Blanco, in Los Angeles. Blanco returns on Christmas Day.

Rodriguez, L. J. 1998. *America is her name.* Illus. C. Vazquez. New York: Curbstone Press. America is a Mixteca Indian girl who lives in a barrio in Chicago. She dreams of the state of Oaxaca in Mexico where she was born. America's father loses his job and her uncle drinks too much. When a poet comes to her class and encourages the students to think of themselves as writers, America encourages her mother and sister to write down their thoughts on paper. This book is appropriate for second and third graders.

Rylant, C. 1998. *Poppleton and friends.* Illus. M. Teague. New York: Blue Sky Press. This book focuses on Poppleton the Pig and his friends. Poppleton learns that if you want to live to be 100, eating grapefruit might help, but having friends definitely will.

Schoen, M. 1990. *Bellybuttons are navels.* Buffalo, NY: Prometheus. As Mary and her brother, Robert, bathe together, they discover that they have similar and different body parts and learn to identify them. This book is designed to develop an acceptance of the body and to help parents and educators initiate discussion and education about the human body.

Seuss, D. 1984. *Butter battle book.* New York: Random House. This story depicts the difficulties of battle and the possible outcomes.

Shyer, M. 1985. *Here I am, an only child.* New York: Scribner. A little boy explains the advantages and disadvantages of being an only child.

Simon, N. 1976. *All kinds of families.* Chicago: Albert Whitman. Exploring in words and pictures what a family is and how families vary in makeup and lifestyle, this book celebrates happy times but also shows that some relationships are troubled ones. Separations and sadness occur, yet the positive values of lives shared endure to provide foundations for future families.

Waxman, S. 1989. *What is a girl? What is a boy?* Culver City, CA: Peace Press. This book describes and illustrates the anatomy of males and females. Although some people may be uncomfortable with the graphic illustrations, information is presented in a matter-of-fact manner. Sex stereotypes are addressed and often refuted.

Williams, V. 1988. *Stringbean's trip to the shining sea.* New York: Greenwillow. A boy sends back postcards from his camping trip across the western United States.

Yolen, J. 1993. *Weather report.* Illus. A. Gusman. Honesdale, PA: Boyds Mill Press. A book of poetry about the weather. Includes poems about rain, sun, wind, snow, and fog.

Zamorano, A. 1997. *Let's eat!* Illus. J. Vivas. New York: Scholastic. A family awaits the arrival of a new baby.

References

Banks, J.A. 1992. Multicultural education for freedom's sake. *Educational Leadership* 49 (4): 32–5.

Bredekamp, S. 1987. *Developmentally appropriate practice in early childhood programs serving children from birth through eight.* Washington, DC: National Association for the Education of Young Children.

Brown, C., and G. Brown. 1985. *Play interactions.* Skillman, NJ: Johnson and Johnson.

Charlesworth, R., and K. Lund. 1990. *Math and science for young children.* New York: Delmar.

Cooper, J. D. 1997. *Literacy: Helping children construct meaning.* 3rd ed. Boston: Houghton Mifflin.

Derman-Sparks, L., and A.B.C. Task Force. 1989. *Anti-bias curriculum.* Washington, DC: National Association for Education of Young Children.

Gilbert, L. 1989. *Do touch.* Mt. Rainier, MD: Gryphon House.

Hamilton, D., and H. Flemming. 1990. *Resources for creative teaching in early childhood education.* 2d ed. Orlando, FL: Harcourt Brace Jovanovich.

Haugland, S. 1995. Classroom activities provide important support to children's computer experiences. *Early Childhood Education Journal 23* (2): 99–100.

Huck, C. S., S. Hepler, J. Hickman, and B. Kiefer. 2001. *Children's literature in the elementary school.* 6th ed. Dubuque, IA: Brown and Benchmark.

Hunt, T., and N. Renfro. 1982. *Puppetry in early childhood education.* New York: Nancy Renfro Studios.

Labbo, L. D., and S. L. Field. 1996. Celebrating culturally diverse families. *Language Arts* 73 (1): 54–62.

Maxim, G. W. 1998. *Social studies and the elementary school child,* 6th ed. Columbus, OH: Prentice Hall.

Norton, D. 1999.*Through the eyes of a child.* 5th ed. Columbus, OH: Merrill.

Piaget, J. 1952. *The origins of intelligence in children.* New York: International Universities Press.

Seefeldt, C. 1997. *Social studies for the preschool primary child.* Columbus, OH: Merrill.

Smith, C. 1982. *Promoting the social development of young children.* Mountain View, CA: Mayfield.

Chapter 5

Reading, Writing, and Discussing

Communicating in Social Studies

Pamela J. Farris
Northern Illinois University

We write and read in order to know each other's responses, to connect ourselves more fully with the human world, and to strengthen the habit of truth-telling in our midst.

—Benjamin DeMott "Why We Read and Write"

Objectives

───────────────○∿○───────────────

Readers will

- understand ways to incorporate language arts and social studies;
- understand the steps of the writing process; and
- be able to generate language arts activities based on social studies and language arts learning goals.

Introduction

Social studies offers many opportunities for reading, writing, and discussing, skills that good citizens need to develop to their fullest. It is essential that the citizenry in a democratic society be well educated, with each citizen able to gain information through reading and to communicate effectively through speaking and writing. As former U.S. Commissioner of Education Ernest L. Boyer (1990, 5) writes,

> While economic purposes are being vigorously pursued, civic priorities also must be affirmed. Indeed, unless we find better ways to educate ourselves as *citizens,* Americans run the risk of drifting unwittingly into a new kind of dark age, a time

103

when specialists control the decision-making process and citizens will be forced to make critical decisions not on the basis of what they know but on the basis of blind belief in so-called "experts."

The interdisciplinary philosophical tenet is based on sharing relevant material from the content area(s) with children. Decision making is promoted as children make choices about how and what they will learn. Children are also encouraged to interact with each other as they learn.

Reading, writing, and discussing allow children the individual freedom to learn as well as maintain a social responsibility to the class to share what has been learned. As Banks (1991–1992, 32) states, "To create and maintain a civic community that works for the common good, education in a democratic society should help students acquire the knowledge, attitudes, and skills they will need to participate in civil action to make society more equal and just." Students are encouraged to challenge and question both themselves and others; therefore, such a classroom is a democratic community.

A democracy is established on the belief that each citizen has worth and can offer something of value to the group. This necessitates the *trust* be gained and maintained if a democracy is to survive. In the classroom, the teacher must first establish the basic principles of democracy. In the areas of reading, writing, and discussing, this means that every child's ideas must be respected.

Support and encouragement must also pave the way if trust is to evolve in the classroom. This is not purely a one-directional matter of teacher to student but also of student to teacher, for the teacher must be willing to submit ideas that the class may openly criticize. For example, when the teacher shares a piece of his or her own writing with a class for the first time, both the teacher and the students are somewhat anxious and uncomfortable. The teacher wants the students to like what he or she has written because writing is very personal. The students feel that the situation is precarious because they are unsure of whether they should make only positive comments. That is, will the teacher consider negative comments to be ill-suited for the occasion? By opening up through sharing his or her own writing with the class, the teacher is demonstrating democratic principles: We all have different talents, we all have feelings, we all have beliefs, and we all can profit by sharing our thoughts and ideals.

According to Alfie Kohn (1996, 499), "If we had to pick a logical setting in which to guide children toward caring about, empathizing with, and helping other people, it would be a place where they would regularly come into contact with their peers and where some sort of learning is already taking place." Laura Schiller (1996), a sixth-grade teacher at Birney Middle School in Southfield, Michigan, teaches a yearlong thematic unit titled "Coming to America: Community from Diversity" to her students. Schiller finds that by having her students investigate their families' heritage and immigration to the United States, many social studies concepts are learned and a sense of community evolves in her classroom.

The San Ramon Valley Unified School District in San Ramon, California, fosters democratic principles by rooting its elementary curriculum in the development of social values (Schaps and Solomon 1990). This school system relies on children's literature and cooperative learning to encourage a caring climate where learning takes place. Quality literature that depicts how values "work" is the basis for reading instruction. For instance, books with themes of fairness and kindness help students develop empathy for others; books about other cultures and circumstances represent universal issues and concerns. Cooperative learning emphasizes collaboration, extensive interaction, division of labor, use of reason and explanation, and consideration of values related to the activity in which the group is engaged. Cooperative learning activities in the social studies often rely on a cycle of discussing reading and writing.

ॐ *Reading*

Research studies in reading indicate that when children can relate their daily life experiences as well as prior knowledge to the content of a textbook, they are better able to understand and assimilate new concepts and knowledge (Alvermann, Smith, and Readance 1985). Thus, the engaging narrative style of a children's book may result in a student's discovery and retention of social studies concepts (McGowan and Guzzetti 1991).

Reading enables children to gather information directly and to gain knowledge through vicarious experiences. By reading a social studies textbook or nonfiction book, students can acquire

Children's literature has a powerful impact on a child.

© Lawrence Migdale

background information about a specific social studies concept or topic; for instance, *Katie's Trunk* (Turner 1992) is a true story of a Tory family at the beginning of the American Revolution. By reading fiction, children can develop empathy for others as well as a better understanding of their own feelings and values. There are numerous award-winning books in this area, including *Letters from Rifka* (Hesse 1992), which depicts a family fleeing Russia in 1919.

Children's Literature

Reading quality children's books is important for children. According to Charlotte Huck (1990, 3),

> Literature not only has the power to change a reader, but it contains the power to help children become readers. Traditionally, we have recognized the influence of literature on our thoughts and feelings, but we have been slower to discover the role that literature plays in *creating readers,* in actually helping children learn to read.

Reading quality children's literature enhances a child's understanding of social studies. According to McGowen and Guzzetti (1991, 18),

> Literary works are packed with conceptual knowledge about the human condition and can supply meaningful content for skill-building experiences. . . . Perhaps more completely and certainly more intensely than with textbooks, a creative teacher can use trade books to engage students in the pursuit of such citizenship competencies as processing information, examining other points of view, separating fact from opinion, and solving problems.

The "Author's Chair" is a place where children may share their own writing with classmates and the teacher.
© Elizabeth Crews

The teacher must take care to provide good books. In recent years, numerous authors have written books that create vivid and accurate historical settings. Joan Lowery Nixon's (1992, 1993, 1994) Ellis Island series depicts the lives of three immigrant girls in the early 1900s—Rebeka, a Russian Jew; Kristyn, an independent Swede; and Rose, whose family was escaping famine in Ireland. A great number of quality children's and young adult books are available that are appropriate for teaching social studies. Each year the National Council for the Social Studies (NCSS) names "Notable Social Studies Trade Books for Young People." This annotated bibliographical list is printed in NCSS's *Social Education* along with subject categories such as biography, contemporary issues, environment, folktales, geography, history and culture, reference, social interactions, and world history and culture. In addition, each book is identified by the social studies themes depicted.

The increased use of children's literature in social studies instruction has provided more relevant textual material for students than the sole use of social studies textbooks. By incorporating both, the classroom teacher can capitalize on the best of both types of reading material.

The proliferation of quality child's literature with a social studies base permits the classroom teachers to enrich and expand a topic by having children read beyond the social studies textbook. For instance, Patricia MacLachlan's *Sarah, Plain and Tall* (1985) outlines a widower's search for a mail order bride to "make a difference" for his young son and daughter. Because of its rich descriptions of the Maine coastline and the Nebraska prairie, the book provides an excellent opportunity for comparing and contrasting the two settings geographically in addition to discussing the differences in the plant and animal life native to each of the two regions.

Economics is the focus of *Lyddie,* a book by Katherine Paterson (1991), set in 1840. Lyddie is a young farm girl who ventures to Lowell, Massachusetts, in search of a better life. She finds work in the mills and discovers the anguish and frustrations of the dangerous mill work. The long hours, low pay, and inadequate living and working conditions are well portrayed by Paterson, providing today's students with insights as to the sacrifices made by workers and, in this case, children during the Industrial Revolution.

Other books encourage students to reflect on their own lives. Cynthia Rylant's *When I Was Young in the Mountains* (1982) is a picture book that introduces children to the simple pleasures Rylant engaged in while growing up in the Appalachian Mountains. Rylant depicts the social and psychological aspects of life there. Ed Lane, a fifth-grade teacher, wrote his reflections about his experiences as a child in the fifth grade and shared them with his class.

> When I was young and in the fifth grade, Mr. Sheffield was my teacher. Mr. Sheffield was six feet, six inches tall. One day Henry broke a classroom rule. Mr. Sheffield picked Henry up and held him against the wall. I NEVER misbehaved in Mr. Sheffield's room.

After sharing what he wrote, Ed had his students write their reflections of being in second grade. Since most of the students attended the same elementary school as second graders, they wrote not only about their own remembrances but also about the culture and history of the school itself. After writing about and editing their memories of second grade, the class went to the second-grade classroom, where each fifth-grade student was paired up with a second grader. Then the fifth graders shared their experiences with the second graders.

Concepts can be introduced by sharing a children's book with students. *How Many Days to America?* by Eve Bunting (1988) describes how a Caribbean family flees to the United States and freedom in a fishing boat. Through a dramatic and touching story, students learn the importance of freedom and the value people from other countries place on it. In *Mark Twain and the Queens of the Mississippi* (Harness 1998), students see the Mississippi River and its steamboats through Twain's own words.

Cultural and sociological differences can also be presented through children's literature. Folktales often provide insight into a different culture. A Russian folktale, *The Enormous Carrot* (Vagin 1998), tells how animals join together to pull a large carrot out of the ground; kindergartners and first graders will delight in this story while learning about the concept of being a community. Upper-elementary and middle school students can also enjoy folktales. *The Crane Wife* (Bodkin 1998) is a retelling of a Japanese folktale about a poor fisherman who gains a beautiful and talented wife in a very moving, touching story. Folklore is the basis of David Wisniewski's (1991) *Rain Player,* a richly illustrated picture book based on Mayan folklore. The author provides extensive information about Mayan history and culture in a note at the end of the book.

Historical fiction that accurately depicts cultural and sociological commonalities and differences are quite useful. In *Choosing Up Sides* (Ritter 1998), Luke, a left-handed preacher's boy in the 1920s finds he lives in a right-handed world. His family considers left-handedness to be the side of Satan and contrary to God. But Luke finds he is a talented left-handed pitcher and struggles not to disgrace his family.

Another example of a folktale appropriate for social studies instruction is a very simple Chinese legend retold by Margaret Greaves (1985) in *Once There Were No Pandas.* A young girl makes a sacrifice for a white bear, which gave the first pandas their unique black markings. The author includes a pronunciation key for the Chinese terms in this simple book. A good companion book is Laurence Yep's (1991) *Tongues of Jade,* a collection of seventeen Chinese folktales.

The use of autobiographies and diaries can be a very effective way of sharing perceptions about people and events throughout history. For instance, *All for the Union* (Rhodes 1991) is a book that middle school students will find interesting. Containing the Civil War diary and letters of Elisha Hunt Rhodes, this book eloquently describes the Civil War through the eyes of a thoughtful soldier. Rhodes's diary is featured in Ken Burns's (1990) PBS television documentary *The Civil War.*

Informational books must be a part of social studies instruction so that children can become familiar with "what really happened." Unfortunately, many school libraries have informational books that are either outdated or present a view from only one perspective. Newly published informational books relating to social studies tend to present a variety of perspectives. For instance, *Pueblo Storyteller* by Diane Hoyt-Goldsmith (1991) depicts the contemporary life of a Cochiti (Pueblo) Indian girl, while David Weitzman's (1982) *Windmills, Bridges, and Old Machines: Discovering Our Industrial Past* relates how specific machines were developed and how they work. Novelist Walter Dean Myers (1991) turned his pen to nonfiction in the book *Now Is Your Time! The African American Struggle for Freedom,* which traces the civil rights movement in America by following African American slaves, soldiers, political leaders, inventors, and artists. Jerry Stanley's (1992) *Children of the Dust Bowl* is a true story of families who were lured to California by a desire for a better life during the Great Depression.

Book Links is a professional journal that provides articles on ways to integrate literature in the curriculum. "Women and the Way West" by Loftis (1996) gives several suggested titles of children's books, including picture books and historical novels, that portray the harsh life of pioneer women. Another article by Scales (1995) outlines ways of studying the First Amendment in middle schools using literature as the primary vehicle.

By acquainting children with literature that contains social studies themes and content, the teacher may find that student motivation is increased. In addition, for these students who find the textbook either too difficult or not very exciting, children's literature may unlock doors to historical events, light a path for geography, or explain in simple terms an economic or sociological concept.

Reading historical fiction can enhance a student's knowledge of geography. Here the student is drawing a map of Boston during the Revolutionary War after reading *Johnny Tremain*.

© Elizabeth Crews

✍ *Writing*

Children enjoy reading about what interests them most; the same is true for writing. Children write best when they write about what is most familiar and interesting to them (Graves 1983). Assigning children topics in which they have little interest makes it difficult for them to write because they not only lack motivation but may have no background in the topics.

Different forms of writing, including expository (descriptive, explanatory, and persuasive), poetic, and narrative, should be used to meet different social studies goals. By using a variety of writing forms, students will maintain their interest in social studies and writing (Walley 1991). Writing gives students the opportunity to reflect on what they have just read or discussed (Abel, Hauwiller, and Vandeventer 1989).

Writing can also help students understand concepts and attain knowledge. For example, Langer and Applebee (1987) found that thinking is enhanced by writing. Kuhrt (1989) conducted a study with sixth graders regarding their acquisition of social studies concepts. She found that writing in learning logs or journals about that they have read in a chapter in a social studies textbook enhanced the students' knowledge of concepts.

The writing process consists of five stages typically referred to as prewriting, drafting, revising, editing, and publishing/sharing (Britton 1978; Farris 2001; Graves 1983; Murray 1998; Tompkins 1998). Figure 5.1 presents a summary of these stages.

Stages of the Writing Process

Prewriting	The teacher needs to provide students with essential background experiences for writing. In addition, the assignment needs to be clearly delineated and explained. At this point the students may brainstorm to discover what they already know about the writing topic and what remains to be learned. Questions may be generated and lists made of possible sources of information. The information is then gathered and organized for the next stage.
Drafting	Drafting involves actually putting the pencil to paper. This stage focuses on content, not mechanics. In essence, it is getting the principal ideas down on paper.
Revising	In the revising stage, the writer rereads the draft and makes changes on the draft itself. Some teachers refer to this as "sloppy copy" in that words are often misspelled or crossed out and lines are drawn to indicate where sentences or paragraphs should be moved or inserted.
Editing	This stage is a polishing stage. Editing also occurs in the prewriting stage as the writer thinks about ideas, adopting some and discarding others. Likewise, editing takes place in the drafting stage as the writer makes decisions about word choice, sentence order, and so on. In the editing stage, the writer reads through the revised draft, correcting errors in both content and mechanics. The piece of writing is then recopied.
Publishing/ Sharing	In this stage the finished product is shared with the class. This may be done by having each child read his or her final draft, by making a class book of all the students' pieces of writing, or by placing all of the final pieces on a bulletin board. The students should discuss each other's work so that they not only learn from each other but also appreciate each other.

FIGURE 5.1   Effective writing is a five-stage process.

Prewriting

In social studies, the teacher may want to give the students a broad topic and allow them to write on a subtopic in which they are interested. In the prewriting stage, the teacher establishes a purpose for the writing and gives students time to think about their individual topics. Each student brainstorms to gather her or his already collected ideas and thoughts about the topic. The student may brainstorm with another student to share information and to formulate questions for which they may both want to find answers.

Some teachers find *graphic organizing,* also called *semantic mapping,* to be a successful prewriting activity (Rico 1983). A concept may serve as the nucleus word or words, with related words or groups of words generated by the students and each placed in a separate circle and linked in a web to the nucleus words. Students then contribute related ideas and information that they already know about the concept or topic. These ideas are also written down, either on the chalkboard if it's a class discussion or in the student's notebook if it's an individual writing assignment. Figure 5.2 shows an example of clustering done by a sixth-grade class in reference to National Women's History Month (March).

Graphic organizers can entail both brainstorming and discussion. For instance, the sixth-grade class brainstormed the primary theme of the cluster: women who have made an impact on society. The result was the various subclusters. These were discussed and refined until the students agreed on those shown in Figure 5.2. The class then identified specific women for each cluster. Some library time was devoted to the project. This proved worthwhile because both well-known and little-known names were included: Agnes de Mille, an innovator in dance choreography, who was responsible for the dances in the musical *Oklahoma!;* Ida B. Wells-Barnett, the first black investigative reporter, who led the effort against the lynching of blacks by white mobs; Julia De Burgos, a Puerto Rican poet; Ch'iu Chin, a Chinese feminist and political leader, who was beheaded for leading an uprising against the Ch'ing dynasty; and Susan La Flesche Picotte, the first Native American female physician. The teacher introduced the class to Fanny Mendelssohn, who was Felix Mendelssohn's sister. Many music historians believe that Fanny was the better composer of the two, but because she was a woman, her works were not given the attention received by her brother's musical compositions. The class discussed the reasons why this occurred and listened to music by both Fanny and Felix.

The prewriting stage may also involve *interviews.* The local community can provide a wealth of individuals who are knowledgeable about specific topics. For instance, Sarah Wheeler's fifth-grade class was studying the Civil War. Living in a fairly remote rural community in Illinois, the students did not have ready access to historians and well-endowed libraries. However, several townspeople were interested in the Civil War. A local minister who collected songs of the Civil War period was interviewed by members of the class. Miller (2000) suggests having older students interview younger students and then write a biography of their partner. Both the upper and lower grade students are challenged to think critically about what goes into the final writing piece.

Students may individually interview community members. First they should prepare a set of questions. This may be done in pairs or in small groups of students. People such as an anthropologist or economist from a local college or university, the manager of a local fast-food restaurant, a political newspaper reporter, a circuit court judge, or a state legislator can provide students with new insights. However, students should also study the particular topic prior to the interview.

Reading is part of the prewriting stage as students seek out information from various textual sources: books, newspapers, magazines, almanacs, and so forth. The

Pioneers
Women who were first in unknown
territory
Innovators

Suffragettes   *Equal Rights Advocates*

Supporters of voting   Supporters of same rights
rights for women   for women as for men

Scientists   *Authors*

Experts in science   Writers of books
Makers of new discoveries   Newspaper reporters
                                Poets

                Impact On Society

Artists   *Political Leaders*   *Educators*

Dancers   World leaders   Supporters of
Painters   Leaders of causes   education
Singers
Actresses

FIGURE 5.2   Identifications and definitions of clusters for Women's History Month.

students should take notes and write down sources. *Viewing* videotapes and laser discs may also be part of the prewriting stage. These are just a few of the various forms of media that can be used in this data-gathering stage.

Drafting

The actual writing of the initial draft of the paper begins when most or all of the research has been complete. As the student writes, it is best if they skip every other line so that they will have ample room for revising later. Some students may refer to the draft as "sloppy copy" or "draft" so that everyone will know that the focus is on content, not mechanics, which they will address in the next stage. In the drafting stage, the teacher should stress content and make no mention of mechanics or spelling.

Pioneers

Amelia Earhart
Clara Barton
Sally Ride
Susan La Flesche Picotte

Suffragettes
Susan B. Anthony
Elizabeth Cady Stanton

Equal rights advocates
Gloria Steinem
Harriet Beecher Stowe
Harriet Tubman

Scientists

Marie Curie
Elizabeth Blackwell

Authors

Emily Dickinson
Helen Keller
Ida B. Wells-Barnett
Julia De Burgos

Impact On Society

Artists

Agnes de Mille
Sarah Bernhardt
Marian Anderson
Grandma Moses

Political leaders

Margaret Thatcher
Shirley Chisholm
Ch'iu Chin

Educators

Mary McLeod Bethune

FIGURE 5.2 (Continued)

Revising

The revising stage occurs when the initial draft is complete and the writer rereads what he or she has written. During this stage, the writer reads the draft, crosses out words and phrases and replaces them with other words and phrases, and circles misspelled words or those the writer believes are spelled incorrectly to be checked for accuracy later.

During the revising stage, the student tries to view the piece as a reader would. This involves asking questions: Is this clear? Is it interesting to read? Is it well organized? Are the facts accurate? Children often have difficulty realizing that not everyone has the same amount of knowledge about a topic as they possess. This in turn may cause difficulty for the reader. Therefore, it is important for the writer to consider the audience for whom the piece is written.

Editing

Editing is the stage in which the piece is polished before publishing/sharing takes place. Some teachers have the students exchange papers and edit each other's writing. Other teachers encourage effective editing by having students, particularly those for whom writing is difficult, read their work out loud to themselves.

After making all the necessary corrections, the students recopy their papers. This ensures that the papers not only look nice to the reader's eye but also are easier to read. When students use computers for writing, spell checkers and grammar checkers are useful in their editing.

Publishing/Sharing

The last stage of the writing process is that of publishing/sharing. In this stage each student shares his or her writing with the class or members of the student's group. When the piece or writing is presented, each student should find something positive to say about it. This helps build trust among classmates.

It is important to note that this stage allows students to learn from each other. Thus, students should be encouraged to ask questions of the writer after the presentation. This also enhances the writer's self-esteem and self-confidence. Having written a piece, the student has expanded his or her knowledge in that particular area.

Portfolios

It is a good idea to date all pieces of writing in the area of social studies and then have each student file his or her piece in a *portfolio* of writing samples. As Kaltsounis (1990) points out, writing in social studies is both a method of assessing students' work and a tool of learning. Titles of books the student has read should also be listed and put in the portfolio. These books will then serve as resources or motivation for the child's own writing.

Periodically, perhaps once every month or evaluation period, the teacher and the students should review the student's progress together by examining the contents of the portfolio. The student can critique the various pieces, thereby engaging in self-evaluation to determine his or her own strengths, weaknesses, likes, and dislikes. Portfolio assessment also enables the child and teacher to establish new goals.

✍ Writing and Social Studies

Four types of writing are appropriate for social studies. These are narrative, poetic, expository, and persuasive writing. *Narrative* writing can be described as story writing; that is, all the elements of a story, including character, plot, and setting, are present. There is a beginning, a middle, and an end. Children between five and eight years old tend to use this form of writing for social studies.

Poetic writing, which is often ignored in content areas such as social studies, should be included in social studies instruction. Some forms of poetry offer natural links to social studies. Two of these are haiku poetry, three-lined poems with five, seven, and five syllables per line respectively, which depict concern for and awareness of the environment, and parallel poetry or definition poems, which examine feelings or concepts. Examples of these two kinds of poetry are shown here.

The sharing of children's literature can serve as a stimulus for writing poetry. For example, the picture book *Nettie's Trip South* (Turner 1987) is a story that was inspired by the diary of the author's great-great-grandmother who, as a young child, took a trip in 1859 from her home in Albany, New York, to the southern states. On

H a i k u

Acid Rain
Rain falls slowly now
Trees will die from the acid
Man destroys nature.
Max, eleven years old

Here is an example of haiku poetry, which focuses on nature. Max has incorporated a social issue, acid rain, with nature in his poem.

P a r a l l e l   P o e t r y

Freedom
Freedom is powerful.
Freedom is being able to vote
for who you want.
Freedom is being able to walk
the streets.
Freedom is sharing the
responsibility for peace.
Freedom means being on
constant guard so no one
can take it away from you.
Group of ten-year-old students

Freedom was the focus of this parallel poem by a group of fourth graders.

Slave Auction

Here I stand on the auction block,
Waiting my turn to be sold.
I clasp my sister's hand tightly,
youth wanting together to
grow old.
Will this be the last time we'll see each
other?
A man pulls her away as she cries and leaves.
We've already lost our father, our mother.
Now we are left to face the world
Alone.

JAKE fith grade

Jake wrote "Slave Auction" after his teacher read *Nettie's Trip South* aloud to the class.

her journey, she viewed a slave auction firsthand. The book is a superb choice to share with students as a part of a Civil War unit. Afterward, the students may, either individually or in small groups, compose poetry that reflects their own thoughts and feelings about what Nettie saw on her trip (Farris 2001).

The preceding poem is by a fifth-grade student whose teacher had read *Nettie's Trip South* to her class.

Expository writing includes writing informational works such as research reports. This type of writing may be done on an individual basis or, for older students, as a collaborative effort (Tompkins 1998). Biographies, including historical biographies, also fall into this type of writing.

Students must narrow their topic for expository writing and develop questions to be answered. Then they should use the library to research the information. After gathering the information, students must organize it, write their first draft, and then revise and edit the piece.

Tompkins (2000) suggests having the students write class collaboration reports as a form of expository writing. They divide their writing approach into six steps.

Formal discussion, either in a debate or in a panel discussion, allows children to research a specific topic of their own choosing.

© Richard Hutchings/PhotoEdit

1. *Choose a broad topic.* For instance, the topic might be the Middle Ages.
2. *Design research questions.* Questions such as these would be appropriate: What kinds of work did people do in the Middle Ages? What kind of political system existed?
3. *Gather and organize information.* The students work in pairs to gather the information.
4. *Draft sections of the report.* Students use their notes to write their section reports. (It is helpful if the students skip every other line so they will have space for revising and editing later.)
5. *Compile the section.* The students put together the sections, and the class as a group under the teacher's supervision writes the introduction, conclusion, and summary.
6. *Publish the report.* The final copy is published on a word processor if the students did not use a word processor for their section reports. Each student receives a copy of the final report.

Figure 5.3 is an example of a rubric used to evaluate expository writing.

Expository writing can also be used to introduce students to the use of references and a bibliography. A simple bibliography can be introduced as early as second grade by having the students write the name of the author and the title of the book on the last page of their reports. Later, a more elaborate bibliographical style can be introduced.

Evaluating Writing: Biography

	Elements of Biography (5)	Ideas (5)	Organization (5)	Sentence Structure (5)	Mechanics (5)
4	All elements of biography developed: Who, Life span Early years (schooling, family) Contributions/ awards/honors Impressions	Fresh, original Focuses on topic Supporting details	Ideas connected Sequenced & logical	Clearly written Complete sentences Compound/ complex sentences Variety of sentence length	Few or no errors: Capitalization Ending punctuation Commas Paragraphs indented Spelling
3	Most elements of biography developed: Who, Life span Early years (schooling, family) Contributions/ awards/honors Impressions	General focus on topic Most supporting details included	Most ideas connected Most ideas sequenced & logical	Most sentences clearly written Most sentences complete Simple sentences Some variety of length	Some errors: Capitalization Ending punctuation Commas Paragraphs indented Spelling
2	Few elements of biography developed: Who, Life span Early years (schooling, family) Contributions/ awards/honors Impressions	Moves away from focus Few supporting details	Some ideas connected Not always sequenced & logical	Some unclear sentences Some run-on, fragmented sentences Little variety	Many errors: Capitalization Ending punctuation Commas Paragraphs indented Spelling
1	Lacks development of elements of biography: Who, Life span Early years (schooling, family) Contributions/ awards/honors Impressions	Unfocused Lacks details	Few ideas connected Little sequence & logic	Sentences not clear Frequent fragmented sentences No variety	Serious errors: Capitalization Ending punctuation Commas Paragraphs indented Spelling
0	No attempt	No attempt	No attempt	No attempt	No attempt

FIGURE 5.3 A rubric to evaluate biographies.

Written by Tyler, B., Tyson, R., & Hightower, W. (1998). Tifton, GA: Northside Elementary School, Tift County Schools.

✒ *Multigenre Writing for Research*

Students may use or include different types of writing genres for a social studies research project. Following are some examples that students may opt to do. They may include three or four of these in their report. Reports may be on individuals (Joan of Arc, Princess Diana, Benjamin Franklin, Albert Einstein, Al Capone, etc.) or an event (the attack on the *Maine,* the Holocaust, the first American in space, etc.).

Newspaper/magazine article: feature story	Trivia Facts
Newspaper article: obituary	Quotes
Newspaper article: column	Play
Newspaper article: personal or want ad	Game
Newspaper article: news story	Book Cover
Newspaper/magazine article: news story	Map
Newspaper (tabloid): cover with headlines and subheadlines	Memo
Newspaper review of movie, book, concert, etc.	Poem
Newspaper letter to editor	Definition
List (achievements, events, names, supplies, etc.)	Recipe
Narrative story	Receipt
Greeting card	
Sheet music	
Personal letter or note	
E-mail dialogue	
Journal/diary entries	
Descriptive paragraph	
Television/radio ad	
Poster (wanted, playbill, concert, movie, etc.)	
Conversation/dialogue	
Dual thoughts (inner dialogue)	
Stream of consciousness	
Photo caption (with photo or illustration)	
Eulogy	
Wedding invitation	
Doctor's report	
Birth certificate	

Persuasive writing includes propaganda. Students in grades 4 through 6 should be encouraged to write persuasive arguments as well as to learn the various devices of propaganda. Persuasive writing requires that the student present a case and take a stance, followed by giving three or four sound reasons for the stance. The student then concludes by restating the problem and proposed reasons and way(s) to resolve it. Typically, a community or school issue provides an excellent opportunity for introducing students to this form of writing as it applies to social studies. Figure 5.4 is an example of a rubric to evaluate persuasive writing.

Evaluating Writing: Persuasive Text

	Elements of Persuasion (5)	Ideas (5)	Organization (5)	Sentence Structure (5)	Mechanics (5)

4	Issue
	Point of view
	Defense
	Conclusion
		Fresh, original
		Focuses on topic
		Supporting
		  conclusion
			Clearly states
			  issue
			Point of view
			  identified
			Clear defense of
			  view
			Brief summary
				Clearly written
				Complete sentences
				Compound/
				  complex sentences
				Variety of sentence
				  length
					Few or no errors:
					Capitalization
					Ending
					  punctuation
					Commas
					Paragraphs
					  indented
					Spelling

3	Issue
	Point of view
	Defense
		Most ideas focus
		  on issue
		Some support
		  of view
			States the issue
			Point of view
			  identified
			Clear defense of
			  view
				Most sentences
				  clearly written
				Most sentences
				  complete
				Simple sentences
				Some variety
				  of length
					Some errors:
					Capitalization
					Ending
					  punctuation
					Commas
					Paragraphs
					  indented
					Spelling

2	Issue
	Point of view
		Few ideas focus
		  on issue
		Moves away from
		  issue
		Lack of support
		  for viewpoint
			States the issue
			Identifies point
			  of view
			Defense is present
				Some unclear
				  sentences
				Some run-on,
				  fragmented
				  sentences
				Little variety
					Many errors:
					Capitalization
					Ending
					  punctuation
					Commas
					Paragraphs
					  indented
					Spelling

1	Issue	Incomplete ideas
		No support
		  of issue
		Lacks detail
			States the issue	Sentences
				  not clear
				Frequent
				  fragmented
				  sentences
				No variety
					Serious errors:
					Capitalization
					Ending
					  punctuation
					Commas
					Paragraphs
					  indented
					Spelling

0	No attempt	No attempt	No attempt	No attempt	No attempt

FIGURE 5.4   An example of a rubric for evaluating persuasive writing.

Written by Spencer, C., Stewart, M., Edwards, S., & Whitehead, D. (1998). Tifton, GA: Charles Spencer Elementary School, Tift County Schools.

❧ *Aesthetic and Efferent Reading and Writing*

Aesthetic and efferent reading and writing were first identified by Louise Rosenblatt (1978) back in the 1930s. Readers have different purposes for reading; for instance, reading for enjoyment and reading for information. Reading for pleasure is referred to as aesthetic reading. Reading to find out information is referred to as efferent reading.

According to Rosenblatt, nearly every reading experience requires a balance between aesthetic and efferent reading. As students read, they move back and forth between the aesthetic and efferent stances. Tompkins (1998) believes that literature, however, should be read primarily from the aesthetic stance. Thus, when having students read picture or chapter books, or historical novels, it is important that teachers keep foremost in mind that the experience be a pleasurable one. This is even true though students will be gaining information, the efferent side of reading, as they read such books.

Likewise, writing has its own aesthetic and efferent sides. Poetry and narratives are considered more aesthetic while expository writing (persuasive, descriptive, and explanatory) is from the efferent stance.

Social studies requires both aesthetic and efferent reading and writing. Researching informational books relies largely on efferent reading as does writing a descriptive report. However, there are several different types of activities that allow students to utilize efferent reading with aesthetic and efferent writing. For instance, fourth graders through middle schoolers are hooked on music. They know the latest CDs and the top tunes on the charts. One way to incorporate music into the social studies is to have the student write lyrics and do a karaoke sing-along. A list of karaoke cassette and CD titles available from Sound Choice can be purchased for one dollar. This company offers the oldies as well as current hits. The address is:

Sound Choice
14100 South Lakes Drive
Charlotte, NC 28273
Web site: *www.soundchoice.com*

Here is an example of a song written by a fifth grader after studying the 1600s in a social studies unit.

In the 1600s

(Sing to the tune of "In the Navy" by the Village People)
In the 1600s, you could sail the seven seas,
In the 1600s, men wore wigs if they pleased.
In the 1600s, London burned to smithereens,
In the 1600s, Elizabeth was Queen.
In the 1600s, Louis XIV ruled France,
In the 1600s, he wore fancy coats and pants.
  (Clap, Clap, Clap
  Clap, Clap, Clap
  Clap, Clap, Clap
  Clap, Clap, Clap, Clap, Clap, Clap)
(CHANT) We want witches!
  We want witches!
  We want witches to burn today! Yeah!
In the 1600s, you could start a war over taxes,
In the 1600s, you could kill your enemies with broad axes.
In the 1600s, women wore long dresses,
In the 1600s, men hunted with blunderbusses.
  (Clap, Clap, Clap
  Clap, Clap, Clap
  Clap, Clap, Clap, Clap, Clap, Clap)
(CHANT) We want witches!
  We want witches!
  We want witches to burn today! Yeah!
  —By Kurtis

This not only is a fun culminating activity for students, but also offers an excellent means of alternative assessment. By having students work with a partner, they can often come up with a wide variety of lyrics based on the content covered in the unit. The teacher can specify the number of facts, etc., to be included.

Poetry formats have versatility, flexibility, and diversity. Poetry is a superb way to link content area concepts and motivation to learn. Writing poetry helps students develop their abilities to record descriptions and visualize ideas. As such, it aids in concept development and retention.

☜ *Historical Documents: Diaries, Journals, Letters, and Newspapers*

Upper-elementary and middle school students can learn a great deal about social studies through reading the diaries, journals, letters, and newspaper articles written during the various periods of history. For instance, reading from the journals and letters of men engaged in the Louis and Clark expedition tells of their harsh journey as they explored the newly purchased Louisiana Territory. Students discover that Meriwether Lewis, well educated, and William Clark, a former army officer, were able to engage in mostly peaceful encounters with various American Indian tribes, something that was lost on later generations of governmental officials. When the expedition was almost at its farthest point west, Lewis and Clark decided to let all of the individuals in the group decide if the party should stay put or attempt to return to St. Louis. Lewis and Clark let every member of their party vote, including Sacajawea, a Shoshone Indian woman, and Clark's servant, a black slave (Devoto 1997). This was unheard of for the period in which they lived, for only white men had the right to vote. Truly this was an important democratic event in our history (Ambrose 1996). Thus, the following social studies themes can be examined: I. Culture; II. Time, Continuity, and Change; III. People, Places, and Environments; IV. Individual Development and Identity; and X. Civic Ideals and Practices. A good book for upper-elementary and middle school students to read is *Off the Map: The Journals of Lewis and Clark* (Roop and Roop 1993), which traces the journey of Lewis and Clark. The book begins with the letter from President Thomas Jefferson authorizing the expedition and continues with excerpts from the men's journals. The editors include an overview of the significance of the expedition.

While students can encounter Lewis and Clark's journals via books, they need to also become aware of how to use actual, authentic historical documents and artifacts. One way is to share your own family's letters, that is, letters from soldiers in World War II, the Korean War, the Vietnam Conflict, the Persian Gulf War, or the War in Kosovo; or letters from family members who moved to another state and described the differences in geography, and so on. Many local libraries and historical societies have letters, diaries, and journals dating back a hundred years or more. It is best to introduce such documents that have been laminated with a protective covering. Then move to the actual document that has been handed down and preserved. Students must be taught how to handle such documents without damaging them. They need to learn to open old newspapers and letters slowly and carefully so they won't tear. Their hands need to be both clean and dry, so allow time for a trip to the restroom to thoroughly wash away dirt and grime from playing on the playground or from leftover lunch spills.

One period that offers a rich source of diaries, journals, letters, and newspapers is that of the Civil War. Upper-elementary and middle school students can compare the letters of the various soldiers as to their views of the war, which lends itself to the fourth standard of Individual Development and Identity. By comparing letters from brothers, students can discern which brother had received the greater education before going off to war. Local historical societies and libraries are good sources of such writings. Students may also locate such materials on the Web site of the Library of Congress.

During the Civil War, children's magazines were published. *Lessons of War: The Civil War in Children's Magazines* (Marten 1998) is a collection of essays, editorials, articles, poetry, short stories, and letters from children's magazines from the period. By reading from this collection students gain insight into what children of the period experienced from raising funds for soldiers to the loss and sacrifice of family members. A sense of the southern and northern cultures during that period of history can be extracted by students as they read actual articles written during that time.

Letters and journals of soldiers can be difficult for young readers to discern. In *Soldier's Heart,* Gary Paulsen (1998) depicts the life of Charley Goddard of Winona, Minnesota, who at fifteen enlisted in the First Minnesota Volunteers. Paulsen relied heavily on Goddard's letters and journals to write the story about the trauma soldiers encountered in battle, and the mental scars left behind for soldiers to endure. This is a superb book for fifth graders as it presents in a simple, straightforward text the problems of a young man facing war. Teachers must be careful in selecting such books to make certain the historical information presented is accurate.

Prior to going to battle, soldiers were asked to write letters to their loved ones. This practice continues today. Here is an excerpt from such a letter. Major Sullivan Ballou, a Union soldier, wrote this letter to his wife, Sarah, while he was stationed in Washington, D.C. Ballous wrote the letter on July 14, 1861, a week prior to Ballou's regiment being engaged in the first battle of Bull Run (or Manassas as it was referred to by the Confederates).

> "Sarah, my love for you is deathless. It seems to bind me with mighty cables that nothing but omnipotence can break. And yet my love of country comes over me like a strong wind and bears me irresistibly with all those chains to the battlefield.
>
> "If I do not return, my dear Sarah, never forget how much I loved you, nor that when my last breath escapes me on the battlefield, it will whisper your name.
>
> "Forgive my many faults and the many pains I have caused you and how thoughtless, how foolish, I have sometimes been. But oh, Sarah, if the dead can

come back to the earth and flit unseen around those they love, I shall always be with you, in the brightest day and the darkest night. Always. Always.

"And when the soft breeze fans your cheek, it shall be my breath; or the cool air your throbbing temple, it shall be my spirit passing by.

"Sarah, do not mourn me dead. Think: I am gone, and wait for me. For we shall meet again."

Ballou died at Bull Run a week after writing this letter. Someone, or, more likely, several people, took care to preserve this wonderful letter.

Another soldier in the Battle of Bull Run was Elisha Hunt Rhodes of Cranston, Rhode Island, who entered the Army of the Potomac as a private in 1861 and participated in every campaign from Bull Run to the surrender proceedings at Appomattox in 1865. Rhodes was a descendant of Roger Williams. Following is Rhodes's letter to his sister after he fought in the Battle of Bull Run (Manassas).

> Camp Clark, Washington, D.C.
> July 28, 1861

"My Dear Sister,

I rec'd your letter last night. I will try to give you all the particulars of the Battle. We left our camp on Sunday, July 21st at 2 o'clock in the morning. We started without breakfast and only a little hardbread in our haversacks. We marched until about 10 o'clock A.M. when our pickets were fired upon. We were on a road with woods on one side. In a few minutes we received a volley and the orders were given for the 2nd R.I. Reg. to charge. We started and charged through the woods into an open field. We had about 700 men. We came out upon about 5,000 of the Rebels who started on the run for the woods on the other side of the valley. We marched to the brow of the hill and fired. Our battery came up and opened fire. The enemy opened fire from several masked forts and cut down our men in great numbers. We loaded and fired as fast as we could. This was the time that Wm. Aborn was shot. He fought bravely when he was shot through the neck. He fell into a dry ditch and then got out and crawled into the woods. He no doubt died immediately as the wound was a bad one. Some of us got separated from our Co. and joined Co. F. We were near a fence. Col. Slocum was with us. He took a prisoner and loaded his gun and fired it. The Co. was ordered to fall back, but I not belonging to it stayed near the Col. He tried to get over the fence and received 3 wounds. I was the only man very near him when he fell. I tried to get him alone, but found I could not carry him a great while. I called for help and an Old Crimea soldier named Thos. Parker came and helped me. We carried him to a house and I was left with him after the firing ceased. When we left I brought his spurs and delivered them to the Lieu. Col. He thanked me very kindly for them. As I rec'd the credit here I did not think of Parker. We drove the Rebels away from the fields, but our powder gave out and they received new men, so we had to retreat. Our two Regiments protected the men as they marched off. The Rebels ran into the field with shots from their artillery and cut us off. They fired several shells at us and killed a good many men. We continued to retreat until we reached Washington."
(Rhodes, 1991, 40–41)

Rhodes fought in twenty battles and rose from the ranks of private to lieutenant colonel and commander of his regiment by the end of the war. After the Civil War was over, Rhodes returned to work in the cotton and woolen mill business. He was elected Brigadier General of the Rhode Island Militia. Rhodes died at age 75 on January 14, 1917.

Another important battle was that of Gettysburg, a bitterly fought engagement in which both sides lost several thousand men. Major General George Picket led fifteen thousand men in the biggest and most deadly cavalry charge of the Civil War. Today it is remembered as "Picket's Charge."

Following is a portion of a journal of the Battle of Gettysburg kept by a nineteen-year-old lieutenant named John Dooley. Like many Southern officers, Dooley had brought along one of his family's slaves to cook, wash, and run errands. Dooley wrote the following entry into his journal as he marched as a member of the Confederate Army. The route the soldiers took was along narrow, rutted dirt roads as they made their way from Richmond, Virginia, north to Gettysburg, Pennsylvania. They passed farmland that had been the scene of a recent battle.

> "Scarce a farmyard that is not stained by human blood. Scarce a field unpolluted
> by the enemy's touch. The fences are burned, the meadows trampled down, the
> cattle all gone and the harvests unharvested; proud homesteads in ruins . . ."

Dooley, by nature a peaceful and gentle person, became angered at seeing the ravaged countryside. He wrote that this was the work of Northern invaders, that "party of brutal men, uneducated, unrefined, unprincipled, inhuman, and criminal" (Murphy 1992, 10).

The realities of the time and the desperate situations that the soldiers and their loved ones faced are presented to students in a much different light when the accounts come from those actually present at the scene. Through diaries, journals, and letters, students learn to develop empathy for soldiers and their families on both sides. A good activity is to have students pretend they were living during the war and have them write letters to friends and family members or keep a journal of their feelings as the war progressed.

Oral History

Oral history offers elementary and middle school students an opportunity to interview people and gain their perspective about a certain event or time period. Oral history can be done with third through eighth graders. It is critical that the teacher first develop students' questioning strategies so that their interviews will go well. It is best for students to begin with recall questions and then move to higher-level questions. The five W's—Who, When, Where, What, and Why—of newspaper and television reporting are a good starting point with students. The teacher should model questions that the students might ask and then have students get into pairs to generate additional questions. Remind students to leave ample space between questions to write the response of the person they are interviewing.

Mary Conner (1998, p. 424), a teacher in Pasadena, California, gives these suggestions to her students for conducting oral history interviews:

- You may wish to tape-record the interview. If you do, ask permission first. Using a tape recorder can intimidate some people.
- Make an appointment with the person. Thirty minutes to an hour of time should be ample for each interview.
- Thank the person in advance for agreeing to help you with your assignment. Follow up with a brief thank-you note after the interview.
- Keep in mind that most adults love to talk about their life experiences.
- The person may not be able to answer all of your questions. If a question makes a person seem uneasy, move on to another question.
- If the person doesn't give you specific details, ask them to tell you more or elaborate.
- If you are uncertain as to what the person is talking about, ask them to explain.

A particular theme or time period should be chosen for the oral history project. Themes may include such topics as immigration, World War II, the space race between the United States and the then country of U.S.S.R., the Vietnam War, or the assassination of Martin Luther King Jr. Themes may be localized; for example, students who live in Florida may interview residents who lived through Hurricane Andrew or California students may interview people about earthquakes or the Rodney King trial. A time period might be when the individual interviewed was an elementary student of the 1960s.

Students can begin the year by interviewing one another to develop and write a biography of another classmate. Using a computer, color printer, and a digital camera, the students can produce biographies complete with color photos of their subjects.

✎ Current Events

Having students become aware of current events is a way that they can become active citizen participants. Ben Bradlee, former editor of the *Washington Post,* once said that a newspaper contained "the first rough draft of history" (Ellis 1998). Newspaper articles are an attempt to record accurately the events of the day. Not every family subscribes to a daily newspaper so many students lack access to one for current events assignments. However, access to television and radio is almost universal for most children. Now the Internet offers yet another source of news events for upper-elementary and middle school students.

Sometimes local newspapers offer free or inexpensive subscriptions for students for a limited time period. These opportunities are invaluable to teachers in social studies instruction. Besides current events, death notices offer the opportunity to teach about culture, grocery and car ads reflect economics, events in other parts of the world provide geographic awareness, editorials give insights into political science, and major news stories may go down as historic events.

In studying the current events, one approach is to coincide the event with a thematic unit. For instance, in science the study of plants can be accompanied by having students gather current events on agricultural conditions, whereas the study of space can be accompanied by having students examine news articles on space travel, NASA's research, and congressional appropriations for further space launches.

One successful activity is to have students select a date in the near future and have them each send fifty cents in dimes to newspapers throughout the nation requesting that the newspaper printed on that particular date be sent to them at their home address. For example, a fifth-grade class choose October 30, 1998, the day after John Glenn was launched into space for the second time. Among the newspapers collected were *The Dallas News, The Washington Post, The New York Times, The St. Louis Post Dispatch, The Los Angeles Times, USA Today,* and from Glenn's home state, *The Cincinnati Enquirer.* The students compared headlines and the stories about the Discovery space shuttle mission. They also noted other national stories and compared and contrasted related articles.

Besides newspapers, electronic news sources can be used for current events. Here are some that students can find via surfing the Internet:

CNBC News   *http://www.cnbc.com*
CNN Interactive   *http://www.cnn.com*
Electronic Newsstand   *http://www.enews.com*
USA Today Top News   *http://www.usatoday.com/news/nfront.htm*
World Newspaper   *http://www.deltanet.com/user/taxicat/epaper.html*

Other sources of current events include faxed statements by politicians indicating their stance on various issues. These may be obtained by contacting state legislators or members of Congress.

◈ *Discussion*

In teaching social studies, the teacher must give children the opportunity to discuss topics of interest to them. This may be done by allowing groups of students to find a topic of common interest and report back to the class about that topic. More formal types of discussion include panel presentations in which students are assigned to or elect to serve in a group of three or four students. Each group member researches a specific aspect of the topic, and all members make the final presentation to the entire class.

A structured form of discussion for older students is the debate. This very democratic process is a formal discussion of a topic, question, or issues in which opposing sides take turns presenting arguments to the audience. A timed format is established in advance for opening statements from both sides and questions from both sides and from the audience. The audience evaluates the debate and votes for the winning team. Debates require the students to research their position and to develop oral language skills.

Through discussion, students develop both listening and speaking skills. They also develop confidence in speaking before their peers, something that is an asset later in life. Literature circles offer students the opportunity to engage in reading the same book, discussing it, and sharing a project based on the book with the class (see Focus Box 5.1).

5.1   Focus Box

Literature Circles

Literature circles are groups of three to eight students who are reading the same story, article, or novel. Since self-selection is part of literature circles, groups change depending on each student's current interest. Thus, students who have selected the same title to read make up a literature circle (Knoeller 1994; Scott 1994). The group usually meets two or three times a week to talk about the book they are reading. On the other days, the students read the assigned readings from the book and complete tasks related to the book. Here are some examples of tasks for literature circles:

- Discussion Leader: Monitors other group members and gives assistance with tasks when needed. Leads the discussion when the group meets together.
- Historian: Traces the major historical events of the chapter.
- Geographer/Cartographer: Draws a map related to the setting of the book and depicts journeys of the main character.
- Word Warrior: Keeps a list of unusual or unfamiliar words from the book along with writing the sentences in which they were used and their definitions.
- Phrase Keeper: Jots down interesting phrases from each chapter, noting the page numbers for each.
- Character Analyst: Compares and contrasts the main characters of the book.

With literature circles, students are assigned a task for their group. Then the students are assigned to read a set number of chapters, usually one to three chapters, and complete their tasks before meeting as a group. The teacher floats around the classroom and intercedes only if a student appears to need assistance. During the group discussion, students share their reactions to the book along with the final results of their assigned tasks. Students then rotate tasks for the next reading assignment from the book.

Students can also engage in other activities as they read the book. Here are two suggestions.

- As a group, make a character web that depicts the main character's relationship with other characters. Discuss the character web at each group meeting and make changes when appropriate (Kauffman and Yoder 1990).
- Each student keeps a literature response journal and shares reactions to the book as part of the group discussion.

The process of reading, doing the assigned tasks, and meeting and sharing with the group continues until the book is finished. At that point a culminating activity takes place. Some examples of culminating activities are:

❧ Reading, Writing, and Discussing as Learning Strategies

It is important to assist children in developing and applying the appropriate strategy for different types of reading material. For instance, in gathering factual information about the economy of the state of Arizona as compared with that of New Mexico, a student may need to read graphs. However, locating information about the capital of the state of Iowa may require a student be able to scan through text. To find the main idea of a political speech, the student must be able to skim for information and then create a summary.

- Rewrite an exciting portion of the book as a play and perform for the class.
- Write and perform a reader's theatre from an important exchange of dialogue in the book.
- Write a critique of the book, using samples of book reviews from the local newspaper.
- Make a mural or diorama depicting a scene from the book.
- Stage a mock interview of major characters in the book.

Tips for Initiating Literature Circles

The teacher needs to select books, usually two to four, that will appeal to the students and that relate to the social studies topic to be covered. The teacher then does a brief read aloud from a portion of each of the available books. The read-aloud may be one or two pages or the prologue of a book. The brief passage may be from the beginning or an interesting point in the middle of the book. The idea is to read enough to whet students' appetites. After reading the passage to the class, the teacher asks the students to react to what has been read and share their thoughts. The class briefly discusses the events shared and makes predictions about what will happen next. Then the teacher goes on to another book and the process is repeated until all the available books have had a portion shared and discussed.

Four or five students is an ideal group size for literature circles. For the first couple of attempts, the teacher should assign the students to their groups as well as to the tasks they are to perform. This will provide some structure and help make certain the reading material and tasks are not overly difficult for some of the students.

Students need to be reminded that literature circles are a collaborative activity. Everyone in the group must read the book and do their assigned task as well as join in the discussion during the group meetings.

References

Kauffman, G., and K. Yoder. 1990. Celebrating authorship: A process of collaborating and creating meaning. In *Talking about books,* edited by K. G. Short and K. M. Pierce, 135–54. Portsmouth, NH: Heinemann.

Knoeller, C. P. 1994. Negotiating interpretations of text: The role of student-led discussions in understanding literature. *Journal of Reading* 37: 572–80.

Scott, J. E. 1994. Literature circles in the middle school classroom: Developing reading, responding, and responsibility. *Middle School Journal* 26 (2): 37–41.

SQ3R

A study strategy introduced more than forty years ago and still in wide use is SQ3R (Robinson 1970). Students independently work through five steps:

1. *Surveying* the material by skimming through the chapter
2. Formulating *questions* by changing the chapter's subheadings into questions
3. *Reading* to answer the questions that were generated
4. *Reciting* answers to the questions after reading the chapter
5. *Reviewing* the answers to the questions

PQRST

A variation of SQ3R is PQRST (preview, question, review, summarize, and test), which was developed by Spache and Berg (1966). This strategy may be used independently or in pairs. It, too, involves five steps:

1. *Previewing* the material to get an idea of the primary emphasis and main points of the chapter or passage
2. Developing *questions* to be answered while reading the material
3. *Reviewing* what was read
4. *Summarizing* either orally or on paper the main points of the passage
5. *Testing* to find out how familiar the student is with the material

Literature Response Journals

Literature response journals allow students the freedom to write down their thoughts about a book as they read it. To identify what passage they are reading when they write down their comments and/or reactions, students jot down the page number in the margin. Students should be instructed to leave four or five lines of space so that the teacher can question or respond to what they have written.

Students may elect to write as if they were the main character in the book or as if they were the main character's good friend. Students may make any comments or illustrations they wish in such journals. The teacher responds by asking short, provocative, nonjudgmental questions.

RAFT

RAFT was designed by Santa, Havens, and Harrison (1989) as a strategy for students to use to write for a specific audience. RAFT is an acronym for the *role* of the writer, *audience* to whom the writing is directed, *format* of the writing, and *topic* of the piece itself.

The student identifies a theme about which to write—such as the Revolutionary War—identifies the audience, and selects a format. Possible formats include advice columns, editorials, advertisements, horoscopes, invitations, diaries, journals, songs, obituaries, and poetry. Thus, a RAFT outline about the Revolutionary War might look like this:

R: Members of the Sons of Liberty
A: King George III
F: A rap song
T: Why people living in the New England colonies should support the separation of the colonies from England

At this point, the students create their own rap song to share with the class.

RESPONSE: An Interactive Approach to Study Skills

RESPONSE is yet another study strategy. Developed by Jacobson (1989), RESPONSE was designed with the purpose of creating interaction between the student and teacher.

The teacher assigns a passage or chapter to be read by the student. As the student reads the text, he or she uses a RESPONSE form to make notations, write down questions, and jot down unfamiliar concepts or names (see Figure 5.5).

Upon receiving the student's RESPONSE sheet, the teacher reviews it, responding to questions or unfamiliar terms that the student has marked with an asterisk. In addition, the teacher clarifies any errant statements or misunderstandings the student may have shown. For instance, in Figure 5.5, Kenny had written under "New Words/Concepts/Terms" "Patrick Henry" followed by "The Great Compromiser." However, Henry Clay was known as the "Great Compromiser," so Kenny had confused the two men. His teacher clarified the differences between Clay and Henry so that Kenny could better understand the contributions of each of these leaders.

By combing all the students' questions and unknown terms, the teacher forms a picture of what the students understand and what is unclear to them. Rather than trusting to instinct, the teacher uses RESPONSE sheets as a more precise measure of what direction the class discussion should take.

By writing notes in the margins of the RESPONSE sheet, the teacher can give positive feedback to a student as well as offer guidance in finding information. In doing this, it is important to personalize the comments by using the student's first name. For instance, Carol Fuhler, Kenny's teacher, wrote this as her final comment to Kenny: "Very Complete, Ken—nice job!"

RESPONSE can be used as a group activity. Each student completes a RESPONSE sheet and shares the information with the other members of the group. The group then discusses each of the important points, questions, and words/concepts and creates a RESPONSE form that summarizes what the group believes is significant. The students hand in their individual forms and the group form to the teacher. Used in this manner, RESPONSE becomes a cooperative learning activity.

Cooperative Learning

Although whole class instruction tends to be the predominant method of instruction, cooperative learning has proved to be an effective, noncompetitive instructional approach that allows for student interaction. According to Gunter, Estes, and Schwab (1990, 169) "Working *cooperatively* . . . may be the most critical social skill that students learn, when one considers the importance of cooperation in the workplace, in the family, and in leisure activities." Reading, writing, and discussing are essential elements of cooperative learning because each student must contribute to the group's overall success. The basic premise of cooperative learning is that each student must contribute for the goal of the group to be accomplished.

Calkins and Harwayne (1991) assert the need for children to be allowed to work cooperatively, in particular, to be given ample opportunities to interact and discuss with each other matters of substance. They point out, "If we were designing schools from start to finish, clearly we'd build in hours and hours of interactive learning. Youngsters need to talk about books, molecules, the Civil War, and current events" (p. 100).

Studies of children who have engaged in cooperative learning activities on a regular basis found that the students gained in self-esteem and were more accepting

Name: *Kenny Maxwell*   Date: *Oct. 27, 1994*

Chapter: *Nine, Section 2*

IMPORTANT POINTS: As you read, write down important information and the page on which you found the information.

p. 174 Patrick Henry and Samuel Adams thought that making the government more powerful would harm the freedoms won in the Revolutionary War

p. 174 The delegates decided to write a new constitution and give more power to the central government.

p. 174 They were called the Founding Fathers and the meeting was known as the Constitutional Convention. They met in 1787

p. 174 Each State had different concerns.

p. 177 Problems were settled by compromises.

p. 177 Congress would have two house—Senate and House of Representatives—both needed to agree on a law—The Great Compromise

p. 177 Three-Fifth Compromise—of every five slaves only three would be counted for tax.

p. 177 National government divided into three parts. Legislative made up of two houses of congress They made the laws. Executive headed by the president. See that the laws of Congress were carried out. Communicated with foreign governments. Judicial the federal courts.

QUESTIONS: As you read, write down any questions that you may have along with the page number. Some questions will be for our class discussion. If you want an answer to a question, place an asterisk (*) by it.

p. 177 How could one part of the government make certain other part followed the law?

NEW WORDS/CONCEPTS/VOCABULARY/NAMES: Write the word or phrase along with the page number on which you found it. Place an asterisk (*) by those you would like to have defined or explained.

p. 174 Patrick Henry, "The Great Compromiser"

* p. 174 Three-Fifths Compromise

FIGURE 5.5   An example of a RESPONSE form.

of cultural and individual differences (Slavin 1983). Augustine, Gruber, and Hanson (1989–1990) are three elementary teachers who have used cooperative learning for several years in their classrooms (grades 3, 4, and 6). They believe that cooperative learning promotes higher achievement, develops social skills, and places the responsibility of learning on the student. According to Augustine, Gruber, and Hanson, "If other educators believe as we do that higher achievement, increased acceptance of differences, improved attitudes towards school, and enhanced self-esteem are valuable goals for all children, then we all need to promote the continued use of cooperative learning" (p. 7). Johnson and Johnson (1993) outlined five elements of cooperative learning. Each element is essential if cooperative learning is to be successfully established as an instructional strategy in a classroom. The elements particularly foster civics education. Here are the five elements:

1. Positive interdependence must be developed. The student must care about each other's learning and understand that "they are responsible for and benefit from one another's learning" (p. 44).
2. Students need lots of opportunities and time to interact with one another to elaborate, bolster, and compromise on issues.
3. Individual accountability must be present in any cooperative learning activity. Students need to realize they are each responsible for their own learning. No free rides are available.
4. Social skills need to be taught for cooperative learning to be successful. Students need to understand how to communicate, serve as an effective group leader, build trust, compromise, and resolve differences.
5. Group processing or group assessment needs to occur on a regular basis so that the group can determine its strengths and weaknesses and can determine how to perform better in the future.

A cooperative learning activity that can be used as part of a social studies unit is roulette writing (Farris 1988). Students in groups of four or five each write about the same topic. After writing for approximately three minutes, each student hands his or her piece of writing to the student at the left. Upon receiving a new writing piece, the student reads what has been written and then continues the piece until the teacher indicates that it is time to pass the paper to the next writer. Each successive writer receives additional time to read what has already been written and to think about how to continue the work. The object of the activity is to continue the same theme and content the first writer in the group used. The last student who writes on the piece writes the conclusion. This is an excellent cooperative learning activity because a student need only contribute one sentence to be a part of a successful activity.

Figure 5.6 shows an example of roulette writing based on a pioneer unit in a fifth-grade class. This group's topic was "The Day Our School Burned Down." Different handwriting indicates where one student stopped writing and the next began.

Group investigation is another cooperative learning strategy that is effective in social studies instruction and relies on the use of reading, writing, and discussion skills. Sharan and Sharan (1989–1990) believe that group investigation focuses on children's individual interests and gives them control over their learning. Children are grouped by common interests, and then they plan what they will study and how. All members of the group plan and discuss what they will research or investigate.

The Day Our School Burned Down

The year was 1870. It was hot, and we found it difficult to pay attention to the teacher in the stuffy class room. The building was all made of wood.

Laura Ingalls was our teacher. She tried disparately to make the day a good one but it was no use, it was just too hot. She dismissed us earlier than usual. We all ran across the lane to the creek.

While playing in the creeks, we noticed a grey cloud of smoke rising above the trees. We followed the smoke to see where it came from. It was our school! Our school was on fire! Miss Ingalls ran to the saw mill down the road to get Pa Ingalls. We and the other mill workers began bringing water down to put out the fire.

But it was too late. The school was gone and so too was the church. Where would we learn and pray? The children cried.

FIGURE 5.6   An example of roulette writing.

The group divides the work, giving each member a task to carry out as part of the overall investigation. The entire group reviews, synthesizes, and condenses into a summary the information gathered through individual research and presents the summary to the entire class.

In group investigation, the teacher initially presents a broad, multifaceted topic to the class for discussion. Groups are formed as subtopics emerge and students indicate their interests. The group members plan how they will investigate their particular subtopic and then carry out their research investigations. Next, the

The adults cried. Then Pa Ingalls prayed for divine guidance. Right then we decided to rebuild. The debris would be cleared tomorrow and the next day everyone would come and help build a new school. The children could do the running, the women the cooking, and the man the building. Yes we would have a bigger and better schoolhouse than before. We'd even have new desks, slates and books. It'd be hard work, but together we could do it.

FIGURE 5.6 (Continued)

groups reconvene to review and discuss all the information gathered as well as to synthesize, analyze, and summarize the information in their final report. Then all groups present the final reports (Sharan and Sharan 1989–1990).

Field Trips

Social studies lends itself to a wide variety of field trips—local community governmental offices, historical museums, visiting senior citizen centers to interview those present about their recollections of a certain period in history, and so on. When deciding on engaging in a field trip with your class, it is important to do some spade work ahead of time. First investigate the location. What are the advantages to having your students visit this site? What are the disadvantages? Is the site age appropriate for your students (look around during your visit to the location and see if children and adolescents your students' age are enjoying themselves and are benefiting from their experience)? Next, find out what the school board policies and procedures are regarding field trips. Some school districts prohibit overnight field trips. Others have time stipulations. For instance, a fifth-grade teacher wanted to take her students to visit the state capital, a four-hour drive one way, on a day trip. Her school district's field trip policy included a provision that the time at the location must be equal to or exceed the travel time. Since her students would have had to be at the capital for eight hours plus the eight-hour bus trip, the teacher opted for an overnight visit. The students were then given the additional opportunity to visit a museum as well.

Most school districts insist upon having signed permission forms or slips from the student's parent or guardian. The letter to the parents and guardians should give details as to what to expect from the field trip. This includes the time and day of departure and return, the reason for the field trip, suggestions as to what their children should wear, whether money is needed to cover expenses or make purchases at a gift shop, and any other information you believe is important to include. You may wish to request parents volunteer as chaperones for the trip as part of your permission form. These letters must be sent out in advance with extra copies made for those students who lose them on the way home from school. A checklist should be kept of the permission slips as they are returned so that those students who still need to return their forms may be reminded to do so. All permission forms should be kept in a secure location.

Field trips require an extra measure of security procedures. Remember that it is the teacher's responsibility to give the bus driver specific directions to the site in advance of the day of the field trip. Keep in mind that a bus cannot be maneuvered as easily as a car or minivan. Make a phone tree of parents and the school's phone numbers in case the bus breaks down delaying the return to school. To be extra safe, take a cellular phone with you on the field trip. Be prepared for early fall field trips to watch out for bee or wasp stings. Some students will be allergic to nuts, chocolate, or strawberries. A trip to the local custard shop might require that they be watched for what they can safely eat. If your class will stop at a gift shop, let the students know in advance. It is usually wise to suggest a modest amount of money to bring or some students will bring a large amount to spend. Gift shops can be tempting to students so be aware that this stop will require additional time.

On the day before the field trip, go over your classroom rules as well as any other rules of behavior you believe the students need to review (thanking museum guides, docents, chaperones, standing quietly and listening to presentations, getting into line without pushing and shoving, staying with their assigned group, being prompt, etc.).

Chaperones are usually parents or grandparents of your students. All chaperones should be trained for the field trip. Give them an outline of the day's events. Describe in detail what they are to do with their group. Try to give each chaperone four or five students at the most. Be certain to provide the chaperones this information a week before the field trip along with your home and school numbers and e-mail address. Then if any questions arise or they cannot attend and need a substitute, they can contact you.

Some schools require students to wear name tags while others think that can cause potential problems as strangers can learn the students' names. Find out what your school district's policy is and follow it. Many schools identify only the student's first name so strangers cannot track them by using the phone book for that area.

The best field trips occur when the students visit a site that they have been studying in social studies. A visit to a Rendezvous after studying about trapping and trading with American Indians can be very enriching. Going to the Rendezvous without having some background can be nothing more than a wasted learning opportunity. Let the students know what to look for during the trip. Giving them small, pocket-size notebooks and pencils they can use to jot down notes along the way can be helpful. Have the class make a K-W-L chart before you depart with the students listing what they already know (K) and what they want to learn (W) on the field trip. The day after the field trip, have the class complete the K-W-L chart with what they learned (L).

Chapter Summary

Reading, writing, and discussion skills are important in social studies instruction. Recently published children's literature offers students new perspectives and insights into the social studies. The literature can be used not only to stimulate reading and discussion but also to suggest ideas for writing as well.

The writing process is composed of five stages: prewriting, drafting, revising, editing, and publishing/sharing. Through these stages, the students reflect on what they want to convey to their audience of readers and how their message will be interpreted. Among the different types of writing are narrative, poetic, persuasive, and expository writing.

An approach similar to the process approach in writing should be introduced in reading. Students need to learn a variety of reading strategies for different types of text.

In developing communication skills, it is important to foster group interaction. Cooperative learning is one way to encourage the interdependence of students when conducting small group activities or projects.

Reading, writing, and discussing are essential in the development and refinement of thinking skills. By encouraging the development of these skills, the classroom teacher can assist students in some very fundamental aspects of being a good citizen. Without these skills, it is questionable whether a democracy can exist.

Children's Books

Ambrose, S. 1996. *Undaunted courage: Meriwether Lewis, Thomas Jefferson, and the opening of the American West.* New York: Simon and Schuster. This book gives a very detailed account of the political and historical aspects of Lewis and Clark's journey. Good reference for a teacher and above-average middle school reader.

Bodkin, O. 1998. *The crane wife.* Illus. G. Spirin. New York: Gulliver. A retelling of a popular love story. Good for all grades.

Bunting, E. 1988. *How many days to America?* Illus. B. Peck. Boston: Clarion Books. Boat people from the Caribbean flee to America.

Devoto, B. (Ed.). 1997. *The journals of Lewis and Clark.* Boston: Houghton Mifflin. The actual journal entries of Meriwether Lewis and William Clark are contained in this volume. Superb source of historical documents for upper-elementary and middle school students.

Glass, A. 1998. *Folks call me Appleseed John.* New York: Dell Yearling. This is the biography of John Chapman who was called Johnny Appleseed. It is told through his own eyes. Good for lower- and upper-elementary students.

Greaves, M. 1985. *Once there were no pandas.* New York: Dutton. A Chinese folktale about the origin of panda bears.

Harness, C. 1998. *Mark Twain and the queens of the Mississippi.* New York: Simon and Schuster. Dramatic panoramas of the Mississippi River and its steamboats are accompanied by quotes from Samuel Clemens writings in this picture book for older students.

Hesse, K. 1992. *Letters from Rifka.* New York: Henry Holt. A journal is kept by a young girl as her family flees the Russian Revolution in 1919.

Hoyt-Goldsmith, D. 1991. *Pueblo storyteller.* Photog. L. Migdale. New York: Holiday House. A young Pueblo Indian girl, the tribal storyteller, tells the old tales of her tribe.

Kellogg, S. 1988. *Johnny Appleseed.* New York: Morrow. This is one of a series by Steven Kellogg of American folk heroes.

MacLachlan, P. 1985. *Sarah, plain and tall.* New York: Harper & Row. Sarah is a mail-order bride who leaves her home in Maine to travel to the plains of Nebraska.

Marten, J. (Ed.). 1998. *Lessons of war: The Civil War in children's magazines.* Wilmington, DE: Scholarly Resources. This is a collection of actual letters, articles, essays, and poetry from children's magazines from both the northern and southern states during the Civil War period. Good for intermediate through middle school.

Micucci, C. 1992. *The life and times of the apple.* New York: Scholastic. A detailed look at apples. This book crosses over between social studies and science. It gives economic information as how many apples are produced by states and countries. Excellent resource for K–8.

Murphy, J. 1992. *The long road to Gettysburg.* New York: Prentice Hall. This book gives an overview of the Battle of Gettysburg as viewed through the eyes of a Confederate officer. Excellent for upper-elementary and middle school students.

Myers, W. D. 1991. *Now is your time! The African American struggle for freedom.* New York: HarperCollins. A nonfiction historical account of African Americans in America.

Nixon, J. L. 1992. *Land of hope.* New York: Bantam Starfire. A young Jewish girl escapes Russia in the early 1900s and yearns for education.

Nixon, J. L. 1993. *Land of promise.* New York: Bantam Starfire. Kristyn, a very independent girl, leaves Sweden for a life on a Minnesota farm in the early 1900s.

Nixon, J. L. 1994. *Land of dreams.* New York: Bantam Starfire. Rose, an Irish Catholic, comes to America to live with her family in Chicago early in the twentieth century.

Paterson, K. 1991. *Lyddie.* New York: Dutton/Lodestar. Lyddie works in the cotton mills of Massachusetts during the Industrial Revolution. Child labor and working conditions are explained in this book.

Paulsen, G. 1998. *Soldier's heart: Being the story of the enlistment and due service of the boy Charley Goddard in the First Minnesota Volunteers.* New York: Delacorte. Charley Goddard enlisted in the Union Army at age fifteen. The book tells of Charley's first battle at Bull Run. Later in the war, Charley fights at Gettysburg. Excellent for fifth graders.

Rhodes, R. H., ed. 1991. *All for the Union: The Civil War diary and journal of Elisha Hunt Rhodes.* New York: Orion. Elisha Hunt Rhodes served in the Army of the Potomac from the Battle of Bull Run through the surrender at Appomattox Courthouse. Superb reference material for middle schoolers.

Ritter, J. H. 1998. *Choosing up sides.* New York: Philomel. Luke tries to please his father but he's a talented southpaw pitcher. And his father, a conservative preacher, believes left-handedness is the devil's work.

Roop, P., and C. Roop, eds. 1993. *Off the map: The journals of Lewis and Clark.* New York: Walker. The journey of William Clark and Meriwether Lewis is traced through their own journal entries as they explored the territory of the Louisiana Purchase.

Rylant, C. 1982. *When I was young in the mountains.* Illus. D. Goode. New York: Dutton. This book portrays life in the Appalachian Mountains.

Stanley, J. 1992. *Children of the Dust Bowl: The true story of the school at Weedpatch Camp.* New York: Crown. True stories of Oklahoma families who lived in Weedpatch Camp in California during the Great Depression.

Turner, A. 1987. *Nettie's trip south.* Illus. R. Himler. New York: Macmillan. The author depicts life in the South before the Civil War as her great-great-grandmother wrote about it in a diary.

Turner, A. 1992. *Katie's trunk.* Illus. R. Himler. New York: Macmillan. The actual experiences of a Tory family at the beginning of the American Revolution.

Vagin, V. 1998. *The enormous carrot.* New York: Scholastic. A well-known Russian folktale about working together to get a deed accomplished.

Weitzman, D. 1982. *Windmills, bridges, and old machines: Discovering our industrial past.* New York: Macmillan. A nonfiction book that relates inventions to industrial efficiency.

Wisniewski, D. 1991. *Rain player.* New York: Clarion Books. A Mayan Indian legend about a young boy who challenges the rain god to a ball game.

Yep, L. 1991. *Tongues of jade.* Illus. D. Wiesner. New York: HarperCollins. Seventeen Chinese folktales are shared in this book.

Web Sites

http://www.historychannel.com

This Web site is the home of the History Channel. Periodically, activities accompanying movies and documentaries are shared for teachers to use with their students.

www.libraryspot.com

This is a superb Web site for upper-elementary and middle school students to use to conduct social studies research. This site is linked to more than 150 major libraries in the United States as well as all fifty state libraries and the Library of Congress.

www.ncss.org

This is the Web site of the National Council for the Social Studies.

http.www.unicef.org/voy

Voices of Youth is an Internet project of the United Nations Children's Emergency Fund (UNICEF). The site offers learning activities and materials. On-line discussions include such topics as child labor, armed conflict, HIV/AIDS, and discrimination.

References

Abel, F., J. Hauwiller, and N. Vandeventer. 1989. Using writing to teach social studies. *Social Studies* 80 (1): 17–20.

Alvermann, D., L. C. Smith, and J. E. Readance. 1985. Prior knowledge activation and the comprehension of compatible and incompatible text. *Reading Research Quarterly* 20 (4): 420–36.

Augustine, D. K., K. D. Gruber, and L. R. Hanson. 1989–1990. Cooperation works! *Educational Leadership* 47 (4): 4–7.

Banks, J.A. 1991–1992. Multicultural education for freedom's sake. *Educational Leadership* 49 (4): 32–5.

Boyer, E.L. 1990. Civic education for responsible citizens. *Educational Leadership* 48 (3): 4–7.

Britton, J. 1978. The composing process and the functions of writing. In *Research on composing: Points of departure,* ed. C. R. Cooper and L. O'Dell. Urbana, IL: National Council of Teachers of English.

Burns, K. 1990. *The Civil War.* Public Broadcasting System. Videocassette series.

Calkins, L.M., and S. Harwayne. 1991. *Living between the lines.* Portsmouth, NH: Heinemann.

Conner, M.E. 1998. The role of the immigrant on United States History. *Social Education* 62 (7): 421–426.

Demott, B. 1990. Why we read and write. *Educational Leadership* 47 (6): 6.

Ellis, A. K. 1998. *Teaching and learning elementary social studies.* 6th ed. Boston: Allyn and Bacon.

Farris, P. J. 1988. Roulette writing. *The Reading Teacher* 42 (1): 91.

Farris, P. J. 2001. *Language arts: Process, product, and assessment.* 3rd ed. Boston: McGraw-Hill.

Graves, D. H. 1983. *Writing: Teachers and children at work.* Portsmouth, NH: Heinemann.

Gunter, M. A., T. H. Estes, and J. H. Schwab. 1990. *Instruction: A model approach.* Boston: Allyn and Bacon.

Huck, C. S. 1990. The power of children's literature in the classroom. In *Talking about books,* ed. K. Short and K. Pierce, 3–16. Portsmouth, NH: Heinemann.

Jacobson, J. M. 1989. RESPONSE: An interactive study technique. *Reading Horizons* 29 (2): 85–92.

Johnson, D. W., and R. T. Johnson. 1993. What to say to advocates for the gifted. *Educational Leadership* 50 (2): 44–7.

Kaltsounis, T. 1990. Interrelationships between social studies and other curriculum areas: A review. *Social Studies* 81 (6): 283–6.

Kohn, A. 1996. *Beyond discipline: From compliance to community.* Alexandria, VA: Association for Supervision and Curriculum Development.

Kuhrt, B. L. 1989. The effects of expressive writing on the composing and learning processes of sixth-grade students on social studies. Ph.D. diss., Northern Illinois University, DeKalb, IL.

Langer, J., and A. Applebee. 1987. *How writing shapes thinking: A study of teaching and learning.* (NCTE Research Report No. 22). Urbana, IL: National Council of Teachers of English.

Loftis, S. S. 1996. Women and the way west. *Book Links* 5 (3): 29–41.

McGowan, T., and B. Guzzetti. 1991. Promoting social studies understanding through literature-based instruction. *Social Studies* 33 (4): 16–21.

Miller, F. 2000. Biography buddy: Interviewing each other. *Social Studies and the Young Child* 12 (3): 13–14.

Murray, D. 1998. *Write to learn.* 6th ed. Orlando: Harcourt Brace.

Rico, G. L. 1983. *Writing the natural way.* Los Angeles: Tarcher.

Robinson, F. P. 1970. *Effective study.* New York: Harper and Row.

Rosenblatt, L. 1978. *The reader, the text, and the poem.* Carbondale, IL: Southern Illinois University Press.

Santa, C., L. Havens, and S. Harrison. 1989. Teaching secondary science through reading, writing, studying, and problem solving. In *Content area reading and learning,* ed. D. Lapp, J. Flood, and N. Farnan, 137–51. Englewood Cliffs, NJ: Prentice-Hall.

Scales, P. 1995. Studying the First Amendment. *Book Links* 5 (1): 20–4.

Schaps, E., and D. Solomon. 1990. Schools and classrooms as caring communities. *Educational Leadership* 48 (3): 38–42.

Schiller, L. 1996. Coming to America: Community from diversity. *Language Arts* 73 (1): 46–51.

Sharan, Y., and S. Sharan. 1989–1990. Group investigation expands cooperative learning. *Educational Leadership* 47 (4): 17–21.

Slavin, R. 1983. *Cooperative learning.* New York: Longman.

Spache, G. D., and P. C. Berg. 1966. *The art of efficient learning.* New York: Macmillan.

Tompkins, G. E. 1998. *Language arts: Content and teaching strategies.* 4th ed. Columbus, OH: Merrill.

Tompkins, G. E. 2000. *Teaching writing.* 3rd ed. Columbus, OH: Merrill.

Walley, C. 1991. Diaries, logs, and journals in the elementary classroom. *Childhood Education* 67 (3): 149–54.

Chapter 6

© James L. Shaffer

Facilitating Learning through Strategic Instruction in Social Studies

Bonnie L. Kuhrt
Carl Sandburg Middle School, Rolling Meadows, Illinois

Pamela J. Farris
Northern Illinois University

Highlighting the Issues
Point:
Above all, textbooks must try to lay bare the fundamental structures of history, geography, health, and science—and in a manner that permits children and youth to grasp the structure.

—Richard Anderson et al.
Becoming a Nation of Readers

Counterpoint:
The report ignores the role of the student as a constructive participant in learning and places the teacher in the role of a giver of information whose task it is to follow the organization of a well-written textbook.

—Bonnie C. Wilkerson
"A Principal's Perspective"

Objectives

―――――――――――――――――――⌘―――――――――――――――――――

Readers will

- understand lower- through higher-level thinking skills as depicted in Bloom's taxonomy;
- be able to apply brain research findings as part of strategic instruction in social studies;
- be able to apply strategies to activate learning;
- understand how to teach strategic sequencing in social studies;
- recognize the need for teaching history as perspective taking; and
- be able to apply Internet reading strategies in social studies instruction.

Introduction

Children need to develop learning strategies that they can apply effectively in social studies as they read, write, and discuss. The student constructs meaning from within. The teacher does not merely facilitate the process but works cooperatively in developing the meaning. Creation of the student's own meaning is also an essential element to the constructivist model identified by Gaskin et al. (1994), which describes how classroom discussion of text can help in the active construction of meaning. However, discussion of text encourages the student to construct personal meaning only when the initiating problem or question allows for a variety of student responses. Increasing the accessibility of the information locked in the expository material of textbooks becomes more important with the increased literacy demands of authentic assessment and the increased language diversity of the students.

The current shift from an overdependence on norm-referenced testing to the higher literacy demands associated with authentic assessment suggests that avoiding expository material is not a viable alternative.

Students are held accountable for the knowledge locked within the expository passages, including some that may not be accessible. By modeling comprehension strategies, Hadaway and Young (1994) suggest, student interaction with textbooks can increase understanding. Resnick and Klopfer (1989, 206–7) suggest that "Knowledge is acquired not from the information communicated and memorized but from the information that students elaborate, question, and use." Therefore, the question becomes: How can the reasoning activities necessary for knowledge acquisition be activated to give students control over their learning in social studies?

―――

☙ *Bloom's Taxonomy*

Benjamin Bloom (1956) believed that the primary purpose of education was to change learners in desirable ways. Thus, the purpose of teaching social studies is to specify how students will be changed during the learning process. As stated in Chapter 3, Bloom developed a taxonomy of education objectives that he believed would greatly improve the effectiveness of assessment. The six levels of

Bloom's taxonomy from the lowest level of thinking required to the highest are as follows:

1. Knowledge—define, distinguish, identify
2. Comprehension—conclude, demonstrate, differentiate
3. Application—apply, classify, develop
4. Analyze—analyze, categorize, compare
5. Synthesis—combine, constitute, derive
6. Evaluation—appraise, argue, assess, judge

Thinking begins with basic or low level units at the knowledge level, which includes recognition or recall of facts and progresses upward to the higher levels of synthesis (creativity) and evaluation (assessment). The basic premise is that learning is additive and that a student must go through the steps from lowest to highest. If a level, or step, is missed, the student must go back and acquire that level.

The preceding levels can be used in questioning students in social studies. Bloom felt that by using such observational objectives with the performance (work examples) of students, students would be challenged as learners. This serves as a student-centered approach to evaluation.

This chapter examines strategies for helping students gather, organize, relate, and retain knowledge in social studies. We look at strategies that activate learning and describe the characteristics of graphic organizers. This chapter provides a basic framework for strategic instruction as well as integration of reading, writing, and reasoning in social studies.

Brain Research and Strategic Instruction in Social Studies

New research in neuroscience gives teachers insights into how social studies instruction can be more effective. Brain research suggests that teachers need to set the stage for learning in order to help student attend to relevant knowledge to be presented in upcoming instruction. Thus, the teacher should ask focusing questions about the topic and have the students recall previous information. The objective of the lesson should be made clear by the teacher (Wolfe 1999). One way to activate prior knowledge is to use an alphabet grid. Make twenty-six boxes on the chalkboard or bulletin board and write a letter of the alphabet in each box. Then have students take turns writing something about the upcoming topic in a box until no one in the class has any more words to put in the boxes. For example, if our topic is China, a student might write "tea" in the box for the letter "t" while another student might write "Great Wall" in the "g" box and yet another writes "Asia" in the "a" box. Some boxes will have more than one word while others may be empty. After everyone in the class has had a chance to write a word, the class can discuss the words and their meanings. By having students with diverse backgrounds or limited abilities go among the first students, the teacher affords those the opportunity to be successful. At the end of the unit, the activity is repeated until the students have exhausted all of their newly gained knowledge and information. The "a" box may have "Asia" and acupuncture, for instance. This can now serve as an evaluation technique for the success of the unit. The alphabet box technique works with grades 2 to 8.

Brain research points out the need to use more than one modality for learning. In fact, the more, the better. In planning a unit of story, the teacher should keep in mind ways to incorporate students' use of their senses. Research indicates that when students use more than one sense, learning increases dramatically. For instance, combining listening and a visual may yield up to 80 percent recall and understanding of a topic. Obviously videos and videodiscs are important supplementary materials. Overhead projectors may be used by both the classroom teacher and students to demonstrate social studies concepts along with an oral explanation. PowerPoint demonstrations are also quite effective ways to present new content and concepts. Social studies offers tactile (artifacts, locating capitals of countries on a globe, relief maps), smell (field trip to demonstration of pioneer village—candle making, blacksmithing, etc.), and taste (class made johnny cakes or applesauce, dishes from various cultures) experiences. Various CDs offer students the chance to be taken to another culture, hear folk songs, or listen to a famous speech. Such stimulation of the learning modalities of seeing, hearing, touching, smelling, and tasting helps to aid the student in understanding and retaining new material.

If a task is either too difficult or too easy, students will have little motivation to continue to do it. Likewise, if students find that the level of stress is too high or too low, learning becomes less efficient (Hunter 1982). Basically, brain research points out that this is "fight or flight" survival tactics by the brain. In other words, teachers need to adopt instruction that reaches out to the emotions of students. If the task seems to have little or no value to the students, they will drop it from their brains. If the emotional content (i.e., stress) is too extreme, thinking processes of the students become less efficient.

Teachers need to be able to break down skills into their subcomponents to explain them piece by piece to students (e.g., how to identify the focus of a passage in a social studies textbook, how to locate a specific longitude and latitude on a map, or how to define the Articles of Confederation). Memory is stored in the brain in different ways. If a student repeatedly practices something wrong, such as saying the capital of Kentucky is Louisville, then the brain cells fire together and are wired together. They eventually become hardwired and fire automatically, in this case spewing out Louisville, rather than Frankfort, as the capital of Kentucky. As Madeline Hunter said, "Practice doesn't make perfect; it makes permanent" (Wolfe 1999, 63).

✎ Strategies to Activate Learning

A learner makes a comparison between personal knowledge of a subject and the new information contained in the text (Jones et al. 1987). This is known as a learner's schemata. Defined as complex knowledge structures that help students process information effectively, the schemata are classified as three distinct types: (1) content and organizational patterns, (2) processes, and (3) conditions. By familiarizing students with expository text structures, recognition of these patterns can promote comprehension. The development of the schemata involves the following phases: (1) activating prior knowledge, (2) monitoring comprehension, (3) evaluating the meaning and inconsistencies with regard to prior knowledge. As students internalize the when and why for the application of these patterns, the conditions for transferring these structures to a new context emerge.

Topic: France

Know	Want to Know	Learned
Country in Europe	What products are manufactured?	Cars, pottery, wine
Mountains	What kinds of farming & agriculture?	Cattle, grain
Produces wine	What kind of government?	Citrus fruits, vegetables, grapes
Produces perfume	What are popular sports?	Parliamentary
Franc is the money		Tennis, soccer, snow skiing
French is the language		French words: broil, sauté, pâté, etc.
		A banking center for the world
		Member of Common Market

FIGURE 6.1   An example of K-W-L by a fourth-grade class.

Finally, the interplay between the process of prediction and verification that takes place during reading suggests strategies to activate prior knowledge and to analyze text material.

K-W-L

One strategy to help students take an active role in reading social studies text is K-W-L (Ogle 1986, 1989) which stands for know, want to know, and learned. This strategy is a three-step approach to help students read and understand informational text such as social studies material. The teacher and each student begin with a chart containing three columns: (1) Know, (2) Want to Know, and (3) Learned. By using K-W-L prior to the whole-class discussion, the student assesses what she or he already knows before the group activity begins (Gaskin et al. 1994). Naive beliefs become apparent during the examination of the new information in the text. Figure 6.1 provides an example of a K-W-L chart constructed on the topic of France; the learning activities associated with this strategy are discussed in the section on strategic sequencing.

Using specific reasoning strategies to activate prior knowledge helps students comprehend the ideas contained in the text. Through this active engagement, readers are able to link new information with their personal knowledge of the subject. By learning to monitor and control such reasoning strategies, students develop an understanding of how they learn. This metacognitive awareness allows them to control the learning process.

Graphic Organizers

When used with social studies textbooks, graphic organizers or sematic maps, help activate student learning. Graphic organizers are also very appropriate for use with non-fiction informational books. When students are reading material that contains a large amount of information, a visual display can help them remember what they have read.

In the Classroom Mini Lesson

K-W-L Informal Assessment

*B*y keeping a matrix with student names recorded on the horizontal lines and using the vertical columns to record the number and quality of responses, McAllister (1994) is able to keep track of each student's rate and quality of responses during the K-W-L activity. Using a recording system of good, average, and poor and inserting comments on the matrix help identify students who need more attention.

The teacher can demonstrate the use of graphic organizers by reading aloud five or six pages from the social studies textbook or an informational children's literature book. Students working in pairs reread the passage the teacher read aloud and begin to map the information. The students identify key information, which is then classified under a heading and related to the nucleus word or words that identify the primary topic.

The graphic organizer shows the learner the relationship patterns developed in the text that have similarities to the structures inherent in the schemata. However, distinctive differences exist between the graphic organizer and reasoning. Although the graphic organizer can activate the reasoning strategies, the learning takes place during the interaction between the learner's prior knowledge, the demands of the graphic organizer, and the information contained in the textbook. Therefore, differences appear in the visual representations created from text material because of variations in the learner's prior knowledge as well as in the reasoning strategies applied.

Using a graphic organizer aids comprehension of the social studies text by making the patterns clear. Designed as a means of organizing text material into relationship patterns, the graphic organizer centers attention on the key information contained in the text. Hadaway and Young (1994) advocate the development of literacy through content and the use of the graphic organizer to promote comprehension. More important, they suggest that the current trend toward more language diversity in the schools necessitates this instructional strategy. By building background knowledge and developing language and content simultaneously, the instructor can promote cooperative problem-solving activities, which is an effective pattern of instruction where language diversity is a consideration. However, Hadaway and Young stress that these activities benefit all children, because the relationship between the concepts and the main ideas is reinforced through the manipulation of text material. With the graphic organizer, students can better control and comprehend large amounts of information.

In examining the impact of the graphic organizer on meaningful learning, Armbruster, (1985) identifies three stages leading to meaningful learning: (1) selection of information from the text, (2) organization into a coherent structure, and (3) integration of the new information. Armbruster applies this model to three basic structural patterns used in social studies texts: (1) description, (2) comparison/contrast, and (3) explanation. Figure 6.2 shows three examples of graphic organizers. These represent three different approaches to feudal societal groups generated by sixth-grade students.

Feudal Society Groups

Clergy	Nobles	Peasants
- teach religion	- govern	- farm land
- help poor and sick	- enforce laws	- provide services
- have more rights	- protect people	- work for clergy and nobles
	- have more rights	- largest group

Believed God wanted it that way →

- few tried to make improvements or change way of life

- remained in groups they were born into

a

	Ties of Loyalty	Duties
Lord	- protected vassals from enemy attack - if he failed to do this, vassal owed no loyalty	- gave vassal a fief - gave symbol of trust - gave right to govern
Vassal	- less powerful noble - fief vassals for life - upon death, passed to son - did not lose respect for seeking protection - gave loyalty to lord - some supported the one likely to win	- helped lord in battle - supplied knights - owed 40 days of battle a year - paid lord when sons became knights and daughters married - paid ransom for lord's release - supplied food and entertainment - decided cases

b

FIGURE 6.2 Sample graphic organizers developed by students.

Residence

Type	Time period	Description
Manor	9-11th centuries	-wooden buildings high wooden fences -1 room, high ceiling and straw floor -all activities -fire for cooking and heating
Castle	12th century	-stone fortress -lookout tower and arches -moat -- soft muddy bottom -drawbridge -- heavy door -portcullis -- heavy oak/iron gate -keep -- tall tower with all, many rooms and dungeon

c

FIGURE 6.2   (Continued)

Armbruster, Anderson, and Ostertag, (1989) expanded the list of patterns by dividing the explanation pattern into (3) sequence, (4) cause-effect, and (5) problem solution. Regardless of the labels, these organizational patterns are used in most social studies text materials. Graphic organizers, as visual representations of these patterns, help the learner focus on the important information within the text and clarify the purpose in reading.

By setting the focus for learning, the graphic organizer gives the student control over the text and assistance in comprehension. The value of these visual models lies in directing the integration of reading, writing, and group work toward a specific learning outcome. The remainder of this chapter applies sequencing strategies and the use of graphic organizers to a seventh-grade geography lesson.

❧ *Strategic Sequencing*

The sequencing of strategies, like the phases of learning, involves (1) prereading to activate prior knowledge, (2) using graphic organizers to monitor comprehension, and (3) evaluating inconsistencies between new information and prior knowledge. These three steps, especially the first one, are central to comprehension of the text materials.

Phase One: Activating Prior Knowledge

Before students read social studies texts, learning theory suggests engaging them in activities that tap their prior knowledge of the topic. Because of the descriptive pattern used in social studies books—particularly when describing geography—the text provides an opportunity to classify specific characteristics of a geographic region. During this initial introduction to a region, students access their prior knowledge. This follows the same logic as the K-W-L strategy (Ogle 1986, 1989). During the prereading stage, students brainstorm about what they already know of the topic. The pooled information is recorded on the class chart under the "Know" column. As students contribute information, some conflicts and disputes will arise. These discrepancies are turned into questions and listed under the "Want to Know" column.

Drawing on the same thinking strategies as the K-W-L, Davidson, (1982) presents another strategy: the whole class uses mapping strategies to assess the group's level of prior knowledge. For this geography unit, the students independently list random associations for Western Europe in their learning logs. The teacher uses an overhead transparency to record student responses about the topic. This activity gives students a model for the process of anticipating the information contained in the chapter.

By mapping the predicted material for the text, students determine what they know, predict what will be discussed, and assess what was learned. They are using the K-W-L thinking strategy in a new format. Students activate their prior knowledge by writing what they know into a learning log. Fulwiler (1978), defines this kind of writing as a means of connecting the personal and the academic functions of writing. This learning log strategy actively engages the student in learning by encouraging rehearsal of ideas and establishing the level of background knowledge prior to the whole-class discussion. Following a time span of three to five minutes, the teacher records the student associations of Western Europe on an overhead transparency (see Figure 6.3). All student associations are recorded regardless of their accuracy. Associations are removed from the list only when they are disproved or are not validated in the textbook. No attempt at classification occurs during this stage. Information is recorded in the random order in which the students present it.

After listing the known information on the overhead projector, the teacher uses another transparency to model the classification of this information. For the topic of Western Europe, the teacher starts with "country" the obvious category of countries. By circling each country and listing it under the category on the

Scandinavia, terrorism, driving on the left side of the road, Cliffs of Dover, cooperating with their money, trying to trade together, Alps & valleys, an underwater tunnel between France & England, the Berlin Wall is coming down, Germany reunited, borders change in Europe, France, Netherlands, Spain, countries are small like some of our smaller states, the countries are close but the cultures are different, Austria, Scotland, & Ireland, densely populated, that's why they came here, England used up all its resources, steel is made in some countries that have iron & coal, you can go on trains all over Europe, landforms protect some of the countries, plains & swamps may be all the landforms, not deserts

FIGURE 6.3   Listing random Western Europe associations.

WESTERN EUROPE

Countries	Land forms	Natural resources	Economics	Transportation	Problems
France	Alps	coal	economic	drive on wrong side	terrorism
Netherlands	valleys	farms	community	of the road	Wall coming down
Germany	Cliffs of Dover	iron ore	cooperate	trains all over	small like states
Austria	swamps	steel	with money	underwater tunnel	England used up
Spain	plains		trade together	between France	resources
Ireland	all types		European Union	and England	densely populated
	no desert		"Eurodollar"		close but different
	can protect				cultures
	countries				borders change

FIGURE 6.4   Classifying associations.

transparency, the teacher demonstrates the classification process. Students continue the process by classifying the information in their learning logs and recording the reasoning for each classification. Finally, the teacher records the students' categories on the transparency (see Figure 6.4) and identifies similar and overlapping categories. Depending on the group's familiarity with the text, categories based on geography concepts may emerge. Following this predictive activity, the students move to the next phase and preview the chapter.

Phase Two: Assessing and Monitoring Comprehension

By comparing the subtopics in the text with their classification categories, students evaluate their initial predictions and determine the need for additional topics. Next, the students generate questions in their learning logs that predict the information presented in the text (see Figure 6.5). Collection of this information during class discussion establishes the purpose for reading. Finally, students read the text to find the information that answers the questions. This strategy combines the thought processes of the K-W-L strategy and the explicit framework of the graphic organizer.

Initially, the students revise their predictions in their learning logs by focusing on the subtopics identified in the text. The teacher directs the evaluation process through questioning. Were any categories overlooked during the brainstorming activity, and is there a need to extend the categories? What possible relationships are seen in the subtopics, and how do they appear to be organized? The teacher gains insight into the group's knowledge of text cues by following student input on these topics.

Students examine the pictures, maps, graphs, and subheadings as they revise their original predictions. Graphic displays used in expository text reinforce the connections between concepts and help students discover patterns. Students can preview the graphic displays (i.e., headings, graphs, maps, bold prints) in the text and discuss what is illustrated. During the group discussion, the teacher guides and clarifies the information. Gillespie (1993, 352) suggests using questioning strategies similar to those used with prose. "What is the main idea? What are the supporting details? What is the purpose of the graph? How are the details related?"

Students may depend on the subheadings of the social studies chapter to suggest concepts presented in the text. Another helpful strategy, however, is to use the introduction and the first sentence of each paragraph to identify central concepts. After this research, students will add to their learning logs and the group will discuss the following question: What signals are found in the chapter introduction, and what organization can be predicted?

Using the text overview, the teacher begins to record the questions that the students believe will be answered in the text. These questions establish the purpose for reading. Taking one subtopic at a time, the teacher records the questions on the overhead transparency as students predict what the material will cover. The students then read the text.

Phase Three: Evaluating Inconsistencies and Written Extensions

Finally, in a class discussion, students reflect on what they have learned. During this time, the students share what they recorded under the column titled "Learned." The teacher moves students to the evaluative level during this final phase of instruction, beginning with an analysis of the classification of associations and the descriptive map of the text. Examination and discussion of the similarities and differences between the predicted structure and the actual text organization help students refine this knowledge and apply this learning to their preview of the next chapter.

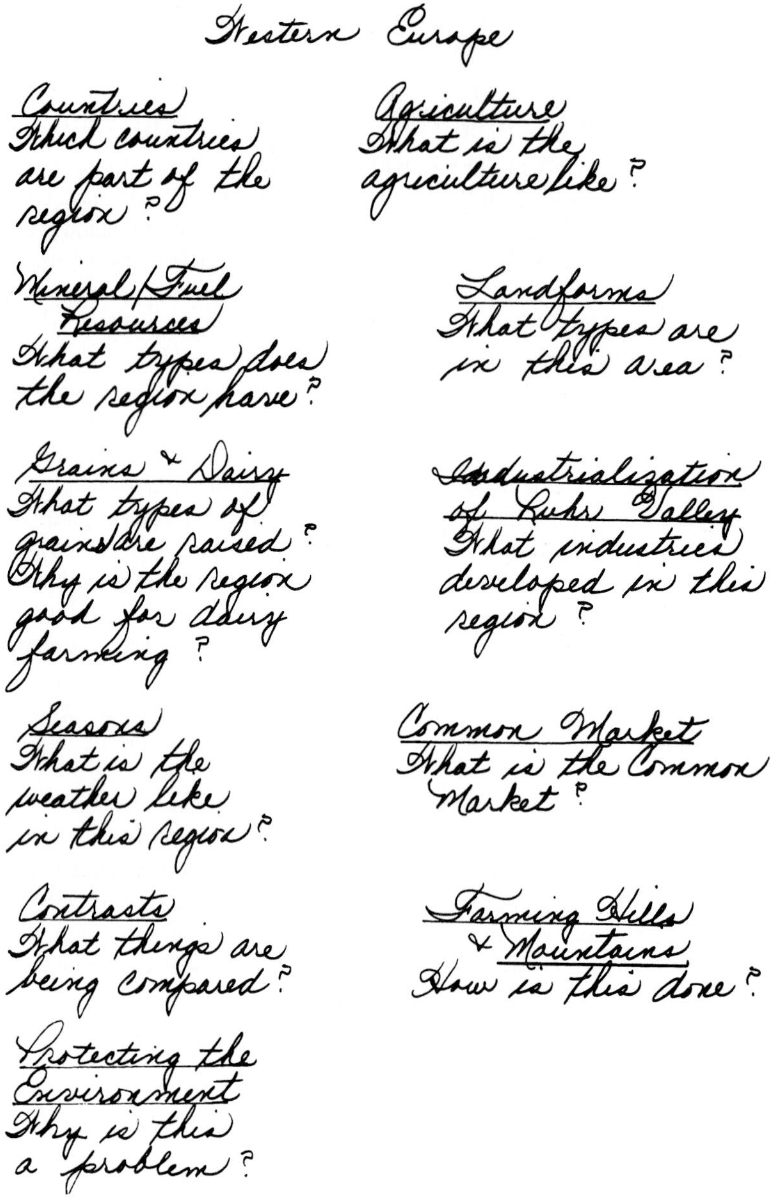

Western Europe

Countries
Which countries are part of the region?

Agriculture
What is the agriculture like?

Mineral / Fuel Resources
What types does the region have?

Landforms
What types are in this area?

Grains & Dairy
What types of grains are raised? Why is the region good for dairy farming?

Industrialization of Ruhr Valley
What industries developed in this region?

Seasons
What is the weather like in this region?

Common Market
What is the Common Market?

Contrasts
What things are being compared?

Farming Hills & Mountains
How is this done?

Protecting the Environment
Why is this a problem?

FIGURE 6.5   Predicted structure of previewed text.

By placing the classification of associations (see Figure 6.4) on the overhead transparency and having students refer to the descriptive map that they created while they were reading the text, the teacher ensures that students can evaluate the effectiveness of their predictions. The focus on this analysis should center on the students becoming more effective in making future predictions. Through the awareness of concepts covered in the first chapter, expectations for future chapters are changed.

As the students examine the descriptive maps, they find that many of the countries originally classified as part of the region were correct. However, their

Students need to learn how to use the Internet to gather research. They also need to learn how to be consumers and gather accurate, appropriate information.

© Elizabeth Crews

classification contained too many countries; two incorrect countries in the original prediction will each appear in other regions. Because the students gave no consideration to the categories of agriculture and climate in their initial classifications, they learn that these categories need to be added to the predictions of future chapters. In this chapter, students find the concept of transportation appears under the category of industrialization. The problems cited in the chapter are more environmental and general than those in TV and radio newscasts, and in newspapers and magazines. Using this critique as a basis, the predictive process can be repeated for subsequent chapters.

Each time the students perform this predictive process, they further refine the organizational pattern for more effective future predictions. Descriptive mapping strategies can extend into group discussion, research, and writing. Students can experience more rehearsal of the material, for example, by manipulating the information on the maps generated for chapters on Northern and Western Europe to write a paper comparing and contrasting the two regions.

The descriptive maps, generated from the expository text, provide a structure for the points of comparison so that students become sensitive to the structure required in expository writing. Signal words cue the reader to the structure of the written product as students make transitions from material on one descriptive map to material on another (see Figure 6.6).

Clues for Teaching Further Thinking Skills

By examining the influence of the descriptive mapping activity on expository writing, one can see how the mapping process gives students control over focus and

Western Europe

Countries
Ireland
France
Germany
Austria
Switzerland
Belgium
United Kingdom
Netherlands
Monaco
Leichinstein
Luxenberg

Agriculture
Yield highest
in the world
Large farms
Migrant workers
rotate with crops
Have fertile crops
because of chemical
advanced machinery
Cooperate farms
(W.W.II)
Average 30 acres

Mineral/Fuel Resources
Rich mineral resources
Well developed trans-
portation
Mining manufacture
Iron ore
Coal

Economics
Common Market
Share economic
opportunity
Free trade
No Tariffs
between common
Market countries
(7 from Western
Europe, 3 aren't)

Landforms
plains
plateaus
hills
mountains

Grains/Dairy
Because of plains
there's large crops
of grain
Wheat, livestock
40% of land is
reclaimed by sea.

Industrialization
Coal deposits
produce steel
from Iron
Transportation
(railroads and
canals) brought
in products from
other countries
Countries are
interdependent
exchange resources

Climate
Seasonal
changes are not
extreme
Precipitation
is moderate and
cool and damp

Farming Hills
Special crops
Good income
Poor soil, cool
Climate
Grapes and fruit
Dairy products
Meat products

Protecting the Enviroment
Dwindling coal supply
Researchers trying
to develop ways
to tap other energy sources
Pollution

Patterns of Living
Country life (rural)
cathedral, castles
Cities industrialized
Variety of jobs
Education, science
Modern architecture

FIGURE 6.6   Student-generated descriptive map by Shannon.

organization. Students use the descriptive maps to identify points of comparison in the text. This establishes the focus and organization of their paper. Once students establish their series of topics in the introductory paragraph, they can go on to isolate each point of comparison and examine it for similarities and differences (see Figure 6.7).

Northern and Western Europe
by Shannon

Have you ever visited Europe? Examination of Northern and Western Europe shows that many similarities and differences can be seen in many areas. By refering to agriculture, resources, climate, contries, and land, you can see just how alike and different they really are.

When comparing Northern European agriculture to Western European agriculture, it becomes clear that there are many similarities and differences. Western Europe prows to be more of an agriculture region, unlike Northern Europe in many ways. Farming in Western Europe is more basic since boulders and rocks soil don't interfere with the flurishing plains and basins. Western Europe produces a large variety of grain, wheat, and livestock, similar to its neighbor, Northern Europe. Northern Europe although it has swamps and marshes, and rocky soil yields more than Western Europe. Northern Europe produces large quantities of daily, grains, and livestock. Such examples are exported cheese, butter, oats, wheat, rye, barley, and livestock products like meat and hide. This conclusion is drawn from the hard workers and the various farming techniques. Northern Europe and Western Europe are similar

FIGURE 6.7 An example of expository writing.

since they both use cooperative farms to help keep costs down. Unlike most Western farmers, in Northern Europe, farmers often share their equipment and profits. Western Europe benefits by having migrant workers rotate with their crops. Also,   crops are more fertile because of chemical advanced machinery.

Resources play a great deal of importance in Northern and Western Europe. While Northern Europe is famous for its fish and forests, Western Europe has rich mineral resources. Both areas produce steel and iron or , although Western Europe also has coal deposits. In order to transport the products, Western Europe has many railroads and canals which have their transportion well developed. In comparison, Western Europe produces more natural resources while Northern Europe stays less industrialized.

Through climate, simalarties and differences became clear in Western and Northern Europe. Northern Europe has a moderate climate, as well as Western Europe, until you reach areas north of the Artic Circle. This area includes long winters and short growing seasons. Western Europe doesn't appear to have extreme seasonal changes and precipitation is moderate. Over all, most of this area is cool and damp.

FIGURE 6.7   (Continued)

Such countries within Western Europe are Ireland, France, West Germany, Austria, Switzerland, Belgium, United Kingdom, Netherlands, Monaco, Liechtenstein, and Luxenburg. Countries located in Northern Europe are Iceland, Norway, Sweden, Finland, and Denmark. These countries make up all the similarties and differences contained in this article.

A distinctive difference between northern and western Europe is the land type. In northern Europe glaciers remain, while marshes and swamps are present. This land permits limited farming because of its infertile soil with boulders and gravel. On the other hand, western Europe has large farms and fertile crops, the average being thirty acres. Landfarms there include plains, plateaus, hills, and mountains.

As concluded from information gathered, many similarities and differences have arisen between the two countries. While western Europe proves more as an agriculture region, northern Europe is big in the fishing industry. Through examination of agriculture, resources, climate, countries, and land a better understanding can be reached about these two famous countries.

FIGURE 6.7   (Concluded)

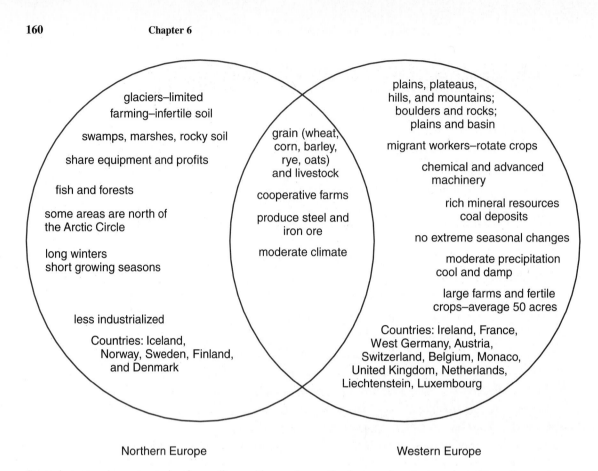

glaciers–limited
farming–infertile soil

swamps, marshes, rocky soil

share equipment and profits

fish and forests

some areas are north of
the Arctic Circle

long winters
short growing seasons

less industrialized

Countries: Iceland,
Norway, Sweden, Finland,
and Denmark

grain (wheat,
corn, barley,
rye, oats)
and livestock

cooperative farms

produce steel and
iron ore

moderate climate

plains, plateaus,
hills, and mountains;
boulders and rocks;
plains and basin

migrant workers–rotate crops

chemical and advanced
machinery

rich mineral resources
coal deposits

no extreme seasonal changes

moderate precipitation
cool and damp

large farms and fertile
crops–average 50 acres

Countries: Ireland, France,
West Germany, Austria,
Switzerland, Belgium, Monaco,
United Kingdom, Netherlands,
Liechtenstein, Luxembourg

Northern Europe   Western Europe

Strategic sequencing—structuring for reading, writing, and reasoning in expository text—using a Venn diagram to compare commonalities and differences between northern and western European countries.

The students make appropriate transitions between the information contained in each chapter to establish these comparisons. As a result, the information drawn from each chapter does not remain isolated facts but emerges as an interrelated information bank. This process of creating connections between the information encourages rehearsal of the information and facilitates long-term retention of the material. The positive impact of this type of manipulation and integration of material is supported by the research of Langer and Applebee (1987) and the results of their three-year study funded by the National Institute for Learning. Moreover, the research of Armbruster, Anderson, and Ostertag (1989) concludes that instruction on text structure has a positive impact on reading and writing expository text. This finding is based on their research on the problem-solution structure with a fifth-grade population. Since expository text is one of the most difficult text structures, the researchers suggest that text structure instruction could be beneficial in learning content area material such as social studies and could have a positive impact on writing as well.

Finally, through the use of their learning logs, students can think about how they evaluate the structure of the information presented in the chapters and how they process that information; in other words, students develop a metacognitive awareness.

In the Classroom Mini Lesson

$\mathcal{W}$ hen Lewis, Wray, and Rospigliosi (1994) work with expository material, they have several strategies to help students transform the information and make it their own.

- By drawing pictures of the steps in a procedure and labeling the process, students can restructure the information obtained from sequential text material.
- Students can synthesize text information into a graphic display that corresponds to the structure of the material. For example, a Venn diagram can be used to reinforce the information drawn from a compare and contrast selection.
- Students can take information from the text and use it to create a newspaper article.

History as Perspective Taking

As students get older, they can better understand history if they take different perspectives. For instance, a third grader may take the perspective as a pioneer going west and then investigate the same topic from the viewpoint of a member of an American Indian tribe. A fifth grader may take the position of a sister of two Civil War soldiers, with one fighting for the Confederate Army and the other for the Army of the Potomac. Each of her brothers could present their sides of the issue of slavery.

Mac Duis, an eighth-grade teacher at Haverford Middle School in Haverford, Pennsylvania, capitalizes on his students' ability to conceptualize and think in abstract terms (Duis and Duis 1998). Students at this age are searching for their own identity, a process which requires that they draw on the present as well as the past. Seventh and eight graders are able to take on the perspectives of others and gain new insights about opinions that may be different from their own. Duis has his students engage in perspective taking in teaching about early American history through an activity he calls the Colonial Convention. This activity is set in the year 1750. Each student adopts the role of a character from the late colonial period and must present the views of that character at the Colonial Convention. Duis gives each student the hometown and background of each character. At this point, the students give their characters' background.

Character Development Planner

Student:
Character's name:
Character's hometown:
Character's occupation:
Character's gender:
Character's age:

Character's religion:
Character's family members and their ages:
Character's family history:
Character's interests:
Character's unique characteristics:
Character's influential experiences:
Character's opinion about colonial trade:
Character's opinion about the "*Indian* problem":
Character's opinion about the role of religion:

Duis has the students research the period. In addition, the students read *The Light in the Forest* (Richter 1995), the classical story about a white boy raised by Native Americans when his parents are killed in a skirmish. The class takes a field trip to a working farm where they engage in such colonial period tasks as carding wool, making crafts, and preparing Early American food dishes.

The students present their characters' views at the Colonial Convention. The other students may question or challenge a student's character on their views if the views seem to change during the presentation. At the end of the Colonial Convention, the students write compositions comparing the views of the colonists from the three different regions: New England, the Middle Colonies, and the South.

The assessment of the students includes three criteria: (1) the thoroughness of the character development planner, (2) historical accuracy of character attributes, and (3) historical appropriateness of stands on issues. Each of these is graded on a three-point scale with the total score being worth nine points. Culminating events can be a class version of a Colonial Newspaper or a fair reflecting the period's foods and crafts (Duis and Duis 1998).

This unit by Duis incorporates several social studies standards. These are listed as follows:

Integrated Instructional Unit
Theme: Colonial America

Standard I. Culture
- a. Compare similarities and differences in the ways groups, societies, and cultures meet human needs and concerns.
- d. Explain why individuals and groups respond differently to their physical and social environments and/or changes to them on the basis of shared assumptions, values, and beliefs.

Standard II. Time, Continuity, and Change
- c. Identify and describe selected historical periods and patterns of change within and across cultures.
- d. Develop critical sensitivities such as empathy and skepticism regarding attitudes, values, and behaviors of people in different historical contexts.

Standard V. Individuals, Groups, and Institutions
- b. Analyze group and institutional influences on people, events, and elements of culture.

Standard X. Civic Ideals and Practices
- c. Locate, access, analyze, organize, and apply information about selected public issues—recognizing and explaining multiple points of view.

d. Practice forms of civic discussion and participation consistent with the ideals of citizens in a democratic republic.

By using these standards as guidelines for his integrated unit of study on Colonial America, Mac Duis strengthens his students' understanding of the social studies.

❧ Technology and Reading Strategies

"New technologies have not diminished our students' need to read. In fact, the arrival of computers and the Internet has increased the importance of reading" (Lewin 1999, 17). As teachers help students develop new reading strategies it is good to use guided reading to assist students in gathering and comprehending information presented on the Internet. An "E-sheet" contains the topic or a related topic to what is being studied (i.e., the Revolutionary War, a comparison of All Soul's Day and The Day of the Dead [Dia de los Muertes]); a specific Web site; five questions related to the Web site; and one question for extra credit (Lewin 1999). The E-sheet serves as a kind of semantic map for the Net-surfing student.

Guided Reading: E-Sheet

Topic: The Punic Wars

Web Site #1: History of Western Civilization, Boise State University

http://www.history.idbsu.edu/westciv/punicwar/

Questions:

1. Who wrote this Web site?
2. Which countries were involved in the Punic Wars?
3. Why did the Romans lose the first Punic War?
4. What role did Hannibal play in the Punic Wars?
5. Describe two war strategies that Hannibal used.

Extra Credit Question:

6. Who was Scipio? Which side he did fight on?

Web Site #2: The University of Virginia

www.cti.itc.Virginia.EDU/~mpm8b/dido/01.html

Questions:

1. Who wrote this Web site?
2. Where was Carthage located?
3. Who was Hannibal?
4. How did Hannibal get his troops to Italy to battle the Romans?
5. Elephants were important in the Punic Wars. How were they used?

Extra Credit Question:

6. What was Fabius's strategy? Was he correct?

Chapter Summary

Students and teachers are held accountable for student performance in social studies as well as in reading and expository writing. Awareness of the active nature of the learner in constructing the meaning of the text suggests direction in addressing this issue. Combining selections from children's literature with the social studies textbook and applying learning strategies may be the most efficient way to help students understand and relate concepts.

Students can use strategic sequencing and graphic organizers to acquire the necessary awareness of text structure. Developing descriptive maps while reading the text helps students compare and contrast the information as well as link the concepts they are learning. This procedure of generating writing from graphic representations enhances students' expository writing by centering their attention on the focus and organization, which are primary traits on most writing assessment measures. Finally, as students use their learning logs in this procedure, they develop the metacognitive awareness necessary to take control of their own learning. By using this learning method, students can facilitate their reading comprehension and improve the focus and organization of their writing.

Children's Books

Richter, C. 1995. *The light in the forest.* New York: Turtleback. When a white boy's parents are killed in a battle with Native Americans, he is taken back and raised by the tribe as True Son. Attitudes toward Native Americans during the colonial period are presented.

References

Anderson, R. C., E.H. Hiebert, J. A. Scott, and I. A. G. Wilkinson, 1984. *Becoming a nation of readers: The report of the commission on reading.* Washington, DC: National Institute of Education.

Armbruster, B. B. 1985. Using graphic organizers in social studies. *Ginn Occasional Papers,* 22.

Armbruster, B. B., T. H. Anderson, J. J. Ostertag. 1989. Teaching text structure to improve reading and writing. *The Reading Teacher* 43: 130–7.

Bloom, B. S., ed. 1956. *Taxonomy of educational objectives: Handbook I. Cognitive domain.* New York: David McKay.

Davidson, J. L. 1982. The group mapping activity for instruction in reading and thinking. *Journal of Reading* 26: 52–6.

Duis, M., S. S. Duis. 1998. Teaching history as perspective taking: The Colonial Convention. *Middle Level Learning* (September, no. 3): M9–M11.

Fulwiler, T. 1978. *Journal writing across the curriculum* (Report No. CS 204 467). Denver, CO: Conference on College Composition and Communication. (ERIC Document Reproduction Service No. ED 161 073)

Gaskin, I., E. Satlow, D. Hyson, J. Ostertag, and L. Six. 1994. Classroom talk about text: Learning in science class. *Journal of Reading* 37: 558–65.

Gillespie, C. 1993. Reading graphic displays: What teachers should know. *Journal of Reading* 36: 350–4.

Hadaway, N., and T. Young, 1994. Content literacy and language learning: Instructional decisions. *The Reading Teacher* 47:522–7.

Hunter, M. 1982. *Mastery teaching.* El Segundo, CA: TIP Publications.

Jones, B. F., A. S. Palincsar, D. S. Olge, and E. G. Carr, 1987. *Strategic teaching and learning: Cognitive instruction in the content areas.* Alexandria, VA: Association for Supervision and Curriculum Development.

Langer, J., and A. Applebee, 1987. *How writing shapes thinking.* Urbana, IL: National Council of Teachers of English.

Lewin, L. 1999. "Site Reading" the World Wide Web. *Educational Leadership* 56 (5): 16–20.

Lewis, M., D. Wray, and P. Rospigliosi, 1994. And I want it in your own words. *The Reading Teacher* 47: 528–36.

McAllister, P. 1994. Using K-W-L for informal assessment. *The Reading Teacher* 47: 510–1.

Ogle, D. 1986. K-W-L: A teaching model that develops active reading of expository text. *The Reading Teacher* 39: 564–70.

Ogle, D. M. 1989. The know, want to know, learn strategy. In *Children's comprehension of text: Research into practice,* ed. K. D. Muth, 205–23. Newark, DE: International Reading Association.

Resnick, L. B., and L. E. Klopfer, 1989. Toward rethinking the curriculum. In *Toward rethinking the curriculum,* ed. L. B. Resnick and L. E. Klopfer. Arlington, VA: Association for Supervision and Curriculum Development.

Wilkerson, B. 1988. A principal's perspective. In *Counterpoint and beyond,* ed. J. Davidson, 79–85. Urbana, IL: National Council of Teachers of English.

Wolfe, P. 1999. Revisiting effective teaching. *Educational Leadership* 56 (3): 61–4.

Chapter 7

© Michael Siluk

Another Time, Another Place

Bringing Social Studies to Life through Literature

Marjorie R. Hancock
Kansas State University

The thread of people's lives weaves through the past, the present, and into the future. . . . through the pages of historical fiction, the past becomes alive.

—Donna E. Norton
Through the Eyes of a Child 5th ed.

Objectives

───────────────── ⌁ ─────────────────

Readers will

- understand how the literary genres of historical fiction, nonfiction, and biography can build students' historical and geographical knowledge and understanding;
- understand how recently published biographies present history in a realistic and entertaining way;
- understand how response journals can be used with historical fiction to help students better understand historical events;
- and, be able to develop thematic units for the teaching of social studies.

Introduction

Just as literature brings life to the philosophy of integrated instruction, so too does literature breathe life into an elementary social studies program. The wealth of literature linked to social studies spans all literary genre and provides a complement, indeed a possible alternative, to the factualized textbook that has long been the mainstay of the traditional social studies curriculum. Levstik (1990, 850) quotes a fifth grader who preferred reading historical novels about the Revolutionary War rather than her social studies textbook. According to this student, the textbook "just says that Americans were right, but doesn't tell you exactly why they were right or why the British fought."

The trend toward integrated instruction and its dependence on literature has obviously influenced an explosive increase in quality children's trade books, many of which are linked to teaching social studies. This new bounty of literature is embellished with rich, realistic detail and historical characters with whom the reader may easily identify; it also provides an unprecedented way to make social studies interesting and meaningful to the elementary reader. Literature has the power to transport readers to another place and allow them to become part of it. Literature provides the opportunity to transport readers to another time and allow them to become a part of history. Literature possesses the magic to bring social studies to life and, at the same time, to bring deeper understanding and meaning to students of social studies.

What young American could resist the detailed research, captivating documentation, and truthful biographies of Russell Freedman, including *The Life and Death of Crazy Horse* (1996) and *Eleanor Roosevelt: A Life of Discovery* (1993)? What child's wonderlust and sense of patriotism would not be aroused by the vivid illustrations of natural landmarks in *Purple Mountains Majesty* (Younger 1998)? What reader's empathy for the trails of the westward pioneers would not be enhanced through the authentic diary entries of Amelia S. Knight in *The Way West: The Journal of a Pioneer Woman* (Knight 1993)? What amazement might result upon reading a historically based account of five-year-old Charlotte May Pierstorff who was mailed to her grandmother in 1914 at a cost of fifty-three cents in *Mailing May* (Tunnell 1997)? What child will not remember the blend of fear and friendship surrounding the Civil War and the power of "touching the hand of Abraham Lincoln" in Patricia Polacco's *Pink and Say* (1994)? What adolescent would not empathize with the pain and courage of Billie Jo in forgiving herself a family tragedy occurring during the dire economic and natural conditions of the Oklahoma Dust Bowl in the Newbery award-winning *Out of the Dust* (Hesse 1997)?

Advocates of integrated instruction have strongly encouraged teachers to expand the use of literature in their classrooms to enhance reading and writing (Cullinan 1987). Now the literature connection is also being extended to the realm of social studies as a means of personalizing and making the social science more relevant to the lives and needs of students (Ammon and Weigard 1993; Ceprano and English 1990; Sanacore 1990). Quality children's literature linked to the social studies curriculum encompasses both geographic and historical concepts. It also encompasses a variety of literary genre (picture books, folklore, poetry, historical fiction, biography, informational books) that have been found to provide effective links to the curriculum (Johnson and Ebert 1992; Moir 1992).

This chapter provides the classroom teacher with a supply of ideas for incorporating literature into an integrated social studies program. Practical reading and writing applications supported by recent research and built around the literary genre of picture books, historical fiction, and biography are suggested. The integrated ideal of thematic units is addressed through sample concept-based units. These integrated applications of literature to an elementary social studies program provide only a beginning for classroom teachers as they start to bring social studies to life through the use of literature. Teachers' personal perspectives, knowledge of literature, and related activities can provide even further impetus for implementing an integrated perspective of elementary social studies.

Across the U.S.A. (and Around the World) with Picture Books

Picture books have been found to be an excellent means of conveying an understanding of both geography and history to elementary-level students (Dowd 1990; Pritchard 1989; Sisson 1990). Once considered the realm of primary grades, picture books now provide a means of adding a lively dimension to social studies teaching whatever the age or grade of the student. Quality picture books can capture student interest in the places associated with characters. Picture books with geographic features motivate students' interest in maps and geographic information (Levstik 1985). As Louie (1993, 17) writes: "Whereas textbooks present factual information and explanation, literature can make geographic concepts come alive for children. When teachers use literature as a medium to teach location, they also extend children's love of stories to geographic concepts."

A challenging means of combining a geography and history trip across the nation (or around the world) is through an exploration of children's picture books with settings in our country (or around the globe). The integration of social studies, reading, and writing is effectively accomplished through a classroom journey in which picture books transport students to another time and another place while providing information about our country or the world today. Although this section of the chapter focuses on our nation's regions, similar activities can be used with a world map and literature related to settings around the world.

A large outline map of the United States is required for this journey. Throughout the unit (or even throughout the school year), names and symbols of books will be added to this map, until it finally becomes a class mural.

A whole class activity built around *Alphabet Annie Announces an All-American Alphabet Book* (Purviance and O'Shell 1988) can serve as an introduction to the entire United States. This alphabet book is composed of a series of alliterative sentences that include the names of American cities and the characteristic traits of each (for example, "Susie Strauss skis, sings, and strums on the slopes of the Sun Valley"). Each city can be located on the classroom map.

Students' initial exposure to a cross-country journey across America can be enhanced by an oral reading, singing, and discussion of *This Land Is Your Land* (Guthrie 1998). The classic folk song is brought to life through richly illustrated folk art spanning the "redwood forest" to the "Gulf Stream waters" and the "wheat fields waving" to the "diamond desert." An unforgettable portrait of the diversity of our land inspires the handing of our national treasure to each succeeding generation.

A sampling of picture books dealing with the various regions and states of the United States is briefly described in the rest of this section.

The Northeast

Let's journey to Maine where Peter Parnell's *Winter Barn* (1986) provides the tranquil setting for the activities of creatures who inhabit a memorable barn during the long,

By reading picture books about different areas across the United States, children learn about the geography and history of the various regions of our country.

© Richard Hutchings/PhotoEdit

cold New England winter. Moving to Vermont, the reader experiences the family tradition of gathering sap for boiling into maple syrup in *Sugaring Time* (Lasky 1983). Chesapeake Bay provides the backdrop for *Waterman's Child* (Mitchell 1997), an intergenerational saga of those who never abandon the sea as their source of livelihood and never forget the importance of family in good times and bad. A sensitive and informative view of the Amish is captured with colored photographs in *Amish Home* (Bial 1993), while the spirit of Amish community inspires Jane Yolen's *Raising Yoder's Barn* (1998). Thomas Locker's paintings enliven the story of a young boy who learns the dangers and excitement of the ice harvest in the Hudson River Valley in days gone by in *The Ice Horse* (Christiansen 1993). *Nothing Here But Trees* (van Leeuwen 1998) creates a warm portrait of a family's struggles in the Ohio wilderness. *In Coal Country* (Hendershot 1987) transports the reader to a small Ohio coal mining town during the depression of the 1930s and captures the pride of a vanishing way of life.

The Southeast

On Grandaddy's Farm (Allen 1989) offers a nostalgic visit to Tennessee in the 1930s. The serene, rustic setting and simple pleasures of olden times evoke a vivid sense of America's past. Although the chores and responsibilities were demanding, there was plenty of time for having fun and making memories for the hardworking farm family depicted in this book.

The folk traditions of Appalachia are captured in a fanciful collection of rhymes, riddles, and verse aptly titled *Granny Will Your Dog Bite? And Other*

Mountain Rhymes (Milnes 1990). These humorous portrayals can be tempered with Cynthia Rylant's serious recollections of the land were she grew up, in *Appalachia: The Voice of Sleeping Birds* (1991). An uncelebrated Kentucky heroine is shared in *Mary on Horseback* (Wells 1998), a story of an extrordinary nurse who brought health care to skeptical mountain people.

Heading farther south, the reader explores the southernmost reaches of our boundaries through a boat trip through the Florida *Everglades* (George 1995). Descriptions and photographs of floods and droughts, crocodiles and panthers, moss and orchids fill the pages of *Sawgrass Poems* (Asch 1997), a celebration of a unique ecosystem to be treasured and preserved.

The Midwest and Great Plains

The agricultural belt of the Midwest and Great Plains is the next stop on our literary journey. Carl Sandburg's poetry blends with the artwork of Wendell Minor in portraying *Grassroots* (1998), celebrating the beauty and ruggedness of middle America. Westward migration through the rugged prairie lands of Missouri, Kansas, and Oklahoma are revealed through *Grandma Essie's Covered Wagon* (Williams 1993), a true tale adapted from the authentic oral history of the author's grandmother. *Mississippi Mud* (Turner 1997) shares journal entries of three children on their Conestoga wagon journey from Kentucky to Oregon across the tallgrass prairie of the Great Plains.

The Oklahoma Land Rush of 1893 and the role of black settlers in westward expansion is told through *I Have Heard of a Land* (Thomas 1998). The author's great-grandparents traveled on a wagon train to stake their claim for land, a symbol of freedom and a new life for many former slaves.

The Southwest

Turning southward, the literary road leads to Texas and *The Best Town in the World* (Baylor 1983). Life in this small country town in the Texas hills around the turn of the century seems little different from that of many American towns of that era. However, its residents take special pride in it. While in Texas, share Tomie de Paola's Comanche tale, *The Legend of the Bluebonnet: An Old Tale of Texas* (1983). The beautiful state flower results from the selflessness of an Indian girl who sacrifices her dearest possession to bring rain to save her people. Steven Kellogg's tall tale of *Pecos Bill* (1986) describes how the title character is raised by a pack of coyotes and grows up to become a legendary Texas cowboy.

The changing faces of the desert area of the Southwest are portrayed through *Storm in the Desert* (Lesser 1997), which lyrically describes an approaching storm and its effect on plant and animal life. *Desert Scrapbook* (Wright-Frierson 1997) utilitizes sketches, journal notes, and artifacts to share the flora, fauna, and fluctuating moods of the Sonoran Desert.

The Far West

The character of the Northwest is often linked to its ties to westward expansion. Our literary journey westward leads us to *Long Ago in Oregon* (Lewis 1987), a series of poetry vignettes set in an Oregon town in 1917. The daily lives of the townspeople in this book reveal their strong character and determination, traits necessary for the settling of seemingly remote part of the country.

Western folklore and legends abound. *The Cremation of Sam McGee* (Service 1987) details the adventures of a Yukon prospector during the Alaskan gold rush. Among the legends about the huge expanse of remote western mountains and valleys is *The Legend of the Indian Paintbrush* (de Paola 1988), the story of a beautiful western flower. Paul Goble's *The Great Race of the Birds and Animals* (1985) recounts a myth describing the Cheyenne's close relationship with nature.

Gathering the Sun (Ada 1997) salutes the migrant workers who for decades have brought in the California harvest through their fortitude and hard work. This alphabetical book blends poetry in both Spanish and English with sun-drenched illustrations to celebrate the harvest and the workers in this warm, year-round climate that produces an abundance of fruits and vegetables.

Linking Regions Together

As teachers read a wide selection of books to their students and students read even more books independently, the mural map will come alive with literary memories of the regions of the United States. Students might record the author, title, location, and time period of each book on a slip of paper and attach it in the proper place on the map. They might also draw a picture or symbol of each story on the map to create a permanent memory of each book read. Barbara Younger's *Purple Mountains Majesty* (1998) is a superb book to share as a culminating read-aloud as it tells the story of Katharine Lee Bates's journey across America as an inspiration for her beloved poem/song "America the Beautiful." *From Sea to Shining Sea* (Cohn 1993) contains a multicultural collection of stories and songs related to all periods of American history. A plentiful list of book titles for travel across the United States for all grade levels can be obtained through the *Exploring the United States through Literature* series (Latrobe 1994).

Discovering our country's geography and history through picture books can be a unit lasting a few weeks. It can also be expanded to cover the entire school year. What is created on the classroom wall map is a collage of literature experiences ranging in location "from sea to shining sea."

Extending Our Journey to the World

Although this section of the chapter focuses on the geography and history of the United States, teachers can easily adapt strategies and locate literature to move beyond our own borders to discover the world through picture books. A good beginning is Anita Lobel's *Away from Home* (1994), which takes us alphabetically to the far corners of the world. This alliterative pattern book becomes a model for your students' own journey across the globe. *How to Make an Apple Pie and See the World* (Priceman 1994) whisks readers to several countries to gather world-class ingredients for a sumptuous apple pie. These two books provide motivating activities that can easily build into a parallel unit for a worldwide trip through picture books. The classroom becomes a collage of literature-based experiences that definitely transport students across the globe.

In the Classroom Mini Lesson

Reflecting on History through Reader's Theatre

*R*eader's theater provides an exciting format for blending oral language, dramatic reading, careful listening, and quality literature into a memorable experience (Young and Vardell 1993). Not only can reader's theater improve reading fluency and attitudes toward reading, but it can also aid in an understanding of historical contexts and attitudes. Whether reading from the text as prepared script or altering the text to afford a reader's theater format, the value of this activity spans the outcomes of language arts and social studies.

Bull Run by Paul Fleischman (1993) suggests a perfect opportunity for dramatic reading by up to sixteen students. The text provides two-page reflections by eight Northern and eight Southern characters of different stature and backgrounds as approaching, during, and after the historic Battle of Bull Run. The perspectives of soldiers, common folk, and leaders reflect the changing thoughts and views about war itself. A mixture of male and female roles provide choice for your performers. The words are powerful and reflect the reality of the period at the onset of the Civil War. Have your students practice to improve reading fluency, articulation, and expression. The performance read from the text will blend the powerful voices as they recur intermittently throughout the script. Encourage your students to let their voices exude the changing tones that the onset of war brings. This activity allows choice and places the reader in the role of a historical character.

Katie's Trunk by Anne Turner (1992) contains a blend of both narrative and dialogue by several characters. With some writing alterations, a script reflecting the tone of the text can be prepared. Based on a true incident that happened to one of the author's ancestors, the reader's theatre will give an exciting glimpse into the beginnings of the American Revolution. Tories, rebels, and patriotic allegiances fill the life of Katie. Papa, Mama, Walter, Hattie, and Katie are joined by the rebellious likes of John Warren and Ruben Otis. History will be brought to life in a dramatic reading of the words of these common people who witnessed the disagreement that led to the fight for America's freedom.

Historical fiction picture books provide an essential resource for script writing for reader's theatre in the intermediate grades. A chapter from historical fiction can provide another opportunity for script writing in the middle school. Literature provides an authentic, integrated language arts activity encompassing reading, writing, listening, and speaking through reader's theatre.

The following list will provide a few picture book titles for your journey:

Chin-Lee, *A is for Asia* (1997)
Dooley, *Everyone Bakes Bread* (1996)
Knight, *Talking Walls: The Stories Continue* (1996)
Lewin, *Market!* (1996)
Onyefulu, *A Is for Africa* (1993)
Sturges, *Bridges Are to Cross* (1998)
Wells, *A to Zen* (1992)

∽ Meeting Famous People Face-to-Face through Biography

Biography has provided a natural literature link to social studies for decades. The serial biographies of the past provided dry, factual information about famous people. Current authors, however, have begun to present authentic, flesh-and-blood individuals to elementary-grade readers by relating interesting historical information in a realistic and entertaining manner. Authors such as Jean Fritz, Russell Freedman, Diane Stanley, and Leonard Everett Fisher have introduced students to the multidimensional characteristics of famous people and their public and private lives.

Children in the intermediate grades seem to be almost magnetically drawn to the achievements of those who have overcome obstacles on their journey toward personal success. According to Levstik (1993), older elementary students link themselves closely with biographical characters. Biographies enable readers to experience real life vicariously by tapping the experiences of achievers while providing a historical context for understanding such people's lives. Biographies are written about people who have had a positive impact on society and therefore leave the reader with an optimistic view of his or her potential as an individual in our society (Zarnowski 1990).

Perhaps Jean Fritz's explanation of the appeal of biography over time and generations best explains why biographical accounts should be included in the social studies curriculum:

> We all seek insight into the human condition, and it is helpful to find familiar threads running through the lives of others, however famous. We need to know more people in all circumstances and times so we can pursue our private, never-to-be-fulfilled quest to find out what life is all about. (Quoted in Commire 1982, 80)

Extending biography beyond famous individuals in American history to those renowned throughout the world can increase student awareness of the traits that characterize past and present global leaders. Two activities can be used to bring children face-to-face with historical figures. The first involves exposing students to picture book biographies and then having the students write biographical poems (bio-poems) describing traits of these famous individuals. The second activity, geared more toward intermediate-level students, involves making biographical comparisons to better understand the researching and writing of biographies of famous figures. Author studies and comparative biographical readings focus on the process of biography and can eventually lead students to biographical composition efforts.

From Simple Biographies to Bio-Poems

A plentiful supply of simple biographies that combine a picture book format with historical data on famous persons are available for third-through fifth-grade students. Reading these biographies, learning the historical background surrounding a famous person, and incorporating a related writing activity is an efficient way to use a whole language approach to social studies. Picture book biographies such as David Adler's *A Picture Book of Benjamin Franklin* (1990), Robert Burleigh's *Flight: The Journey of Charles Lindbergh* (1992), and James Cross Giblin's *George Washington* (1992) are brief but accurate accounts of the lives of famous Americans. Diane Stanley and

Peter Vennema's *Cleopatra* (1994) and Aliki's *The King's Day: Louis XIV of France* (1989) introduce young readers to famous world leaders.

A related writing activity emerging naturally from a study of historical figures involves composing a nine-line "bio-poem" (Danielson 1989) about the individuals portrayed in picture book biographies. Here is the format of the nine-line bio-poem:

Line 1:   First name of biographical subject
Line 2:   Four Adjectives describing the subject
Line 3:   Husband/wife/sibling, etc., of . . .
Line 4:   Lover of . . . (three people, places, things)
Line 5:   Who feels . . . (three things)
Line 6:   Who fears . . . (three things)
Line 7:   Who would like to see . . . (three things)
Line 8:   Resident of . . . (city, state, country)
Line 9:   Last name of biographical subject

Following the reading of *Good Queen Bess* (Stanley and Vennema 1990), Sarah, a sixth-grade student, composed the following bio-poem highlighting the personality and achievement of Queen Elizabeth I of England.

> Elizabeth I
> Well-educated, intelligent, cautious, loyal
> Daughter of Henry VIII and Anne Boleyn
> Lover of England, Robert Dudley, and her
> loyal subjects
> Who feels more powerful than most men,
> capable of ruling her homeland, and
> proud to serve her people
> Who fears her imprisonment in the Tower,
> leaving no heir to the throne, and the
> treasonous Mary Queen of Scots
> Who would like to see the defeat of the
> Spanish Armada, the flowering of the
> Elizabethan Age, and herself remembered
> as a great monarch
> Resident of London
> Queen of England 1558–1603.

By writing and sharing biographical poetry about famous leaders, students gain greater insights into historical figures (Danielson 1989).

A collection of such bio-poems may be displayed on a "Who's Who" bulletin board. A class discussion often elicits common traits, goals, and accomplishments of famous people. The bio-poem provides an encapsulated view of these people.

Becoming an Expert on Biographers and Their Subjects

Becoming a "biography buff" (Zarnowski 1990) involves not only learning about famous historical figures but also learning about the literary genre of biography in the process. Students can become biography buffs by reading (1) biographies of different subjects written by the same author and (2) biographies about the same subject written by different authors. Some specific examples and suggestions should help further this use of biography in the social studies curriculum.

Several children's authors have become known for their special treatment of historical figures in their well-written, award-winning biographies. Ingri and Edgar d'Aulaire, Jean Fritz, Milton Meltzer, F. N. Monjo, and Diane Stanley have each written a number of high-quality biographies of historical figures.

An interesting interdisciplinary idea is to study not only the historical characters that biographers portray in their works but to become an expert on the biographers themselves. Students can do this by reading several biographies by the same author. For example, Jean Fritz is known for her motivating titles of books about the Revolutionary War heroes, including *And Then What Happened, Paul Revere?* (1973), *Can't You Make Them Behave, King George?* (1982), *Where Was Patrick Henry on the 29th of May?* (1975), *Why Don't You Get a Horse, Sam Adams?* (1974), and *Will You Sign Here, John Hancock?* (1976). Students not only learn from and enjoy the unique portrayals of these historical subjects but may come to understand the significance and style of biography itself. An analysis of Fritz's books for writing style, sense of humor, historical accuracy and documentation, characterization, and theme can provide students with some general insights into Fritz's process of writing her biographies.

Ideas gleaned from a similar analysis of several works by the same author may inspire a young writer of biography to research and construct a biographical sketch of a favorite historical personality. Other authors to study include F. N. Monjo, who often tells his stories from an outsider's point of view as in *Poor Richard in France* (1973), told from his grandson's point of view. Milton Meltzer is another biographer famous for his use of authentic voices and words from the past, as in *Voices from the Civil War* (1989), with excerpts from documents, diaries, interviews, and speeches. Russell Freedman's photobiographic essays, including *Indian Chiefs* (1987a) and *Franklin Delano Roosevelt* (1990), provide another means of sharing biography. Kathryn Lasky's (2000) *Vision of Beauty: The Story of Sarah Breedlove Walker* tells the success story of a girl born to former slaves in the language Walker would have used. The varied techniques of these biographers introduce exemplary styles and models for young biographers in the elementary classroom.

Another way to become a biography buff is to become a expert on one historical figure by reading several biographies of the same person. A compare and contrast chart can be used to determine each author's portrayal of the individual's strengths and weaknesses, use of authentic materials for conveying the story (maps,

Social Studies enables students to collaborate on projects. These girls are doing a project that involves writing a report and mapping a region of the United States.

© Elizabeth Crews

documents, photographs, etc.), style of writing (point of view/tone), documentation, and type of biography (complete or partial). Such comparisons and contrasts may reveal a variety of information, even conflicting information, on the subject. As a culminating activity, students might share their findings by dressing and speaking in the first-person voice of their subject.

For example, through the years, many authors have attempted to capture the life of Abraham Lincoln in their own special styles. The d'Aulaires' (1957) classic illustrated portrayal of the life of Lincoln is a good place to begin. In contrast, Russell Freedman won a Newbery Medal for *Lincoln: A Photobiography* (1987b). Other authors have presented portions of Lincoln's life, including Carl Sandburg in *Abe Lincoln Grows Up* (1985) and Richard Kigel in *The Frontier Years of Abe Lincoln* (1986). These titles serve as a beginning for developing expertise on this great statesman. Students' comparisons and contrasts will begin to clarify their own preference for biographical portrayal and lead them toward the development of their own written portrayal of Lincoln or another figure.

Another example might carry the reader back in time and beyond our borders to the Middle Ages in France and the story of Joan of Arc. Two fine picture book biographies, *Joan of Arc* (Poole 1998) and *Joan of Arc* (Stanley 1998) provide well-researched information and a humanistic portrayal of this young heroine. Comparing and contrasting facts, illustrations, and historical notes provide an adventure through the eyes of historian, researcher, and artist.

The possibilities seem unlimited as integrated instruction and the genre of biography work together in a meaningful reading and writing interaction. The emphasis of integrated instruction on process supports the use of authors' studies and comparative studies to assist young writers in developing their own writing style. The integration of reading and writing through the use of biography epitomizes the philosophy of integrated instruction.

❧ Sharing Personal Responses to Historical Fiction through Journals

Historical fiction has long-held literary ties to the social studies curriculum. The benefits of using historical fiction to enhance social studies instruction have been enumerated (Cianciolo 1981; Gallo and Barksdale 1983). Historical fiction can help children "experience the past—to encounter the conflicts, the suffering, and the despair of those who lived before us. . . . Well-written historical fiction offers young people the vicarious experience of participating in the life of the past" (Huck, Hepler, Hickman, and Kiefer 1997, 600). The case for historical fiction has been convincing indeed. Teachers have traditionally responded by reading historical fiction aloud to their classes and by assigning book reports on historical fiction.

A response-based view of the role of children's literature in the elementary classroom, however, has been brought to the attention of researchers and teachers (Galda 1988); that is, children are encouraged to respond to literature by writing as they read. Researchers inform us that written language captures ideas concretely and may even influence the development of reading (Langer and Applebee 1987).

The need for encouraging personal responses to literature has been supported by Louise Rosenblatt (1976, 1978), whose transactional theory of reader response articulates the essential reciprocal relationship between the reader and the literary text. Likewise, children as readers have their own story to tell as they interact with the pages of the book. The reader response theory further suggests that readers be active participants in making meaning from the literature they encounter (Probst 1984).

Too often, when teachers assign historical fiction "book reports," students choose a book from a list and summarize the content after they have read the book. But what about the informative thoughts they experienced while reading the book? What about these connections students have made with the historical facts that have become part of their reading schema? How can those connections be captured so that teachers and students alike can experience the link between historical fiction and historical fact?

Responding to historical fiction by writing in a variety of journal formats is an effective way of capturing this personal interaction of the reader with a part of history brought alive through quality children's literature. The textbook may be essential for presenting the facts of a historic period, but the catalyst that can bring those facts to life may be books of historical fiction that place "real" characters in "authentic" periods of history allowing the reader to "live through" the life and times portrayed.

The insightful interactions of the reader with historical fiction may be lost if thoughts, emotions, and responses are not permanently captured throughout the reading of the book. The solution, therefore, is to capture the internal connections between historical fact and historical fiction by writing a journal. A historic response journal, a character journal, or both aid students in connecting fact and fiction by allowing them to vicariously experience an unfolding piece of history as they read historical fiction.

Historical Fiction Response Journals

A response journal is a place for students to express their thoughts, insights, feelings, reactions, questions, connections, and opinions while reading a book (Hancock 1993c). According to Hancock (1993b, 467), "Written response to literature is a powerful means of preserving those special transactions with books that make reading a rewarding, personal journey." The teacher might give brief talks on a variety of historical fiction books geared to a particular period of American or world history. After the students have personally chosen one of these books, the teacher should encourage them to record their individual thoughts while they are reading the book. Students must be assured that the journals will not be graded and that spelling and punctuation will not be corrected. Emphasis should be on the free expression of ideas as the students interact with literature.

The resultant journal entries may include a transfer of the reader to another time and place in history. Readers tend to bring life to fictional characters, and the students may talk to, advise, and judge the actions of a character within the context of history in their journal entries. The student may also make mention of historical facts and names that are part of the background for reading and discuss the historical setting. In reading journal entries, the teacher may discover the personal connection with history as a student assumes the guise of a fictional character. Identification with a character can transport the reader to a historical period that is brought alive through reading.

Some teachers find it difficult to turn students loose with an assignment as free as the foregoing. They prefer giving students a list of response prompts that focus their responses more on the historical aspects of the books they are reading. Here are a few sample response prompts:

What historical facts are mentioned in the book that you already knew from our
   study of this historical period?
What new and interesting historical facts were presented?
How does the life of the main character fit into the historic period (education, dress,
   expectations of society)?
How do the actions of the main character fit into the standards of the historical
   period?
What impression of life during this historic period is projected?

If teachers prefer prompts to free expression and impressions, it is still essential to capture responses to these prompts *while* the students are reading the book rather than retrospectively after they have completed it. Growth of understanding of the historical period can only be indicated through the unfolding reactions of the reader during the reading process.

Suggested historical fiction trade books for the literature response journal include:

Avi, *Beyond the Western Sea, Books 1 & 2* (1996)
Avi, *The True Confessions of Charlotte Doyle* (1990)
Conlon-McKenna, *Under the Hawthorn Tree* (1990)
Cushman, *The Ballad of Lucy Whipple* (1996)
Cushman, *Catherine, Called Birdy* (1994)
Hesse, *Out of the Dust* (1997)
Paulsen, *Soldier's Heart* (1998)
Porter, *Treasures in the Dust* (1997)
Salisbury, *Under the Blood Red Sun* (1994)

Character Journals

Another interesting way of extending response to historical fiction while ensuring the reader's vicarious interaction with history is to have the student write in a character journal (Hancock 1993a). The character journal encourages the reader to "become" the main character. Entries in the journals are written as if the reader/writer were that character. Entries are usually written down at the end of each chapter in diary form.

An excellent book that models a character journal is *Letters from Rifka* (Hesse 1992). Written in the first person narrative style, the story is presented as a series of journal entries written by Rifka in the margins of the treasured book of poetry by Russian author Pushkin. In these entries, Rifka reveals her hopes and dreams as well as the obstacles she and her Jewish family had to overcome to reach America in 1919. Strong examples of a character journal are title in the *Dear America* and *My Name is America* series (Scholastic). For example, *The Journal of William Thomas Emerson: A Revolutionary War Portrait* (Denenberg 1998) shares first-person journal entries filled with the authentic voice of a twelve-year-orphan who joins the cause of the patriots in the prerevolutionary Boston. This well-researched fictional journal format provides a model for character journals for intermediate and middle-level students.

The type of historical fiction that lends itself best to character journals must have a strong main character with whom the reader can identify. The character and plot must be closely linked, and a strong sense of the historical period should be present.

Suggested historical fiction trade books for the character journal include:

Conrad, *Prairie Songs* (1985)
DeFelice, *The Apprenticeship of Lucas Whitaker* (1996)
Giff, *Lily's Crossing* (1997)
Hahn, *Stepping on the Cracks* (1991)
Houston, *Bright Freedom's Song* (1998)
Morpurgo, *Waiting for Anya* (1991)
O'Dell, *My Name Is Not Angelica* (1990)
Paterson, *Lyddie* (1991)
Paterson, *Jip* (1996)

Putting It All Together: Thematic Social Studies Unit

Because interdisciplinary instruction advocates the teaching of integrated rather than the isolated pieces of information, the thematic unit becomes an essential component of social studies teaching. The selection and elaboration of a social studies theme or concept through literature, reading, and writing symbolize the synthesis of integrated instruction. A similar concept-based interdisciplinary approach to teaching social studies with literature has been introduced by James and Zarrillo (1989). Thematic units built around a central theme can lead students beyond facts and dates to a deeper understanding of a concept (Lipson et al. 1993; Manning, Manning, and Long 1994).

Designing classroom instruction based on related titles and planning an array of response-based literature activities associated with them provide a solid base for effective teaching (Pappas, Kiefer, and Levstik, 1996). Hancock (2000) enumerates several benefits to teaching thematic units through a literature base:

- Thematic units expose students to all literary genre.
- Thematic units based on literature contain multiage possibilities.
- Thematic units provide a broader vision and higher-level exploration of a topic.
- Thematic units naturally use fact and fiction for both enjoyment and learning.

Hancock (2000) also suggests the following five steps for planning a thematic unit:

1. Choose a broad-based theme and title.
2. Brainstorm titles of related children's literature.
3. Locate additional children's books through library searches or Internet Web sites.
4. Create a graphic web or organizer reflecting the connectedness of the literature or subthemes.
5. Plan literature-based activities for the whole class, small group, and individual participation.

Two thematic social studies units are described on the following pages. The first, *Change,* is appropriate for students in the primary and early-intermediate grades and is closely tied to the NCSS themes on Time, Continuity, and Change. The second, *In Quest of Freedom,* is suited for children in the upper-intermediate and middle school levels and links to the NCSS themes of People, Places, and Environments, Individuals Development and Identity, and Power, Authority, and Governance. Although these units focus on social studies concepts, the literature, reading, and writing activities incorporate a true integrated, interdisciplinary instructional perspective.

Thematic Concept: Change

The world is changing constantly. The Soviet Union no longer exists; the two German states have been reunited. In the United States, suburbs creep into farmlands, local roads become interstate highways, and small towns grow into booming cities.

For some people, change signals progress. For others, including children, change can be stressful and disappointing. The more personal aspect of our daily life also change. New jobs, moves to a new location, and the fluid structure of the family unit can be unsettling for both ourselves and the students we teach.

Reading about the change in familiar ways of life can help children put change in a proper perspective. Books can help them understand the loss of something special while coming to understand that places and people are always evolving. Literature about change in towns, communities, and cities can lead to insightful discussions and activities that may help young children cope with the unsettling changes that take place around them. A thematic unit built on quality literature and enhanced by writing and discussion activities can awaken students to this broad concept that will sweepingly affect their future.

City changes, although expected, can seem overwhelming over time. *New Providence: A Changing Cityscape* (Von Tscharner and Fleming 1987) looks at the development of the downtown area in a fictitious city between 1910 and 1987. The town is viewed historically through changing architecture, vehicles, and storefronts. One building, for example, changes from a dry goods store to a pharmacy to a computer outlet during its seventy-seven-year history. The book provides a natural extension for gathering photographs, maps, and newspapers from your own city or town to discover how history had been reflected over the years in its development. Economic and sociological changes as well as political influence over time might also be examined.

Alice and Martin Provensen's *Shaker Lane* (1987) follows the evolution of a community from farmland to growing rural area to sprawling suburb on the shores of a new reservoir. While the community changes, some people like Old Man Van Sloop, stay and adjust to the changes. To complete this book, the class might invite a longtime resident of the community to share an oral history of change. Some students might be encouraged to interview several longtime residents and record their perspectives in a permanent written record of community reflections.

The classic *The Little House* by Virginia Lee Burton (1942) can serve as a transitional book from an urban to a rural perspective of change. The encroachment of the city on the country is portrayed through the house that stood on the hill and watched day by night as the seasons passed. Gradually a road is built, traffic increases, and a city surrounds the little house. A happy ending is ensured because the house is relocated by the great-great-granddaughter of the man who built it.

The Little Black Truck (Gray 1994) faces a similar fate. After spending a lifetime as a useful part of a rural existence, a rusty pickup gets a second chance at life when she is discovered and restored by the grandson of her former owner. These simple, yet sensitive stories can foster a discussion on change and its personal effect on people. Although these characters are inanimate, their imaginary emotions parallel those of some residents of a changing community.

The rural perspective of change is also represented in children's literature. *Toddlecreek Post Office* (Shulevitz 1990) takes the reader to a small town whose small post office serves as the activity center for townspeople and dogs. Although the kindly postmaster, Vernon Stamps, has spent years listening to people's joy and woes on their daily visits, his mail dispersal becomes inefficient. The locals lose their gathering place, and the building is eventually torn down. This portrait of vanishing small-town America possibly reflects a deeper vanishing American way of life. Related activities might include a debate on changes in one's own community and whether they are beneficial.

A personal connection to change is shared by reading *Letting Swift River Go* by Jane Yolen (1992). In the middle of this century, many towns across America were purchased by the government and drowned in order to form reservoirs. This dramatic event is captured by a west Massachusetts child's perspective as her childhood memories are submerged so urban areas can be supplied with water. Sally Jane recalls playing by the Old Stone Mill, harvesting maple sap, and walking to school down a country road. Although her vivid memories have been transformed by progress, Sally learns that memories become part of life forever. Students can speculate on exploring the history of their own towns, roads, and geographic surroundings. The interaction of facts and speculation provide an exciting outlet for exploring change in the students' own environment.

Although cast in a farm setting, *Time to Go* (Fiday and Fiday 1990) captures a child's emotion about moving and giving up a special place. This story of loss of a family farm describes a child's feelings as he recalls a happy past on the day that it is time to go and accept change. Our nation has become increasingly mobile, and children need to know they are not alone in their feelings of loss. A written, chronological reflection of change on a child's life can provide personal insights to the classroom teacher. Voluntary sharing of such reflections can help children cope when it is "time to go."

A historical perspective on change can be viewed through the eyes of immigrants who left their homes and traveled to a strange, new land during the past century. While they chose to create a new identity, they retained bits of their culture and traditions as they helped blend the country that today is America. *Journey to Ellis Island* (Bierman 1998) showcases the authentic account of the author's father's immigration to America from war-torn Russia. This story details a family's courageous journey to a new land and their adaptation and preservation of their own identities within the context of their newfound home. In a fictional account, *When Jessie Came Across the Sea* (Hest 1997), Jessie must travel alone to America leaving her grandmother behind. Transcending time and culture, this title is a tribute to all who seek a better life and see change as a positive reward.

A higher-level comparison on change occurs through the reading, examination, and reflection on *Dateline: Troy* (Fleischman 1996). A retelling of the classic story of the Trojan War is juxtaposed with newspaper clippings of modern news events. Guided discussion can lead to the discovery of the tragic parallels between ancient and modern history and the realization that change does not necessarily mean progress, but that history repeats itself.

The foregoing books and suggested extension activities provide a simple beginning for a thematic unit on change. Although limited to personal and historical perspectives on change, these resources provide a model of how interdisciplinary teaching and learning transcends the traditional textbook. The unit could last a couple weeks or be expanded to include the additional perspectives over a period of several weeks. The concept of change will be better understood because the students' own lives and community will have become an integrated part of the study. Reading, writing, researching, reflecting, and discussion activities that augment quality literature will give students a multidimensional perspective on change in the community and their own lives.

An Investigative Thematic Unit: The Quest for Freedom

A journey through history provided a multitude of views on the struggle for the attainment of freedom. A thematic unit based on the general concept of freedom can provide a thought-provoking perspective for studying the effects of people striving to achieve independence, emancipation, civil liberty, or autonomy that ultimately leads to self-respect and self-determination. Throughout history, the quest for freedom has spanned the globe and the ages. Exploring personal stories of difficult struggles to achieve freedom provides an exciting vehicle from which to study this broad historical topic. Although this thematic unit will be limited, it can be covered in from three to nine weeks, depending on teacher augmentation and student motivation.

This particular unit is designed to be used with three groups of students within a classroom. Each group of students should investigate one type of freedom from a specific historical perspective: political freedom (based on the Revolutionary Period, 1773–1785), personal freedom (based on the struggle of African Americans for equality), and freedom from persecution (based on the Holocaust of World War II).

Researching

Each group begins the unit by defining its type of freedom, discussing what group members already know about it, and deciding what they would like to learn from their research and reading. Although the initial work involves research from textbooks and encyclopedias, findings should be geared toward answering the following questions from a variety of literature:

What were the causes of this quest for freedom?
What effects did lack of freedom impose on the individual involved?
What steps did those involved directly take up to move toward freedom?
What individuals emerged as catalysts in supporting the quest for freedom?
What outcome prevailed as a result of this quest?
Does this quest for freedom still continue today? And if so, how? If not, why not?

The three groups come together at the end of their investigation and share the information they have discovered, citing the literature that led them to their discoveries. All groups compare and contrast their answers to the foregoing guideline questions. Commonalties and generalities often emerge as students engage in higher-level reasoning and thinking.

Reading

Along with informational books and encyclopedias, a wealth of literature of all genre can assist students in achieving a fuller understanding of the quest for each type of freedom. The following lists suggest a variety of literary genre that can be used in this investigative unit.

Political Freedom for a Nation

Anticaglia, *Heroines of '76* (1975) (biography)
Avi, *The Fighting Ground* (1984) (historical fiction)

Prior to letting students loose to do a report or project, the teacher should inform the students of the expectations for the task. Often, such expectations are established as part of the class discussion.

© Elizabeth Crews

Brenner, *If You Were There in 1776* (1994) (informational)

Clapp, *I'm Deborah Sampson: A Soldier in the War of the Revolution* (1977) (biography)

Collier and Collier, *My Brother Sam is Dead* (1985) (historical fiction)

Longfellow, *The Midnight Ride of Paul Revere* (1990) (picture book/poetry)

Meltzer, *The American Revolutionaries: A History in Their Own Words, 1750–1800* (1987) (diaries/documents)

Peacock, *Crossing the Delaware: A History in Many Voices* (1998)

Rinaldi, *Cast Two Shadows: The American Revolution in the South* (1998) (historical fiction)

Personal Freedom and Individual Equality

Hamilton, *Anthony Burns: The Defeat and Triumph of a Fugitive Slave* (1988)(biography)

Jurman, *Freedom's sons: The True Story of the AMISTAD Mutiny* (1998) (informational)

Lester, *To Be a Slave* (1968) (firsthand accounts)

Lester, *From Slave Ship to Freedom Road* (1998) (art/response)

McKissick and McKissick, *Christmas in the Big House, Christmas in the Quarters* (1994) (informational picture book)

Meltzer, *The Black Americans: A History in Their Own Words, 1619–1983* (1984) (letters, speeches, diaries, documents)

In the Classroom Mini Lesson

Literature-Based Time Lines

A collaborative method of recording the wealth of social studies related literature shared during a unit or throughout the entire academic year is by keeping
a cumulative literature-based time line. The following steps will help your students
achieve a chronological log of trade books recorded through a historical perspective.

1. From the content of a single unit or the coverage of your social studies
   curriculum, determine the time span that the time line will cover. (Consider the
   time units of the U.S. History Standards for American History.)
2. Create a time line around the upper walls of your classroom with yarn, colored
   strips of paper, or a roll of twelve-inch-wide shelf paper.
3. Let students calculate appropriate units and appropriate mathematical spacing
   of prominent historical events during the chosen time span. Use a social studies
   textbook as an anthology for dates and events.
4. Use word processing and computer-generated graphics to mark years and
   selected images of chosen historical events.
5. Each time a student reads a book within the unit or curricular span (biography,
   historical fiction, informational), add a self-illustrated drawing of the historical
   message of the text. Under the drawing, copy one quote from the text that best
   represents the historical context of the book.
6. Prepare a three-by-five-inch index card that includes the author and title
   of the book.
7. Attach the drawing and the index card to the time line within the appropriate
   historical time frame.
8. As the time line fills in with literature, students place dates and events in a
   historical framework. They also remember and connect the related literature
   experiences that helped bring history to life.

Paulsen, *Nightjohn* (1993) (fiction)
Rappaport, *Escape from Slavery: Five Journeys to Freedom* (1991) (informational)
Van Steenwyck, *My Name Is York* (1997) (fictionalized biography)

Freedom from Persecution—The Holocaust

Bitton-Jackson, *I Have Lived a Thousand Years: Growing up in the Holocaust*
        (1997) (autobiographical memoir)
Jiang, *Red Scarf Girl: A Memoir of the Cultural Revolution* (1997)
        (autobiographical memoir)
Levine, *A Fence Away from Freedom: Japanese Americans and World War II*
        (1995) (informational narrative)
Matas, *Daniel's Story* (1993) (fiction)
Meltzer, *Never Forget: The Jews of the Holocaust* (1976) (quotes/journal entries)
Mochizuki, *Passage to Freedom: The Sughara Story* (1997) (picture book)
Tunnell, and Chilcoat, *Children of Topaz* (1996) (informational/diary)

Writing

Each group of students incorporates the information compiled from the various types of literature into a newspaper explaining the struggle for freedom. Group members cooperatively choose an appropriate name for their newspaper. Each student then writes a feature or column on information gleaned from a particular book that was read or shared. The newspaper may be a mix of fact and fiction, but it must stay within the historical context of the quest for freedom. Diary entries, personal vignettes, and anecdotes can be written to capture the human spirit of individuals struggling toward freedom.

The use of word processing or software programs in newspaper format is highly desirable. Duplication of each newspaper for each member of the class will provide a means to share and compare information from each group. The cooperative group effort required during this unit not only provides a wealth of information on the topic of freedom and the spirit of those who fought for it but may also increase each student's desire to further explore an aspect of freedom surveyed by other members of the class.

The development of thematic units is limited only by the desire of the teacher to integrate reading, writing, and social studies in the curriculum. An interdisciplinary approach enables the classroom teacher to tear down traditional curricular boundaries while providing meaningful integration through unit teaching.

Chapter Summary

Integrated instruction has provided classroom teachers with a justification to introduce quality literature across the curriculum. The realm of social studies has always been associated with biography and historical fiction, but integrated instruction has provided inclusion of these genre with related writing and discussion activities. In addition, the world of picture books provides an extension of literature into both geographic and historical concepts.

Literature linked to social studies widens a child's world by providing the opportunity to participate in new experiences, visit new places, and be a genuine part of the past. The rich resources of literature available for use in interdisciplinary instruction brings social studies to life through literary journeys that offer meaningful links to the child's own life and world.

Children's Books

Ada, A. F. 1997. *Gathering the sun: An alphabet in Spanish and English.* Trans.
 R. Zubizaretta. Illus. by S. Silva. New York: Lothrop. Sun-drenched paintings and
 twenty-eight poems transport the reader to the fields and orchards of California where
 migrant workers create the harvest each year.

Adler, D. 1990. *A picture book of Benjamin Franklin.* New York: Holiday House. Survey of
 the life of Benjamin Franklin, highlighting his work as an inventor and statesman.

Aliki. 1989. *The king's day: Louis XIV of France.* New York: Crowell. The daily ceremonial
 rituals in the life of King Louis XIV at Versailles.

Allen, T. B. 1989. *On grandaddy's farm.* New York: Knopf. Events from the 1930s, when the author and his cousin spent summers on their grandparents' farm in the hills of Tennessee.

Anticaglia, E. 1975. *Heroines of '76.* New York: Walker. A chronicle of the involvement of fourteen outstanding women in the Revolutionary War.

Asch, F. 1996. *Sawgrass poems: A view of the Everglades.* Photographs by T. Levin. San Diego, CA: Harcourt Brace. Poetry celebrates the wonder and mystery of the Florida Everglades as words and photos capture the isolation, solitude, soul, and spirit of this ecosystem.

Avi. 1984. *The fighting ground.* Philadelphia: Lippincott. Thirteen-year-old Jonathan goes off to fight in the Revolutionary War and discovers the real war is being fought within himself.

Avi. 1990. *The true confessions of Charlotte Doyle.* New York: Orchard Books. As the lone young women on a transatlantic voyage in 1832, Charlotte learns of a murderous captain and a rebellious crew.

Avi. 1996. *Beyond the western sea—Book one: The escape from home.* New York: Orchard. A brother and sister seek to escape an Ireland devastated by famine only to become involved in a serial adventure involving colorful characters and a ship to America.

Avi. 1996. *Beyond the western sea—Book two: Lord Kirkle's money.* New York: Orchard. The saga of the escape from Ireland continues with a dangerous voyage and interesting series of events upon arrival in Lowell, Massachusetts.

Baylor, B. 1983. *The best town in the world.* Illus. R. Himler. New York: Scribner. Life in a small country town in the Texas hills around the turn of the century poetically reveals the "best" of everything.

Bial, R. 1993. *Amish home.* Boston: Houghton Mifflin. A sensitive and informative view of the spirit and beliefs of the Amish told through color photographs.

Bierman, C. 1998. *Journey to Ellis Island: How my father came to America.* Illus. L. McGraw. New York: Hyperion. An account of the ocean voyage and arrival at Ellis Island of Julius Weinsten who immigrated from Russia in 1922 told through paintings, family photographs, period postcards, and exceptional text.

Bitton-Jackson, L. 1997. *I have lived a thousand years: Growing up in the Holocaust.* New York: Simon & Schuster. An unforgettable memoir that details the horrible experiences of Auschwitz and the perseverance and twists of fate that allow Elli Friedmann to survive the death camp.

Brenner, B. 1994. *If you were there in 1776.* New York: Bradbury Press. A wealth of information on the Revolutionary times from what colonists ate for dinner to the tool they used to pick lice from their wigs.

Burleigh, R. 1992. *Flight: The journey of Charles Lindbergh.* Illus. M. Wimmer. New York: Philomel Books. Picture book biography that portrays the length and impact of Lindbergh's historic flight in *The Spirit of St. Louis.* 1992 Orbis Pictus Award.

Burton, V. L. 1942. *The little house.* Boston: Houghton Mifflin. A country house is unhappy when the city, with all its buildings and traffic, grows up around it.

Chin-Lee, C. 1997. *A is for Asia.* Illus. Y. Heo. New York: Orchard. A panoramic glimpse into a continent that covers one-third of the earth through an alphabetic format.

Christiansen, C. 1993. *The ice horse.* Illus. T. Locker. New York: Dial Books for Young Readers. Beautiful oil paintings capture the excitement and danger of the ice harvest in the Hudson River Valley.

Clapp, P. 1977. *I'm Deborah Sampson: A soldier in the war of the revolution.* New York: Lothrop. Real-life adventure of a New England woman who, posing as a man, served for more than a year in the Continental Army.

Cohn, A., ed. 1993. *From sea to shining sea.* New York: Scholastic. This multicultural collection contains stories and songs related to all periods of American history. Illustrations by Caldecott winners accompany the text.

Collier, J., and C. Collier. 1985. *My brother Sam is dead.* New York: Four Winds. A family is divided by the Revolutionary War as the protagonist is caught between his loyalist father and his rebel brother.

Conlon-Mckenna, M. 1990. *Under the hawthorn tree.* New York: Holiday House. Three children journey across Ireland during the famine of 1848 in an attempt to locate their only living relatives.

Conrad, P. 1985. *Prairie songs.* New York: Harper and Row. Louisa's life in a loving pioneer family in Nebraska prairie is altered by the arrival of a new doctor and his beautiful, tragically ill wife.

Cushman, K. 1994. *Catherine, called Birdy.* New York: Clarion. Authentically shared against a language and setting backdrop of the Middle Ages, Birdy must adapt to her impending marriage to an older man at the wishes of her father.

Cushman, K. 1996. *The ballad of Lucy Whipple.* New York: Clarion. The rough life of a California mining town provides the backdrop for Lucy's initial reluctance to adapt to the gold rush and her growing maturity as she finds her way home.

d'Aulaire, I., and E. P. d'Aulaire. 1957. *Abraham Lincoln.* Rev. ed. New York: Doubleday. Classic children's biography of Lincoln from his birth through the Civil War by a famed author-illustrator team.

DeFelice, C. 1996. *The apprenticeship of Lucas Whitaker.* New York: Farrar Straus Giroux. After his family dies of consumption in 1849, Lucus becomes Doc Beecher's apprentice and exposes the macabre practices for fighting tuberculosis.

Denenberg, B. 1998. *The journal of William Thomas Emerson: A Revolutionary War portrait. (My name is America* series). New York: Scholastic. A young tavern boy overhears the activities of the committee while proving himself a true patriot during prerevolutionary days.

de Paola, T. 1983. *The legend of the bluebonnet: An old tale of Texas.* New York: Putnam. A retelling of the Comanche lesson of how a little girl's sacrifice brought the bluebonnet to Texas.

de Paola, T. 1988. *The legend of the Indian paintbrush.* New York: Putnam. Little Gopher becomes an artist for his people and brings the colors of the sunset down to earth as his paintbrushes are transformed into brilliantly colored western flowers.

Dooley, N. 1996. *Everyone bakes bread.* Illus. P. J. Thornton. Minneapolis, MN: Carolrhoda. A tour of the globe reveals many countries and cultures with commonalities in culinary traditions.

Fiday, B., and D. Fiday. 1990. *Time to go.* Illus. T. B. Allen. San Diego: Gulliver. As a child and his family prepare to leave, he takes one last look at the family farm.

Fleischman, P. 1993. *Bull Run.* Illus. D. Frampton. Woodcuts. New York: HarperCollins. The voices of sixteen characters before, during, and following the historic Civil War battle bring life and personal commitment from people from all walks of life—slaves, free people, soldiers. Includes notes from the book to be used as a reader's theatre.

Fleischman, P. 1996. *Dateline: Troy.* Collages by F. Frankfeldt and G. Morrow. Cambridge, MA: Candlewick Press. A retelling of the story of the Trojan War juxtaposed with newspaper clippings of modern news events revealing the tragic parallels of ancient and modern history.

Freedman, R. 1987a. *Indian chiefs.* New York: Clarion. Famous Native American leaders of the old West are depicted.

Freedman, R. 1987b. *Lincoln: A photobiography.* New York: Clarion. An absorbing look into Lincoln's career shown through numerous photographs, prints, and reprints of original documents. The 1988 Newbery Medal winner.

Freedman, R. 1990. *Cowboys of the wild west.* New York: Clarion. Photos of cowboys in the late 1800s along with narration about their lifestyle, cattle drives, and the hardships they faced.

Freedman, R. 1990. *Franklin Delano Roosevelt.* New York: Clarion. A photobiography of our longest serving president.

Freedman, R. 1993. *Eleanor Roosevelt: A life of discovery.* New York: Clarion. Eleanor Roosevelt's life as spouse of a major historical figure and as a well-known humanitarian is described in this book.

Freedman, R. 1996. *The life and death of Crazy Horse.* New York: Holiday House. An engaging narrative of the life of Crazy Horse from his youth to his death, including interviews from the 1930s, maps, and pictorial records of his tribe's history.

Fritz, J. 1973. *And then what happened, Paul Revere?* Illus. M. Tomes. New York: Coward, McCann. Description of the well-known and lesser-known details of Paul Revere's life and exciting ride.

Fritz, J. 1974. *Why don't you get a horse, Sam Adams?* Illus. M. Tomes. New York: Coward, McCann. The blatant defiance of British authority is exemplified by the behavior of this noble statesman.

Fritz, J. 1975. *Where was Patrick Henry on the 29th of May?* Illus. M. Tomes. New York: Coward, McCann. A brief biography of Patrick Henry that traces his progress from planter to statesman.

Fritz, J. 1976. *Will you sign here, John Hancock?* Illus. T. S. Hyman. New York: Coward, McCann. John Hancock's vanity and penchant for flourishes is captured in this brief biography.

Fritz, J. 1982. *Can't you make them behave, King George?* Illus. T. de Paola. New York: Coward, McCann. Unpopular English monarch George III is viewed through a humorous, yet historical perspective.

George, J. C. 1995. *Everglades.* Illus. W. Minor. New York: HarperCollins. A storyteller relates the beginnings of the Everglades and the human impact on the area.

Giblin, J. C. 1992. *George Washington: A picture book biography.* Illus. M. Dooling. New York: Scholastic. Washington's dedication to his nation is evidenced through evocative oil paintings and expressive text, which captures the leader who shaped democracy in our nation.

Giff, P. R. 1997. *Lily's crossing.* New York: Delacorte. Albert, a Hungarian refugee, and Lilly, a spoiled socialite, form a friendship while hiding secrets during World War II.

Goble, P. 1985. *The great race of the birds and animals.* New York: Bradbury. A retelling of the Cheyenne Sioux myth about the Great Race, a contest called by the Creator, to settle the question of whether man or buffalo should have supremacy as the guardian of Creation.

Gray, L. M. 1994. *The little black truck.* Illus. E. Sayles. New York: Simon and Schuster. Mary Ann, the little black truck, spends s lifetime as a part of a happy rural existence. She gets a second chance at life when she is discovered and restored by the grandson of her former owner.

Gregory, K. 1996. *The winter of the red snow: The Revolutionary War diary of Abigail Jane Stewart.* (*Dear America* series) New York: Scholastic. Fictionalized journal entries written in Valley Forge, Pennsylvania, in the winter of 1777–78 enhanced by authentic portraits, drawings, and documents from the period.

Guthrie, W. 1998. *This land is your land.* Illus. K. Jakobsen. Boston, MA: Little, Brown. This well-known folk song and tribute to Woody Guthrie is accomplished by folk art that guides the reader on a coast-to-coast tour of America.

Hahn, M. D. 1991. *Stepping on the cracks.* New York: Clarion Books. Preoccupied with World War II and their own brothers in the military, preadolescent best friends discover the sixth-grade bully is hiding his brother, who is an army deserter, in a hut in the woods.

Hamilton, V. 1988. *Anthony Burns: The defeat and triumph of a fugitive slave.* New York: Knopf. A biography of the slave who escaped Boston in 1854, was arrested at the instigation of his owner, whose trail caused a furor between abolitionists and supporters of the Fugitive Slave Act.

Hendershot, J. 1987. *In coal country.* Illus. T. B. Allen. New York: Knopf. A child growing up in a coal mining community finds both excitement and hard work in life deeply affected the local industry.

Hesse, K. 1992. *Letters from Rifka.* Rifka, a Russian Jewish girl in the early twentieth century, writes about her hopes in immigrating to America.

Hesse, K. 1997. *Out of the dust.* New York: Scholastic. Set in Oklahoma Dust Bowl during the Great Depression, this free verse novel tells of Billie Jo's struggle to forgive herself and heal her heart when a family tragedy overwhelms her spirit.

Hest, A. 1997. *When Jesse came across the sea.* Illus. P. J. Lynch. Cambridge, MA: Candlewick Press. An inspiring tale of a young immigrant girl's life in America and the threads that bind her to her European heritage.

Houston, G. 1998. *Bright freedom's song: A story of the underground railroad.* San Diego, CA: Harcourt Brace. Bright is slowly drawn into her family's secret work transporting slaves on the underground railroad and fears the consequences if she is caught.

Jiang, J. 1997. *Red scarf girl: A memoir of the Cultural Revolution.* New York: HarperCollins. A young girl remembers the chaotic events in Mao's China in the mid-60s and the emotional impact on herself and her family.

Jurman, S. 1998. *Freedom's sons: The true story of the AMISTAD mutiny.* New York: Lothrop, Lee & Shepard. The story of the only successful slave revolt in history in 1839 as fifty-three Africans broke out of chains, took over the ship, and challenged the Supreme Court who ultimately set them free.

Kellogg, S. 1986. *Pecos Bill.* New York: Morrow. Incidents from the life of the legendary cowboy, from his life among the coyotes to his unusual wedding day.

Kigel, R. 1986. *The frontier years of Abe Lincoln: In the words of his friends and family.* New York: Walker. The years of Lincoln's childhood and young adulthood are viewed from the point of view of those who knew him best.

King, C., and Osborne, L. B. 1997. *Oh, freedom! Kids talk about the civil rights movement with the people who made it happen.* New York: Knopf. Voices young and old explore the feelings, experiences, and events during the civil rights movement through interviews conducted by children with family members, friends, and activists.

Knight, A. S. 1993. *The way west: The journal of a pioneer woman.* Illus. by Michael McCurdy. New York: Simon and Schuster. The diary of a pioneer woman during the Westward movement is shared.

Knight, M. B. 1996. *Talking walls: The stories continue.* Illus. A. S. O'Brien. Tilbury House. A sequel to *Talking walls* (1992) takes the reader around the world to revere the role famous walls have played in past and current history.

Lasky, K. 1983. *Sugaring time.* Illus. C. G. Knight. New York: Macmillan. The record of how a Vermont family carries on the tradition of gathering sap for boiling into maple syrup is enhanced by black-and-white photographs.

Lasky, K. 2000. *Vision of Beauty: The Story of Sarah Breedlove Walker.* Boston: Candlewick. Illus. N. Bennett. The first child born to a family after slavery was abolished, Sarah was orphaned at age 7. She went on to design hair products and became wealthy.

Leitner, K. 1992. *The big lie: A true story.* New York: Scholastic. A stark, autobiographical account of how the author's family was rounded up in Hungary and taken to Auschwitz, where her mother and younger sister died.

Lesser, C. 1997. *Storm in the desert.* Illus. T. Rand. San Diego: Harcourt Brace. Poetic narrative and dynamic watercolors describe the effects of a desert storm on the landscape and inhabitants.

Lester, J. 1968. *To be a slave.* New York: Dial. The verbatim testimony of former slaves is combined with the author's own commentary on the conditions and inequality of slavery.

Lester, J. 1998. *From slave ship to freedom road.* Illus. R. Brown. New York: Dial. Presents a series of paintings that depict the horror and hope of slavery from its beginnings to hard-won freedom and eloquent text that reflects the pain, grief, humiliation, and triumph of slaves.

Levine, E. 1995. *A fence away from freedom: Japanese Americans and World War II.* New York: Putnam. Japanese Americans imprisoned in relocation camps following the bombing of Pearl Harbor tell their stories of hurtful discrimination, extraordinary courage, and unexpected kindness.

Lewin, T. 1996. *Market!* New York: Lothrop, Lee & Shepard. From the chilly Andes Mountains to the sultry jungles of Africa, from the souks of Morocco to the New York waterfronts . . . people come to market to buy and sell what they grow, catch, or make.

Lewis, C. 1987. *Long ago in Oregon.* Illus. J. Fontaine. New York: Harper and Row. A collection of poetic vignettes describe a year in the life of a young girl living with her family in a small Oregon town in 1917.

Lobel, A. 1994. *Away from home.* New York: Greenwillow Books. This around-the-world journey follows the alphabet to the far corners of the world. Alliterative sentences share names, action verbs, and cities of the world.

Locker, T. 1998. *Home: A journey through America.* San Diego, CA: Harcourt Brace. This tribute to America blends selected writings and poems that vividly describe the landscape where writers call home with Locker's oil paintings for a vision of our varied and special land.

Longfellow, H. W. 1990. *The midnight ride of Paul Revere.* Illus. T. Rand. New York: Dutton. Illustrated version of the narrative poem re-creating the famous event of 1775 in which Revere warned the people of the Boston countryside that the British were coming.

Matas, C. 1993. *Daniel's story.* New York: Scholastic. Published in conjunction with the opening of the United States Holocaust Memorial Museum, this novel tells the composite story of millions of children who lived through the Holocaust.

McKissack, P. C., and F. L. McKissack. 1994. *Christmas in the big house, Christmas in the quarters.* Illus. J. Thompson. New York: Scholastic. The documented text compares and contrasts how Christmas was celebrated in the big Virginia plantation house and the slave quarters in the period just before the Civil War.

Meltzer, M. 1976. *Never forget: The Jews of the Holocaust.* New York: Harper & Row. A history of the atrocities committed against the courageous Jews documented by historical sources.

Meltzer, M. 1984. *The black Americans: A history in their own words, 1619–1983.* New York: Cromwell. A history of African Americans in the United States told through authentic documents and eyewitness accounts.

Meltzer, M. 1987. *The American revolutionaries: A history in their own words, 1750–1800.* New York: Cromwell. Letters, diaries, memoirs, interviews, ballads, newspaper articles, and speeches depict life and events in the colonies before, during, and after the American Revolution.

Meltzer, M. 1989. *Voices from the Civil War: A documentary history of the great American conflict.* New York: Cromwell. Authentic source material documents the life and events of the four years of the Civil War.

Milnes, G. 1990. *Granny will your dog bite? And other mountain rhymes.* Illus. K. Root. New York: Knopf. A collection of rhymes and songs about various aspects of life in the Appalachians.

Mitchell, B. 1997. *Waterman's child.* Illus. Bu D. San Souci. New York: Lothrop. A saga of a close-knit family on Chesapeake Bay who never abandon life on the ocean.

Mochizuki, K. 1997. *Passage to freedom: The Sugihara story.* Illus. D. Lee. New York: Lee & Low. Against the order of the government, a Japanese diplomat issues thousands of visas to Jewish refugees to escape the wrath of the Nazis.

Monjo, F. N. 1973. *Poor Richard in France.* Illus. B. Turkle. New York: Holt, Rinehart, and Winston. Benjamin Franklin's trip to France is revealed from the view of his seven-year-old grandson.

Morpurgo, M. 1991. *Waiting for Anya.* New York: Viking. The daring exploits of Jo and Benjamin as they plan the escape of twelve Jewish children from France to Spain during World War II.

Murphy, J. 1996. *A young patriot: The American Revolution as experienced by one boy.* New York: Clarion. Fifteen-year-old Joseph Plumb Martain shares his experience in the army from 1776 to 1783 in his own words including the leadership of Washington, Lafayette, and Steuben, the battle of Yorktown, and the winter at Valley Forge.

O'Dell, S. 1990. *My name is not Angelica.* New York: Dell/Yearling Books. Raisha and her betrothed, Konje, an African tribal chief are captured and sold into slavery in the West Indies. Konje escapes and becomes a leader of a band of runaway slaves, while Raisha, called Angelica by her owner, waits their reunion.

Onyefulu, I. 1993. *A is for Africa.* Boston: Cobblehill. The author shares fond memories of Nigeria through colorful photographs that show a variety of African lifestyles.

Parnell, P. 1986. *Winter barn.* New York: Macmillan. A dilapidated old barn shelters a wide variety of animals during the subzero temperatures of a Maine winter.

Paterson, K. 1996. *Jip.* New York: Dutton. A Vermont orphan finds his roots while befriending a mentally unstable prisoner.

Paterson, K. 1991. *Lyddie.* New York: Dutton. A Vermont farm girl goes to work in deplorable conditions of a factory during the Industrial Revolution in Lowell, Massachusetts.

Paulsen, G. 1993. *Nightjohn.* New York: Delacorte. Nightjohn, an escaped slave, believes that reading is the key to freedom. He returns to the South where beatings and mutilations never deter him from his goal of teaching slaves to read.

Paulsen, G. 1998. *Soldier's heart.* New York: Delacorte. The enlistment and service of Charlie Goddard in the First Minnesota Volunteers during the Civil War focuses on death, destruction, and mental anguish that touches those who serve their cause.

Peacock, L. 1998. *Crossing the Delaware: A history in many voices.* Illus. W. L. Krudop. New York: Atheneum. Narrative, letters, and true accounts dramatize Washington's crossing the Delaware during the harsh winter of 1776 and build appreciation of the import of the Battle of Trenton and the true spirit of '76.

Polacco, P. 1994. *Pink and Say.* New York: Philomel. This Civil War story of friendship and fear has been passed through Polacco's family. It celebrates shared humanity in a war-torn nation.

Poole, J. 1998. *Joan of Arc.* Illus. A. Barrett. New York: Knopf. Meticulously researched, this chronology of the events surrounding Joan's remarkable life captures her courage and humanity while sharing the drama, triumph, and tragedy of her crusade.

Porter, T. 1997. *Treasures in the dust.* New York: HarperCollins. The two voices of Annie May Weightman and Violet Cobble of Cimmaron County, Oklahoma, blend to reveal the triumph of friendship in the face of struggles during the depression era of the dust bowl.

Priceman, M. 1994. *How to make an apple pie and see the world.* New York: Knopf. Readers are whisked around the world to gather the necessary ingredients for a sumptuous apple pie. Social studies, math, and taste buds are integrated when the recipe becomes reality.

Provensen, A., and M. Provensen. 1987. *Shaker Lane.* New York: Viking. When the town decides to build a reservoir on its land, the residents of Shaker Lane move away rather than fight to keep their homes.

Purviance, S., and M. O'Shell. 1988. *Alphabet Annie announces an All-American alphabet book.* Boston: Houghton Mifflin. An alphabetical tour of characters performing various activities in American cities makes for an interesting array of alliterative rhymes.

Rappaport, D. 1991. *Escape from slavery: Five journeys to freedom.* Illus. C. Lily. New York: HarperCollins. Five stories of African American slaves who reached freedom before the Civil War also reveals the dangerous work of abolitionists on the Underground Railroad.

Rinaldi, A. 1998. *Cast two shadows: The American Revolution in the South.* San Diego, CA: Harcourt Brace. Claiming she wants no part of war, Caroline Shitaker endures much heartache as her family is torn apart and her best friend is hanged during 1780 with a differing view of the war than that fought in the North.

Rylant, C. 1991. *Appalachia: The voices of sleeping birds.* San Diego: Harcourt Brace Jovanovich. Poetic collections of the author growing up in Appalachia are enhanced by evocative, full color portraits of the region.

Salisbury, C. 1994. *Under the blood red sun.* New York: Delacorte. Friendships and Japanese American family ties are strained following the bombing of Pearl Harbor.

Sandburg, C. 1985. *Abe Lincoln grows up.* Illus. J. Daugherty. San Diego: Harcourt Brace. Reprinted from Sanburg's *Abraham Lincoln: The prairie years.*

Sandburg, C. 1998. *Grassroots.* Illus. W. Minor. San Diego, CA: Harcourt Brace. Beautiful oil paintings blend with the treasured poetic voice of Sandburg to share timeless observations of the Midwest—America's heartland.

Service, R. 1987. *The cremation of Sam McGee.* New York: Greenwillow. An illustrated version of a well known poem that captures the mystery and romance of the Alaska gold rush and tells the tale of an interesting Yukon prospector.

Shulevitz, U. 1990. *Toddlecreek post office.* New York: Farrar, Straus, and Giroux. Vanishing small-town America is portrayed as the local post office, the center of town activity, is closed down and a town faces a lost identity.

Stanley, D. 1998. *Joan of Arc.* New York: Morrow. At seventeen she rode into battle and was proclaimed the savior of France; at nineteen she was condemned to a terrible death; five hundred years later she becomes a saint. History is brought to life through rich narrative and gilded illustrations.

Stanley, D., and P. Vennema. 1990. *Good Queen Bess.* New York: Four Winds. The life of the strong-willed queen of England during the time of Shakespeare and the defeat of the Spanish Armada is presented through beautiful illustrations and text.

Stanley, D., and P. Vennema. 1994. *Cleopatra.* Illus. D. Stanley. New York: Morrow Junior Books. A picture book biography that delves into the life and times of this great ruler.

Sturges, P. 1998. *Bridges are to cross.* Illus. G. Laroche. New York: Putnam. A journey to famous bridges around the globe reflects the significance of bridges as cultural symbols, celebrations, and solutions in our world.

Thomas, J. C. 1998. *I have heard of a land.* Illus. F. Cooper. New York: HarperCollins. The Oklahoma Territory invited the strength and determination of men, women, and newly freed African Americans to stake their claim in quest of a new life and courageous dream.

Toll, N. S. 1993. *Behind the secret window: A memoir of a hidden child during World War II.* New York: Dial Books. When she was eight, the author and her mother were hidden from the Nazis by a Gentile couple in Poland. The sixty-four authentic watercolors illuminate the experiences of a child in hiding.

Tunnell, M. O. 1997. *Mailing May.* Illus. T. Rand. New York: Greenwillow. A true story of a five-year old Charlotte May Pierstorff who was "mailed" to her grandmother from Grangeville to Lewiston, Idaho, in 1914 for fifty-three cents!

Tunnell, M. O., and Chilcoat, G. 1996. *The children of the Topaz: The story of a Japanese American internment camp based on a classroom diary.* New York: Holiday House. Based on a teacher's diary as a primary source, the book deals with the impact of forced imprisonment on Japanese Americans during World War II and includes diary reproductions and authentic information on the conditions at Topaz.

Turner, A. 1992. *Katie's trunk.* Illus. R. Himler. New York: Macmillian. The two sides of the American Revolution confront each other as Katie finds that true friendship extends beyond the lines drawn by war.

Turner, A. 1997. *Mississippi mud: Three prairie journals.* Illus. R. Blake. New York: HarperCollins. Through poetic journal entries, Amanda, Caleb, and Lonnie reveal different dreams and personalities on their journey from Kentucky to Oregon.

Van Leeuwen, J. 1998. *Nothing here but trees.* Illus. P. Boatwright. New York: Dail. The great forest of Ohio provides a challenge to a family who must do their best to carve a new life and home from this wild land.

Van Steenwyck, E. 1997. *My name is York.* Illus. B. Farnsworth. Rising Moon. The slave of William Clark tells the story of the Lewis and Clark expedition from his own perspective as he dreams of attaining his own freedom.

Von Tscharner, R., and R. Flemming. 1987. *New Providence: A changing cityscape.* San Diego: Harcourt Brace. A visual treatment of the emerging urban environment as an imaginary town moves through economic, political, and architectural changes from 1910 to 1987.

Wells, R. 1992. *A to Zen.* Illus. Yoshi. New York: Picture Book Studio. This alphabet book is illustrated with Japanese characters and explores twenty-six aspects of traditional and modern Japanese culture.

Wells, R. 1998. *Mary on horseback: Three mountain stories.* New York: Dial. Nurse Mary Breckenridge traveled on horseback to the isolated mountains of Kentucky and exhibits the goodness and vitality of an undercelebrated heroine.

Williams, D. 1993. *Grandma Essie's covered wagon.* Illus. W. Sadowski. New York: Knopf. A vivid account of the joys and challenges of a move from Missouri to Kansas to Oklahoma in the late 1800s. Adapted from the authentic oral history of the author's grandmother.

Wright-Frierson, V. 1997. *A desert scrapbook.* New York: Simon & Schuster. The flora and fauna of the Sonoran desert is portrayed through sketches, journal entries, painted snapshots, and watercolored artifacts of this ever-changing habitat.

Yolen, J. 1992. *Letting Swift River go.* Illus. B. Cooney. Boston: Little, Brown. Sally Jane experiences changing times in rural America as the Swift River town in western Massachusetts is enveloped by a water reservoir. The story eloquently reveals that while change is constant, the memory of a place can stay with you forever.

Yolen, J. 1998. *Raising Yoder's barn.* Illus. B. Fuchs. Boston: Little, Brown. A strong community allegiance prevails when a devastating fire ravishes the barn of an Amish family in Pennsylvania.

Younger, B. 1998. *Purple mountains majesties: The story of Katharine Lee Bates and "America the beautiful."* Illus. S. Schuett. New York: Dutton. A summer cross-country train trip inspires scholar/poet/professor Bates to write her famous tribute to the beauty and grandeur of the nation's physical blessings—mountains, plains, and shining seas.

Web Sites

www.win.tue.nl/cs/fm/engels/discovery
  Discovers Web–Exploration from Roman Empire Period to twentieth century. (Gr. 5–8)
http://lcweb2.gov/ammem/
  American Memory: Historical Collections for the National Digital Library. (Gr. 4–8)
http://www.execpc.com/~dboals
  History and social studies Web site for K–12 teachers.
http://www.pagesz.net/~stevek/resources.html
  Resources for historians. (Gr. 5–8)
http://www.pages.net/~stevek/history.html
  What is history? A sampler.
http://www.cr.nps.gov/nr/twhp/home.html
  National Register of Historical Places (good for showing local historical places to Gr. 2–8).
http://library.advanced.org/10966/index.html
  The Revolutionary War: A Journey Towards Freedom. (Gr. 5–8)
http://users.southeast.net/~dixe/amrev/index.htm
  The American Revolution: On-Line
www.isu.edu/~trinmich/Oregontrail.html
  The Oregon Trail—contains Fantastic Facts and Historic Sites sections. (Gr. 3–8; excellent supplement to Oregon Trail CD-ROM)
www.sunsite.utk.edu/civil-war/warweb.html
  American Civil War home page: Comprehensive site. (Gr. 5–8)
http://lincoln.lib.niu.edu
  Lincoln/Net: Official Abraham Lincoln Web site of Illinois. (Gr. 7–8)
www.ellisisland.org
  Ellis Island: Immigration history. (Gr. 4–8)
www.grolier.com/wwii/wwii_mainpage.html
  World War II: Comprehensive Web site. (Gr. 5–8)
www.stanford.edu/group/King
  Martin Luther King, Jr.: Biography

Children's Literature Listservs
Child_Lit<listserv@email.rutgers.edu>
  This children's Literature Criticism and Theory group is the most academic of the listservs. This discussion group fosters the sharing of ideas by researchers engaged in scholarship on any topic.
Kidlit_Lit<listserv@bingvmb.cc.binghamton.edu>
  Children's literature supporters discuss teaching, innovative ideas, current research and share ideas, questions, and stories with the group.

CCBC-Net<listserv@ccbc.cc.binghamton.edu
> The Cooperative Children's Book Center at the University of Wisconsin focuses on a monthly theme, author, subject, or issue.

Other Literature-Related Web Sites for Teachers

http://www.aaronshep.com/rt/RTE.html
> Aaron Shepard's Reader's Theatre Editions
> Stories including humor, fantasy, and retold tales from different cultures are adapted into reader's theatre scripts for third grade and above.

http://ericir.syr.edu
> AskERIC Home Page
> Literature-based lesson plans, virtual libraries, full texts of fairy tales and fables, bibliographies, and links to other Web sites are available through this home page.

http://bdd.com/teachers
> BDD Books for Young Readers
> The Teachers Resource Center shares teaching tools to bring quality books to life for young readers.

References

Ammon, R., and J. Weigard. 1993. A look at other trade book topics and genres. In *The story of ourselves,* ed. M. O. Tunnell and R. Ammon. Portsmouth, NH: Heinemann.

Ceprano, M., and E. B. English. 1990. Fact and fiction: Personalizing social studies through the tradebook-textbook connection. *Reading Horizons* 30:66–77.

Cianciolo, P. 1981. Yesterday comes alive for readers of historical fiction. *Language Arts* 58:452–61.

Commire, A., ed. 1982. *Something about the author.* Detroit, MI: Gale Research.

Cullinan, B. E. 1987. *Children's literature in the reading program.* Newark, DE: International Reading Association.

Danielson, K. E. 1989. Helping history come alive with literature. *Social Studies* 80:65–8.

Dowd, F. 1990. Geography is children's literature math, science, art and a whole world of activities. *Journal of Geography* 89:68–73.

Galda, L. 1988. Readers, texts, contexts: A response-based view of literature in the classroom. *The New Advocate* 1: 92–102.

Gallo, D. R., and E. Barksdale. 1983. Using fiction in American history. *Social Education* 47: 286–9.

Hancock, M. R. 1993a. Character journals: initiating involvement and identification through literature. *Journal of Reading* 37:42–50.

Hancock, M. R. 1993b. Exploring and extending personal response through literature response journals. *The Reading Teacher* 46 (6): 466–74.

Hancock, M. R. 1993c. Exploring the meaning-making process through content of literature the content of literature response journals. *Research in the Teaching of English* 27:335–68.

Hancock, M. R. 2000. *A celebration of literature and response: Readers, books, and teachers in K–8 classrooms.* Columbus, OH: Prentice-Hall/Merrill.

Huck, C. S., S. Helper, J. Hickman, and B. Z. Kiefer. 1997. *Children's literature in the elementary school.* 6th ed. Madison, WI: Brown & Benchmark.

James, M., and J. Zarrillo. 1989. Teaching history with children's literature: A concept-based, interdisciplinary approach. *Social Studies* 80:153–8.

Johnson, N. M., and M. J. Ebert. 1992. Time travel is possible: Historical fiction and biography—Passport to the past. *Reading Journal* 45:488–95.

Langer, J., and A. Applebee. 1987. *How writing shapes thinking: A study of learning and teaching.* Urbana, IL: National Council of Teachers of English.

Latrobe, K. H., series ed. 1994. *Exploring the Untied States through literature* series. Phoenix, AZ: Oryx Press (seven volumes include: Northeast, Southeast, Great Lakes, Plains, Southwest, Mountain, and Pacific States).

Levstik, L. 1985. Literary geographic and mapping. *Social Education* 77:38–43.

Levstik, L. S. 1990. Research directions: Mediating content through literary texts. *Language Arts* 67:848–53.

Levstik, L. S. 1993. "I wanted to be there": The impact of narrative on children's thinking. In *The story of ourselves,* ed. M. O. Tunnell and R. Ammon. Portsmouth, NH: Heinemann.

Lipson, M. Y., S. W. Valencia, K. K. Wixson, and C. Peters. 1993. Integration and thematic teaching: Integration to improve teaching and learning. *Language Arts* 70:252–63.

Louie, B. Y. 1993. Using literature to teach location. *Social Studies and the Young Learner* 5:17–18, 22.

Manning, M., G. Manning, and R. Long. 1994. *Theme immersion: Inquiry-based curriculum in elementary and middle schools.* Portsmouth, NH: Heinemann.

Moir, H., ed. 1992. *Collected perspectives: Choosing and using books for the classroom.* Boston: Christopher Gordon.

Norton, D. E. 1999. *Through the eyes of a child.* 5th ed. Columbus, OH: Merrill.

Pappas, C., Kiefer, B., & Levstik, L. (1996). *An integrated language perspective in the elementary school: Theory in action.* 2nd ed. New York: Longman.

Pritchard, S. F. 1989. Using picture books to teach geography in the primary grades. *Journal of Geography* 88:126–7, 137.

Probst, R. E. 1984. *Adolescent literature: Response and analysis.* Columbus, OH: Merrill.

Rosenblatt, L. 1976. *Literature as exploration.* New York: Appleton-Century-Crofts.

Rosenblatt, L. 1978. *The reader, the text, the poem.* Carbondale, IL: Southern Illinois University Press.

Sanacore, J. 1990. Creating the lifetime reading habit in social studies. *Journal of Reading* 3:414–8.

Sisson, J. 1990. Read you way across the U.S.A. *Journal of Geography* 89:175–7.

Young, T., and S. Vardell. 1993. Weaving readers' theatre and nonfiction into the curriculum. *The Reading Teacher* 46:396–406.

Zarnowski, M. 1990. *Learning about biographies: A reading-and-writing approach for children.* Urbana, IL: National Council of Teachers of English.

Chapter 8

© David Frazier Photolibrary

Geography

Exploring the Whole World through Interdisciplinary Instruction

Maria P. Walther
Gwendolyn Brooks Elementary School, Aurora, IL

What is needed is a mutual commitment to the learning of geography and to understanding the learning of geography. It is our common agenda.

—*Anne K. Petry*
"Future Teachers of Geography: Whose Opportunity?"

Objectives

─────────────────────────────ᴄᴠᴐ─────────────────────────────

Readers will
- understand the geography for life standards;
- demonstrate competency in applying the six essential elements of geography;
- be able to utilize children's literature in the teaching of geography; and
- be able to incorporate Internet sites throughout the world in the teaching of geography.

Introduction

Geography surrounds us. Without thinking about it, we make decisions based on geographical knowledge every day—we dress appropriately for the weather, plan the quickest route for doing errands, and draw maps to places we want others to find. There is an ongoing interaction between humans and the geography that surrounds them. It is this interaction that teachers must share with their students. Geography should come to life in the classroom, and the 1994 National Geography Standards reflect this idea in the title *Geography for Life*. The Standards state, "Geography is for life in every sense of that expression: lifelong, life sustaining, and life enhancing.

Geography is a field of study that enables us to find answers to questions about the world around us—about where things are and how and why they got there. We can ask questions about things that seem very familiar and are often taken for granted" (Geography Education Standards Project 1994, 11).

It is important to note that the whole thrust of the Standards is on questioning why things are the way they are. There is no better way to get students thinking, discussing, and analyzing information than through the use of children's literature and because "all students can learn if they are engaged in meaningful activities that move from whole to part, build on students' interests and backgrounds, serve their needs, provide opportunities for social interaction, and develop their skills in both oral and written language" (Freeman and Freeman 1991, 29). Children can travel to other lands and be a part of the events that shaped our world. Literature is an excellent way for students to gain the geographical knowledge that they need in order to be productive citizens in a global community. "Geographers believe that their goal of understanding how all of the parts of the world are globally interrelated is very important for today's citizens" (Sunal and Haas 2000, 269). Literature encourages questioning and discussion. It provides a common ground for continued study. As Louie (1993, 18) states, "Whereas textbooks present factual information and explanation, literature can make geographic concepts come alive for children." It is through the use of quality children's literature and literature-based reading, writing, thinking, and listening activities that geography will come to life in the classroom.

This chapter gives practical ideas on how to incorporate geographic subject matter, skills, and perspectives—as identified by the 1994 National Geography Standards—into a social studies classroom through the use of children's literature activities, research and writing activities, and thematic units. A beginning step for both teachers and students when incorporating geography in their classroom and in their lives is to adjust their mind-set about what geography is. In this chapter, geography comes to life through the use of the many excellent books available. Educators must reinforce the ideas that the Standards (1994, 18) espouse: "Geography is not a collection of arcane information. Rather, it is the study of spatial aspects of human existence. Geography has much more to do with asking questions and solving problems than it does with rote memorization of isolated facts." Boehm and Petersen (1994, 211) expand on this idea when they state: "Geography is an eclectic subject that ranges from the physical sciences through the social sciences to the arts and humanities." By integrating geography into all subject areas of the curriculum, students will begin to see that geography truly plays a part in all aspects of their lives.

A Look at the Geography for Life Standards

The Standards (1994) provide teachers with a clear picture of what students should know and be able to do at the end of three benchmark grades: four, eight, and twelve (see Focus Box 8.1). They were developed through a consensus process by geographers, teachers, parents, and others. The Standards are based on the five fundamental themes that were identified in 1984 in the *Guidelines for Geographic Education: Elementary and Secondary Schools* (Committee on Geographic Education). "The five themes have become an integral element of social studies education, appearing in all geography textbooks and most social studies programs

8.1   *Focus Box*

Six Essential Elements and Eighteen Geography Content Standards

The geographically informed person knows about and understands:

The World in Spatial Terms

1. How to use maps and other geographic represen-tations, tools, and technologies to acquire, process, and report information from a spatial perspective.
2. How to use mental maps to organize information about people, places, and environments in a spa-tial context.
3. How to analyze the spatial organization of peo-ple, places, and environments on Earth's surface.

Places and Regions

4. The physical and human characteristics of places.
5. That people create regions to interpret Earth's complexity.
6. How culture and experience influence people's perceptions of places and regions.

Physical Systems

7. The physical processes that shape the patterns of Earth's surface.
8. The characteristics and spatial distribution of ecosystems on Earth's surface.

Human Systems

9. The characteristics, distribution, and migration of human populations on Earth's surface.
10. The characteristics, distribution, and complexity of Earth's cultural mosaics.
11. The patterns and networks of economic interde-pendence on the Earth's surface.
12. The processes, patterns, and functions of human settlement.
13. How the forces of cooperation and conflict among people influence the division and control of Earth's surface.

Environment and Society

14. How human actions modify the physical environment.
15. How physical systems affect human systems.
16. The changes that occur in the meaning, use, distribution, and importance of resources.

The Uses of Geography

17. How to apply geography to interpret the past.
18. How to apply geography to interpret the present and plan for the future.

---

as a context for geographic education" (Boehm and Petersen 1994, 211). The themes are (1) location, (2) place, (3) relationships within places (human-environ-mental interaction), (4) relationships between places (movement), and (5) regions. The five themes were meant to convey to the nation's teachers the message that it is no longer acceptable to stop teaching geography after teaching only location and place (Boehm and Petersen 1999). The Standards expand on the five themes and as-sist educators in answering two important questions: What is most worth knowing about geography? and What content, skills, and perspectives are essential for stu-dents to know and use? The five themes give meaningful guidance to educators and curriculum developers about what good geography is (Bednarz and Bednarz 1994).

The study of geography comprises three interrelated and inseparable parts: sub-ject matter, skills, and perspectives. The subject matter of geography is the essential knowledge that students must have. It is on this essential knowledge that the skills are based. The skills include asking geographic questions, acquiring, organizing, and ana-lyzing geographic information, and answering geographic questions. The knowledge and skills must be viewed from two perspectives: spatial and ecological. Students must master all three components of geography to become geographically informed citizens (Geography Education Standards Project 1994).

෴ *The Geographic Skills*

The geographic skills can be used as a framework for developing lessons. A brief explanation of each skill and a sample activity follows:

1. **Asking geographic questions.** Students will find the answers to the questions Where? and Why There?

   After fifth-grade students read the book *Follow the Drinking Gourd* (Winter 1988), the teacher and students can identify the locations of the underground railroad stations that are hinted at in the lyrics. Then the class can discuss why those locations were chosen as part of the Underground Railroad (Louie 1993). When teaching the same concept to younger students it is important that they understand that the Underground Railroad was not a train, but a series of safe hiding places for escaping slaves. Two excellent picture books that introduce the concept of the Underground Railroad to young learners are *Barefoot: Escape on the Underground Railroad* (Edwards 1997) and *Secret Signs Along the Underground Railroad* (Riggio 1997).

2. **Acquiring geographic information.** Students will gather information from a variety of sources and in a variety of ways.

   When acquiring geographic information, students should be involved in fieldwork. Fieldwork could involve students conducting research in the community by distributing questionnaires, taking photographs, recording observations, interviewing citizens, and collecting samples (Geographic Education Standards Project 1994). Another source of geographic information that students can utilize is the wealth of resources located on the Internet (see the Web Sites section at the end of the chapter).

3. **Organizing geographic information.** Students will organize and display information in ways that help with analysis and interpretation of data. They must be able to both decode and encode maps.

   Introducing middle school students to the picture book *Hottest, Coldest, Highest, Deepest* (Jenkins 1998), which describes the remarkable natural wonders on earth, is one way to begin a "Top Ten" project. Students could then work in groups to collect, organize, analyze, and display information about their chosen top ten natural wonders. Other books that would be helpful for this project are *America's Top Ten Rivers* (Tesar 1998b), *American's Top Ten Mountains* (Tesar 1998a), and *America's Top Ten Natural Wonders* (Ricciuti 1998).

4. **Analyzing geographic information.** Students will look for patterns, relationships, and connections.

   After fourth grade students study a map of the Oregon Trail and read from the many diaries available, they can draw inferences and suggest reasons why people migrated and why they chose particular routes. One such diary is *Rachel's Journal* (Moss 1998), which gives a fictional account of a ten-year-old girl traveling from Illinois to California and provides young readers with a sense of what it would have been like to journey on the Oregon Trail.

5. **Answering geographic questions.** Students will develop generalizations and conclusions based on geographic knowledge.

   Students choose a topic of interest to them (e.g., the best place to go in-line skating, where the town should build a bike trail) and research the topic by doing fieldwork. They compile the research by using charts, maps, and graphs and present their findings to the class or to the agency that could implement their ideas.

❧ The Six Essential Elements

The Standards identify six essential elements that can be used to plan and organize themes in the classroom. Of course, as with any integrated theme or unit of study, the subject matter will reach far beyond geography. Following are brief descriptions of each element to help in the selection of related themes.

1. **The World in Spatial Terms**—Studying the relationship between people, places, and environments by mapping information about them in a spatial context.
2. **Places and Regions**—Discovering how the identities and lives of individuals are rooted in particular places and in human constructs called regions.
3. **Physical Systems**—Examining the physical processes that shape Earth's surface and that interact with plant and animal life to create, sustain, and modify ecosystems.
4. **Human Systems**—Looking first at population, and then at the human activities, from culture to economics, to settlement, and to conflict and cooperation.
5. **Environment and Society**—Understanding the intersection of physical and human systems.
6. **The Uses of Geography**—Learning how geography, when taken as a whole, helps us understand the past, interpret the present, and plan for the future (Geography Education Standards Project 1994).

   The remainder of this chapter addresses each of these six elements and demonstrates how teachers, through the use of literature activities, can incorporate each element into their existing themes and units. For each element, a sample theme, unit, or list of activities is offered. It is my hope that these themes and ideas will start teachers on the road to becoming geographically informed citizens who will in turn provide students with plenty of opportunities to experience, question, and make decisions based on their geographical knowledge.

❧ The World in Spatial Terms

Around the World with Exciting Books

Children are fascinated with travel and far away places. Kapp (1991) explains an excellent way to introduce the concept of travel to young children. After reading Shel Silverstein's poem "Magic Carpet" found in *A Light in the Attic* (1981), students sit on an oriental rug and tell about their choice of a travel spot. These choices are recorded on a chart and saved for future reference. Kapp discovered

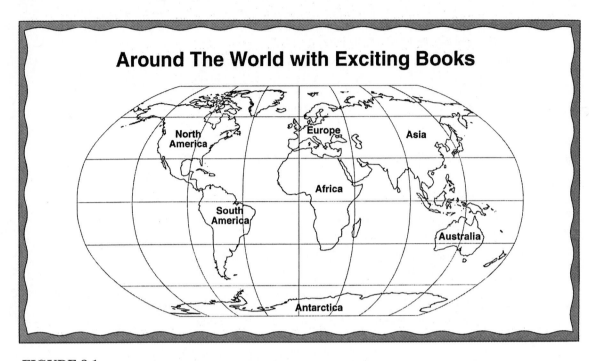

FIGURE 8.1   Around-the-world bulletin board.

that "by the end of the year in which geography was regularly infused into the curriculum, the chart demonstrates that students have expanded their horizons" (1991, 174). Children who, at the beginning of the year, chose either Walt Disney World or Grandma's house were now choosing places from other continents. One way to infuse geography in the classroom is through the use of a read-aloud called "Around the World with Exciting Books." As an addition to the regular read-aloud, books from around the world can be read once a week and charted on a world bulletin board (see Figure 8.1). As children travel from continent to continent through great literature, they can write descriptions of the continents from the information gathered in the books. They can also draw an illustration of each book read. These descriptions and illustrations can be posted on the bulletin board. For intermediate students this activity can be utilized as a way to encourage independent reading in a variety of genre. Students can keep track of their own reading using an individual world map where they record the titles and authors of both fiction and nonfiction books they read about each continent. Following is a list of books for primary and intermediate grade children that represent each continent in our world.

Africa—Primary

de Paola, *Bill and Pete Go Down the Nile* (1987) (Egypt)
Feelings, *Jambo Means Hello: A Swahili Alphabet Book* (1974)
Hoffman, *Boundless Grace* (1995)
London, *Ali: Child of the Desert* (1997)
Musgrove, *Ashanti to Zulu: African Traditions* (1976)

Africa—Intermediate

Smith, *Thunder Cave* (1995)

Antarctica—Primary

Glimmerveen, *A Tale of Antarctica* (1989)

Antarctica—Intermediate

McMillan, *Penguins at Home: Gentoos of Antarctica* (1993)

Asia—Primary

Dolphin, *Our Journey from Tibet* (1997)
Levinson, *Our Home Is the Sea* (1988) (China)
Tejima, *Bear's Autumn* (1986) (Japan)

Asia—Intermediate

Neuberger, *The Girl-Son* (1995)

Australia—Primary

Baker, *Where the Forest Meets the Sea* (1987)
Factor, *Summertime* (1987)
Fox, *Possum Magic* (1983)
Wheatley and Rawlins, *My Place* (1988)

Australia—Intermediate

Oodgeroo, *Dreamtime: Aboriginal Stories* (1994)

Europe—Primary

Bemelmans, *Madeline* (1939) (France)

Europe—Intermediate

Brewster, *Anastasia's Album* (1996)
Krasilovsky, *The Cow Who Fell in the Canal* (1957) (Netherlands)
Krasilovsky, *The First Tulips in Holland* (1982) (Netherlands)

North America—Primary

Ancona, *Pinata Maker/El Pinatero* (1994) (Mexico)
Binch, *Gregory Cool* (1994) (Caribbean)
MacLachlan, *All the Places to Love* (1994)
Winslow, *Dance on a Sealskin* (1995) (Alaska)

North America—Intermediate

Jacobs, *A Passion for Danger: Nansen's Arctic Adventures* (1994)

South America—Primary

Alexander, *Llama and the Great Flood* (1989)
Cherry, *The Great Kapok Tree: The Tale of the Amazon Rain Forest* (1990)
Dorros, *Tonight Is Carnaval* (1991)

South America—Intermediate

Kurtz, *Miro in the Kingdom of the Sun* (1996)

Mental Maps

"The Standards redefine place-location literacy as having an accurate mental map. A mental map is a picture of the world and its features carried by individuals in the 'mind's eye'" (Bednarz and Bednarz 1994, 194). Mental maps can be effective tools for students and teachers. Providing students with various opportunities to draw mental maps freehand as part of their class work will help them to see maps as instruments for expressing ideas. It gives them a tool for both learning and demonstrating knowledge (Hayes 1993).

An idea for introducing mental maps to seventh graders, called "Write It! Map It! Sail It!" (Hollister 1994, 279), engages students in both describing a route in writing and drawing a map. Students choose a location familiar to them and write detailed directions for reaching that place. They then give these directions to a classmate who draws a map from the written directions. The maps are displayed for all students to comment on. Through this activity, students discover that it is difficult to verbally describe how to get somewhere clearly enough for someone else to map.

Mental maps can also be used in the middle school to represent ideas found in books. For example, *Anno's U.S.A.* (Anno 1983) can be used to give students a more in-depth understanding of the United States. Students can use their prior knowledge of U.S. geography to trace the traveler's route and discuss the characteristics of the different locations in terms of landscape, history, and story settings (Louie 1993).

Middle school teachers can also use mental maps as instructional tools to illustrate geographic ideas and work through problems associated with places. Mental maps are very useful because they emphasize key information and eliminate irrelevant details often found on wall maps and textbooks (Hayes 1993).

Students in third and fourth grades will find it a challenge to map the activities of the canoeists in the book *Three Days on a River in a Red Canoe* (Williams 1981). Using the map in the book that shows the first day's activities, students can make maps of the activities that the families engage in on the remaining days (Louie 1993).

Children in the early primary grades can also use mental maps. There are many excellent books that lend themselves to the use of mental maps. "In the early grades, students should come to see maps, like the written word, as a source of information about their world" (Geography Education Standards Project 1994, 63). Children can draw a map of the route the characters took when they were looking for Miss Nelson in the book *Miss Nelson is Missing* (Allard 1977). After reading the book *Around the Pond: Who's Been Here* (George 1996), youngsters can draw a map of the route Cammy and William took on their walk, then compare it with the map in the book. The multicultural tale of *My Little Island* (Lessac 1984) can be mapped to show the different places the boy visits when he returns home, and the charming story of *The Little Band* (Sage 1991) lends itself to a map showing the places the band passed on its march through the town. Finally, the humorous story *The Scrambled States of America* (Keller 1998) would be a wonderful introduction to mentally mapping the United States.

Using Literature to Teach Mapping Skills

There are many outstanding and informative nonfiction books for teaching students of all grade levels about how maps are made and how to use maps. The following list gives just a few:

Berger and Berger, *The Whole World in Our Hands: Looking at Maps* (1993)
Carey, *How to Use Maps and Globes* (1983)
Clouse, *Puzzle Maps, U.S.A.* (1990)
Crewe, *Maps and Globes* (1996)
Hartman, *As the Crow Flies: A First Book of Maps* (1991)
Knowlton, *Maps and Globes* (1985)
Lye, *Measuring and Maps* (1991)
Sipiera, *Globes* (1991)
Weiss, *Getting from Here to There* (1991)

There are also fiction books that lend themselves to teaching various map skills. The difficult skill of recognizing and using symbols can be introduced to young children in the book *My Camera: At the Aquarium* (Marshall 1989). Students can follow the photographer's footprints on a map of the aquarium to see the many different sea creatures. They can then make symbols for each sea creature on their own map of the aquarium (Louie 1993). Intermediate students can practice measuring distance on maps using the nonfiction book *Measurement* (Sammis, 1998) where, through activities, they learn to make distance measurements on maps using scale bars, color keys, and contour lines. The story *Jeremy's Tail* (Ball 1990) is an excellent book for helping young children discover the similarities and differences between people in their community and the people Jeremy meets in the book. Using the clues in the illustrations, the teacher can use a globe to trace Jeremy's journey. The class can also map the same journey on a flat map and collect postcards and other travel information from the different locations (Louie 1993). Intermediate students can also enjoy tracking a story's progress on a map. The book *Paddle to the Sea* (Holling 1991) is full of maps that guide the reader along the way as the canoe named Paddle journeys from Canada through inland waterways and finally crosses the Atlantic Ocean. Students can use a large reference map to chart the canoe's progress.

Treasure Maps

Another way to entice students into the creation and use of maps is through a unit on buried treasure. Two intermediate fiction books that will get students thinking about hidden treasure are Hobbs's *Ghost Canoe* (1997) and Fleischman's *The Ghost in the Noonday Sun* (1989). Both books contain young protagonists involved in looking for treasure. Two excellent nonfiction books that describe true stories of

In the Classroom Mini Lesson

Mapping Ideas

1. As a homework assignment during Fire Prevention Week, ask students and parents to plan a safe escape route from their home and a meeting place outside the house. They can make a map of this route to share with the class.

2. Using a map with five major cities on it, middle school students can imagine that they are a bus driver and have to pick up and deliver passengers to all five cities. First, students can determine the most efficient route. Next, create a passenger schedule for one bus based on this route. Finally, they can create a schedule using two buses (Gregg 1997).

3. When a new student joins your class, middle school students can draw a map of the school to help the new child find his or her way.

4. Students can make a three-dimensional map of the classroom. Have students save half pint milk containers from their lunches; tell them to cut the top off where it meets the side, so the box is open, then turn it over and cut away parts of the sides with scissors so that it resembles the legs of a desk (see Figure 8.2). Students decorate their desks and place them on a large piece of

paper on the floor. Ask students to bring various size boxes from home; students use them to make the other furniture in the room. The class then works together to arrange the three-dimensional map (Maxim 1998). An excellent follow-up to this activity would be the book *Roxaboxen* (McLerran 1991), where Marian and her playmates build an imaginary town on a hill.

5. Younger students can make "Me Maps." With a partner, students take turns tracing each other's body shape on large pieces of paper. The children then label their body parts using agreed on symbols for eyes, nose, mouth, ears, waist, and elbows in the correct location on their body maps (Sunal and Haas 2000). An excellent book to get young children started on this activity is *My Map Book* (Fanelli 1995).

6. Using the book *Me on the Map* (Sweeny 1996) as a model, students can make a diagram showing their global address. Beginning with a world map, they can mark the continent that they live on, then the country within that continent, then the state within that country, and finally, the city within that state.

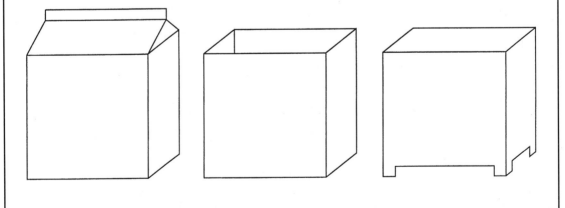

FIGURE 8.2   Milk carton desk.

hidden treasure are *True-Life Treasure Hunts* (Donnelly 1984) and *The Children's Atlas of Lost Treasures* (Reid 1997). Students can use the information gained from the nonfiction books and ideas in the fiction books to write their own treasure hunt stories. These stories should include maps that lead to the treasure their main character is trying to find. Another fun activity for older students is to hide "treasures" for younger students and draw simple treasure maps to help guide the younger hunters to the treasure.

❧ Places and Regions—A Primary Unit about Native American Regions

The Native Americans of North America are excellent examples of groups of people who identified regions based on geography. By studying different Native American groups, students will understand the concept that a region is an area of the earth's surface with unifying geographic characteristics and that these characteristics affected the humans that inhabited the region. A primary unit on Native American regions would follow a format such as the one described here. The students would be studying three Native American regions: the Eastern Woodlands, the Southwest, and the Plains (see map in Figure 8.3). For each region, students would obtain information by listening to both fiction and nonfiction books set in that region. After gathering information about each group, students would use these facts to fill in the following expository writing frame.

The _____ Native Americans lived in _____.

Their homes were _____ made of _____.

They ate _____.

They _____ and _____.

The frame helps students organize their information and shows them the basic elements of report writing. It also serves as a way to compare and contrast the different regions.

Many excellent fiction books are available to help students gather information. *The Rough-Face Girl* (Martin 1992) is the Algonquin Cinderella tale and shows children how the Woodland Native Americans lived. The beautifully illustrated story *Arrow to the Sun* (McDermott 1974) shows the brilliant colors the Southwest Native Americans used in their artwork. *The Legend of the Indian Paintbrush* (de Paola 1988) shows how Plains Native Americans used symbols when writing about events that occurred. The book *Children of the Earth and Sky* (Krensky 1991) tells five stories about different Native American children and is an excellent book for summarizing the three regions. The Native Americans who lived in these three regions have many similarities and differences and after students have studied and written reports about each group, they can participate in making a class Venn diagram (see Figure 8.4) to organize their information and compare and contrast the three Native American Regions.

FIGURE 8.3   Map of Native American Regions.

❧ *Physical Systems—How Climate and Weather Affect Our Lives*

Physical process can be grouped into four categories according to where the process operates: (1) atmosphere (climate and meteorology), (2) lithosphere (plate tectonics, erosion, and soil formation), (3) hydrosphere (the circulation of the oceans and the hydrologic cycle), and (4) biosphere (plant and animal communities and ecosystems). Children must understand the interaction within and between these categories of physical processes (Geography Education Standards Project 1994). The study of atmospheric processes of climate and meteorology provides an excellent basis for an integrated social studies unit on weather and its effect on human beings. As the Standards (p. 76) point out, "Climate and weather affect more than just personal decision-making on a daily basis. They are major factors in understanding world economic conditions over longer periods." Through the study of weather and different weather events, students are given an opportunity to use other data-collecting tools to represent their ideas. In primary classrooms, many teachers graph the daily weather on a weather chart. Teachers must take this graph-

teepees
ate buffalo
made teepees with animal skin
followed the buffalo, moved their home
horses helped them catch buffalo
lived by a lot of grass

Plains

Woodland

wigwam
made of branches and bark
made wampum
carved canoes
ate fish, oysters & clams
made masks of wood
lived near the water and forest
women were proud of their black hair
used spears

used animal skins for clothes
ate squash

corn
hunted
holes in top of their homes
sign language
used bow and arrow
built own homes

pueblos
made of adobe
they met in a Kiva.
made clothes out of cotton
lived in the desert
danced for rain.
made pottery

Pueblo

Venn Diagram

FIGURE 8.4 Venn diagram.

ing activity a step further and begin to ask students questions about how the weather is affecting their lives. If it has been raining for a week straight, for example, teachers can ask their students, How has the weather affected the place that you choose to play after school? This idea can then be broadened to include climates in other places—How does the climate in the desert affect the plant and animal life there? A book that illustrates the delicate balance between plants and animals in the desert is *Desert Trip* (Steiner 1996). Using a large, shallow cardboard box, the class can make a desert diorama with sand and models of desert plants and animals. The diorama can be used as a springboard for writing activities and discussion about desert climate and its effects. Nonfiction titles at various grade levels are also available. Beginning readers will learn many facts from the *Rookie Read-About Science Series* book *It Could Still Be a Desert* (Fowler 1997) and for older readers Gail Gibbons's (1996) *Deserts* is an excellent source of information.

The Cloud Book (de Paola 1975) will give primary students basic information about the ten most common cloud types and what they tell about coming weather changes. The class can then observe the clouds each day and record on a chart or

Children need access to current materials and learning tools.
© Photo by Jean-Claude LeJeune

graph the types of clouds they see. They can write their daily prediction about the weather in a learning log and check their prediction the following day. Teachers can extend the concept of clouds and cloud formation into a creative writing and art activity by reading *It Looked Like Spilt Milk* (Shaw 1947), giving students torn pieces of white paper mounted on nine-by-twelve-inch sheets of blue paper, and having them write what their "cloud" looks like.

Older students can discover how devastating tornadoes can be to both the land and the people when they read *Night of the Twisters* (Ruckman 1988). Some excellent nonfiction books for middle readers that explain the causes, the behavior, and the way meteorologists track tornadoes are *Storm Chasers: Tracking Twisters* (Herman 1997), *Tornadoes* (Murray 1996), and *Tornado Alert* (Branley 1988). Another violent weather event that affects both the environment and the people living in the area is a hurricane. The book *The Day the Hurricane Happened* (Anderson 1974) describes a family's experience when they encounter a hurricane on the Caribbean island of St. John. Two nonfiction books that explain hurricanes, thunderstorms, and other weather events are *Wild, Wet and Windy* (Llewellyn 1997) and *I Didn't Know that People Chase Twisters and Other Amazing Facts about Violent Weather* (Petty 1998). A class can be divided into two groups: one studying tornadoes and the other, hurricanes. Both groups use fiction and nonfiction sources to research their weather events. Each group then conveys to the other—through the use of maps, charts, graphs, and written or oral reports—what causes each type of storm, how it affects both the people and the environment, and what safety measures can be taken to help survive violent weather.

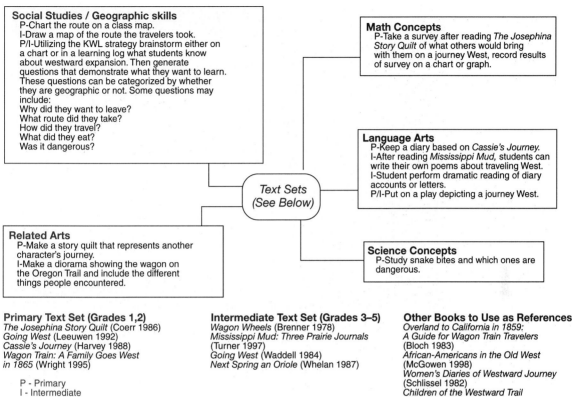

Social Studies / Geographic skills
P-Chart the route on a class map.
I-Draw a map of the route the travelers took.
P/I-Utilizing the KWL strategy brainstorm either on
a chart or in a learning log what students know
about westward expansion. Then generate
questions that demonstrate what they want to learn.
These questions can be categorized by whether
they are geographic or not. Some questions may
include:
Why did they want to leave?
What route did they take?
How did they travel?
What did they eat?
Was it dangerous?

Math Concepts
P-Take a survey after reading *The Josephina Story Quilt* of what others would bring with them on a journey West, record results of survey on a chart or graph.

Language Arts
P-Keep a diary based on *Cassie's Journey.*
I-After reading *Mississippi Mud,* students can write their own poems about traveling West.
I-Student perform dramatic reading of diary accounts or letters.
P/I-Put on a play depicting a journey West.

Text Sets (See Below)

Related Arts
P-Make a story quilt that represents another character's journey.
I-Make a diorama showing the wagon on the Oregon Trail and include the different things people encountered.

Science Concepts
P-Study snake bites and which ones are dangerous.

Primary Text Set (Grades 1,2)
The Josephina Story Quilt (Coerr 1986)
Going West (Leeuwen 1992)
Cassie's Journey (Harvey 1988)
Wagon Train: A Family Goes West in 1865 (Wright 1995)

P - Primary
I - Intermediate

Intermediate Text Set (Grades 3–5)
Wagon Wheels (Brenner 1978)
Mississippi Mud: Three Prairie Journals (Turner 1997)
Going West (Waddell 1984)
Next Spring an Oriole (Whelan 1987)

Other Books to Use as References
Overland to California in 1859: A Guide for Wagon Train Travelers (Bloch 1983)
African-Americans in the Old West (McGowen 1998)
Women's Diaries of Westward Journey (Schlissel 1982)
Children of the Westward Trail (Stefoff 1996)

FIGURE 8.5   Interdisciplinary Literature Unit.
Standard #12: The Processes, Patterns, and Functions of Human Settlement.
Theme: Westward Expansion in the United States.

Human Systems—Westward Expansion in the United States

In an interdisciplinary unit on westward expansion, students will use maps, diaries, and fiction and nonfiction books to draw inferences about why people migrated and why they chose certain routes. As Rocca (1994, 114) states, "Students will benefit from tracing migration routes and learning why these movements were necessary." The interdisciplinary unit illustrated in Figure 8.5 can be taught in the primary grades using the primary text set or in the intermediate grades using the intermediate text set. Children in the intermediate grades can be divided into small groups to read the various texts, and the teacher in the primary grades can share the various books with the students.

In the Classroom Mini Lesson

Creative Road Trips

Students need to learn how to read maps. In particular, they need to become familiar with their own state. Most state tourism departments will provide enough state maps for your students. After making certain your students can locate the major cities on the map, have them make up "creative road trips." These can then be written on cards and shuffled. A student can read the cards while the other students locate the two cities. An atlas can be used to expand the activity to the entire United States or the world. Here are some examples:

Weed Patch, California, to Garden Grove, California
Accident, Maryland, to Rescue, Virginia
Speed, North Carolina, to Trooper, Pennsylvania
Doctor Phillips, Florida, to Medicine Hat, Alberta, Canada
Sleepy Eye, Minnesota, to Coffee, Georgia
Ball Club, Minnesota, to Diamond, Illinois
Talent, Oregon, to Hollywood, California
Hamburg, New York, to Fries, Virginia

A variation for middle school students is to use cities named for names of capitals and countries.

Havana, Illinois, to Cuba, New Mexico
Moscow, Idaho, to Russia, Indiana

Historical events can also be used for yet another variation.

Napoleon, Ohio, to Waterloo, Iowa
Custer, Kentucky, to Little Bighorn (National Monument), Montana

❧ Environment and Society—Protecting Our Earth

When studying the environment and society, students must become aware of how human actions modify the physical environment. They must understand the causes and implications of different kinds of pollution, resource depletion, and land degradation. A unit on environment and society can be divided into three parts: endangered species, endangered environment, and pollution. Students can use children's literature to explore each topic and decide what steps they can take, either as individuals or as a whole class, to address each environmental issue. Students can put their suggestions on posters to put up around the school and the community. The following books paint vivid pictures of the dangers our society will encounter if we do not take steps to protect our earth:

Endangered Species

Suess, *The Lorax* (1971)
Wallwork, *No Dodos: A Counting Book of Endangered Animals* (1993)

Endangered Environment

Baker, *Where the Forest Meets the Sea* (1987)
George, *Everglades* (1995)

Pollution

Peet, *The Wump World* (1970)
Van Allsburg, *Just a Dream* (1990)

❧ The Uses of Geography— Reflective Decision Making

National Council for the Social Studies (1993, 213) states: "The primary purpose of the social studies is to help young people develop the ability to make informed and reasoned decisions for the public good as citizens of a culturally diverse, democratic society in an interdependent world." Students must use the knowledge, skills, and perspectives they have gained through the study of geography to make informed decisions. This decision-making process must be practiced regularly in the schools. Reflective decision making asks students to use what they have learned in a new way. Students have to solve problems, make predictions, write essays, and hypothesize. Throughout this chapter have been examples showing how students can use children's literature and other resources to gain information and organize this information to demonstrate their knowledge. The next step is for students to use this knowledge in a new way. Through reflective decision making, students apply what they have learned in order to make intelligent and responsible decisions. The challenge of reflective decision making is to perceive a problem in its broadest possible context so that its many faceted implications are apparent. The problem selected for the classroom must be directly connected to the interests of the students. Students then go through the following steps, leading them to social action:

1. Identifying and defining the problem
2. Identifying value assumptions
3. Identifying alternatives
4. Predicting consequences
5. Reaching decisions and justifying decisions
6. Realizing the tentativeness of decision making
7. Acting on the decision

Students should work in small groups with others who have the same concerns. Freeman and Freeman (1991) state that when students study topics in social studies cooperatively, they begin to view issues critically and plan social action. "But what is crucial is for social studies to result in social action, in really doing social studies" (p. 32). We must model this decision-making process for our students and show students that we value their active participation in reflective decision making. It is important to give students credit for engaging in the process of learning as well

In the Classroom Mini Lesson

Latitude and Longitude Activities

To have a firm understanding of the concept of latitude and longitude (the system of east–west lines, called parallels of latitude, and north–south lines, called meridians of longitude), students must begin by understanding the grid system as a place location device. After they gain this understanding, they then can begin to transfer it to latitude and longitude. The parallels of latitude measure distances in degrees north and south of the equator (designated as zero degrees latitude). The meridians of longitude converge at both poles and measure distances in degrees east and west of the prime meridian (designated as zero degrees longitude). The following activities build on each other and strengthen a child's concept of latitude and longitude:

1. Prepare a simple grid with squares along the top identified by numbers and squares along the side identified by letters. Design a simple shape—heart, pumpkin, house—by coloring in certain squares. Give students blank copies of the grid and by using coordinates (A-1, B-2, C-3, and so on), instruct students to color in all the squares to create the shape.
2. Provide students with a basic outline map of the world. The map should include the lines of latitude and longitude and a simple compass rose. Play "Find a Continent" by giving coordinates and having students locate the nearest continent.
3. Before reading a book about another country, provide students with coordinates of longitude and latitude that fall within the boundaries of the country in the book. Ask students to use the coordinates to identify the country; have them color in the country on their own outline map of countries they have read about.
4. Write an itinerary for a journey to various cities in the world. Instead of naming the cities, identify them only by longitude and latitude. Have students plot each city on a world outline map and determine a route for the journey.
5. After reading the book *Sarah, Plain and Tall* (MacLachlan 1985), students can compare and contrast Sarah's home in Maine and the Whitting's home on the prairie. Each student can choose a city, determine its latitude and longitude, and describe its prominent features.

MacLachan, P. 1985. *Sarah, Plain and Tall.* New York: Harper and Row.

as credit for the products they make as individuals or in a group (Freeman and Freeman 1991).

Chapter Summary

The use of stories in social studies is a powerful way to engage students' interest and provide readers with opportunities to develop personal understandings. By developing deeper understanding through reflection on what they have read and felt, social studies students form positions about what they value in life and choose the actions they will perform (Common, 1986). As Oden (1992, 151) points out, "Children love books. Through carefully chosen books, geography can be integrated into the curriculum in a way that will stimulate and excite young students. Geography concepts can be emphasized and strengthened easily and painlessly through the use of literature." The use of quality children's literature to teach geographic knowledge and skills opens for students a world of excitement and information.

Children's Books

The Geographic Skills

Edwards, P. 1997. *Barefoot: Escape on the underground railroad.* Illus. H. Cole. New York: HarperCollins. In this dramatic picture book, the forest animals help Barefoot, an escaped slave, elude his pursuers.

Jenkins, S. 1998. *Hottest, coldest, highest, deepest.* Boston: Houghton Mifflin. Describes some of the most amazing wonders of the world, including the places that holds the records for the hottest, coldest, windiest, and rainiest.

Moss, M. 1998. *Rachel's journal.* New York: Harcourt Brace. In her journal, Rachel describes her family's adventures while traveling by covered wagon on the Oregon Trail in 1850. This fictional journal is based on actual experiences of overland emigrants between 1846 and 1868.

Riggio, A. 1997. *Secret signs along the underground railroad.* Honesdale, PA: Boyds Mills Press. A young deaf boy must pass along important information about a new hiding place on the Underground Railroad by using his artistic talent and painting a picture of the new "safe haven" on a panoramic egg.

Ricciuti, E. 1998. *America's top ten natural wonders.* Woodbridge, CT: Blackbirch Press. Introduces ten unique and natural formations in the United States, including the Grand Canyon, Devil's Tower, and Niagara Falls.

Tesar, J. 1998a. *America's top ten mountains.* Woodbridge, CT: Blackbirch Press. Discusses ten of America's most unique mountains, including the Grand Tetons, Mauna Kea, and Mount Rainier.

Tesar, J. 1998b. *America's top ten rivers.* Woodbridge, CT: Blackbirch Press. Explores ten unique rivers in the United States, including the Mississippi, Yukon, and Rio Grande.

Winter, J. 1988. *Follow the drinking gourd.* New York: Alfred A. Knopf. An old sailor named Peg Leg Joe teaches the runaway slaves a song called "Follow the Drinking Gourd," which gives directions along the Underground Railroad to freedom in Canada.

Winter J. 1988. *Follow the drinking gourd.* New York: Knopf. Based on a true story of how a carpenter shared a song with slaves, a song that led them to freedom on the Underground Railroad.

The World in Spatial Terms
Around the World with Exciting Books

Silverstein, S. 1981. *A light in the attic.* New York: Random House. An anthology of humorous poems on a variety of topics.

Africa

de Paola, T. 1987. *Bill and Pete go down the Nile.* New York: Putnam. The crocodile pupils in Ms. Ibis's class study the history and geography of Egypt and the Nile River.

Feelings, M. 1974. *Jambo means hello: A Swahili alphabet book.* Illus. T. Feelings. New York: Dial Books. An alphabet book containing Swahili phonetic spellings, a map of the countries where Swahili is spoken, and descriptive information about Africa.

Hoffman, M. 1995. *Boundless Grace.* Illus. C. Binch. New York: Dial. In this sequel to the book *Amazing Grace,* Grace is invited to visit her father and his new family in Africa.

London, J. 1997. *Ali: Child of the desert.* Illus. T. Lewin. New York: Lothrop. While Ali and his father are crossing the Saharan Desert on camels a fierce sandstorm separates them. Ali has to decide what would be the best way to find his father.

Musgrove, M. 1976. *Ashanti to Zulu: African traditions.* Illus. L. Dillon and D. Dillon. New York: Dial Books. Following letters from A to Z, this source explains traditions and customs of twenty-six African tribes and includes a map of Africa.

Smith, R. 1995. *Thunder cave.* New York: Hyperion. When fourteen-year-old Jacob travels alone to remote Kenya to find his Native American father, he is drawn into an exciting adventure that revolves around the effects of drought and poaching on the African elephant.

Antarctica

Glimmerveen, U. 1989. *A tale of Antarctica.* New York: Scholastic. A story from the penguins' point of view about what happens to their world when humans arrive.

McMillan, B. 1993. *Penguins at home: Gentoos of Antarctica.* Boston: Houghton Mifflin. Children will learn the ways in which gentoo penguins are perfectly adapted to the harsh environment of the Antarctic Peninsula.

Asia

Dolphin, L. 1997. *Our journey from Tibet.* Illus. N.J. Johnson. New York: Dutton Children's Books. This moving book, illustrated with photographs, tells the story of a nine-year-old girl who escapes Tibet through the mountains of the Himalaya so that she can go to school.

Levinson, R. 1988. *Our home is the sea.* New York: Dutton. A young Chinese boy hurries through a crowded market to his family's houseboat in the Hong Kong harbor to join his father and grandfather in their family profession of fishing.

Neuberger, A. E. 1995. *The girl-son.* New York: Carolrhoda. A true story of a courageous mother in turn-of-the-century Korea who fights prejudice and tradition to educate her daughter.

Tejima, K. 1986. *Bear's autumn.* La Jolla, CA: Green Tiger Press. In Hokkaido, the northern island of Japan, a bear cub makes his first dive to catch and eat tasty salmon.

Australia

Baker, J. 1987. *Where the forest meets the sea.* New York: Greenwillow. On a camping trip in an Australian rain forest, a young boy wonders about the future ecology of the region.

Factor, J. 1987. *Summertime.* Illus. A. Lester. New York: Viking Kestrel. The author takes her readers on a trip to Australia in December, when it is summertime.

Fox, M. 1983. *Possum magic.* Illus. J. Vivas. San Diego: Harcourt Brace. When Grandma Poss turns little Hush invisible, she forgets the secret food needed to make Hush visible again. So the two of them set off on a journey to the major cities of Australia to find the remedy.

Oodgeroo. 1994. *Dreamtime: Aboriginal stories.* Illus. B. Bancroft. New York: Lothrop. This book is divided into two parts. In the first half, the author shares stories of her childhood; the second half consists of Aboriginal folktales.

Wheatley, N., and Rawlins, D. 1998. *My place.* Australia: Collins Dover. This story takes place on a street in Australia and through narrative text and illustrations, it chronicles the neighborhood's changes from 1988 back to 1788.

Europe

Bemelmans, L. 1939. *Madeline.* New York: Viking. The classic story of Madeline, who lives in a boarding house in France near the Eiffel Tower and Seine River.

Brewster, H. 1996. *Anastasia's album.* New York: Hyperion. Through the use of real photographs and letters, readers get a glimpse into the private world of the last Romonavs.

Krasilovsky, P. 1957. *The cow who fell in the canal.* Illus. P. Spier. London: World's Work. A picture book that features the landscape, canals, windmills, and quaint village scenes of the Netherlands.

Krasilovsky, P. 1982. *The first tulips in Holland.* New York: Doubleday. Beautiful drawings about spring in Holland.

North America

Ancona, G. 1994. *Pinata maker/El pinatero.* New York: Harcourt Brace. This Spanish/English photoessay describes how Don Ricardo, a craftsman from Southern Mexico, makes piñatas for the special fiestas held in his village.

Binch, C. 1994. *Gregory cool.* New York: Dial Books for Young Readers. Young Gregory learns to relax and enjoy the differences in cultures when he travels from his home in America to Tobago, a Caribbean island, to visit his grandparents.

Jacobs, F. 1994. *A passion for danger: Nansen's Arctic adventures.* New York: Putnam. This story takes readers on a journey with Fridtjof Nansen, a Norwegian, who traveled to unexplored regions of the world in the 1800s.

MacLachlan, P. 1994. *All the places to love.* Illus. M. Wimmer. New York: HarperCollins. This beautifully illustrated book pays tribute to the American farm.

Winslow, B. 1995. *Dance on a sealskin.* Illus. T. Sloat. Alaska: Alaska Northwest. This book takes readers back in time to the ancient culture of the Alaskan Yupik Eskimo and introduces them to the ritual of "the first dance."

South America

Alexander, E. 1989. *Llama and the great flood.* New York: T.Y. Crowell. A Peruvian folktale similar to the Noah's Ark story. The illustrations include mountainous Peruvian landscape and the colorful Peruvian Indian dress.

Cherry, L. 1990. *The great kapok tree: The tale of the amazon rain forest.* New York: Harcourt Brace Jovanovich. A man threatens the natural habitat of the tropical rain forest animals when he comes along to chop the great kapok tree down.

Dorros, A. 1991. *Tonight is carnaval.* New York: Dutton Children's Books. Illustrated with arpilleras sewn by the members of the Club de Madres Virgen del Carmen of Lima, Peru, this book tells the story of a family in South America that is eagerly preparing for the excitement of Carnaval.

Kurtz, J. 1996. *Miro in the kingdom of the sun.* Illus. D. Frampton. Boston: Houghton Mifflin. An Inca folktale, illustrated with woodcuts, tells the tale of a young Inca girl who succeeds where her brothers and others have failed, when her bird friends help her find the special water that will cure the king's son.

Mental Maps

Allard, H. 1977. *Miss Nelson is missing.* Illus. J. Marshall. New York: Houghton Mifflin. A humorous story about Miss Nelson's class, who learn to appreciate their nice teacher after having "The Swamp" as a substitute.

Anno, M. 1983. *Anno's U.S.A.* New York: Philomel Books. This wordless book, illustrated by the author, records a traveler's journey from the West Coast of the United States to the East. Anno places his character in both historical and fictional scenes as he stops in villages, towns, and cities.

George, L. B. 1996. *Around the pond: Who's been here?* New York: Greenwillow. While picking blueberries on a summer afternoon, two children see signs of unseen animals including footprints, a dam, and a floating feather. Other books in this series include: *In the Snow: Who's Been Here? and In The Woods: Who's Been Here?*

Keller, L. 1998. *The scrambled states of America.* New York: Henry Holt. A humorous tale of the time that Kansas got bored and invited all the states to the biggest party ever. When all the states then decided to switch spots, they discovered there is no place like home.

Lessac, F. 1984. *My little island.* New York: Harper and Row. A young boy goes with his best friend to visit the little Caribbean island where he was born.

Sage, J. 1991. *The little band.* Illus. K. Narahashi. New York: Margaret K. McElderry Books. A little band of children from various cultures marches through a town and brings joy and music to the people.

Williams, V.B. 1981. *Three days on a river in a red canoe.* New York: William Morrow. Two children and their mothers spend three days on a river, experiencing and observing nature around them.

Using Literature to Teach Mapping Skills

Ball, D. 1990. *Jeremy's tail.* Illus. D. Rawlins. New York: Orchard Books. Jeremy is blindfolded while playing "Pin the Tail on the Donkey" but on his way to the donkey he travels halfway around the world.

Berger, M., and G. Berger. 1993. *The whole world in our hands: Looking at maps.* Illus. R. Quackenbush. Nashville, TN: Ideal Children's Books. Explains what maps are and how to use them, discusses map symbols and their meanings, and includes maps of a house, community, city, state, country, and the world.

Carey, H. H. 1983. *How to use maps and globes.* New York: Watts. Explains how maps and globes are designed and how to get the most out of them, including special-purpose maps. Discusses how maps can be used to make written and oral reports more interesting.

Clouse, N. L. 1990. *Puzzle maps U.S.A.* New York: H. Holt. Introduces the fifty states and their shapes, showing the states in various configurations aside from their normal arrangement.

Crewe, S. 1996. *Maps and Globes.* Illus. R. Turvey & S. Tourret. New York: Children's Press. A thorough introduction to maps, globes, and how to use them.

Fanelli, S. 1995. *My map book.* New York: HarperCollins. A collection of maps provides a childlike view of the owner's bedroom, school, playground, and other places farther away.

Hartman, G. 1991. *As the crow flies: A first book of maps.* Illus. H. Stevenson. New York: Bradbury Press. A look at different geographical areas from the perspectives of an eagle, rabbit, crow, horse, and gull.

Holling, H. C. 1991. *Paddle to the sea.* Boston: Houghton Mifflin. This book maps the journey of a toy canoe named Paddle, beginning in Canada north of Lake Superior through the inland waterways across the continent to the Gulf of St. Lawrence and finally across the Atlantic Ocean.

Knowlton, J. 1985. *Maps and globes.* Illus. H. Barton. New York: Harper and Row. A brief history of mapmaking, a simple explanation of how to read maps and globes, and an introduction to the many different kinds of maps that exist.

Lye, K. 1991. *Measuring and maps.* New York: Gloucester Press. Discusses the science of geography as measured by globes, maps, latitude, longitude, and map symbols and presents related projects.

McLerran, A. 1991. *Roxaboxen.* Illus. B. Cooney. New York: Lothrop, Lee, and Shepard Books. Marian and her playmates build an imaginary town on the hill, complete with houses, stores, and playfields. This book is based on true events in the childhood of the author's mother.

Marshall, J. P. 1989. *My camera: At the aquarium.* Boston: Little, Brown. Young readers visit different sea creatures in this book by using a map of the aquarium marked with the photographer's footprints.

Sammis, F. 1998. *Measurement.* New York: Benchmark Books. From a series of books entitled *Discovering Geography,* this book explains and gives suggested activities for measuring distance on maps through the use of scale bars, color keys, and contour lines.

Sipiera, P. P. 1991. *Globes.* Chicago: Children's Press. Describes the usefulness of globes to show the roundness of Earth and the various consequences of that shape.

Sweeny, J. 1996. *Me on the map.* New York: Crown Publishers. This book describes a child's global address beginning with her room and ending with her universe.

Weiss, H. 1991. *Getting from here to there.* Boston: Houghton Mifflin. Discusses various aspects of maps, including direction, distance, symbols, latitude and longitude, how maps are made, and special-purpose maps and charts.

Treasure Maps

Donnelly, J. 1984. *True-life treasure hunts.* Illus. C. Robinson. New York: Random House. Compelling stories of pirates, sunken treasure, the Sacred Well at Chicén Itzá in the Yucatán, and King Tut's tomb in Egypt get children interested in hunting for treasure. Includes U.S. lost treasure maps showing where sunken ships and other loot are reportedly hidden.

Fleischman, S. 1989. *The ghost in the noonday sun.* Illus. P. Sis. New York: Greenwillow Books. Twelve-year-old Oliver tries to escape from pirates, who take him to an island to find the ghost and treasure of Gentleman Jack.

Hobbs, W. 1997. *Ghost canoe.* New York: Morrow Junior Books. Fourteen-year-old Nathan, fishing with the Makah in the Pacific Northwest, finds himself holding a vital clue when a mysterious stranger comes to town looking for Spanish treasure.

Reid, S. 1997. *The children's atlas of lost treasures.* Brookfield, CT: Millbrook Press. This book surveys lost treasures around the world, including pirate loot and treasures lost in wars and natural disasters.

Places and Regions—A Primary Unit about Native American Regions

de Paola, T. 1988. *The legend of the Indian paintbrush.* New York: Putnam. Little Gopher is not like the rest of the boys in his tribe. He will never be a great warrior or hunter, instead, he records events in brilliant colors on animal hides.

Krensky, S. 1991. *Children of the earth and sky.* Illus. J. Watling. New York: Scholastic. Depicts traditions and life-styles in five different tribes of northern Native Americans through vignettes set almost two hundred years ago, when they still had much of the continent to themselves.

Martin, R. 1992. *The rough-face girl.* Illus. D. Shannon. New York: G.P. Putnam's Sons. In this Algonquin version of the Cinderella story, the Rough-Faced Girl and her two beautiful but heartless sisters compete for the affections of the Invisible Being.

McDermott, G. 1974. *Arrow to the sun.* New York: Puffin Books. An adaptation of the Pueblo myth that explains how the spirit of the Lord of the Sun was brought to the world of men.

Physical Systems—How Climate and Weather Affect Our Lives

Anderson, L. 1974. *The day the hurricane happened.* Illus. A. Grifalconi. New York: Charles Scribner's Sons. On the Caribbean island of St. John, a family experiences the drama, danger, and destruction of a hurricane.

Branley, F. 1988. *Tornado alert.* Illus. G. Maestro. New York: Crowell. The often-asked questions of what causes tornadoes, how they move, and what to do if you are near one are all handled in a clear and unsensationalized fashion.

de Paola, T. 1975. *The cloud book.* New York: Holiday House. Introduces the ten most common types of clouds, the myths that have been inspired by their shapes, and what they tell about coming weather changes.

Fowler, A. 1997. *It could still be a desert.* New York: Children's Press. Describes the characteristics of deserts, the animals and plants that live in them, and their constantly changing nature.

Gibbons, G. 1996. *Deserts.* New York: Holiday House. An introduction to the characteristics of deserts and the plants and animals that inhabit them.

Herman, G. 1997. *Storm chasers: Tracking twisters.* Illus. L. Schwinger. New York: Grosset & Dunlap. A short chapter book that describes the behavior of tornadoes and how meteorologists track these powerful storms.

Llewellyn, C. 1997. *Wild, wet and windy.* Cambridge, MA: Candlewick Press. Gives information about all types of storms and weather, includes a true/false question on every page.

Murray, P. 1996. *Tornadoes.* New York: The Child's World, Inc. Full-color photographs and clear text help to explain the fascinating phenomenon of tornadoes to children.

Petty, K. 1998. *I didn't know that people chase twisters and other amazing facts about violent weather.* Illus. P. Roberts and J. Moore. Brookfield, CT: Copper Beech Books. Provides interesting information about violent weather phenomena such as thunderstorms, lightning, blizzards, monsoons, and sandstorms. Includes glossary and index.

Ruckman, I. 1988. *Night of the twisters.* New York: Harper and Row. A fictional account of the night that freakish and devastating tornadoes hit Grand Island, Nebraska, as experienced by a twelve-year-old, his family, and his friends.

Shaw, C. 1947. *It looked like spilt milk.* New York: Harper and Row. An imaginary look at clouds and the shapes that they form.

Steiner, B. 1996. *Desert trip.* Illus. R. Himler. San Francisco, CA: Sierra Club Books for Children. As a young girl and their mother hike through the desert they discover the rich variety of life that thrives in the dry desert heat.

Human Systems—Westward Expansion in the United States

Bloch, L. M. 1983. *Overland to California in 1859: A guide for wagon train travelers.* New York: Bloch. This book includes quotes from sources actually used by pioneers, especially *Marcy's The Prairie Traveler,* which tells routes, tracking and pursuing Native Americans, deer hunting, rattlesnake bites, and much more. An excellent background book for students who are writing their own short stories or diaries about travelling West.

Brenner, B. 1978. *Wagon wheels.* Illus. D. Bolognese. New York: HarperCollins. Three young black brothers follow a map to their father's homestead on the western plains to take advantage of the free land offered by the Homestead Act.

Coerr, E. 1986. *The Josefina story quilt.* Illus. B. Degen. New York: Harper and Row. An easy-reader book about Faith, who leaves in May of 1850 on a covered wagon from Missouri to California. Faith brings her pet chicken, Josefina, even though it does not lay eggs and is too tough to eat. Faith keeps a record of her trip by sewing a quilt.

Harvey, B. 1988. *Cassie's journey: Going West in the 1860's.* Illus. D. K. Ray. New York: Holiday House. A picture book that contains a first-person account of a girl who travels by covered wagon from Illinois to California and encounters buffalo, terrible weather, illness, snakebites, and death.

Leeuwen, J.V. 1992. *Going west.* Illus. T. B. Allen. New York: Dial Books for Young Readers. Follows a family's emigration by prairie schooner from the East across the Plains to the West.

McGowen, T. 1998. *African-Americans in the old west.* New York: Children's Press. Describes the important role of freed slaves and other African Americans in the settlement of the West.

Schlissel, L. 1982. *Women's diaries of westward journey.* New York: Schocken. Contains diaries of three women. Also includes a table that lists the characteristics of women who traveled west between 1851 and 1859.

Scott, L. H. 1987. *The covered wagon and other adventures.* Lincoln: University of Nebraska. The author tells of her family's trip by wagons from St. Paul, Minnesota, to Thermopolis, Wyoming, in 1906 and a later trip to Oregon.

Stefoff, R. 1996. *Children of the Westward trail.* Brookfield, CT: The Millbrook Press. Describes what life was like for those children who were uprooted from their midwestern homes and transported by their families across the frontier in wagons and on horseback.

Turner, A. 1997. *Mississippi mud: Three prairie journals.* New York: HarperCollins. Amanda and her two brothers share their hopes and fears in their journals as they travel west. Each entry is written in the form of a poem.

Waddell, M. 1984. *Going West.* Illus. P. Dupasquier. New York: Harper and Row. This book contains nine-year-old Kate's diary of a trip across the United States in a covered wagon.

Whelan, G. 1987. *Next spring an oriole.* Illus. P. Johnson. New York: Random House. Ten-year-old Libby travels west by covered wagon with her family for two months and one thousand miles from Virginia to Michigan in 1837. When the family befriends a Potowatomi child with measles, the Native Americans repay the family's kindness by helping them survive the winter with gifts of corn and smoked meat.

Wright, C. C. 1995. *Wagon train: A family goes west in 1865.* Illus. G. Griffith. New York: Holiday House. This book tells the story of Ginny and her African American family as they travel from Virginia to California using the Oregon Trail.

Environment and Society—Protecting Our Earth

Baker, J. 1987. *Where the forest meets the sea.* New York: Greenwillow. A boy remembers the past inhabitants of the fantastic forest on a beautiful island but wonders if it will all be lost to land development.

George, J. C. (1995). *Everglades.* Illus. W. Minor. New York: HarperCollins. A Seminole storyteller narrates this story of the river and its vanishing inhabitants. A pictorial symbol chart of vanishing species in the Everglades is included.

Peet, B. 1970. *The wump world.* Boston: Houghton Mifflin. The spunky, pudgy wumps live happily on a lush green planet until the Pollutians come from outer space to take over.

Suess, Dr. 1971. *The Lorax.* New York: Random House. A sadder but wiser Once-ler tells how he exploited and ruined the local environment in spite of the warnings of the Lorax.

Van Allsburg, C. 1990. *Just a dream.* Boston: Houghton Mifflin. A nightmarish trip into a polluted future motivates a boy to be concerned for the environment.

Wallwork, A. 1993. *No Dodos: A counting book of endangered animals.* New York: Scholastic. A simple picture book illustrating endangered animals. The endnotes provide detailed information about the threats to the featured animals.

Teaching Resources

Books

Fromboluti, C. S. 1990. *Helping your child learn geography.* Washington, DC: Office of
Educational Research and Improvement.
This publication is filled with good ideas for parents and educators of young children.

National Organizations

National Council for the Social Studies
3501 Newark Street NW
Washington, DC 20016

NCSS has a Geographic Education Special Interest Group composed of K-12 teachers,
curriculum developers, and researchers interested in developing and integrating
geography.

National Council for Geographic Education
Department of Geography and Regional Planning
Indiana University of Pennsylvania
Indiana, PA 15705

NCGE is the only organization for teachers that is exclusively devoted to improving
geographic education. NCGE produces the *Journal of Geography* and distributes
geography education materials published by the Geographic Education National
Implementation Project (GENIP), a coalition of geographical organizations. GENIP
publishes geography education materials and a newsletter that is free of charge for
teachers who request it from: Association of American Geographers, 1710 16th
St. NW, Washington, DC 20009.

National Geographic Society
P.O. Box 2895
Washington, DC 20077-9960

In an effort to improve geography awareness and education, National Geographic has
instituted the Geography Education Program, which offers teacher training and
assistance through workshops and model classroom experimentation. Curriculum
guidelines and suggestions and a quarterly newsletter inform teachers of classroom
ideas and techniques. For a copy of the National Geography Standards, write to:
National Geographic Society, P.O. Box 1640, Washington, DC 20013-1640 or call
1-800-368-2728.

Software

Where in the World Is Carmen Sandiego? (Broderbund) (Mac/Windows)
Expands students' knowledge of world geography and cultures as they travel to 50
countries, gather clues and take guided tours through scrolling landscapes. Designed
for grades 4–8. Also available Junior Detective Edition for grades PreK–3.
(www.broderbund.com)
Where in Time Is Carmen Sandiego? (Broderbund) (Mac/Windows)
This program, designed for grades 4–8, includes eighteen historical puzzles which
allow students to track Carmen from ancient Egypt to the 1960s space race. Along the

way they will meet historical figures and be able to explore in greater depth each historical event they are witnessing. (www.broderbund.com)

Web Sites

(The) CityLink Project
http://www.neosoft.com/citylink/default.html
This site is a comprehensive listing of WWW pages featuring states and cities. Its easy-to-use format provides students with information about various cities including what to see, what to do, and how to find out more information about the city. It would be helpful in creating travel brochures.

City.Net World Map
http://wings.buffalo.edu/world/vt2/
This site offers general information, tourist guides, and pictures for thousands of places.

Earth Day
http://www.erl.noaa.gov/EarthDay/
This eye-pleasing site offers links to environmental information and projects for the classroom.

Global Learning and Observations to Benefit the Environment
http://www.globe.gov/ghome/invite.html
Students from more than sixty countries help scientists record climate changes.

GORP - National Historic Trails
http://www.gorp.com/gorp/resource/us_trail/historic.htm
Students can access this site to find maps and detailed descriptions of the old pioneer routes such as the Oregon Trail.

International Trees and Forests Project
http://www.zip.com.au/~elanora/trees.html
This site guides classrooms from around the world in learning from the trees near their schools.

MapQuest
http://www.mapquest.com
Get customized maps for places all over the world using this interactive atlas.

National Geographic
http://www.nationalgeographic.com
The National Geographic site includes several world-class projects on the environment, wildlife, and preservation.

National Geographic Society Map Machine
*http://www.nationalgeographic.com/ngs/maps/cartographic.htm*l
A shortcut to National Geographic Society Map Machine is http://www.nationalgeographic.com/mapmachine
When students need a quick map, facts about a country, state, or province, or a picture of its flag, choose this site with its Map Machine Atlas.

Online Photo Archive
http://ap.accuweather.com
An exciting archive of more than 400,000 photos of news, as well as thousands of historical photos of people, places, and events.

References

Bednarz, S., and R. Bednarz. 1994. The standards are coming! *Journal of Geography* 93 (4): 194–6.

Boehm, R. G., and J. F. Petersen. 1994. An elaboration of the fundamental themes in geography. *Social Education* 58 (4): 211–3.

Committee on Geographic Education. 1984. *Guidelines for geographic education: Elementary and secondary schools.* Washington, DC: Association of American Geographers and National Council for Geographic Education.

Common, D. L. 1986. Students, stories and social studies. *The Social Studies* 77 (5): 246–8.

Freeman, D. E., and Y. S. Freeman. 1991. "Doing" social studies: Whole language lessons to promote social action. *Social Education* 55 (1): 29–32, 66.

Geography Education Standards Project. 1994. *Geography for life: National geography standards.* Washington, DC: National Geographic Research and Exploration.

Gregg, M. 1997. Seven journeys to map symbols: Multiple intelligences applied to map learning. *Journal of Georgraphy* 96 (3): 146–52.

Hayes, D. A. 1993. Freehand maps are for teachers and students alike. *Journal of Geography* 92 (1): 13–5.

Hollister, V. G. 1994. Arriving where we started: Using old maps in a middle school social studies classroom. *Social Education* 58 (5): 279–80.

Kapp, B. M. 1991. A magic carpet trip to learning geography. *Journal of Geography* 90 (4): 174–8.

Louie, B. Y. 1993. Using literature to teach location. *Social Studies and the Young Learner* 5 (3): 17–8, 22.

Maxim, G. W. 1998. *Social studies and the elementary school child.* 6th ed. Columbus, OH: Merrill.

National Council for the Social Studies. 1993. NCSS Position Statement. A vision of powerful teaching and learning in the social studies: Building social understanding and civic efficacy. *Social Education* 57 (5): 213–23.

Oden, P. 1992. Geography is everywhere in children's literature. *Journal of Geography* 91 (4): 151–8.

Petry, A. K. 1995. Future teachers of geography: Whose opportunity? *Journal of Geography* 51: 487–94.

Rocca, A. M. 1994. Integrating history and geography. *Social Education* 58 (2): 114–6.

Sunal, C. S., and M. E. Haas. 2000. *Social studies and the elementary/middle school student.* Orlando: Harcourt Brace Jovanovich.

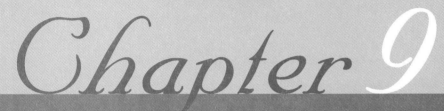

Chapter 9

© Bob Daemmrich/Uniphoto

Civic Education in a Democratic Society

Richard A. Fluck
Northern Illinois University

Democracy is not simply a system whereby people elect those who govern them, but a system in which every member of the community participates in self-governance.

—Walter C. Parker
"Participatory Citizenship: Civics in the Strong Sense"

Objectives

———————————————————— ✺ ————————————————————

Readers will

- understand how to create a democratic classroom;
- appreciate and understand the role of the citizen in a democratic society;
- comprehend the role of civic life, politics, and government;
- be able to apply critical thinking skills in teaching civic education;
- understand brain research as it relates to character education; and
- appreciate the need to teach about human rights for all citizens.

Introduction

"The essential purpose of social studies is to develop competent and caring individuals who can make decent decisions for the common good," according to Tedd Levy (Rasmussen 1999, 1), former president of the National Council for the Social Studies and middle school social studies teacher. This means that students should become responsible citizen actors who take responsibility for making decisions. In our changing global society, the importance of America and its role as the leading democratic society was put forth by Becker (1992, 83–4):

As citizens living in a large, influential, multicultural, democratic society, our actions have an impact on others as well as on the physical and social environment. . . . Citizen power seems to be on the rise [in the world]. Are we preparing our citizens for a new world order?

Thus, for teachers in the twenty-first century, civic education becomes a challenge they must address. In 1994, the Center for Civic Education (CCE) published *National Standards for Civics and Government* (Center for Civic Education 1994). These standards were grouped into five different categories: civic life, politics, and government; the foundations of the U.S. political system; the values and principles of U.S. constitutional democracy; the relationship of U.S. politics to world affairs; and the role of the citizen (see the standards at the end of this chapter).

Creating a Democratic Classroom

"Despite the importance of social studies, experts worry that we are failing to prepare students to participate in their neighborhoods, cities, states, nation, and the world" (Rasmussen 1999, 1). It is up to the classroom teacher to plan experiences in which students can engage in active citizenship.

A democractic classroom has several goals. First, the teacher should be a role model. According to Fernlund (1997, 220–1):

A teacher's actions have a profound influence on the behavior and attitudes of students. If the teacher models democratic practices, the children will absorb powerful lessons. The teacher who shows respect for students when they are expressing their ideas is communicating the importance of each individual's contribution. The teacher who regularly includes alternative points of view in the curriculum is preparing students to live with diversity and to question the truth of just one source of information.

A second goal of a democratic classroom is to foster an open and supportive climate where all ideas and views are given consideration. A third goal is to encourage multiple perspectives and sources. Students learn that knowledge gained through one source alone may not be accurate. They also learn the value of diversity with this goal. A fourth goal is respect and cooperation as both are essential for a productive learning climate. A fifth goal is the idea of shared goals and rules. The last goal of a democratic classroom is that of group decision making (Fernlund 1997).

From the first day of school the teacher can involve students in establishing classroom rules of conduct (Metzger 2000). Kindergartners may decide that they should respect others and their property. As one five-year-old said, "Don't touch somebody else or their things and don't use mean words that hurt." Classroom rules work best if the teacher and the class discuss potential problems at the beginning of the year. Together they come up with a short, clear, and concise list of rules, maybe only three or four. In this way, the students not only feel they have engaged in setting the limits and have ownership but since the rules are few, they can better keep them in mind.

Students should be encouraged to present different sides of an issue and then respond to questions.
© Photo by Jean-Claude LeJeune

Beginning at the third grade level, classes can develop their own classroom constitution. A good way of initiating the school year is to read aloud *Shh! We're Writing the Constitution* (Fritz 1987), which gives insights into the 1787 Constitutional Convention in Philadelphia. When students learn that a constitution is "a set of important rules people have discussed and agreed to live by," they are ready to discuss and decide on rules for their own classroom. This is also a good time to introduce the concept of majority rule with a simple majority being more than 50 percent. Stricter requirements of two-thirds majority can also be explained to students. A constitution should have a preamble, or the reason for the constitution. An example would be "We, the students and teacher in 4–K, in order to learn and work together, have agreed to follow the rules listed below." Students and the teacher should all sign the constitution. It is best to hold the discussions and votes on rules when the entire class is present if the constitution is to work effectively. Any new student can have the constitution explained to him or her and they may sign it as well.

Throughout the year there are several opportunities to embrace democracy in the classroom. Students may vote on the kind of projects they want to do that will be displayed for Parent's Night or the historical novel that the entire class reads for the Civil War period. Although these are not major issues to adults, they provide the opportunity for students to participate in an election process. They do learn the importance of a single vote (see Focus Box 9 .1).

9.1   Focus Box

How Much Is One Vote Worth?

In 1645, one vote gave Oliver Cromwell control of England.

In 1649, one vote caused Charles I of England to be executed.

In 1845, one vote brought Texas into the Union.

In 1868, one vote saved President Andrew Johnson from impeachment.

In 1876, one vote changed France from a monarchy to a republic.

In 1876, one vote gave Rutherford B. Hayes the presidency of the United States.

In 1933, one vote gave Adolph Hitler leadership of the Nazi Party.

In 1960, one vote changed in each precinct in Illinois would have denied John F. Kennedy the presidency.

—**March Fong Eu,**
California Secretary of State, 1984

Quoted in Riggs, Janet. 1995, March. *Good News.* RUMC, Rochelle, IL.

Role of the Citizen

Students must learn that freedom is accompanied by the responsibilities of citizenship. As such, students need to develop personal skills (Engle and Ochoa 1988). Students must learn to express their own personal convictions. This includes being able to communicate their own beliefs, feelings, and convictions. Being able to adjust their own behavior in group situations is yet another skill. Group interaction skills need to be honed so that they can contribute to a supportive climate in working in small or large groups. Another group interaction skill is the ability to participate in making rules and guidelines as well as to be a good group leader or follower. Being able to delegate tasks and duties in addition to organizing, planning, making decisions, and taking an action are other group interaction skills, all of which lend themselves to strong workplace skills when the students enter the workforce.

A good citizen keeps informed on issues that affect society. Hence the classroom teacher should make certain that students are abreast of the news—local, state, national, and international. Events should be shared on a developmental basis. For instance, in early 1999, the impeachment trial of President Bill Clinton involved several aspects that parents and teachers had difficulty addressing. However, the impeachment issue depended on two very simple issues that elementary and middle school students can readily understand: (1) Did the President lie under oath? and (2) did he try to cover up his lies? In a national poll of fourth graders taken during the impeachment trial, the children surveyed overwhelmingly voted that President Clinton should be removed from office because he lied.

Another social and participation skill that students need to develop is the ability to identify situations in which they themselves should take social action. This may be a service learning project that the class undertakes such as cleaning up a neighborhood park and planting flowers or collecting money through a recycling program (Wade 2000). A class of fifth graders decided to show their support for a fellow student who had cancer by cutting their own hair. The boys got "buzz cuts" while the girls had their hair trimmed. The result was the boy felt he was a part of the group rather than the only one with no hair. Obviously such a drastic move required that the teacher take part in the hair cutting himself as well as get parental input and support for the students' decision.

When students are encouraged to work individually or with others to decide on a course of action, they are taking responsibility for improving society. By assisting or guiding them, the teacher can point out ways in which they can influence those individuals who are in positions of power to strive for extensions of freedom, social justice, and human rights (Engle and Ochoa 1988).

Civic Life, Politics, and Government

Students need to have the opportunity to "learn and practice essential citizenship skills, respect for human dignity, and the value of the democratic process" (National Council for the Social Studies 1996, 307). Student government can be having students create a panel of students elected by the class who rule on misbehavior as in conflict resolution. Having a student council for the school has long been a good way to promote and encourage citizenship. J. R. Bolen (1999) went a step farther and developed a student government based on the model of the three-branch U.S. government (legislative, judicial, and executive) at La Mesa Middle School in La Mesa, California. The legislative branch consisted of a Senate and a House of Representatives. Since the middle school was divided into seven teams of learners separated by grade levels, the students decided it would be logical to treat each team as being the equivalent of states. Each team elected two senators who represented them in the Team Senate. Each team was divided into four to six smaller advisories, each of which elected a representative to the House of Representatives. Three committees were created for the Senate and another three for the House of Representatives. The Senate and House of Representatives met together in joint session to vote on approval of any bills that had come through the committee structure.

The judicial branch was comprised of a panel of four student members and three members of the school staff including the principal or vice-principal of the school. The Judiciary Panel had to abide by current student conduct rules of the school and school district. A case heard by the Judiciary Panel included when the president pro tem of the Team Senate was suspended from school for fighting. Under the school code, a student suspended from school cannot take part in any extracurricular activities such as student government. The Judiciary Panel ruled that the student could not participate in student government since the Student Body Constitution stated that a member could be removed from office for not fulfilling his or her duties.

The third branch of student government was the executive branch. The students decided to divide the executive branch into two parts: an Executive Board

In the Classroom Mini Lesson

The Three Branches of Government

A recently published book that describes in detail the executive, legislative, and judicial branches of government is Betsy and Giulio Maestro's (1996) *Voice of the People: American Democracy in Action.* This nonfiction book is appropriate for fifth through eighth graders as it describes the functions of each of the three branches of government. It goes into great detail in explaining how the President of the United States is elected, including how the political conventions and the electoral college work.

Students can be assigned to report on various aspects of the democratic process. For instance, small groups or pairs of students could be assigned to the following topics: House of Representatives, the Senate, how bills are passed, the President's duties and powers, the Supreme Court, the Chief Justice of the Supreme Court, the appellate court system, etc.

Maestro, Betsy, and Maestro, Giulio, (1996). *Voice of the People: American Democracy in Action.* New York: Morrow.

consisting of the president and other officers elected annually by popular vote, and the Student Council made up of the Executive Board, cabinet members (who were appointed by the Executive Board) and elected Team Leaders (governors). The executive branch had limited power under this structure and served to support legislative acts and oversee student activities. The executive branch was responsible for holding bimonthly school spirit assemblies and informing the student body of current events.

A variety of bills were passed by Congress, including the School Safety Act in which students were not allowed to mentally or physically harass other students on their birthdays. Just the airing of this as a problem proved to be a major step for the student body and student behavior changed as a result.

One student asked Mr. Bolen if he supported another person's bill, whether he or she could have the other person vote for his or her bill. Mr. Bolen told the student that this was appropriate and was known as lobbying. Obviously learning about government through active participation helps students to gain insights about governmental processes.

Developing Critical Thinking Skills

While the development of thinking skills has been addressed in an earlier chapter (see Chapter 6 "Facilitating Learning through Strategic Instruction in the Social Studies"), civics education necessitates that students develop the higher-level thinking skills to make judgments and evaluations. The inquiry process of constructivism, sometimes referred to as the scientific method or problem solving, is one approach teachers can use to have students develop new generalizations and correct faulty ones. Students engage in observing, questioning, and even challenging what they already know as they develop a new generalization that is accurate. The teacher sets the stage by providing sets of data surrounding a problem for the students to consider. Students then create their own hypotheses about the likely cause of an event, what is generally true in some area of society, or what might solve a problem. Then the teacher designs a series of activities such as simulations, review of newspaper articles, and so on, in which the students gather data to confirm or dispute their hypotheses. As the students collect the information, some pieces they discard as being not relevant (Parker and Jarolimek 1997).

Perhaps the easiest and most relevant way to introduce students in third grade on up through eighth grade to critical thinking is by having a unit on political advertising during elections. Sharing Web sites and videotapes of TV ads with a class and having the students determine which statements were facts and which were opinions, they will begin to understand the need to have valid data. At this point, the various types of propaganda approaches can be introduced. These are:

Appeal to the elite—the advertiser uses flattery to persuade the listener to buy something.
Bandwagon—the ad appeals to people's desire to belong to the group
Card stacking—the ad presents only one side of an issue
Glittering generality—the ads make broad and dazzling claims but they are not backed up with facts
Name-calling—the ad, usually political, calls something or someone else by a negative term
Plain folks—the ad is designed to appeal to the common person
Rewards—"free" prizes or reduced costs are advertised
Testimonial—a well-known person serves as a product spokesperson
Transference—the ad features a famous person using the product

Playing videos of each of the preceding types of propaganda techniques as found in TV ads or Web sites of opposing candidates and having the students identify them help develop a sensitivity to what is factual and what is opinion or fiction. Second graders can identify the basic propaganda techniques such as name-calling, which occurs on the playground, or rewards. By fourth grade, students should be able to identify bandwagon, card stacking, and testimonial. The remaining propaganda techniques can be addressed in fifth grade. For middle schoolers, films, recordings, and posters of political ads from World War II from the U.S. Army, Nazi Germany, and Tokyo Rose can serve to distinguish how propaganda was used during the war both at home and abroad.

✍ Character Education and Brain Research

Character education has been around for centuries. Historically many leaders such as Aristotle, Quintilian, Muhammad, Martin Luther, Johann Herbart, Horace Mann, and John Dewey advocated character education in schools. Numerous labels have been used for character education including values clarification, moral education, transmission of cultural values, and socialization. Terms commonly used in character education include the following:

Character—refers to a person's moral constitution or a cluster of virtues
Ethical—refers to universal standards and codes of moral principles
Moral—the rightness or wrongness of something based on what a community
     believes to be good or right in conduct or character
Values—refers to what we desire, a sense of feeling about things
Virtue—refers to moral qualities, such as courage or generosity

According to Ella Burnett (2000), "We have a set of learned, internal norms that tell us what is appropriate behavior in a given setting and what is not. We are not usually aware of these norms, which are formed early in our upbringing. We use norms to make sense out of social experiences." (p. 20) Character education helps children to acquire the norms of society.

Brain research by Daniel Goleman (1995) has found that children with what he refers to as "emotional intelligence," or ability to understand other people and manage their own emotions, are better able to get along with others. Goleman believes that all children can develop emotional intelligence. His research findings indicate that children with high emotional intelligence are better learners, have fewer behavior problems, feel better about themselves, and are better able to resist peer pressure. Goleman's research also indicated that such children were better at resolving conflicts and were happier, healthier, and more successful. They tended to possess empathy toward others and, as a group, were less violent than their peers.

Goleman has five basic skills of emotional intelligence. Children need to develop self-awareness of what they are feeling and why. A second skill is the ability to manage their own mood, like anger or stress. A third skill is self-motivation, or directing emotions and energy toward goals. The fourth skill is developing empathy toward others. And the last skill is handling relationships, understanding them, resolving conflicts, and being a friend. Some suggestions of activities to help students build their emotional intelligence include the following:

- Have the class visit a nursing home. Keep the visit short and cheerful.
- Have the class collect cartoons and jokes they like for a bulletin board.
- When a child uses a negative label, help the student think of the opposite word (i.e., lose/win, stupid/smart, crybaby/courageous).
- When a child makes a mistake, help the child figure out how to fix it.
- Have jobs in the classroom so students learn responsibility.
- When a child is frustrated and ready to give up, have the student think of two other ways to accomplish the task at hand.
- Have students play charades using body language to depict emotions.
- Have each student give a positive aspect about a topic (school, recycling, etc.).

Critics of character education argue from two viewpoints. Some argue that schools are not teaching moral principles and values. Other critics state that the values taught in schools are different from their own.

R. Freeman Butts (1988) believes that students should be taught the rights and obligations of citizenship. According to Butts, obligations of citizenship include justice, equality, authority, participation, truth, and patriotism. Rights of citizenship in a demo-

Civics education involves learning traditions of a country. Here second grade Latino students in a San Diego elementary school are learning the Pledge of Allegiance to the U.S. flag.

© Elizabeth Crews

cratic society include freedom, diversity, privacy, due process, property, and human rights. A primary mission of public school education has long been and continues to be citizenship education (Allen and Stevens 1998).The Center for Civic Education (1994, 12) describes effective citizenship as being values for the public good and those of freedom, diversity, and individual rights: "We believe that civic virtue embraces thinking and acting in such a way that individual rights are viewed in light of the public good and that the public good includes the basic protection of individual rights."

Activities for character education begin with kindergartners as we teach them the Pledge of Allegiance. This pledge is the sharing of values, principles, and beliefs that Americans share. Symbols of the shared values, principles, and beliefs of Americans include the flag, the Statue of Liberty, Uncle Sam, the bald eagle, and the national anthem. In addition, certain holidays such as Labor Day, Thanksgiving, Veterans Day, Martin Luther King's Birthday, and Presidents' Day should be celebrated and discussed with students. Character education at the kindergarten level also includes respect for others and their property. This gets into the rights as well as the obligations of individuals.

How we treat others is an important aspect of character education. A book that primary children enjoy is *Snail Started It* by Katja Reider (1998). This circular story includes a lesson about the use of harmful words that hurt others feelings. Virtue is explored in *The Paper Dragon* (Davol 1998), a book for primary and intermediate levels. This book includes the Chinese characters for courage, loyalty, love, and sincerity that underscore the book's theme of love.

As students progress through the grades, they learn about other values, symbols, and principles of basic documents such as the Declaration of Independence, United States Constitution, and Bill of Rights. Students study national and state symbols. Students may nominate and vote on a classroom animal, flag, song, flower, tree, bird, and so on. These can be displayed in the classroom throughout the year.

Older students can delve into the obligations and rights of citizenship. For instance, to open February and Black History month, a fourth- or fifth-grade teacher may want to share *From Slave Ship to Freedom Road,* a picture book by Julius Lester (1998). The book presents several scenarios about the lives of slaves, from their capture in west Africa to the escape along the Underground Railroad. The author, Lester, points out that millions of Africans were captured and chained in very confined quarters on the slave ships, placed side by side on wooden shelves like stacks of books. Those who died during the three-month voyage across the Atlantic Ocean to the New World were tossed overboard. So many dead bodies were thrown overboard that sharks swam alongside slave ships. In the book, Lester provides imagination exercises for African Americans and white people. Engaging students in the simulations presented in the book will help students examine their own feelings and values. For black students, Lester challenges them for being resentful that they are descendants of slaves. For white students, Lester dares them to consider how they would feel if a space ship landed and took them away from their parents and later sold them to people to be their slaves and do their work without pay. As slaves they weren't even allowed to keep their own names as their owners would give them new ones. How would they react? At the end of the book, Lester defines freedom as having several meanings. Freedom is "to be responsible for oneself and one's time; to own oneself; to be one's own master; and, as a promise we are still learning how to keep" (38). This leads well into a class discussion of freedom as a right. Two other picture books that tie in well are *A Place Called Freedom* (Sanders 1998), a story of a family of freed slaves who settle in Indiana. Each winter the father helps slaves escape and settle near them. The community takes the name of Freedom. *The Strength of These Arms: Life in the Slave Quarters* (Bial 1998) gives haunting photographs of the stark contrast between the homes of the plantations owners and the slave quarters.

Through literature, children can gain vicarious experiences and learn about character and virtue. *Gettin' through Thursday,* a picture book by Melrose Cooper (1998), tells the story of Andre, who dreads Thursdays. His mother gets paid on Fridays and by Thursday, the family has little or no money left. His mother tells Andre that if he makes the honor roll, he'll have a party with presents and cake. Andre is pleased until he realizes that report card day falls on a Thursday. But his family plans an imaginary celebration with an imaginary cake and candles for Andre to blow out. They even give him make-believe presents. The next day is payday and the family has a real party with real cake, candles, and presents. Children can relate to this warm story as they themselves have had to wait until payday until their family can afford to buy something they dearly want. Another good book about character is *The Ballad of Lucy Whipple* (Cushman 1996). Lucy's parents dream of living in California. When Lucy's father and little sister die, her mother takes the remaining children to California during the gold rush. Lucy hates the idea of living in California and works to save money to return east. After encountering a former slave and numerous people from different walks of life who had come in search of their own dreams, Lucy decides she is needed in California. She stays and opens a library.

Following is a list of children's books that focus on character and citizenship:

Armstrong, W. H. 1989. *Sounder.* New York: Harper and Row (Gr. 7–8, respect, caring, citizenship)

Bauer, M. D. 1986. *On My Honor.* New York: Clarion (Gr. 6–8, trustworthiness)

Brewster, P. 1988. *Bear and Mrs. Duck.* New York: Holiday House (Gr. K–3, diversity)

Bunting, E. 1983. *The Wednesday Surprise.* Boston: Houghton Mifflin (Gr. K–4, understanding, respect)

Cohen, B. 1983. *Molly's Pilgrim.* New York: Lothrop, Lee & Shepard (Gr. K–3, citizenship)

Cowen-Fletcher, J. 1994. *It Takes a Village.* New York: Scholastic (Gr. K–5, citizenship)

de Paola, T. 1981. *Now One Foot, Now the Other.* Toronto: General Publishing (Gr. K–3, kindness, compassion, respect)

Flournoy, V. 1985. *The Patchwork Quilt.* New York: Dial (Gr. K–3, respect)

Fox, P. 1984. *One-Eyed Cat.* New York: Bradbury (Gr. 6–8, responsibility, trustworthiness)

Garland, S. 1995. *The Summer Sands.* San Diego: Harcourt Brace (Gr. 3–5, citizenship, responsibility)

Garland, S. 1998. *My Father's Boat.* New York: Scholastic (Gr. K–3, citizenship, responsibility, family)

Giff, P. R. 1998. *Lilly's Crossing.* New York: Delacorte (Gr. 5–7, citizenship, responsibility)

Hemphill, P. M. 1991. *Sally Thomas: Servant Girl.* New York: Winston-Derek (Gr. 4–6, citizenship, responsibility)

Kingsolver, B. 1993. *Pigs in Heaven.* New York: HarperCollins (Gr. 8, justice, fairness)

Konigsburg, E. L. 1993. *T-backs, T-shirts, Coat and Suit.* New York: Atheneum (Gr. 5–8, values, justice)

Konigsburg, E. L. 1997. *The View from Saturday.* New York: Atheneum (Gr. 5–8, citizenship, loyalty, values)

Lowry, L. 1994. *The Giver.* Boston: Houghton Mifflin (Gr. 6–8, citizenship, justice, responsibility)

Murphy, J. 1990. *The Boys War.* New York: Scholastic (Gr. 4–8, courage, citizenship)

Park, B. 1995. *Mick Harke Was Here.* New York: Scholastic (Gr. 4–6, courage, responsibility, family)

Paterson, K. 1991. *Lyddie.* New York: Lodestar (Gr. 6–8, courage, responsibility)

Rathmann, P. 1995. *Officer Buckle and Gloria.* New York: Putnam (Gr. K–2, responsibility, citizenship)

Sachar, L. 1998. *Holes.* New York: Farrar, Straus & Giroux (Gr. 7–8, justice, responsibility, courage)

Shannon, D. 1998. *No, David.* New York: Scholastic (Gr. K–2, responsibility, caring, family)

Silverstein, S. 1964. *The Giving Tree.* New York: HarperCollins (Gr. K–5, caring)

Suess, Dr. 1940. *Horton Hatches the Egg.* New York: Random House (Gr. K–1, trustworthiness)

Taylor, M. 1976. *Roll of Thunder, Hear My Cry.* New York: Dial (Gr. 5–8, fairness, justice)

Taylor, T. 1969. *The Cay.* New York: Doubleday (Gr. 5–8, respect, caring, trustworthiness)

Walsh, J., and S. Williams. 1992. *When Grandma Came.* New York: Puffin Books. (Gr. K–3, family, caring, responsbility)

White, E. B. 1952. *Charlotte's Web.* New York: HarperCollins. (Gr. 3–5, fairness, responsibility, caring, friendship)

Every year numerous children's books are published that have themes based on character and/or citizenship. Keeping in close contact with the school librarian or the children's literature buyer at a local bookstore can be helpful to teachers looking for additional reading materials in this social studies strand.

✎ *Human Rights*

The Convention on the Rights of the Child (CRC), an international treaty, was adopted by the United Nations in 1989. The three main categories that are included are (1) the right to provision of basic needs such as food, shelter, and health care; (2) the right to protection from exploitation, armed conflict, and other threats to health and safety; and (3) the right to participation through expression of opinion, access to information, or in practice of one's culture, religion, and language. Human rights education encourages students to become responsible citizens. For instance, "children learn to respect the rights of others in a classroom where guidelines are established cooperatively, expression of opinion is encouraged and taken seriously, problems are discussed openly, and responsibilities are shared by all" (Schmidt and Manson 1999, P3).

Many children's books share the importance of human rights. The picture book *Uncle Willie and the Soup Kitchen* (DiSalvo-Ryan 1991) gives students an introduction to a community soup kitchen where volunteers work to feed those less fortunate. After sharing this book, students may volunteer in a local soup kitchen or collect canned goods to be used in a soup kitchen or food pantry for disadvantaged members of the community. *Supergrandpa* (Schwartz 1991) is the true story of a sixty-six-year-old man who wanted to enter a 1,000-mile bicycle race, the tour of Sweden. When the judges refused to let him enter, Gustav decided to participate anyway. While the other bikers rode the train to the starting point, Gustav rode his bike—a 600-mile journey. While the younger racers rode their sleek bikes during the day, Gustav pedaled his old bike during the cooler hours of the day. People along the route fed him. With a handmade red zero sewed to his vest, Gustav was first to cross the finish line. The judges ruled he had not won. But the people protested and the king invited Gustav to join him at the palace. Being denied opportunities is also the theme of *I Am Rosa Parks* (Parks and Haskins 1997), the autobiography of the civil rights heroine. In this book she describes segregation in the South and the Montgomery bus boycott.

Students need to see that famous individuals can be generous to those who are less fortunate than they. Children interested in sports will enjoy *Lives of the Athletes: Thrills, Spills (And What the Neighbors Thought)* (Krull 1997), which tells what makes these individuals great sports figures and interesting human beings. Older children might enjoy learning about Gandhi and his campaign for self-rule using nonviolent means in *Gandhi, Great Soul* (Severance 1997). These books and others can help students understand the need for standing up for human rights for all people.

Chapter Summary

The teacher plays an important role in assisting students in learning to become responsible citizen actors. By teaching about democracy and the rights and obligations of citizenship as well as serving as a role model, the teacher can help children learn the basic rudiments of a democratic government in early elementary school. By the intermediate and middle school grades, civic education and character education can be further refined. Harriet Lipman Sepinwall (1999, P5) writes about young children, "They need to acquire and practice skills for resolving conflicts peacefully and for living together in a spirit of mutual cooperation and appreciation for the contributions of others. Teachers of young children have an opportunity to lay a foundation . . . which . . . can help to make this a better world."

Children's Books

Bial, R. 1998. *The strength of these arms: Life in the slave quarters.* Boston: Houghton Mifflin. Photographs of plantation homes and slave quarters are described.

Cooper, M. 1998. *Getting through Thursday.* Illus. N. Bennett. New York: Lee and Low. Andre dreads Thursdays—the day each week when the family has no money.

Cushman, K. 1997. *The ballad of Lucy Whipple.* New York: Clarion. Lucy balks at having to live in a California mining town during the gold rush.

Davol, M. W. 1998. *The paper dragon.* Illus. R. Sabuda. New York: Atheneum. Love, courage, loyalty, and sincerity are examined in this book.

DiSalvo-Ryan, S. 1991. *Uncle Willie and the soup kitchen.* New York: Morrow. Uncle Willie and his friends work hard as volunteers to help those less fortunate.

Fritz, J. 1987. *Shh! We're writing the Constitution.* Illus. T. De Paola. New York: Putnam. The Constitutional Convention in Philadelphia is recreated in this historically accurate book.

Krull, K. 1997. *Lives of the athletes: Thrills, spills (and what the neighbors thought).* San Diego: Harcourt Brace. A Notable Children's Book in Social Studies selection tells about the human side and generosity of famous athletes.

Lester, J. 1998. *From slave ship to freedom road.* Illus. R. Brown. New York: Dial. Through simulations and vivid paintings, what it was like to be a slave is portrayed in this moving book.

Parks, R., and J. Haskins. 1997. *I am Rosa Parks.* Illus. W. Clay. New York: Dial. This is a picture book autobiography of Rosa Parks.

Reider, K. 1998. *Snail started it.* Illus. Angela von Roehl. New York: North-South Books. Six characters learn a lesson on the use of harmful words.

Sanders, S. R. 1998. *A place called freedom.* Illus. T. B. Allen. New York: Atheneum. Families of freed and runaway slaves settle in Freedom, Indiana.

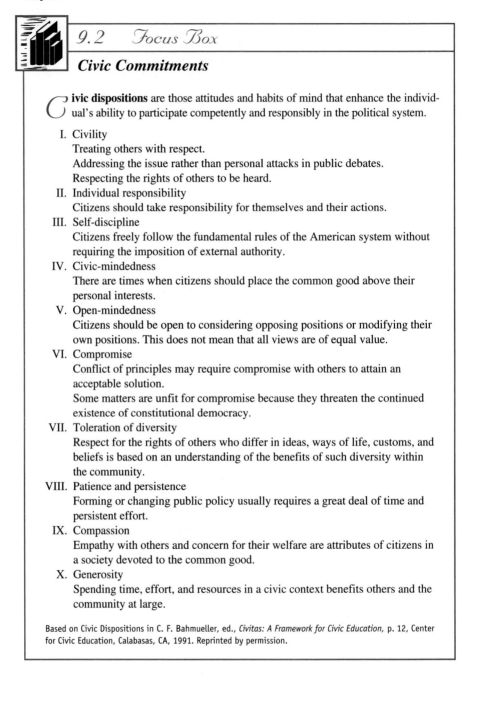

9.2   Focus Box

Civic Commitments

*C*ivic dispositions are those attitudes and habits of mind that enhance the individual's ability to participate competently and responsibly in the political system.

I. Civility
Treating others with respect.
Addressing the issue rather than personal attacks in public debates.
Respecting the rights of others to be heard.

II. Individual responsibility
Citizens should take responsibility for themselves and their actions.

III. Self-discipline
Citizens freely follow the fundamental rules of the American system without requiring the imposition of external authority.

IV. Civic-mindedness
There are times when citizens should place the common good above their personal interests.

V. Open-mindedness
Citizens should be open to considering opposing positions or modifying their own positions. This does not mean that all views are of equal value.

VI. Compromise
Conflict of principles may require compromise with others to attain an acceptable solution.
Some matters are unfit for compromise because they threaten the continued existence of constitutional democracy.

VII. Toleration of diversity
Respect for the rights of others who differ in ideas, ways of life, customs, and beliefs is based on an understanding of the benefits of such diversity within the community.

VIII. Patience and persistence
Forming or changing public policy usually requires a great deal of time and persistent effort.

IX. Compassion
Empathy with others and concern for their welfare are attributes of citizens in a society devoted to the common good.

X. Generosity
Spending time, effort, and resources in a civic context benefits others and the community at large.

Based on Civic Dispositions in C. F. Bahmueller, ed., *Civitas: A Framework for Civic Education,* p. 12, Center for Civic Education, Calabasas, CA, 1991. Reprinted by permission.

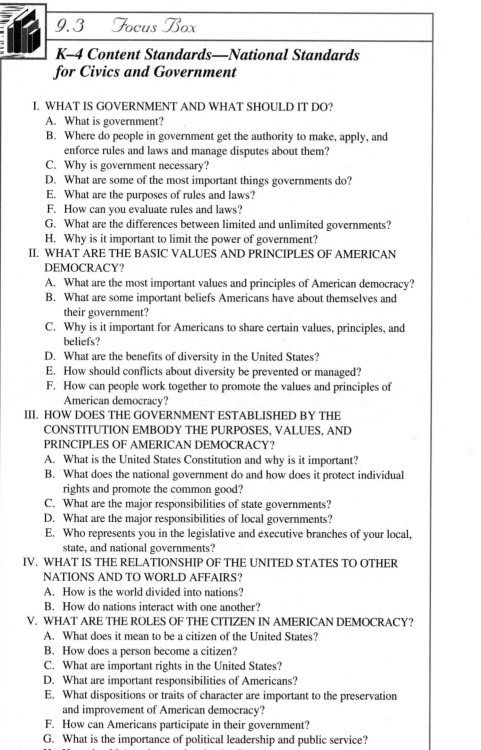

9.3   Focus Box

K–4 Content Standards—National Standards for Civics and Government

I. WHAT IS GOVERNMENT AND WHAT SHOULD IT DO?
  A. What is government?
  B. Where do people in government get the authority to make, apply, and enforce rules and laws and manage disputes about them?
  C. Why is government necessary?
  D. What are some of the most important things governments do?
  E. What are the purposes of rules and laws?
  F. How can you evaluate rules and laws?
  G. What are the differences between limited and unlimited governments?
  H. Why is it important to limit the power of government?

II. WHAT ARE THE BASIC VALUES AND PRINCIPLES OF AMERICAN DEMOCRACY?
  A. What are the most important values and principles of American democracy?
  B. What are some important beliefs Americans have about themselves and their government?
  C. Why is it important for Americans to share certain values, principles, and beliefs?
  D. What are the benefits of diversity in the United States?
  E. How should conflicts about diversity be prevented or managed?
  F. How can people work together to promote the values and principles of American democracy?

III. HOW DOES THE GOVERNMENT ESTABLISHED BY THE CONSTITUTION EMBODY THE PURPOSES, VALUES, AND PRINCIPLES OF AMERICAN DEMOCRACY?
  A. What is the United States Constitution and why is it important?
  B. What does the national government do and how does it protect individual rights and promote the common good?
  C. What are the major responsibilities of state governments?
  D. What are the major responsibilities of local governments?
  E. Who represents you in the legislative and executive branches of your local, state, and national governments?

IV. WHAT IS THE RELATIONSHIP OF THE UNITED STATES TO OTHER NATIONS AND TO WORLD AFFAIRS?
  A. How is the world divided into nations?
  B. How do nations interact with one another?

V. WHAT ARE THE ROLES OF THE CITIZEN IN AMERICAN DEMOCRACY?
  A. What does it mean to be a citizen of the United States?
  B. How does a person become a citizen?
  C. What are important rights in the United States?
  D. What are important responsibilities of Americans?
  E. What dispositions or traits of character are important to the preservation and improvement of American democracy?
  F. How can Americans participate in their government?
  G. What is the importance of political leadership and public service?
  H. How should Americans select leaders?

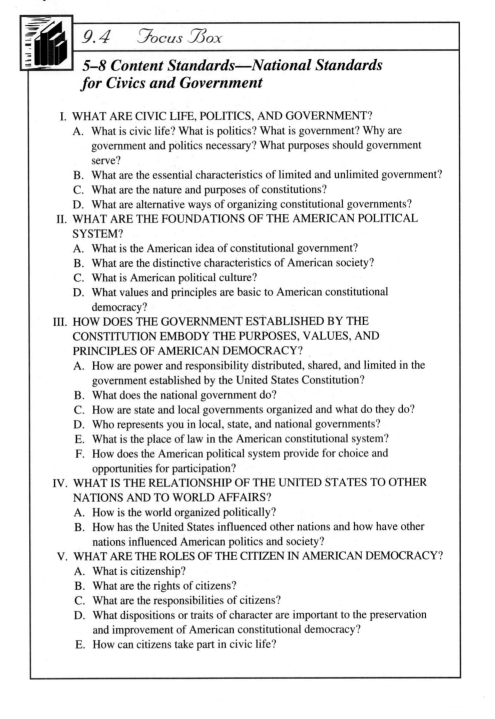

9.4   Focus Box

5–8 Content Standards—National Standards for Civics and Government

I. WHAT ARE CIVIC LIFE, POLITICS, AND GOVERNMENT?
   A. What is civic life? What is politics? What is government? Why are government and politics necessary? What purposes should government serve?
   B. What are the essential characteristics of limited and unlimited government?
   C. What are the nature and purposes of constitutions?
   D. What are alternative ways of organizing constitutional governments?
II. WHAT ARE THE FOUNDATIONS OF THE AMERICAN POLITICAL SYSTEM?
   A. What is the American idea of constitutional government?
   B. What are the distinctive characteristics of American society?
   C. What is American political culture?
   D. What values and principles are basic to American constitutional democracy?
III. HOW DOES THE GOVERNMENT ESTABLISHED BY THE CONSTITUTION EMBODY THE PURPOSES, VALUES, AND PRINCIPLES OF AMERICAN DEMOCRACY?
   A. How are power and responsibility distributed, shared, and limited in the government established by the United States Constitution?
   B. What does the national government do?
   C. How are state and local governments organized and what do they do?
   D. Who represents you in local, state, and national governments?
   E. What is the place of law in the American constitutional system?
   F. How does the American political system provide for choice and opportunities for participation?
IV. WHAT IS THE RELATIONSHIP OF THE UNITED STATES TO OTHER NATIONS AND TO WORLD AFFAIRS?
   A. How is the world organized politically?
   B. How has the United States influenced other nations and how have other nations influenced American politics and society?
V. WHAT ARE THE ROLES OF THE CITIZEN IN AMERICAN DEMOCRACY?
   A. What is citizenship?
   B. What are the rights of citizens?
   C. What are the responsibilities of citizens?
   D. What dispositions or traits of character are important to the preservation and improvement of American constitutional democracy?
   E. How can citizens take part in civic life?

Schwartz, D. 1991. *Supergrandpa.* Illus. B. Dodson. New York: Lothrop. When an elderly man decides to enter the Tour of Sweden, the judges refuse to let him. He enters the race anyway—and wins! Great book for all ages.

Severance, J. B. 1997. *Gandhi, great soul.* New York: Clarion. The life of Mahatma (which means "great soul") Gandhi is documented accompanied by numerous photographs.

Web Sites

http://www.civiced.org
This is the Web site for the Center for Civic Education.

References

Allen, M. G., and R. L. Stevens. 1998. *Middle grades social studies.* 2nd ed. Boston: Allyn and Bacon.

Becker, J. 1992. A new world order. *Educational Leadership* 49 (5): 83–4.

Bolen, J. R. 1999. Taking student government seriously. *Middle Level Learning* January/February (4): 6–8.

Burnett, E. M. G. 2000. Conflict resolution: Four steps worth taking. *Social Studies and the Young Child* 12 (3): 20–23.

Butts, R. F. 1988. *The morality of democratic citizenship: Goals for civic education in the republic's third century.* Calabasas, CA: Center for Civic Education.

Center for Civic Education. 1994. *National standards for civics and government.* Calabasas, CA: Center for Civic Education.

Engle, S., and A. Ochoa. 1988. *Education for a democratic citizenship.* New York: Teachers College Press.

Fernlund, P. M. 1997. Civic education: Building participation skills in a democratic society. In *Elementary and middle school social studies: A whole language approach* 2nd ed., ed. P. Farris and S. Cooper, 207–28. Boston: McGraw-Hill.

Goleman, D. 1995. *Emotional intelligence: Why it can matter more than IQ.* New York: Bantam.

Metzger, D. 2000. Young citizens: Partners in classroom management. *Social Studies and the Young Learner,* 12 (4): 21–23.

National Council for the Social Studies. 1996. NCSS guidelines and principles for student government: NCSS position statement. *Social Education* 60 (5): 307.

Parker, W.C., and J. Jarolimek. 1997. *Social studies in elementary education.* 10th ed. Upper Saddle River, NJ: Prentice-Hall.

Rasmussen, K. 1999, Winter. Social studies: A laboratory for democracy. *ASCD Curriculum Update,* 1–3, 8.

Schmidt, J. and P. Manson. 1999. Human rights education: A Framework for social study from the interpersonal to the global. *Social Studies and the Young Child,* 11 (3): P1–P4.

Sepinwall, H. L. 1999. Incorporating Holocaust education into the K–4 curriculum and teaching in the United States. *Social Studies and the Young Learner,* 11 (3): P5–P8.

Wade, R.C. 2000. Beyond charity: Service learning for social justice. *Social Studies and the Young Learner,* 12 (4): 6–9.

Chapter 10

Economics Education

Ways and Means

Steven L. Layne
Butler Junior High, Oak Brook, IL

Jill E. Scott-Cole
Henry-Senachwine Elementary School, Henry, IL

Scarcity is the fundamental concern of economics.

—**Tom V. Savage and David G. Armstrong**
Effective Teaching in Social Studies (4th ed.)

Objectives

―――――――――――――――∾―――――――――――――――

Readers will

- understand that economics is based on the concept of scarcity;
- understand that students need to develop decision making in order to become good consumers; and
- be able to incorporate literature in the teaching of economics.

Introduction

A housewife in a small town in Indiana opened the mail to find she had been granted a credit card in her own name. She hadn't requested the card nor the $10,000 credit line offered to her. She called the credit card company, not to thank them, but to ask a question: How can your company offer a $10,000 line of credit to a woman who has no job? The answer: This is America.

This story should not be surprising. According to the Concord Coalition (Scott 1995), the U.S. government has a national debt of $4.7 trillion that increases $9,600.00 every second. Likewise, the average American family is more indebted now than at any previous time in history. In the United States, money is easy to spend and everyone is encouraged to do so. Recently, one family reported that even the family pet was mailed a credit card!

Given the current status of economics in our country and the "spend now—pay later" mentality of a large portion of society, it is imperative that our children be educated to understand economics. The children of today are our only hope for change. If change is what we seek, then a working knowledge of economic systems, both past and present, is the best tool educators can provide.

Imagine for a moment that you have just arrived at an elementary school faculty meeting. The principal announces that everyone will spend time working on writing new curricular units during staff in-service days this year and provides a list of topics that need attention. Teachers are to volunteer for the topics they are most interested in researching. Chances are that if "economics" is one of the choices, there will not be an overabundance of volunteers. Economics is a subject area viewed by many adults as dull and highly technical. Many elementary teachers might feel that they "don't have the working knowledge to teach economics," yet they are actually seasoned professionals in using many of the economic principles that children in elementary school are ready to learn.

This chapter shares information on the most significant tools available to assist teachers in communicating and expanding economic knowledge to their young charges. In other words, we're going to tell you about many books you can use with students to make teaching and learning economics a great experience. Through the use of good literature, you can help your students discover how much a million really is, what it would be like to live during the Great Depression, or how one grain of rice could turn a peasant into the richest man in all of Japan (Pittman 1986)!

✤ What Is Economics?

Economics is two things: a body of knowledge and a way of thinking (Banaszak 1987). It involves the questions of what, how, how much, and for whom. The analysis of what goods and services should be produced, how they are produced, how much is produced, and for whom the goods and services are produced is the study of economics (Allen and Stevens 1998; Warmke and Muessig 1980). In teaching economics to students, we are instructing them on the terms and concepts of the field, but also on a mind-set that will help them become successful consumers in our society. The study of production, distribution, exchange, and consumption is very important to help students understand the basics of economics, but these concepts need to then be related to the decision-making skills students will use as they grow to adulthood. We must keep in mind that the purpose for having our students study economics is to enable them to use the concepts in their real lives and become informed, competent citizens (Wentworth and Schug 1993).

Economics is based on a concern about scarcity. People often want more than the available resources can provide, and then decision-making skills become necessary (Dillingham, Skaggs, and Carlson 1992). It is important that students understand that in making a decision, they are either acting on or reacting to the economy. Students

10. 1 Focus Box

Economic Terms

*E*conomics education can be divided into three facets. The first may be termed *personal economics* and deals with helping students become aware of terms and concepts they need in the economics of their individual, day-to-day lives. Personal economics deals with individual households, companies, and markets. Here are some examples of this category.

Money—Students need to be aware that money can be used for good or poor choices. Decision-making skills involving money are crucial.

Budgeting—Even young children can develop a budget for allowance money or class money. A budget answers the question. How am I going to spend this money?

Banking—The basics of banking can easily be brought into the classroom via a field trip or a guest speaker. Other terms than can be taught while discussing banks are interest, credit, loans, checking accounts, and savings accounts.

Careers—As students discuss personal economics, the topic of careers is sure to be broached. It's valuable to get students thinking about how they would like to earn a living when they are adults. Related terms are wages and benefits.

The next three terms give students some strategies for determining their personal choices and for using good decision-making skills. The terms themselves might not be used with younger children, but the concepts are very valuable.

Scarcity—This refers to the situation where there are limited resources to meet unlimited wants. Decisions and choices must be made.

Opportunity cost—This term describes a student's second choice for a scarce resource.

Cost-benefit analysis—This is a decision-making process in which the student would weigh the benefits and costs of certain personal choices.

need to be shown how good economic decisions can bring satisfaction and poor economic decisions can bring disappointment.

The determination of specific economic concepts most important to learn will vary by which economist or educator is being consulted (Laney 1993). This chapter provides lists of economic terms (see the Focus Boxes) that may be helpful in structuring an economic curriculum that focuses on the nurturing of decision-making strategies and the ability to make good choices.

Classroom Economics

The crux of economics is about choices and decision making. According to Dillingham, Skaggs, and Carlson (1992, 2), "It is not possible for all people to satisfy all their wants in a world of scarce resources; it is impossible to avoid making choices." Perhaps the teacher can take a moment and reflect on classroom routines already in place that would lend themselves to economic study and decision making. It may be surprising how many everyday classroom procedures can be related to economics with just a change in emphasis or a rearrangement of activities. Sometimes all it takes is an aware teacher ready to teach economics through regular class work, with just a word to the students to make them aware as well.

For example, as our classrooms make the journey from teacher-directed to child-centered, giving choices to students is essential. We are not leaving the classroom totally up to the students, but we are providing options so students can determine their preferences and priorities and make appropriate decisions. Every day, students are faced with choices. The advantages and disadvantages of each should be presented, discussed, and weighed. The students should then make the ultimate decision, and the consequences, whether good or bad, should be noted and discussed. Only through consistent practice can students gain the competence in decision making that will make the process easier and more successful for them as adults.

The classroom provides unlimited opportunities for decision making. Students can make choices of food and games to have at a class party, of poems or plays to learn and share with another class, of which friend to read with, or what topic to use for writing workshop. As students become competent at decisions such as these, they can be given even more responsibility in the classroom. Teachers may allow students a choice among books to be studied during reading workshop, various response actitivies to a book, the amount of time to be spent daily in sustained silent reading, and topics that the class will study together. The teacher may also want to provide math, social studies, and science manipulatives and activities for students to choose between to supplement their learning in those areas as well.

Economic education has been largely considered a discipline better suited for secondary students, not elementary and middle school students. In 1997, the National Council on Economic Education issued the *Voluntary National Standards in Economics*. Sixteen of these standards are appropriate for introduction at the elementary or middle school level. These standards "encompass the most important and enduring ideas, concepts, and issues in the field. Each is a principle of economics that economists, economic educators, and teacher consider essential for students to know" (Meszaros and Engstrom 1998, p. 7.). The following list includes the sixteen content standards that apply to elementary and middle school curriculum and a suggested children's book for each (National Council on Economic Education 1997; Kehler 1998, 26–29).

Content Standard 1: Productive resources are limited. Therefore, people cannot have all the goods and services they want; as a result, they must choose some things and give up others.
Hutchins, *The Doorbell Rang* (1986)

Content Standard 2: Effective decision making requires comparing the additional costs of alternatives with the additional benefits. Most choices involve doing a little more or a little less of something; few choices are all-or-nothing decisions.
Williams, *Something Special for Me* (1983)

Content Standard 3: Different methods can be used to allocate goods and services. People, acting individually or collectively or through government, must choose which methods to use to allocate different kinds of goods and services.
Cosgrove, *The Muffin Muncher* (1978)

Content Standard 4: People respond predictably to positive and negative incentives.

Kroeger, *Paperboy* (1996)

Content Standard 5: Voluntary exchange occurs only when all participating parties expect to gain. This is true for trade among individuals or organizations within a nation, and among individuals or organizations in different nations.

Viorst, *Alexander, Who Used to be Rich Last Sunday* (1978)

Content Standard 6: When individuals, regions, and nations specialize in what they can produce at the lowest cost and then trade with others, both production and consumption increase.

Hall, *Ox-Cart Man* (1979)

Content Standard 7: Markets exist when buyers and sellers interact. This interaction determines market prices and thereby allocates scarce goods and resources.

Jaffrey, *Market Days: From Market to Market* (1995)

Content Standard 8: Prices send signals and provide incentives to buyers and sellers. When supply or demand changes, market prices adjust, affecting incentives.

Merrill, *The Toothpaste Millionaire* (1972)

Content Standard 9: Competition among sellers lowers costs and prices and encourages producers to produce more of what consumers are willing and able to buy.

Hall, *The Milkman's Boy* (1997)

Content Standard 10: Institutions evolve in market economies to help individuals and groups accomplish their goals. Banks, labor unions, corporations, legal systems, and not-for-profit organizations are examples of important institutions. A different kind of institution, clearly defined and well-enforced property rights, is essential to a market economy.

Giff, *Count Your Money with the Polk Street School* (1994)

Content Standard 11: Money makes it easier to trade, borrow, invest, and compare the value of goods and services.

Wells, *Bunny Money* (1997)

Content Standard 13: Income for most people is determined by the market value of the productive resources they sell. What workers earn depends, primarily, on the market value of what they produce and how productive they are.

Stevens, *Tops and Bottoms* (1995)

Content Standard 14: Entrepreneurs are people who take the risks of organizing productive resources to make goods and services. Profit is an important incentive that leads entrepreneurs to accept the risks of business failure.

Seuss, *The Sneetches* (1961)

Content Standard 15: Investment in factories, machinery, new technology, and the health, education, and training of people can raise future standards of living.

Mitchell, *Uncle Jed's Barbershop* (1993)

Content Standard 16: There is an economic role for government to play in a market economy whenever the benefits of a government policy outweigh its costs. Governments often provide for national defense, address environmental concerns, defend and protect property rights, and attempt to make markets more competitive. Most government policies also redistribute income.
Hager and Pianin, *Balancing Act* (1998)

Decision making should permeate the curriculum and become a natural process for students. The purpose of economics education is to help prepare students to make choices that will improve their lives, and one way to do that is to include the everyday aspects of economics and decision making in the students' classroom life.

❧ *Primary Thematic Unit: Money*

A good place to begin teaching economic concepts to our primary students is with money. "Money is linked to changes in economic variables that affect all of us and are important to the health of the economy" (Mishkin 1995, 3). Even the youngest students have come in contact with money and its power. It is part of their own personal economics because it affects them in their everyday life. Since that is the case, it is never too soon to begin teaching not only how much each coin is worth, how to buy items, and how to figure change, but the economic significance of money as well.

The topic of money is taught from the preschool years on up. Most of the time the focus of the lessons is mathematically based, and students are encouraged to manipulate coins and bills in order to count, add, subtract, and exchange money correctly. We should be adding to this list activities that encourage thinking, defining choices, and making decisions. Although it is very important for students to be able to use money accurately, in our society today it is also crucial to use money wisely.

The following example of a thematic unit on money stresses the importance of thinking about the use of money and the choices and decisions that go along with that process. It is our belief that the medium that can promote such thinking best is children's literature. However, although literature is presented as the base from which this unit grows, it can be used in addition to and entwined with the traditional mathematics unit on money that is often included in the primary curriculum.

Immersion in the Concept of Money

One effective way to introduce students to a concept is to immerse them in physical representations of the topic to be covered. In a classroom where the students are about to study money, you might see posters of coins and bills, money manipulatives set out for children to explore, books about money displayed attractively, and poems about money on chart paper. There should be a mix of informational and fiction books, letting children know that the characters they read about offer interesting facts to learn as well as practical applications to their lives.

In the Classroom Mini Lesson

Activities for Economics Lessons

Listed here are some additional ideas for bringing decision making and economics into the classroom.

1. Students can help decide on a money-making project for their class. They should be involved in every step of the project, including the decision of what to spend the money on when the project is complete.

2. Near Christmastime, let students write their Christmas wishes to Santa, and then have them prioritize the list and give reasons.

3. Set up a class store that has commonly needed items for sale: pencils, pens, erasers, crayons, etc. Students can use real money or class money they have earned through class activities to buy items they need. Keep the store running throughout the school year, stopping often to evaluate and discuss successes, failures, and changes that need to be made.

4. Have a class garage sale. Ask students to bring small items from home that they don't want anymore. They can make posters to advertise their booth, determine prices for their merchandise, and invite other classrooms to their sale. Throughout the activity, discuss supply and demand, goods and services, competition, propaganda, and the use of money.

5. Discuss the difference between using money and bartering. Let students experience both of these systems using the class store and discuss advantages and disadvantages of each.

6. Take a field trip to a local business and ask someone to explain the economic concerns of the business and perhaps how the students can participate or help.

7. Play board games that use money or economic concepts and discuss strategies and choices as the children play.

8. Give each student in the room a job and discuss how the jobs provide goods and services and how they interact with each other and support each other.

9. Bring in several travel brochures and travel sections from the Sunday newspaper, complete with hotel fees and airfares. Divide the class into groups of three students each, and give each group an imaginary $5,000 to spend on an imaginary vacation. Have each group plan a vacation and give reasons why they selected what they did. You may even arrange for a travel agent to visit the classroom at the beginning of the project.

10. Pair up students and give them each an imaginary $1,000. Give the students a conversion table for foreign currencies. Let the students choose a country and convert their $1,000 into the new currency.

As discussed earlier, if the teacher takes the approach that the everyday routines of the classroom can be used to teach the topic at hand, money can become a part of everything done in the classroom. Storytime can include books and poems relating to money, sharing time can encourage "money stories" from the children, and writing workshop can promote pieces where children describe some of their money-spending decisions. These pieces may then be dramatized to practice the use of concrete coins and dollars and to instill the notions of choices and decision making.

10.2   Focus Box

Consumer Economics Terms

Older students who have had experience with personal economics are ready for an introduction to the second facet of economics, *consumer economics.* Consumer economics encompasses our nation as a whole and demonstrates how individuals and groups fit into our economy. Some valuable terms follow.

Supply and demand—A teacher may use a balance scale to demonstrate supply and demand. As the demand for goods goes up, supply goes down. Then as the supply goes down (scarcity), prices go up, which in turn causes the demand to go down again. This reestablishes the balance.

GNP—The gross national product is the sum total of goods available in the country. It can be a yardstick of the economy's performance.

Inflation—Students may be able to understand inflation through this scenario: If you buried $100 in the ground and dug it up ten years later, would you be able to buy more or less with that same $100? If you can buy fewer goods, inflation has occurred. Deflation has occurred if you can buy more goods.

The stock market—Stocks are ownership of a company. Stocks go up and down based on the perceived value of the company. The stock market is where shares of stock are bought and sold.

Goods and services—The following activity may help students understand the difference between goods and services. Ask each student what jobs his or her parents hold. On the chalkboard, categorize each job as providing a good or a service.

Import/export—Our country imports goods from other countries, and we export goods to other countries. A demonstration may be held between two classrooms. One class has apples, the other has bananas. It would get boring eating only one kind of fruit, so one class imports bananas from the other class and exports their own apples. That way, both classes can enjoy both kinds of fruits.

Teaching the Concept of Money through Literature

One book that introduces money as well as the existence of choices and the necessity of decision making is *Alexander, Who Used to be Rich Last Sunday* (1978) by Judith Viorst. In this book, Alexander receives a dollar from his grandparents and then makes some choices about spending the money. At the end of the story, Alexander has no money left and is disappointed in the decisions he made. This is a wonderfully humorous book, but it can also encourage discussions of the choices Alexander made. Which were good choices and which were not? Which choices would the students have made themselves? What advice would they give Alexander? How would the students spend the money if they had received the same amount from their grandparents? How do they think Alexander will spend his money next time?

Not only does this book provide rich exchanges concerning decision making, but it also includes money math as well. Each time Alexander spends money, the students can subtract the amount from the original dollar he received from his grandparents. A chart may be made to keep track of Alexander's expenditures with one column reserved for the class' opinion of the choice (See Figure 10.1).

This book also lends itself to dramatization. One student could act out the part of Alexander while other children could play Alexander's brothers, parents,

Decision	Amt. Spent	Class opinion	Better choice
Bubblegum	15¢	OK	just buy one piece
Bets	15¢	poor	Don't bet!
Rented snake	12¢	good	—
Bad words	10¢	Very bad	Don't say bad words.

FIGURE 10.1   Young students can make a class economic chart to determine the best financial choices.

friends, grandparents, and the storekeepers he visits. Act One may show Alexander making the choices described in the book; Act Two may show the students making their own choices of how to spend the money and how Alexander's satisfaction with his choices could change.

A book that combines mathematical facts about money and thinking strategies as well is David M. Schwartz's *If You Made a Million* (1989). Each page shows an amount of money from one penny to a million dollars and humorous ways to earn it. The book also introduces such concepts as interest, denominations of bills, checks, banking, loans, down payments, and income tax. It entices students to count money, compare it, and think about its use in our world today. The last page states that money involves choices, and the question posed to the children is, what would you do with a million dollars?

This certainly leads directly into a writing project. The students can make their own personal lists of what they would do with one million dollars and prioritize the list, thinking about what they value most and what they feel would constitute wise choices. Then they can move into small groups where they are instructed that they no longer personally have a million dollars, but that their group has a million dollars. Since they can't have all the items on their separate lists, some decision making is required. Which items will stay on the groups' list and which will be abandoned? Then the class can reconvene and the students are advised once more that their groups do not have a million dollars, but their class as a whole does. Again, decision making comes into play, and choices have to be made. As the class discusses the situation, the students need to come up with those items that are going to stay on the list and those that can be left off. These choices can be prioritized on the board and a discussion can ensue about what the children find as the most important and valuable ways to spend a million dollars.

After this role-playing activity, it may be appropriate to present the class with some real money and an authentic decision-making situation. If the students have participated in a moneymaking project or have run a class store for a while, perhaps this is a good time to discuss some options for the profits. Encourage them to apply the knowledge they learned from the previous activity to the real-life choices they can make with the money their class really does have!

Another favorite book for this unit is the Caldecott Honor Book *The Treasure* (1978) by Uri Shulevitz, which promotes reflection about money and how it can be used. The story, which takes place in historic Eastern Europe, tells about an old man named Isaac. In a dream, a voice tells the poverty-stricken old man to look for a treasure under the bridge by the Royal Palace. He travels a long way to the city where the Royal Palace stands. Once there, he talks to the captain of the guard who laughs at the old man's dream. Then the guard reveals his own dream in which he is told to look for a treasure under the stove in the house of a man named Isaac. Isaac returns home to find the treasure under his own stove. In gratefulness, he builds a house of prayer and sends the captain of the guard a priceless gift. Isaac is never poor again.

This book combines *personal* and *social economics* in its plot and theme. Isaac made choices about searching for wealth and spending his treasure once he'd found it, but the theme of the story also encompasses the social polarity between wealth and poverty. All of this makes for excellent discussion and thinking about money.

As a response to this book, perhaps the students could have their own treasure hunt in the classroom. The teacher could hide a "treasure" (e. g., money to spend at the class store, a food treat, a new book for the classroom library, or certificates for extra time for free reading) and give the students clues to its whereabouts. This would not necessarily be a competition, but a cooperative project, and the whole class would share in the treasure. When the treasure is found, its value can be discussed and ideas for its distribution debated.

These are just three of the books rich in ideas to teach the basics of money, weighing choices, and decision making. Other books that correlate with these subjects are included in the annotated bibliography at the end of this chapter.

Using Poetry to Teach the Concept of Money

Poetry can play a large role in helping children understand a variety of topics, money being no exception. Sharing poetry in the classroom can give students a new perspective on the topic as well as foster an ongoing enjoyment of poetry. The whimsical poem below can be an introduction to money that will capture children's imagination and prepare them to discuss money and what it means to them.

I Asked My Mother

I asked my mother for fifty cents
To see the elephant jump the fence.
He jumped so high that he touched the sky
And never came back 'til the Fourth of July.

—Anonymous

This next poem was cowritten by a first-grade class and their teacher. After reading many poems about money, they decided they wanted to write one of their own. As they did, they had some wonderful discussions about the significance of money, and how the children proposed to use money in their everyday lives.

Money

Money, money, money, money,
Coins, a dollar bill.
Put some money in the bank
Save it if you will.

Money, money, money, money,
Penny, nickel, dime.
A quarter is twenty-five
And all of them are mine!

Another poem written by a nine-year-old comments on an everyday experience common to all schoolchildren—keeping track of lunch money. Students will certainly be able to commiserate with the poet and may be inspired to write their own lunch money "blues."

Lunch Money

I'm in the lunch line.
I have ten dollars. Ten is fine.
A bully takes two. That makes eight.
Eight's still great.
I trip and hit my knee, out falls three.
That makes five. Will I survive?
My friend begs me, so I give her three.
Now I have two. What will I do?
I give it to the lunch lady.
It is just enough.
Boy, getting lunch is really tough.

—Nina, age 9

Additional poems related to money may be found in various poetry anthologies. Listed here are poems that students might enjoy.

"The Animal Store" by Rachel Field
"Barter" by Sara Teasdale
"The Coin" by Sara Teasdale
"The Falling Star" by Sara Teasdale
"The Fairies Never Have a Penny to Spend" by Rose Fyleman
"For Sale" by Shel Silverstein
"Market Square" by A. A. Milne
"Smart" by Shel Silverstein

Culminating the Unit on Money

As the students close their unit on money, it may be timely to expand their knowledge beyond their own classroom and into other countries around the world. Armstrong and Burlbaw (1991, 143) state that "money fascinates" and this may be even more true as students have the opportunity to look at currency from other countries.

Although the primary student would not study foreign banknotes in detail, the understanding that money is used around the world but may take different forms helps the children develop an appreciation of various cultures, perhaps even some represented in the classroom.

Samples of foreign currency may be obtained from several sources. Students may have some coins or bills at home they could bring to school, or teachers, friends, and acquaintances may have some that could be borrowed. Put the word out around school and the community that you are looking for examples of foreign money, and you may receive plenty to culminate the class's study of money. Following is the address of a supplier where you may purchase selections of world banknotes or catalogs of world paper money. Catalogs may be available for as little as $1.00 and banknote selections for approximately $17.00 (Armstrong and Burlbaw 1991). An especially helpful guide available from Morris Lawing is *Collector's Guide and Catalogue of World Paper Money* by John Aeillo.

Morris Lawing
P.O. Box 9494
Charlotte NC 28299

Suggested activities with world currency include finding locations on the map that match the foreign money the class is observing, using the pictures on paper money to determine things of value to that country, noting heroes of particular countries from their pictures on the money, listing differences and similarities between the foreign currency and U.S. currency, and being aware of the fact that money can reflect a country's economic values and history. Through participating in these activities, students come to understand their own money system better, as well as learning about the world around them.

Although the thematic unit on money may be concluding in the classroom, the study of money and its relationship to economics can continue throughout the school year. Money, its power, and its problems come into students' lives daily. The choices and decisions facing students are unlimited and deserve the attention of the teacher sensitive to economic issues. As the teacher incorporates decision making into the fabric of the classroom routines, students study economics all year long.

Here are some additional titles relating to money:

Berenstain and Berenstain, *The Berenstain Bears and the Trouble with Money* (1983)
Berger and Berger, *Round and Round the Money Goes* (1993)
Briers, *Money* (1987)
Brittain, *All the Money in the World* (1979)
Elkin, *Money* (1983)
Facklam and Thomas, *The Kids' World Almanac of Amazing Facts About Numbers, Math, and Money* (1992)
Frank, *Tom's Lucky Quarter* (1990)
Giff, *Count Your Money with the Polk Street School* (1994)
Hoban, *Twenty-Six Letters and Ninety-Nine Cents* (1987)
Maestro and Maestro, *Dollars and Cents for Harriet* (1988)
Maestro and Maestro, *The Story of Money* (1993)
McMillan, *Jelly Beans for Sale* (1996)

McNamara, *Henry's Pennies* (1972)
Medearis, *Picking Peas for a Penny* (1990)
Mitgutch, *From Gold to Money* (1985)
Williams, *A Chair for My Mother* (1982)
Zimelman, *How the Second Grade Got $8,205.50 to Visit the Statue of Liberty* (1992)

Web Sites for Information on Money

www.treas.gov/currency
www.making-sense.com/history.htm
www.sys.virginia.edu/~wwwle/jun/lesson.html
www.kidsbank.com/index_2.html
tqjunior.advanced.org/3643/smartbuying.html
www.aplusmath.com/cgi-bin/flashcards/money

❧ Intermediate Thematic Unit: The Great Depression

Vocabulary related to content area study can often be technical and intimidating. Students may feel that economic terms such as *inflation* or *depression* hold little relevance to their daily lives. Creating an interest and motivation in students to learn about economic concepts can best be achieved by incorporating literature into the curriculum.

The power of literature to put students in touch with another time and place is the vehicle by which even the most technical concepts may be introduced and explored. Students are more willing and able to learn the meanings of economic terms if they are able to associate them with their own lives, the lives of someone they know, or the experiences of a character they meet in a book. Careful integration of children's literature into a study of economics can ensure that every student will be able to relate to the concepts being studied.

One way of addressing some higher-level economic concepts is through a study of the Great Depression that began in the United States in 1929. The historical importance of the Great Depression is primarily due to the economic turmoil with which it is associated. Many students will find learning about economic principles easier if they can make comparisons between what they know about our economy today and what they understand it to have been like many years ago. Students can develop an understanding of the nation's economy during the Great Depression by looking at how it affected the lives of people who lived during those years. Good literature is one way to provide that understanding.

Introducing the Concept with Literature

A strength in the introduction of any concept is to begin with what the children already know. Often students will reveal their knowledge readily when they are relating to a story. A good read aloud on the Great Depression is *Uncle Jed's Barbershop*

10.3 Focus Box

Social Economic Terms

A third facet of economics is *social economics.* Social economics refers to ways the economy affects or is affected by the conditions of our society. Some terms related to social economics include:

War—Historically affects all societies by increasing the need for supplies and decreasing the available laborers. Rationing may occur so that needed goods are available for those involved in combat.

Welfare—Society's system for providing necessities to those who are unemployed and lacking a source of income.

Lottery—Instituted in some parts of the country as a way for local or state government to fund various projects while promising an economic windfall to the correct ticket holder.

Homeless—A condition of being without residence, which is becoming an increasing problem for which no viable solutions have been found.

Wealth—Descriptor indicating a high level of economic and social status.

Poverty—Descriptor indicating a low level of economic and social status.

Inflation—A rise in price level related to an increased volume of spending and/or credit with a loss in the value of the currency.

Depression—Economic condition in which employment, business, and stock market values severely decline.

(Mitchell 1993), which depicts the true story of an African American barber who loses his savings when the bank collapses during the economic crisis. A perfect novel for a unit on the Great Depression is Mildred Taylor's *Song of the Trees* (1975). This book, Taylor's first, tells the story of the Logan family suffering through the depression in rural Mississippi. The father has gone to Louisiana because there is no work in Mississippi, and a white man is pressuring the Logan children's grandmother to sell some of her land. This white man intends to chop down all the beautiful trees and, because of the depression, is offering very little money for the land.

Quite early in the story, it is discovered that seven-year-old Christopher-John has been up at night eating cornbread. His mother gently chastises him and explains that the family must eat only when they are truly hungry. She gives her young son a simple explanation of the family's limited finances, including the reason why his father has left the family in Mississippi to go to work laying railroad tracks in Louisiana. This simple explanation of the family's economic situation and the concept surrounding it provides an easy introduction to the term *depression.* Students can then focus on other events from the story that they feel might be associated with the depression.

Taylor's book is very short, making it an ideal springboard into the topic of the Great Depression. Teachers can introduce graphic organizers or other aids to assist students in charting information as they receive it. Economic terms appropriate for discussion following *Song of the Trees* include: unemployment, inflation, and depression. A good follow-up to *Song of the Trees* is Zilpha Snyder's *Cat Running* (1994), which describes the fate of rural children during the Great Depression. Homelessness and wanderers such as the Okies are depicted.

Advancing the Concept with Literature

It may be difficult for students today to directly relate to the desperation that comes with an economic depression. James Lincoln Collier's *Give Dad My Best* (1976) offers them the opportunity to vicariously experience the lengths to which poverty can drive an individual. Jack Lundquist is fourteen years old and watching helplessly as his unemployed father allows poverty to overtake the family. Jack's father, a trombone player, made quite a living during the Roaring Twenties. Now the twenties are over and the widowed Mr. Lundquist spends his days waiting for things to get better.

Jack faces considerable inner turmoil as he watches his father lie to his sister, Sal, about buying her a dress for the school play. Later, Jack tries to quell his own fears that his father is spending the precious rent money on jazz albums and beer, until he learns that the family is about to be evicted. To keep the family together, Jack acts on an idea he has considered throughout the entire novel: theft.

Students will see in Jack how truly desperate life can become during an economic depression. When the hero of the novel is driven to thievery by forces beyond his control, the reader is forced to consider the causal factor. Collier's book prepares students to intelligently discuss an economic depression. This book offers teachers a tremendous opportunity for promoting critical thinking about economics by leading students into a discussion of how Mr. Lundquist might have planned his finances and spending more carefully prior to the Great Depression. Likewise, students may discuss the alternatives that they see for the family to remain together. Students may find, as they read and study further, that the alternatives they suggest may or may not have been possible during this time in history.

Phyllis Reynolds Naylor's *Walking Through the Dark* (1976) is a true testimony to the courage of people living in America during the 1930s. This novel provides a disturbing yet poignant look at the effects of the Great Depression on the Wheeler family. Ruth Wheeler, a young teenager, is sick of hearing about "hard times" as the novel opens. In a sense, Ruth is like many of our students; she is uninvolved and uninterested in economic events that have not directly affected her family.

As the story unfolds, Ruth and her family are forced to endure conditions they never could have dreamed possible. Each family member is forced into a form of humility that erases all distinction of economic status. The story is told in such a manner that readers cannot help but feel a sense of guilt for any abundance they enjoy.

Walking Through the Dark will give students a taste of just how devastating the effects of the Great Depression were. Phyllis Reynolds Naylor uses Ruth Wheeler's diary as an introduction to many chapters, and it is through this diary that we begin to see the growth and maturity that hard times often bring. Asking students to keep a character journal would be an ideal way of bringing students into a more affective relationship with the Wheeler family. In addition, this particular novel lends itself to the creation of a time line (see Figure 10.2). Students creating a time line of the changes forced on the Wheelers by the economy are interacting with the text in a critical manner.

Extending the Concept with Literature

Milton Meltzer is a name well known in the field of children's literature. His ability to represent America's past in simple language with attention to historical accuracy

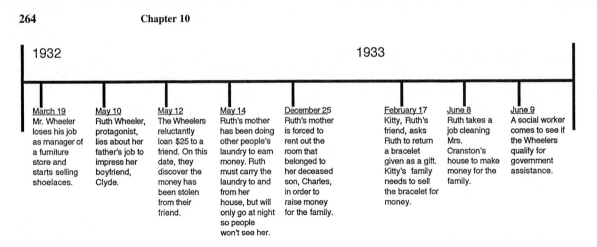

FIGURE 10.2   Chronological Time Line of the Effects of the Great Depression on the Wheeler Family. Lauren Sprieser, a fifth grader, created this time line as she read *Walking Through the Dark* (Naylor 1976).

From: Lauren E. Sprieser, Brook Forest School, Grade 5.

has garnered him praise from critics and numerous literary awards. Meltzer's *Brother Can You Spare a Dime?* (1969) is a nonfiction book based on eyewitness accounts of the Great Depression. Included in this book are detailed descriptions of life during the depression from people who really lived through it, as well as photographs, songs, and political propaganda from the period. Although this type of information might not appeal to students initially, after experiencing the depression through the characters in some fine pieces of literature, students' interest levels are sure to be heightened.

If fictional characters—such as those previously mentioned—can become real to a reader, a natural motivation for learning is created because the reader cares about the people who are experiencing hardship. In Collier's book, students may find music to a song played by Jack's father in *Give Dad My Best* or see a photograph showing a room for rent like the one put out by the Wheelers in *Walking Through the Dark*. The literature used to introduce and advance students' knowledge now provides fuel for them to make connections with more complicated nonfiction material.

Although Meltzer's book is a tremendous nonfiction resource, students should be encouraged to continue their exploration with other readings of expository material. Source ideas include chapters or sections from social studies textbooks at different grade levels, newspaper and magazine articles discussing the Great Depression, or adult books that have some sections appropriate for intermediate students. In addition, the plethora of picture books flooding the publishing market is sure to include some that address the Great Depression.

Suggestions for Further Reading

The following titles offer opportunity for further reading on the Great Depression and the economic difficulties faced by families during the 1930s.

Antle, *Hard Times: A Story of the Great Depression* (1993)
Curtis, *Bud, Not Buddy.* (1999)
Evans and Rylant, *Something Permanent* (1994)

In the Classroom Mini Lesson

Economic Activities for Intermediate and Middle School Students

The following ideas may be used to integrate or extend a study of economics in the intermediate or middle school classroom.

1. Create checkbooks for students with registers and a "deposit" system. Allow them to write checks to purchase any number of things, such as time for free reading or the privilege to sit in a special chair. Work with them to balance and maintain accurate records.

2. Research the economic conditions of a country in need. As a class, choose to sponsor the care of a child from that country through an organization. Students should budget expenses to cover the summer months and work to organize moneymaking projects to support the child.

3. Engage students in a study of propaganda techniques. Have them decide which methods they find most persuasive. Ask them to create advertisements for books in the school library using the propaganda techniques they have studied. Keep track of the number of times these titles are checked out and find out which methods were most successful.

4. Have students interview their parents or grandparents on the topic of the economy. The class can formulate general questions that they wish everyone to respond to, and students can write individual questions seeking personal testimony from the persons they are interviewing.

5. Invite a guest speaker in to discuss the stock market with the class. Have this person assist the class in selecting a stock to invest in as a simulation and instruct them on the buying and selling of their stock. Teach students to "read" the stock market report and discuss any decisions they may wish to make regarding their stock.

6. Have students select an item, such as gasoline, that is critical to the daily life of people in our country and chart the price increases and decreases of that item over several weeks. Ask them to hypothesize reasons for these price changes. Consider as a class what would happen if the price increased or decreased drastically. What conditions would cause this to happen? How would people most likely respond? How would society's response help or hurt the situation further?

7. Go to a card shop that sells custom cards called something like "on the day you were born." Select the date that you plan to introduce the unit and request copies from different decades (January 15, 1900; January 15, 1910; January 15, 1920; and so on). Have students discuss the differences in prices for bread, milk, gasoline, and cars. During which two decades did the prices increase the most? What could be the reason for the large increase?

Friedrich, *Leah's Pony* (1996)
Hesse, *Out of the Dust* (1997)
Karp, *Nothing Rhymes with April* (1974)
Koller, *Nothing to Fear* (1991)
Meyers, *Red-Dirt Jessie* (1992)

Stanley, *Children of the Dust Bowl* (1992)
Thesman, *The Storyteller's Daughter* (1997)

Web Sites for Information on the Great Depression

www.escape.com/~paulg53/politics/great_depression.shtml
www.scruz.net/~kangaroo/Timeline.htm
www.sos.state.mi.us/history/museum/explore/museums/hismus/1900-75/
    deressn/labnews2.html
drylands/nasm/edu:1995/bowl.html

Literature as a Basis for Economic Comparison

A thematic study is guided by the teacher, who has clearly defined purposes and emphases for the unit. As students look in depth at the Great Depression, the teacher will focus on terminology and concepts that suit the needs of the curriculum. Middle school teachers might focus heavily on the stock market crash that led to the depression while upper-grade elementary teachers might choose only to mention the crash and emphasize instead the crucial elements of decision making in a depressed economy.

Whatever the emphasis, the opportunities for comparison between the economy "then" and "now" are ripe. Picture books or novels that reflect our society as it currently exists offer multiple opportunities for drawing comparisons to a more depressed economy. Students can be asked to focus on a character's appearance in a picture book set in the 1990s and compare it with photographs from Meltzer's book. Similarly, students may be asked to compare descriptions of the community and characters described in Neal Shusterman's contemporary novel *The Shadow Club* (1988) with those of the Lundquist family in *Give Dad My Best.* An additional source of comparison for middle school students is to use the futuristic seeing of Lois Lowry's *The Giver* (1993) as a basis for comparison with that of the Wheeler Family in *Walking Through the Dark.* Each of these stories has endless possibilities for economic comparison if students are guided to focus on what the text and photographs communicate about the economy.

✒ *Using Literature to Teach Economics*

The amount of children's literature available that can be related to economic concerns is almost unlimited. The teacher who is interested in augmenting the economic curriculum with literature will find that almost any quality children's book can be used toward this purpose. Economics is an everyday concern—thus, the everyday actions described in a good plot would most likely relate to some aspect of economics. Good children's literature gives us insights into the lives of characters and into our own lives as well. Economics is an important part of life and can be illuminated through the characters and plot of a good book.

The following questions can be used to focus students' attention on economic concerns while children's literature is being studied in the classroom. These questions are open-ended. More specific questions may be designed according to the piece of literature being used and to meet the needs of a particular group of students.

How is scarcity represented in this book?
How do the characters deal with scarcity?
What resources are involved in the plot?
What are the economic systems described in the story?
What goals do the characters have?
What decisions do the characters make to try to reach their goals?
What choices are made?
How do the characters in the story depend on each other in various ways?
How does money play a role in the book?
What economic lessons do the main characters learn?
What economic terms are used?
What feelings do the characters display in connection with economic successes or failures?

Chapter Summary

Economics education is an important ingredient in developing students who have the kind of decision-making skills necessary to live happy and productive lives. Although economic concepts may intimidate some teachers, careful examination of economic tasks associated with daily living will demonstrate that all educators have the necessary experience to instruct students in some economic principles.

Quality children's books can be effective tools in helping students explore economic concepts and understand the economies of past decades. Using literature allows students to consider the choices made by the characters they have read about and to critically evaluate whether more productive alternatives were possible. Students must carry with them knowledge of economies past and present if they are to lead us into a new age.

Children's Books

Antle, N. 1993. *Hard times: A story of the Great Depression.* Illus. J. Watling. New York: Viking. This historical novel is about an Oklahoma family during the Great Depression.

Berenstain, S., and J. Berenstain. 1983. *The Berenstain bears and the trouble with money.* New York: Random House. Brother and Sister Bear learn how to save and spend money.

Berger, M., and G. Berger. *Round and round the money goes.* Illus. J. McCreary. Nashville, TN: Hambleton-Hill. This book describes how people have used money, from the times of trading to the invention of coins to the use of paper bills. It ends with a discussion of how money is used in our society today.

Briers, A. 1987. *Money.* New York: Bookwright Press. Chapters in this nonfiction book include, "Coins and Paper Money," "Money Around the World," and "Using Money in the Future."

Brittain, B. 1979. *All the money in the world.* New York: Harper Trophy. What happens when Quentin Stowe, a very ordinary boy, catches a leprechaun? He wishes for all the money in the world, of course! This hilarious novel is entertaining while it touches on the real value of money.

Collier, J. L. 1976. *Give Dad my best.* New York: Four Winds. During the depression, young Jack Lundquist tries to hold his family together despite the seeming indifference of his unemployed father.

Cosgrove, S. 1978. *The muffin muncher.* Los Angeles: Price Stern Sloan. A dragon threatens to burn down the drawbridge if the villagers don't leave him a pile of muffins each day. When the villagers run out of resources, the dragon comes up with a new production plan that results in muffins for everyone.

Curtis, C. P. 1999. *Bud, not Buddy.* New York: Delacorte. A young boy searches for his father, a musician, during the Great Depression.

Elkin, B. 1983. *Money.* Chicago: Children's Press. The focus of this book is the history of money, but it also includes kinds of money, why we use money, and what we do with it.

Evans, W., and C. Rylant. 1994. *Something permanent.* San Diego: Harcourt Brace. The stories of ordinary people living during the Great Depression are told through poetry and photographs.

Facklam, M., and M. Thomas. 1992. *The kids' world almanac of amazing facts about numbers, math, and money.* New York: Pharos Books. This fun-filled book is packed with tips, tricks, and shortcuts to help students understand the use of numbers in our world. One chapter is devoted to money.

Frank, H. 1990. *Tom's lucky quarter.* Illus. P. Mangold. Ada, OK: Garrett Educational Corporation. Tom receives a quarter from his father for washing the car. This story follows Tom's quarter from the bookstore where Tom spends his money to buy a book, to the bakery, to the chimney sweep, to the music man, to the bank, to a restaurant, to Tom's father, and then back to Tom!

Friedrich, E. 1996. *Leah's pony.* Illus. M. Garland. Honesdale, PA: Boyds Mill Press. Leah sells her beloved pony in an attempt to save her family's farm. Moved by her personal sacrifice, the neighbors refuse to bid against her as she buys back the tractor her father needs to farm.

Giff, P. R. 1994. *Count your money with the Polk Street School.* New York: Dell. Ms. Rooney's class is learning all about money and saving. If they learn their lessons well, they'll take a trip together. This easy-to-read chapter book also includes a money board game.

Hager, G. and E. Pianin. 1998. *Balancing Act.* New York: Vintage. Describes how the President works with Congress to pass a balanced budget. For middle school and up.

Hall, D. 1979. *Ox-cart man.* New York: Puffin. Each member of a colonial period family works to produce something the father can trade at the Portsmouth market once a year.

Hall, D. 1997. *The milkman's boy.* New York: Walker. The Graves family has a small dairy and deliver milk house-to-house. The family faces competition from other dairies.

Hesse, K. 1997. *Out of the dust.* New York: Scholastic. Fifteen-year-old Billie Joe struggles to escape the guilt she feels over the death of her mother while enduring the hardships of life in the Oklahoma dust bowl during the depression. Billie Joe's free verse adds a unique dimension to the story.

Hoban, T. 1987. *Twenty-six letters and ninety-nine cents.* New York: Greenwillow Books. Photographs are used to show numerals and their corresponding coin values.

Hutchins, P. 1986. *The doorbell rang.* New York: Mulberry Books. Cookies represent an economic concept—scarcity and choice.

Jaffrey, M. 1995. *Market days: From market to market around the world.* Boston: Bridgewater. This is a colorful book that gives students a glimpse of the wares sold at marketplaces around the world.

Karp, N. J. 1974. *Nothing rhymes with April.* Illus. P. Johnson. New York: Harcourt Brace. Set in the 1930s, this story tells of young Mollie Stone. Mollie enters a poetry contest in hopes of winning a secondhand bicycle her family cannot afford.

Koller, J. F. 1991. *Nothing to fear.* San Diego: Harcourt Brace. When his father moves away to find work and his mother becomes ill, Danny struggles to find a way to help the family during the depression.

Kroeger, M. K. 1996. *Paperboy.* New York: Clarion. Willie Brinkman sells newspapers to help his family. But how do you sell papers carrying news that no one wants to read?

Lowry, L. 1993. *The giver.* Boston: Houghton Mifflin. Young Jonas, a member of a futuristic community, is assigned the task of holding all memories of emotion and sensation for the members of a seemingly perfect society.

Maestro, B. 1993. *The story of money.* Illus. G. Maestro. New York: Clarion. This book tells the history of our money system and includes many interesting and useful facts.

Maestro, B., and G. Maestro. 1988. *Dollars and cents for Harriet.* New York: Crown Publishers. Five stories describe how Harriet the elephant earns five dollars to buy something special.

McMillan, B. 1996. *Jelly beans for sale.* New York: Scholastic. This picture book includes realistic, colorful photographs of real children, jelly beans, and the coins it would take to buy the jelly beans. The history of jelly beans, how to make flavored jelly beans, a note from the author, and information on free jelly bean kits for the classroom are also included.

McNamara, L. 1972. *Henry's pennies.* Illus. E. McCully. New York: Crown. Henry decides how to spend his pennies. He wants to buy a real elephant at a white elephant sale, but he ends up purchasing a white rabbit instead.

Medearis, A. S. 1990. *Picking peas for a penny.* New York: Scholastic. Angeline and John are picking peas for a penny during the Great Depression. This is a rhythmic biographical story that shows just how much a penny can mean.

Meltzer, M. 1969. *Brother can you spare a dime? The Great Depression 1929–1933.* New York: Alfred A. Knopf. Meltzer's historically accurate chronology of events during the Great Depression are told through eyewitness accounts.

Meyers, A. 1992. *Red-dirt Jessie.* New York: Walker. Growing up in the dust bowl during the depression, Jessie struggles to help her father recover from a nervous breakdown while trying to tame an abandoned dog that has become wild.

Merrill, J. 1972. *The toothpaste millionaire.* Boston: Houghton Mifflin. Twelve-year-old Rufus Mayflower protests the high price of toothpaste by producing his own.

Mitchell, M. K. 1993. *Uncle Jed's barbershop.* Illus. J. Ranome. New York: Simon and Schuster. This touching story tells of Uncle Jed traveling throughout southern counties cutting hair and saving money for his dream: his own barbershop.

Mitgutch, A. 1985. *From gold to money.* Minneapolis: Carolrhoda. This book tells the history of money from bartering to paper money.

Naylor, P. R. 1976. *Walking through the dark.* New York: Atheneum. Diary entries provide the vehicle for this poignant account of the effects of the Great Depression on a family, particularly the eldest daughter.

Pittman, H.C. 1986. *A grain of rice.* New York: Hastings House. Clever peasant Pong Lo saves the life of the Emperor's daughter but is denied the right to marry her because he is poor. Thus, he asks for one grain of rice to be doubled every day for one hundred days which makes him a rich man.

Schwartz, D. 1989. *If you made a million.* Illus. S. Kellogg. New York: Lothrop, Lee & Shepard. This humorous book considers choices children have for spending.

Seuss, Dr. 1961. *The sneetches.* New York: Random House. Sylvester McMonkey McBean is an entrepreneur who sells stars as well as removes them for higher and higher prices. This is a good tale for social structure as well.

Seuss, Dr. 1971. *The lorax.* New York: Random House. A Community comes together to set rules to protect the environment.

Shulevitz, U. 1978. *The treasure.* New York: Farrar, Straus and Giroux. Isaac has a dream that tells him to go to the city to find a treasure. Although he travels there, he eventually finds the treasure in his own home.

Shusterman, N. 1988. *The Shadow Club.* Boston: Little, Brown. In this novel, "second best" high school students play anonymous pranks on their rivals and allow vengeance to get out of control.

Snyder, Z. K. 1994. *Cat running.* New York: Delacorte. Cat is a girl growing up in a rural setting during the Great Depression. The big race is coming up and she wants to beat the fastest boy in school, an Okie who lives in a cardboard hut.

Stanley, J. 1992. *Children of the dust bowl.* New York: Crown. Photobiographical account of poor migrant workers from Texas and Oklahoma who traveled to California during the 1930s and opened a school for their children.

Stevens, J. 1995. *Tops and bottoms.* San Diego: Harcourt Brace. Lazy Bear agrees to let Hare farm his land in exchange for splitting the harvest. Hare has Bear choose tops or bottoms. Depending on what Bear chooses, Hare plants crops that produce opposite of Bear's choice.

Taylor, M. D. 1975. *Song of the trees.* Illus. J. Pinkney. New York: Dial. Based on a true story, white lumbermen try to force the Logan family to sell the beautiful trees on their land.

Thesman, J. 1997. *The storyteller's daughter.* Boston: Houghton Mifflin. Quinn, the middle child in a working-class family, copes with life during the Great Depression. She learns secrets about her father's strength and optimism.

Viorst, J. 1978. *Alexander, who used to be rich last Sunday.* Illus. R. Cruz. New York: Macmillan. Alexander's grandparents come to visit and bring Alexander a dollar. Will he spend it wisely?

Wells, R. 1997. *Bunny money.* New York: Dial. Max and Ruby go shopping with their savings. So many choices!

Williams, V. 1982. *A chair for my mother.* New York: Greenwillow. A child and her waitress mother save their money to buy a comfortable armchair.

Williams, V. 1983. *Something special for me.* New York: Greenwillow. Rosa has saved money to buy a birthday present for herself. Instead she chooses something everyone can enjoy.

Zimelman, N. 1992. *How the second grade got $8,205.50 to visit the Statue of Liberty.* Morton Grove, IL: Albert Whitman. The second grade experiences many hilarious setbacks and triumphs as they try to raise money for their trip. In the end, victory is sweet!

Software

Classroom Storeworks by Tom Snyder Productions   1-800-342-0236
Students plan their own store from the ground up in this exciting simulation. Tasks include stocking shelves, accepting coupons on goods, keeping track of inventory, monitoring costs, making change, and reviewing sales reports. (Gr. 2–6)

Coin Changer by Heartsoft   1-800-624-2926
Students practice identifying coins and learn money values in this beginning money software. (Gr. 1–4)

Coin Critters by Nordic   1-800-624-2926
Students work through various lessons and skill levels of coin identification, purchasing, and counting change. Tokens can be earned for completing lessons, and the reward is a coin-munching maze game. (Gr. K–6)

Dollars and Cents Series by Attainment   1-800-624-2926
Three levels of this talking software program engage students in essential money skills. Level I is for beginners needing to practice coin identification and counting money, Level II focuses on spending money and shopping, and Level III involves students in purchasing situations and counting change. (Gr. K–8)

Hot Dog Stand: The Works by Sunburst   1-800-321-7511
Students use different tools to run their own business in a real-world challenge they're sure to enjoy. Students are required to accurately compute, interpret graphs, work backward, analyze data, and estimate as they gather information, make purchasing decisions, keep records, and handle unexpected events. (Gr. 5 and up)

Money Challenge by Gamco   1-800-624-2926
This is a tic-tac-toe game that involves answering questions and earning money to buy squares on the game board. There are twenty-four skill levels in combinations of pennies, nickels, dimes, quarters, half dollars, and dollar bills. (Gr. K–4)

Money Town by Davidson/Simon & Schuster   1-800-624-2926
The Greenstreet Town Park has been closed due to a lack of funds! Students will work, sing, and laugh along with colorfnl characters to earn and save money to reopen the park. (Gr. K–3)

Monopoly by Hasbro Interactive   1-800-771-3772
The classic game of money is now available in computer software. (Gr. 4 and up)

Oregon Trail III by MECC   1-800-685-6322
Students engage in various decision-making processes traveling west on the Oregon, California, or Mormon Trail. The level of expertise is student-selected so the adventure always varies. (Gr. 4 and up)

Prime Time Math by Tom Snyder Productions   1-800-342-0236
This exciting program engages students in math as it relates to real-life situations including wilderness search and rescue operations, crimes, medical emergencies, and fires. (Gr. 4–9)

SimCity 2000 by Maxis   1-800-550-0056
All new scenarios in the lastest version of the classic SimCity program make it especially compelling for young learners as they take over running and planning the ultimate city! (Gr. 7 and up)

SimFarm by Maxis   1-800-550-0056
Students experience the joys and tribulations of running a farm. Lots of good decisions must be made in order to run a farm successfully—this program gives students every opportunity! (Gr. 5 and up)

Web Sites

http://www.economicsamerica.org/standards.html
This is the Web site of the National Council on Economic Education. It includes the standards and benchmarks of the twenty suggested economic standards.

References

Allen, M. G., and R. L. Stevens. 1998. *Middle grades social studies: Teaching and learning for active and responsible citizenship.* 2nd ed. Boston: Allyn and Bacon.

Armstrong, D., and L. Burlbaw. 1991. Cashing in on students' interest in money. *The Social Studies* 82:143–7.

Banaszak, R. 1987. *The nature of economic literacy.* Bloomington, IN: Clearinghouse for Social Studies/Social Science Education. ERIC Digest No. 41.

Dillingham, A. E., N. T. Skaggs, and J. L. Carlson. 1992. *Macroeconomics.* Needham Heights, MA: Allyn and Bacon.

Kehler, A. 1998. Capturing the "economic imagination": A treasury of children's books to meet content standards. *Social Studies and the Young Learner* 11:26–9.

Laney, J. 1993. Economics for elementary school students. *The Social Studies* 84:99–103.

Meszaros, B., and L. Engstrom. 1998. Voluntary national standards in Economics: 20 enduring concepts and benchmarks for beleaguered Teachers. *Social Studies and the Young Learner* 11:7–12.

Mishkin, F. S. 1995. *The economics of money, banking, and financial markets.* New York: HarperCollins College Publishers.

National Council on Economic Education. 1997. *Voluntary national content standards in economics.* New York: National Council on Economic Education.

Savage, T. V., and D. G. Armstrong. 1996. *Effective teaching in social studies.* 3rd ed. New York: Macmillan.

Scott, W. 1995. Personality Parade. *Parade Magazine,* 12 February, 2.

Warmke, R. and R. Muessig. 1980. *The study and teaching of economics.* Columbus, OH: Merrill.

Wentworth, D., and M. Schug. 1993. Fate vs. choices: What economic reasoning can contribute to social studies. *The Social Studies* 84:27–31.

Chapter 11

© David Young-Wolff/
PhotoEdit

Drama in the Social Studies

Gateway to the Past, Pathway to the Future

Pamela A. Nelson
Dominican University

The wise teacher capitalizes on children's natural urge to imitate adult life by making creative dramatics an integral part of social studies instruction.

—*George W. Maxim*
Social Studies and the Elementary School Child, (6th ed.)

Objectives

---ᴄⳟ⳹---

Readers will

- understand the role of drama in social studies instruction;
- discover the role of drama and diversity;
- be able to develop dramatic activities as part of social studies; and
- become familiar with sources and ideas for drama based on the thematic strands of the social studies curriculum.

Introduction

Tim was small of stature, and at age thirteen his face still bore more resemblance to a child than an adult. He wore T-shirts emblazoned with the insignias of a heavy metal rock group, and he carried an enormous black, lizard-grained, three-ring binder to class. According to a student teacher, this was a bit puzzling to the regular teachers because, although the binder measured three inches thick, it was always empty. Tim did not complete assignments and only rarely arrived at the classroom with required materials and supplies. In general, Tim did not do well on examinations, and his participation in class discussion was minimal.

Although Tim consistently lost points for not completing daily assignments, his involvement in a program associated with the study of the period prior to the Civil War was complete and positive. For that program the students traveled from their classroom to a local museum village. There the class met with museum staff members to work with primary source materials that indicated the views of local families on issues of slavery and the Union. The students then proceeded to homes or business staffed by volunteers who portrayed three homemakers of the 1850s. They met the wife of a new attorney and supporter of the Compromise of 1850; the wife of a blacksmith, who was an ardent abolitionist; and the wife of the editor of the newspaper, who strove to remain neutral on political and religious issues of the day.

During their visits with each of the women, the students assumed the role of children in 1856 and engaged in tasks that were common to children of that time. They helped prepare for the visit of a famous Illinois senator, Stephen A. Douglas. They mended clothing for fugitives who were being hidden by "conductors" on the Underground Railroad. They sorted type as apprentices at the newspaper. When they gathered at the schoolhouse to rehearse the choral reading for Douglas's visit, they encountered a fugitive slave and heard the story of his escape and journey to freedom in Canada. In the closing portions of the program, the students were faced with their duty in regard to the Fugitive Slave Law. That law stated that it was illegal to aid fugitives from labor in their flight, and that those who knew of such fugitives were legally bound to make their presence known to appropriate law enforcement agents.

A woman who enacted the role of one of the wives was also involved as a volunteer at Tim's school. Upon her return to the classroom, she was greeted by a number of students with comments on the program. None was more surprising than Tim's. He approached the volunteer and said, "I didn't know. I didn't know. I didn't know all that was going on. All that just livin' and decidin'. It was really hard."

Unfortunately, Tim's initial response to history as a part of the social studies is not that uncommon. Sewall (1988) found that students at all grade levels considered social studies to be their most boring subject, largely blaming dull social studies textbooks as the primary reason. According to Goodlad (1984), junior and senior high students view social studies as the least useful subject in relation to their present and future needs. He also reports that elementary school students perceive social studies to be the most difficult and least liked subject in their curriculum. After stating these findings, Goodlad puzzles over the responses because he believes that the topics covered in the social studies seem intrinsically associated with great human interest and drama. He charges that "something happens to them on the way to the classroom" (212).

The National Council for the Social Studies (NCSS; 1984, 1989a, 1989b) has responded to concerns such as this through a variety of task forces that have reported their findings in the council's journal, *Social Education*. Two regular and respected contributors to that journal, Levstik (1990) and Thornton (1990), believe that resources must be devoted to encouraging and supporting classroom teachers and students as agents of change by identifying vital content and selecting, creating, and evaluating resources and methodologies in the teaching of social studies.

This chapter describes how classroom teachers can use drama as a medium through which students may confront history.

❧ *Drama As It Is Used in Social Studies*

Dorothy Heathcote (Heathcote and Herbert 1985) is generally credited with the new focus on drama as a teaching tool or method that can be used in content areas in the pursuit of knowledge and understanding of key concepts. Teachers who involve students in this type of drama are not as concerned with dramatic elements or performance as they are in providing a means through which students may gain empathetic understanding of the complexity of historical events and problems and a desire to explore and reflect on particular contemporary themes and topics more deeply. According to Huck, Hepler, and Hickman (1996, 784), "The child broadens living and learning experiences by playing the roles of people in the past, in other places, and in different situations."

Drama cannot be said to enable students to access the attitudes and feelings that people of former times had about certain events (Shand, May, and Linnell 1990). It may, however, make it possible for students to generate feelings and meanings that relate to those former times or other situations. Drama enables students to construct and approach the multiple realities that are believed to have existed at different times and in different cultures and to do so in very concrete and tangible ways (Leigh and Reynolds 1997).

The most recent use of drama may hold the most promise in the social studies classroom when one considers the current emphases on reaching the process of historical inquiry and developing accurate content knowledge (Bradley Commission 1989; Egan 1986; NCSS 1994; Ravitch and Finn 1987).

Drama relates to preparing students for participatory citizenship as problem solvers and decision makers who can consider events or issues from multiple perspectives. First, drama provides a nurturing environment for the development of the attitudes and values that may encourage children into active participation as citizens. Second, drama provides an environment that permits and encourages individuals to represent and respond to experience in a variety of ways and from multiple perspectives. Finally, drama provides an environment in which students must work together and make decisions that will truly affect the course of action in the drama itself.

When we turn to the development of attitudes and values, we enter a unique domain. Kohlberg (1976), Selman (1971), and Taba (1955) have provided the theoretical and research support for methods that facilitate the development of attitudes, values, and the ability to consider issues empathetically from a variety of perspectives. Their findings indicate that in promoting the development of attitudes and empathetic perspective taking, teachers need to present students with dilemmas in story form that involve characters to whom the students can relate in some way. Students then need opportunities to discuss the dilemmas and consider choices made and options available from their perspectives as observers and as participants in the dilemma situations. Opportunities to draw conclusions, to propose possible solutions, and then to reflect on and discuss what has been proposed are essential.

Putnam (1991) relates her observations of a kindergarten dramatization of the concept of civil rights based on the true story of Rosa Parks. Over a three-day period, children heard the story of the seamstress who was arrested for her refusal to move to the back of a city bus. They learned of subsequent events that served as the beginning of the civil rights movement of the 1960s. The students then assumed

Drama affords students the opportunity to develop empathy for others. In this case, students are in a one-room schoolhouse on the prairie. Through involvement, children transform factual information into meaningful schemata.

© Martin Mitchell Museum

and enacted the roles of Parks, Martin Luther King Jr., the police chief, and members of the community—both African American and white. As students reenacted the drama and changed roles, they had repeated opportunities to vicariously experience the event from different perspectives.

Knight (1989) and Lee (1983) provide additional support for the significance of perspective taking and empathy in the development of historical and social understanding. In particular, Lee believes that while mature historians and social scientists must merely be willing to entertain different beliefs and value system, children who are studying the same events or issues may need to first share the point of view of the individuals involved if they are later to move to the more mature position. If children are not encouraged to develop the skill of empathizing early in life, Lee fears that they will find it difficult, if not impossible, to develop a mature sense of empathy or perspective taking.

In regard to the development of multiple intelligences, Howard Gardner (1983, 1991) recommends approaches that would permit students to become deeply involved in a topic so that they can acquire a rounded view of a situation. According to Gardner,

> Students must have the frequent opportunities to adopt multiple perspectives and stance with reference to the material in question. In the absence of such opportunities, students seem fated to maintain a one-dimensional view of the topic or material. When students are given numerous chances to approach the materials through a variety of disciplinary and personal stances, however, the limits of [stereotypes] should become increasingly clear to them and the complexity entailed in any phenomenon should become increasingly apparent." (237)

Levstick and Barton (1996) also support these earlier views when they speak of drama as one of the arts that demands that students empathetically consider multiple facets of a situation within complex contexts. Through drama, students willingly consider alternative perspectives and possible motives in relation to historic events as they situate themselves in these events, considering how it would have felt and what choices were open to the people of a particular period, including the leaders.

Drama affords students the opportunity not only to consider choices and options that were or are available to individuals at a particular point in time but also to "try out" the options and "live through" the consequences of those choices in a protected environment.

Drama As a Medium That Offers Alternative Forms of Response to Content

Jerome Bruner (1966) identifies three systems through which human beings represent their experiences for consideration, storage, retrieval, and application. He calls these systems, or forms, the enactive, the iconic, and the symbolic. In the enactive form, knowledge is translated into action because it is difficult to express in words. Humans represent experience in this form when it is easier to demonstrate, show, or act out what they know. In the iconic form, knowledge or understanding is translated into visual or other sensory organizational systems. Pictures, charts, and diagrams are examples of iconic representation of experience. The third form of representation, the symbolic, is the most sophisticated of the three systems and is the last to develop. It is best represented by both written and spoken language. Written records, oral histories, and stories are examples of experience that are preserved through symbolic representation. It is in this form that children come into contact with history most often in school and society. Bruner is quick to point out that while adults have command of all three forms, the first two are the most developed in children. He encourages those who work with and for children to recognize the importance of accepting all three forms as valid and appropriate ways of representing experience.

According to Bruner (1977, 13),

> It is only when . . . basic ideas are put in formalized terms as equations or elaborated verbal concepts that they are out of reach of the young child, if he has not first understood them intuitively and had a chance to try them out on his own. The early teaching of science, mathematics, social studies, and literature should be designed to teach these subjects with scrupulous intellectual honesty, but with emphasis upon the intuitive grasp of ideas and upon the use of these basic ideas. . . . They can grasp the idea of tragedy and the basic human plight represented in myth. But they cannot put these ideas into formal language or manipulate them as grownups can.

Drama permits students to make use of all three forms of representation as they express their ideas or understanding of historical events. Drama allows students to show others what they understood or wonder about through their dramatic play, through drawings and construction, and through research and writing (Myers and Philbin 1990; Vass 1992).

✎ *Drama As a Basis for Interaction with Others*

Students must truly engage with one another when drama is used in the classroom, thereby avoiding being what Stahl (1992, 8) refers to as "academic loners." Participation in drama allows students to work as creators, directors, and decision makers and to respond to the work and suggestions of others in functional, meaningful, and relevant contexts (Lehr 1983). Students also have the opportunity to share and celebrate the work of others and to better reflect their own work (Heathcote and Herbert 1985; O'Neill 1985). In improvisational dialogues, students become attuned to seeking meaning. They can also become more involved with an author's thoughts or those of a character and can better reflect on their own point of view (Booth 1985).

Diversity and Drama

Drama also allows children from different ethnic and economic backgrounds and achievement levels to work together in small groups. This finding was noted by Johnson (1983) and Ritchie (1991) in regard to cross-cultural understanding. Gimmestad and DeChiara (1982) found that participation in ethnic drama decreases children's verbalizations of prejudices. Most important, they found that "when small heterogeneous groups of children are asked to work together on learning tasks where some success is guaranteed, they tend to develop positive attitudes toward each other" (49).

Drama participation gives students the only opportunity to use language for purposes and in ways that may not be available to them in everyday life. In assuming roles, students speak, act, and think as their character would regardless of how unlike themselves those characters may be. Students also find themselves in circumstances that they may never have had the opportunity or misfortune to encounter in real life.

During periods provided for planning and reflection when students are out of role, they use language to convey their thoughts to others and to learn the thoughts of others. Students have opportunities to use language to let others know what they need, to control others, to establish relationships, to express pride, to question, to convey information, to negotiate rules and regulations, to record what has happened, to imagine, and to make jokes. Dramatization gives students opportunities to use the various functions of language in cooperative groups as they negotiate with classmates. Johnson and Johnson (1992) and Slavin (1983) have found that such opportunities for students produce greater feelings of self-efficiency and involvement among students as well as increase mastery of content.

When we consider these findings, we see a basis of support for using drama in the social studies classroom. As Johnson and O'Neill (1985, 90) state:

> Dramatizing makes it possible to isolate an event or to compare one event with
> another, to look at events that have happened to other people in other places and
> times perhaps, or to look at one's own experiences after the event, within the
> safety of knowing that just at this moment it is not really happening. We can,
> however, feel that it is happening because drama uses the same rules we find in

life. People exist in their environment, living a moment at a time and taking those decisions which seem reasonable in light of their present knowledge about the current state of affairs. The difference is that in life we have many other things to consider at the same time and often cannot revise a decision taken, except in the long term. So drama can be a kind of playing at or practice of living, tuning up those areas of feelings-capacity and expression-capacity as well as social-capacity.

Drama can provide opportunities for students to explore the attitudes, values, and perspectives that others hold and also to consider their own. Drama allows students to interpret and respond to historical content intuitively through movement, construction, and words. It also provides the opportunity for students to use language and problem-solving skills for real and authentic purposes as they work with peers in their classrooms.

Journals offer children an opportunity to reflect before they become involved in a drama.

© Lawrence Migdale

❧ *Initiating Drama in the Classroom*

In preparing to use drama in the social studies classroom, it is helpful to work through three planning phases and then plunge in, returning to the same three phases again and again. First, teachers need to engage in a preparation period of reflection on the strengths and needs of their students and on their personal weaknesses. Second, teachers need to investigate possible topics and resources related to selected and required topics. Third, teachers need to become familiar with new planning formats that will guide them in their work with students in the classroom.

Preparatory Reflection

Journaling helps many teachers during the initial phase of adding drama to the social studies program. Reflection is often aided by asking and writing about very basic questions.

Teachers must first consider the students who will be the choreographers of the drama once it has begun:

- What are their interests?
- Which issues seem to be of greatest concern to them?
- What topics might be accessible to or developmentally appropriate for these students in terms of their social and emotional characteristics, knowledge base, or academic skills in working with data?

In the Classroom Mini Lesson

Helping Students Through the Doorway to the Past

1. Select a theme or event.
2. Share related literature, films, and artifacts with the class.
3. Create a dialogue or improvisation based on the theme or event with a colleague as a model.
4. Show or tell about the resources that helped you develop your role.
5. Make resources available to the students in the classroom.
6. Present the basic idea of the plot or problem.
7. Work with students to develop the setting in which the drama will take place.
8. Have each student work to develop his or her character.
9. Divide students into partners. Have students assume their roles and do dialogues with their partners.
10. Give the starting point of the drama and begin.

Teachers must then consider the unique perspectives, talents, and abilities that they themselves bring to the classroom:

- What life experiences, course work, and networks throughout the community, nation, and world can they offer to the classroom?
- What former travels or occupations might yield new insight and understanding about people as well as the regions and cultures in which those people live?
- To what areas might they bring unique perspectives?

Teachers must consider the required curriculum and local sources:

- Which topics are most associated with high interest and ready resources— human, media, artifacts, and time?
- Which topics from the curriculum have been especially appealing to the students?
- How much time would it take to add drama to one unit?
- Which goals and objectives of the current curriculum are essential and which may be considered lower priority?
- Which of those goals and objectives might better be met through work in drama?
- What readily available objects or artifacts from homes, the community, or the school might be springboards to drama?

Finally, teachers must find others who have expertise in using drama with children or who are interested novices:

- Are there other individuals in the building, district, local college, or community who have expertise or interest?
- When and where could meetings for sharing take place?

Teachers who have used drama with their classes stress the need for support from and collaboration with other teachers. Such support groups offer ideas and encouragement as well as sounding boards to teachers who are interested in trying something new. Atwell (1998), Graves (1983), and Routman (1994), among others, have emphasized this and have outlined the benefits of such support systems for teachers.

At the end of this planning phase, classroom teachers should have additional insights about their students and themselves, have identified a topic or theme to investigate, and have made contact with others who are engaged in the same process.

Investigating Resources

Egan (1986, 47) said, "The educational achievement is not to make the strange seem familiar, but to make the familiar seem strange. It is seeing the wonderful that lies hidden in what we take for granted that matters educationally." Teachers must be willing to look at a topic or concept through a variety of lenses so that the wonder of the ordinary can be appreciated and brought from the textbook into personal focus.

Some of the resources to be examined and gathered will be traditional. Teachers and students need background information. This is most often provided by secondary sources—textbooks, trade books, the Internet—that give overviews of topics or events. In working with drama, however, teachers must also locate resources that will give individual perspective and a sense of the dramatic to the topic.

Quite often such resources come from fiction and personal narratives, primary source material, and artifacts. Literature for children or young adults that deals with social studies topics is plentiful and of high quality. Each year, listings and reviews of the outstanding children's books for the social studies are published in the April/May issue of *Social Education,* the journal of the National Council for the Social Studies. Examples of primary sources would be letters, diaries, court transcripts, oral histories, and so on. A number of these—for example, the narratives of those who were enslaved, which were collected by the Works Project Administration writers during the 1930s—are excellent sources. If excerpts are carefully chosen and organized, many are readable and accessible to upper-elementary-level students. Artifacts or objects may be found in thrift shops or borrowed from museums or libraries. The children themselves may be able to bring in or make objects that are like those used by people of earlier times. Artifacts, when analyzed and studied, serve as primary sources for students who then begin to order and structure their own personal understanding of the past (Levstik and Barton 1996; Nelson, 1992).

Teachers need to talk about topics with colleagues, asking them for suggestions of material and approaches to use. Talking with others provides insights on what has been done and where gaps occur. Discussion with colleagues often provides a base from which to begin.

Librarians may also be a great help. Teachers may begin with the learning center specialist of the children's librarian at the local library. In addition, librarians in the adult departments of the local library—for example, the reference librarians and those in charge of government documents, interlibrary loans, media, and microfilms—are often willing to give their time and share their considerable expertise. Once they are given an idea of what was initially interesting and compelling about the topic and the unit objective, they can be a great asset to planning.

Most communities also contain a considerable number of resource persons or groups who are often forgotten in terms of resource location and development (see the Teaching Resources section at the end of the chapter). Teachers find that resources from the community come serendipitously, so they need to be prepared and prepare others to seize opportunities when they surface. For example, an important resource for the pre–Civil War program described at the beginning of this chapter was a bill of sale for two slaves: a seven-year-old girl and her three-year-old brother. This item was brought in by a resident who read about the forthcoming program in the local newspaper.

Fines and Verrior (1974) and Morgan and Saxton (1987) insist on the importance of teachers becoming familiar with the most current and valid information and resources on selected topics so that students can be guided toward sources that represent and accurately portray a variety of perspectives. Levstik (1986) also cautions that the emotional loading of narratives used in studying particular issues may lead students to identify with the main characters of the narratives to the exclusion of other views. The teacher's ability to present students with alternative views and rationales for those views, Levstik believes, will help students move beyond a myopic approach to issues and topics. Print, media, and artifacts that support insights into many facets of issues need to be available to students who are using drama as a learning tool.

Developing and Utilizing Specialized Planning Approaches

The planning formats with which teachers are most familiar (Ausubel 1960; Gagne, Briggs, and Wager 1988) were designed to enhance the learning, retention, and retrieval of large amounts of verbal material and skills in relatively short periods of time. They may not be the most effective planning guides when working with drama in the classroom. Egan (1997, 1986) offers one alternative planning model, the "story form model," that may provide a more effective planning tool for experience with drama.

Egan suggests that selected topics be considered as stories to be told rather than information to be disseminated. The most compelling stories, he notes, involve powerful and universal life themes that attract students. In using Egan's model, the teacher's first task is to identify those life themes or big ideas that may be involved in required or supplementary content. The Underground Railroad program mentioned at the beginning of this chapter coordinated closely with the state goals and benchmarks, local goals, and the textbook. The life theme that was considered was the duty of ordinary citizens of a democracy who found the laws of the state in conflict with what they considered to be a higher law.

Stories have identifiable trouble and often compelling characters. They also have a rhythm: a beginning, in which the topic or theme is introduced; a middle, in which something happens to complicate things; a climax, in which some sort of resolution action takes place; and a conclusion, which brings a degree of closure. The teacher's second task is to make use of story rhythm in planning and generating options for events.

The following questions provide guidelines for the teacher in this process of character and story development:

- Who are the people who took part in this event?
- Who are the people who were affected by this?
- What were their ordinary lives like?
- How old were they?
- Who were their friends and relatives?
- What role or roles should the teacher assume?
- What will be the exact words and stimuli used to introduce the drama to the students?
- What objects or artifacts might be used to draw the students in?
- What will compel this particular group of students to participate?
- What areas of the classroom, buildings, or grounds will be used?
- How will space, light, or furniture be arranged in the area or areas?
- Where will the teacher and students look to find supplies, resources, pictures, and objects to help develop understanding of the characters or the situation?
- How best may students be helped through the initial phases of the drama?
- How may the drama be moved if it gets stuck?
- How may the teacher help students bring the drama to a conclusion?

The teacher's final task must be to reflect on the drama—on what has occurred. Students need to be allowed to reflect on their experiences. The teacher must determine the structure of that opportunity and determine what guidance will be offered:

- Where will it take place?
- What options will be offered for students to respond to the drama?
- Will students talk, write, or draw about their experiences?
- How much time will be allotted to individual response and to group response?
- Will students share their impressions with those who participated in the drama or with other significant individuals in the school or community who were not present?
- How will students be led from the drama to demonstrate competencies related to national, state, local, and personal thematic strands and goals?

The importance of the final guide for reflection cannot be underestimated. It supports the call for a balanced approach in the process of utilizing story and drama in the social studies of VanSledright and Brophy (1992). As a result of their research they say:

> [Lessons] might include dramatic, story-like accounts that could provide the formal or syntactic structure for developing historical understanding, but it would need to include patterns and details to provide the substantive content of the chronological precursors to U.S. history. In this way, the students would learn a more balanced and reflexive process for combining the formal (storytelling) and substantive (evidence-based) dimensions, a process in which they already are partially engaged, that would contextualize their growing elaborations with appreciation of the fact that history [social studies] is not just more of the fictional storytelling that they have become familiar with through several years of language arts instruction. (1992, 853)

Swartz (1988) emphasizes that after initial planning, drama should be added gradually so that experiences can be as positive as possible for both teachers and students. The next section provides suggestions and resources for such beginnings.

ᔆ Resources and Ideas for Drama

The suggestions offered in this section use a variety of dramatic techniques to involve students with historical and contemporary topics common to most social studies curricula. In each case, the topic is introduced or developed through young adults and children's literature. The suggestion may be developed more fully to form entire units. Each highlights "big ideas," or key concepts and generalizations in the social studies (Banks, Banks, and Clegg 1998). These big ideas should not be identified for the students prior to engaging in the drama itself. The topics also relate to the thematic strands that have been identified as organizers for the social studies curriculum by the most recent curriculum task force of the National Council for the Social Studies (1994).

ᔆ Drama and Thematic Strands of the Social Studies Curriculum

I. Culture

Social studies programs should develop ideas concerning the unique systems that human beings have created, learned, or adapted to meet their needs so that they will be better able to relate to people in our nation and the world (NCSS 1994, 21).

KEY CONCEPT: Traditions

GENERALIZATION: All societies have a set of traditions that help maintain group solidarity and identity.

Literature Stimulus
Crews, *Big Mama's* (1991)
Dooley, *Everybody Cooks Rice* (1991)
Garza, *Family Pictures/Cuadros de Familia* (1990)
Rylant, *The Relatives Came* (1985)

Dramatic Roles
After reading these books, have students pretend that many years have passed. A scrapbook of the events has been found. Have one student assume the role of an elderly relative who participated as a child. Have another student assume the role of a child who will hear the stories associated with the family gatherings. As an option, students may gather stories about their own family members or individuals whom they are studying, make a scrapbook, and then retell the incidents that are illustrated.

KEY CONCEPT: Rite of passage

GENERALIZATION: All societies have traditional ceremonies and rituals to signal and mark important status changes in a person's life.

Literature Stimulus
Cha, *Dia's Story Cloth: The Hmong People's Journey to Freedom* (1996)
Fournot, *The Patchwork Quilt* (1985)
Guback, *Luka's Quilt* (1994)
Shea, *The Whispering Cloth: A Refugee's Story* (1995)
Freedman, *A Cloak for the Dreamer* (1994)

Dramatic Roles:
In each of the preceding stories, the children of the family are given or assume the task of creating a needlework masterpiece. After reading the stories, arrange students in groups of five and then have them assume roles of other family members—siblings, parents, uncles, aunts, cousins. At that point the "family members" should discuss the changes that they have seen in the main character since the completion of the project. After the role plays, have the group share the changes that they have talked about.

II. Time, Continuity, and Change

Social studies programs should help students understand their historical roots and locate themselves in time. Students should be given opportunities to learn the processes that historians use as well as to gather information about what has happened in the past and its effects on the present and future (NCSS 1994, 22).

KEY CONCEPT: Historical bias

GENERALIZATION: Historians attempt to reconstruct past events based on sources and artifacts that have been left behind. They must judge the accuracy and authenticity of the data. Their work is influenced by personal biases as well as those of the time in which they live and the audience for whom they are working.

Literature Stimulus

Ballard, *Exploring the Titanic* (1988)
Burgess, *Indians of the Northwest: Traditions, History, Legends, and Life* (1997)
Goor and Goor, *Pompeii: Exploring a Roman Ghost Town* (1986)
Reinhard, *Discovering the Inca Ice Maiden* (1998)
Teele, *Step into the Chinese Empire* (1998)

Dramatic Roles

Use an artifact very much like those items that are described in the books. After reading one of the books, have two students assume the roles of workers who have made a great discovery during the exploration. Have another assume the role of the leader of this particular expedition who wants to take the artifacts back to the museum that is underwriting the cost of the work. Have a fourth student assume the role of a famous local archaeologist who does not want artifacts moved from the site. Have the remaining class members assume roles of residents of the nearby community who have come to the site after hearing of the discovery.

KEY CONCEPT: Continuity and change

GENERALIZATION: Although there are constants that run through time, human society is also characterized by change. Conflicts, which have some negative effects, are often the impetus for effective change.

Literature Stimulus
Coles, *The Story of Ruby Bridges* (1995)
Golenbock, *Teammates* (1990)
Lester, *To Be a Slave* (1968)
Lyons, *Letters from a Slave Girl: The Story of Harriet Jacobs* (1992)
McKissack and McKissack, *Black Diamond: The Story of the Negro Baseball
      Leagues* (1994)
Turner, *Follow in Their Footsteps* (1997)

Dramatic Roles
The books suggested for this section represent stories of African Americans in both the nineteenth and twentieth centuries in the United States. Following the sharing of the book, ask one child to assume a role like that played by Works Project Administration workers who gathered the narratives of African Americans. Have another student assume the role of one of the main characters. Have several others assume the roles of individuals who witnessed the events. In each case, it is now fifty years later. Have the writers interview the main characters or witnesses regarding their memories of the actual events and of the impact of those events on the present.

III. People, Places, and Environments

Social studies programs should help students locate geographic regions, towns, cities, and natural and man-made features. Students should also learn of relationships that exist between human beings and the environment (NCSS 1994, 23).

KEY CONCEPT: Human–environment interactions

GENERALIZATION: People work to meet their needs and create places that reflect cultural values and ideas within geographic regions that have certain features.

Literature Stimulus
Begay, *Navajo: Visions and Voices Across the Mesa* (1995)
The Dine of the Eastern Region of the Navajo Reservation, *Oral History Stories of
      The Long Walk: Hweeldi Baa Hane* (1990)
O'Dell, *Sing Down the Moon* (1970)
Sneve, *The Navajo: A First Americans Book* (1993)

Dramatic Roles

After locating the reservation area on a map and discussing the physical features of the area, read O'Dell's *Sing Down the Moon*. Have the students pantomime packing and saying farewell to their homes and their land as they begin the march to Fort Sumner. After their pantomimes, have students share their feelings as well as the list of items they'd try to take with them.

IV. Individual Development and Identity

Social studies programs should help students understand the ways in which they learn and make choices. They also need opportunities to come to know how personal identity and decision-making processes are shaped by culture, groups, and institutions (NCSS 1994, 24).

KEY CONCEPT: Immigration

GENERALIZATION: When people believe that their basic needs and wants may be better or more safely met in another region, they may choose to move. That decision is influenced by personal, cultural, and institutional values and mores.

Literature Stimulus

Bierman, *Journey to Ellis Island: How My Father Came to America* (1998)
Bunting, *A Day's Work* (1994)
Caseley, *Apple Pie and Onions* (1987)
Fraser, *Ten Mile Day and the Building of the Transcontinental Railroad* (1993)
Jacobs, *Ellis Island: New Hope in a New Land* (1990)
Levinson, *Watch the Stars Come Out* (1985)
Strom, *Quilted Landscape: Conversations with Young Immigrants* (1996)

Dramatic Roles

After reading the books, have half of the students assume the roles of relatives, children, and friends of people who have decided to leave their homelands. Have the other half assume the roles of individuals who will be leaving their homes for the United States. Have those students tell their friends and relatives why they have decided to risk leaving, how they will deal with hardships, and what they have as goals or hopes.

V. Individuals, Groups, and Institutions

Social studies programs need to help students know how institutions are formed, what controls and influences them, how they control and influence individuals, and how they can be maintained or changed (NCSS 1994, 25).

KEY CONCEPT: Social organization

GENERALIZATION: Every society consists of smaller units such as classes, families, clubs, communities, and so on. Each of these social units participates in different ways in the total culture to help people meet their needs or to provide for the basic needs and wants of those in the society.

A drama may evolve from a portion of a children's literature book such as the spinning of wool.
© Martin Mitchell Museum

Literature Stimulus
Gates, *Blue Willow* (1972)
Hesse, *Out of the Dust* (1998)
Hunt, *No Promises in the Wind* (1970)
Stanley, *Children of the Dust Bowl: The True Story of the School at Weedpatch Camp* (1992)

Dramatic Roles
Have three or four students be photographers and journalists who have come to do stories so the plight of these individuals can be addressed. Divide the remaining students into groups so that each photographer and journalist has a group of students to photograph and to talk with as the characters go about their daily business. Have the students role-play common activities mentioned in the books.

VI. Power, Authority, and Governance

Social studies programs should help students understand the historical development of structures of power, authority, and governance in this country as well as in other parts of the world. This would include the study of the role of individuals in a democratic society (NCSS 1994, 26).

KEY CONCEPT: Authority

GENERALIZATION: When authorities feel that the ideology or general well-being of their political system is threatened, they may take extreme action against individuals and groups, denying them the basic rights guaranteed under the laws of the state.

Literature Stimulus

Hamanaka, *The Journey: Japanese Americans, Racism and Renewal* (1990)
Mochizuki, *Baseball Saved Us* (1993)
Spier, *We the People: The Constitution of the United States of America* (1987)

Dramatic Roles

Two of the books deal with the treatment of Japanese Americans in the United States during World War II. The third book offers a pictorial interpretation of the Constitution and of the rights and responsibilities that individuals have in our country. Conduct a congressional hearing on the internment. Have a group of five to ten students assume the role of government officials who will conduct the hearings. Have at least ten other students assume roles of spectators and reporters. Have the remaining students assume roles of Japanese American people who were interned at one of the camps during World War II and who have been asked to tell of their experiences.

VII. Production, Distribution, and Consumption

Social studies programs should help students examine questions of what is to be produced, how production is to be organized, how goods and services are to be distributed, and how unlimited wants and needs will be met with limited resources (NCSS 1994, 27).

KEY CONCEPT: Resources, wants, and needs

GENERALIZATION: Producers of goods and services exchange with others to get resources. Since resources are limited, and wants and needs are relatively unlimited, the situation creates a need for decision making. Choices are based on the individual's value system and the relative scarcity and need for goods, services, or resources.

Literature Stimulus

Field, *General Store* (1988)
Freedman, *Kids at Work* (1994)
Parker, *Stolen Dreams: Portraits of Working Children* (1998)
Spedden, *Polar: The Titanic Bear* (1994)

Dramatic Roles

The preceding books deal with children who lived at the turn of the century and in the twentieth century. The lives of children who worked for a living differed greatly from those of children of the wealthy. Help students create a "general store" from the time period by drawing murals based on Rachel Field's poem and the description of stores in Spedden's book. After reading the books, have one-half of the students assume roles of children who worked. Have the other half assume the roles of the wealthy. Give each ten cents. Have them pantomime their selection process in the store you have created. After their experience, have students share what they discovered about their choices.

VIII. Science, Technology, and Society

Social studies programs should provide students with opportunities to consider the implications of technology in our lives and of the ethical issues surrounding its use (NCSS 1994, 28).

KEY CONCEPT: Technological change

GENERALIZATION: Technological change alters established relationships among cities, towns, people, and the environment.

Literature Stimulus

Cherry, *A River Ran Wild* (1992)
Hiscock, *The Big Rivers: The Missouri, the Mississippi, and the Ohio* (1998)
Jackson, *Turn of the Century* (1998)
Millard, *A Street Through Time: A 12,000 Year Walk Through History* (1999)
Von Tscharner, Fleming, and The Townscape Institute, *New Providence: A Changing Cityscape* (1987)

Dramatic Roles

Have each student assume the role of a person who grew up in one of the towns, moved away, and has returned for a high school reunion. Have the students design picture postcards that might have been available at the time of the visit. While they are still in role, have them write messages to friends who weren't able to come to the reunion. In those messages they should tell about the changes they've noticed in the community because of new technologies.

IX. Global Connections

Social studies programs should offer students opportunities to understand the increasingly important and diverse global connections among world societies. They should be able to identify national interest and global priorities and how those may contribute to or offer solutions to problems throughout the world (NCSS 1994, 29).

KEY CONCEPT: Exploration

GENERALIZATION: Explorations that people made into what were, to them, strange territories resulted in tremendous cultural exchange as well as conflict between different cultural and ethnic groups. In general, more technologically advanced cultures have assimilated or destroyed cultures that were less technologically developed.

Literature Stimulus
Sis, *Follow the Dream: The Story of Christopher Columbus* (1991)
Yolen, *Encounter* (1992)
Johnson, *Tomatoes, Potatoes, Corn, and Beans: How the Foods of the Americas
    Changed Eating Around the World* (1998)

Dramatic Roles
After reading the books, which tell of Columbus's journey across the ocean, have the students assume the roles of the Taino people who were present for the initial meeting with the Spanish and for the exchange of gifts. The teacher may assume the role of the elder. The improvisation should be conducted in the hope of determining a course of action toward the outsiders. The question might be whether to continue to work to develop relationships with these newcomers or to imprison or kill them.

X. Civic Ideas and Practices
Social studies programs should offer students an understanding of the civic ideals and practices of citizenship in our democratic republic and of other forms of political organization in other parts of the world (NCSS 1994, 30).

KEY CONCEPT: Political participation

GENERALIZATION: Private citizens act by voting, lobbying, campaigning, attending political meetings, preparing petitions, and running for office.

Literature Stimulus
Blos, *Old Henry* (1987)
Bunting, *Smoky Night* (1994)
Martin, *The Green Truck Garden Giveaway: A Neighborhood Story
    and Almanac* (1998)
Provensen and Provensen, *Shaker Lane* (1987)

Dramatic Roles
These stories tell of the lives of citizens in this country, and the events they experience in their communities. In each of these cases, the neighbors have prejudices regarding each other, and they ultimately come together. Select one of the stories and have each student assume the role of a member of one of the communities. Arrange for each student to have a partner who is from the "other" community. Move the students beyond the ending of the story to subsequent days. What will happen?

KEY CONCEPT: Pressure Groups

GENERALIZATION: Individuals and groups resort to extreme methods to change public policy when they believe that authorities are unresponsive to their needs or that legitimate channels for the alleviation of grievances are ineffective.

Literature Stimulus

Bachrach, *Tell Them We Remember: The Story of the Holocaust* (1994)
Cox, *Fiery Vision: The Life and Death of John Brown* (1998)
Haskins and Benson, *Bound for America: The Forced Migration of Africans to the New World* (1998)
Innocenti, *Rose Blanche* (1985)
Oppenheim, *The Lily Cupboard* (1992)

Dramatic Roles

Ask one of the students to assume the role of a child who sees his or her best friend being arrested or taken away. Have a second student assume the role of the soldier or slaver, and a third student assume the role of the friend. Have four or five other children involved as friends and observers who happen to be nearby.

Chapter Summary

Drama used in the social studies classroom may contribute significantly to the development of the attitudes, values, and group skills that promote healthy interrelationships and cooperation among our families, schools, communities, the nation, and the world. Used in conjunction with literature and other resources, drama can bring back the human characteristics and concerns—the faces—that textbooks and expository teaching methods may strip from history and social studies in attempts to ensure coverage. When Louise Rosenblatt (1982, 1985) refers to the process of evoking meaning from text she speaks of two stances that could be assumed by the individual who is reading or listening to text. One stance involves individuals in a meaning-making process in which the goal is "carrying away" needed information. The other involves students in "living through" the experiences described. Rosenblatt (1983) believes that her transactional view of the meaning-making process offers much to the development of citizens because it acknowledges and values the importance of both stances. She goes on to say:

> Of all the elements which entered into the educational process—except, of course, the actual personal relationship and activities which make up the community life of the school—literature possesses the greatest potentialities for . . . direct assimilation of ideas and attitudes. For literature offers the closest approach to the experiences of actual life. It enables the youth to "live through" much that in abstract terms would be meaningless to him. He comes to know intimately, more intimately perhaps than would be possible in actual life, many personalities. He shares vicariously their struggles and perplexities and achievements. He becomes a part of strange environments, or he sees with new emotions the conditions and the lives about him. And these vicarious experiences have at least something of the

warmth and color and emotion that life itself possesses. . . . literature can be an important means of bringing about the linkage between intellectual perception and emotional drive that we have agreed to be essential to any vital learning process (Rosenblatt 1983, 214–5)

In teaching history within social studies, whether we deal with written or spoken words, we have been most focused on those aspects that enable students to "carry away" information. We tend not to value as highly those stances that permit and encourage students to live through experiences described in text. Yet it is those experiences that may stimulate the interest of students to find out more about the past and provide for the development of perspective-taking abilities so critical to citizens in a democracy.

Drama also makes the "living through" of content possible for students who may not make connections as they read or prepare daily assignments. Drama was the stepping-stone for Tim, described at the beginning of this chapter. He engaged in a decision-making process like that of the three women of the nineteenth century. He came to know one fugitive slave who had made the decision to flee toward an uncertain future rather than stay with the security of what was well known. Tim had to struggle with the dilemma of whether his obligation as a citizen was to obey or oppose laws that he believed to be unjust, knowing that it was those very laws that protected his rights to protest them. Drama helped this student to view the past, his present, and possibly situations that he will encounter in the future in new ways.

Children's Books

Bachrach, S. 1994. *Tell them we remember: The story of the Holocaust.* Boston: Little, Brown.

Ballard, R. 1988. *Exploring the Titanic.* New York: Scholastic.

Begay, S. 1995. *Navajo: Visions and voices across the mesa.* New York: Scholastic.

Bierman, C. 1988. *Journey to Ellis Island: How my father came to America.* New York: Hyperion.

Blos, J. 1987. *Old Henry.* New York: William Morrow.

Bunting, E. 1994. *A day's work.* New York: Clarion Books.

Bunting, E. 1994. *Smoky night.* New York: Harcourt Brace.

Burgess, T. (Ed.) 1997. *Indians of the Northwest: Traditions, history, legends, and life.* Philadelphia, PA: Petre Press.

Caseley, J. 1987. *Apple pie and onions.* New York: Greenwillow.

Cha, D. 1996. *Dia's story cloth: The Hmong people's journey of freedom.* New York: Lee and Low.

Cherry, L. 1992. *A river ran wild.* New York: Harcourt Brace.

Coles, R. 1995. *The story of Ruby Bridges.* New York: Scholastic.

Cox, C. 1998. *Fiery vision: The life and death of John Brown.* New York: Scholastic.

Crews, D. 1991. *Big Mama's.* New York: Greenwillow Books.

The Dine of the Eastern Region of the Navajo Reservation. 1990. *Oral history stories of The Long Walk: Hweeldi Baa Hane.* Washington, DC: U.S. Department of Education.

Dooley, N. 1991. *Everybody cooks rice.* Minneapolis: Carolrhoda Books.

Field, R. 1988. *General store.* New York: Greenwillow.

Fournot, V. 1985. *The patchwork quilt.* New York: Dial.

Fraser, M. 1993. *Ten mile day and the building of the transcontinental railroad.* New York: Henry Holt.

Freedman, A. 1994. *A cloak for the dreamer.* New York: Scholastic.

Freedman, R. 1994. *Kids at work.* New York: Clarion Books.

Garza, C. L. 1990. *Family pictures/Cuadros de familia.* Emeryville, CA: Children's Book Press.

Gates, D. 1972. *Blue Willow.* New York: Viking.

Golenbock, P. 1990. *Teammates.* New York: Harcourt Brace.

Goor, R., and N. Goor. 1986. *Pompeii: Exploring a Roman ghost town.* New York: Thomas Y. Crowell.

Guback, G. 1994. *Luka's quilt.* New York: Greenwillow.

Hamanaka, S. 1990. *The journey: Japanese Americans, racism and renewal.* New York: Orchard Books.

Haskins, J., and Benson, K. 1998. *Bound for America: The forced migration of Africans to the New World.* New York: Lothrop, Lee & Shepard.

Hesse, K. 1998. *Out of the dust.* New York: Scholastic.

Hiscock, B. 1998. *The big rivers: The Missouri, the Mississippi, and the Ohio.* New York: Atheneum.

Hunt, I. 1970. *No promises in the wind.* New York: Tempo Books.

Innocenti, R. 1985. *Rose Blanche.* Mankato, MN: Creative Education.

Jackson, E. 1998. *Turn of the century.* Watertown, MA: Charlesburg Publishing.

Jacobs, W. 1990. *Ellis Island: New hope in a new land.* New York: Charles Scribner's Sons.

Johnson, S. 1998. *Tomatoes, potatoes, corn, and beans: How the foods of the Americas changed eating around the world.* New York: Atheneum.

Lester, J. 1968. *To be a slave.* New York: Dial.

Levinson, R. 1985. *Watch the stars come out.* New York: E. P. Dutton.

Lyons, M. 1992. *Letters from a slave girl: The story of Harriet Jacobs.* New York: Charles Scribner's Sons.

Martin, J. 1998. *The green truck garden giveaway: A neighborhood story and almanac.* New York: Simon & Schuster.

McKissack, P., and F. McKissack. 1994. *Black diamond: The story of the negro baseball leagues.* New York: Scholastic.

Millard, A. 1999. *A street through time: A 12,000 year walk through history.* New York: DK Publishing.

Mochizuki, K. 1993. *Baseball saved us.* New York: Lee and Low.

O'Dell, S. 1970. *Sing down the moon.* New York: Dell.

Oppenheim, S. 1992. *The lily cupboard.* New York: HarperCollins.

Parker, D. 1998. *Stolen dreams: Portraits of working children.* New York: Lerner.

Provensen, A., and M. Provensen. 1987. *Shaker Lane.* New York: Viking Kestrel.

Reinhard, J. 1998. *Discovering the Inca ice maiden.* New York: National Geographic Society.

Rylant, C. 1985. *The relatives came.* New York: Collier Macmillan.

Shea, P. 1995. *The whispering cloth: A refugee's story.* Honesdale, PA: Boyds Mills Press.

Sis, P. 1991. *Follow the dream: The story of Christopher Columbus.* New York: Random House.

Sneve, V. 1993. *The Navajo: A first Americans book.* New York: Holiday House.

Spedden, D. 1994. *Polar: The Titanic bear.* New York: Madison Press.

Spier, P. 1987. *We the people: The Constitution of the United States of America.* New York: Doubleday.

Stanley, J. 1992. *Children of the dust bowl: The true story of the school at Weedpatch Camp.* New York: Crown.

Strom, Y. 1996. *Quilted landscape: Conversations with young immigrants.* New York: Simon & Schuster.

Teele, P. 1998. *Step into the Chinese Empire.* New York: Loprenz Books.

Turner, G. 1997. *Follow in their footsteps.* New York: Dutton.

Von Tscharner, R., R. Fleming, and The Townscape Institute. 1987. *New Providence: A changing cityscape.* New York: Harcourt Brace.

Yolen, J. 1992. *Encounter.* New York: Harcourt Brace.

Teaching Resources

The following list of resources is offered as a starting point from which to develop a network:

Community Resources

Libraries (census reports, microfilms of daily and special interest newspapers, published diaries, cookbooks, art books, maps, files of community organizations and resource people)

Historical societies (photographs, maps, diaries and letters, artifact kits, reproduction items from the gift shop, resources materials on using artifacts and primary sources with children)

Courthouses (transcripts of trails, records of political figures, health records of disease control, dates of major epidemics in the area)

Churches (parish list of births and deaths, sacramental records, descriptions of services, statements of positions on local and national issues, cookbooks with household tips produced at different time periods in that community, artifacts associated with various time periods)

Professional organizations (Association of Newspaper Publishers, local chamber of commerce, service organizations, American Bar Association, American Medical Association)

University Libraries

Microfilm and microfiche (area and national newspapers, special collections of documents and publications associated with local and national movements, bound periodicals)

Government documents and publications (congressional records, presidential papers, contemporary biographies and photographs of political figures, National Park Service travel brochures, current national and international maps prepared by the CIA, transcripts, posters, diaries, indexes for material available from various departments of the federal government)

Special collections (rare books, displays, oversized books, recordings, private papers of individuals associated with the institution)

Artifacts

Printed materials (price lists of commonly purchased goods, recipes, time lines of related events, actual or fictional diary accounts or letters, broadsides [posters or handbills], photocopies or reproduction newspaper accounts or documents, patterns for clothing, photographs [photocopied or actual], reprints or artwork, amps, songs, music, dances from the period)

Real or reproduction household objects (stencil patterns, stencil brushes, wooden spoons and bowls, dishpans, tin plates and cups, kettles or buckets, lye soap, cloth towels, scrub boards and washtubs, boilers, candles and holders, cookie cutters or molds, lanterns, quilts and blankets, carders and wool, flax and cotton samples, spices, slates, and slate pencils, *McGuffey's Readers* and Webster's *"Blue Backed Spellers,"* pens, copybooks, 100 percent cotton paper, tools, horseshoes, hoops, type)

Reproduction toys (whimmy diddles, hoops and sticks, cornhusk and corncob dolls, peach pits, rag balls, marbles, jacks, string, feathers, reproduction paper dolls, bandannas)

Clothing (skirt, blouses, old hats, ribbons, belts, suspenders, bandannas, drawstring bags, hoop skirts, aprons, waist cinchers, collars)

National Resources

National Archives,
Education Branch Office of Public Programs
Washington, DC 20408

Earth Sciences Information Centers
U.S. Geological Survey
507 National Center Reston,
VA 22092

National Public Radio Audience Services
2025 M Street NW
Washington, DC 20036

United States Patent and Trademark Office
Commissioner of Patents and Trademarks
Washington, DC 20231

Web Sites

http://www.mysticseaort.org/alhfarm
Association for Living Historical Farms and Agricultural Museums Web site
http://www.house.gov
U.S. House of Representatives
http://www.yahoo.com/Economy
Yahoo! Business and Economy
http://sunsite.unc.edu/govdocs.html
Government documents (SunSITE)
http://www.whitehouse.gov/ WH/Cabinet/html/cabinet_links.html
The President's Cabinet
http://www.whitehouse.gov
The White House
http://www.si.edu
Smithsonian Institution home page
http://www.law.cornell.edu/supct/supct.table.html
Decisions of the U.S. Supreme Court

http://www.usgs.gov/lien/doi_edu.html
   Department of Interior Education and Outreach
http://www.undp.org/un/index.html
   United Nations Information
http://www.ncss.org/
   National Council for Social Studies
http://www.historychannel.com/index2.html
   History Channel
http://www.execpc.com/~dboals
   History and social studies Web sites for K–12 teachers
http://hanksville.phast.umass.edu/misc/Naresources.html
   Karen Strom's Index of Native American Resources
http://www.pagesz.net/~stevek/resources.html
   Resources for historians
http://coombs.anu.edu.au/WWWVL-SocSci.html
   Social studies virtual library
http://www.nara.gov/
   National Archives
http://www.cr.nps.gov/nr/twhp/home.html
   National Register of Historic Places
http://www.nativeweb.org/
   Native Web
http://www.lib.berkeley.edu/TeachingLib/Guides/Internet
   University of California Library Web
http://www.mit.edu:8001/people/sorokin/women/index.html
   Women's Studies

The above Web Sites were taken from Edinger and Fins (1998), Heide and
   Stilborne (1996), and Vacca & Vacca, 1999.

References

Atwell, N. 1998. *In the middle: Writing, reading, and learning with adolescents.* 2nd ed.
   Portsmouth, NH: Heinemann.
Ausubel, D. P. 1960. The uses of advanced organizers in the learning and retention of
   meaningful verbal material. *Journal of Educational Psychology* 51:267–72.
Banks, J., C. A. M. Banks, and A. Clegg. 1998. *Teaching strategies for the social studies.*
   5th ed. New York: Longman.
Bolton, G. 1985. Changes in thinking about drama in education. *Theory into Practice* 24:
   151–7.
Booth, D. 1985. Imaginary gardens with real toads. *Theory into Practice* 24:193–8.
Bradley Commission on History in Schools and P. Gagnon. 1989. *Historical literacy: The
   case for history in American education.* New York: Macmillan.
Brandt, P., and Wade, R., eds. 1995. Made for each other: Social studies and children's
   literature. *Social Studies and the Young Learner* 8:18–19, 26.
Bruner, J. 1966. *Toward a theory of instruction.* Cambridge, MA: Harvard University Press.
Bruner, J. 1977. *The process of education.* Cambridge, MA: Harvard University Press.
Edinger, M., and Fins, S. 1998. *Far away and long ago: Young historians in the classroom.*
   York, Maine: Stenhouse Publishing.

Egan, K. 1986. *Teaching as story telling—An alternative approach to teaching and curriculum in the elementary school.* Chicago: University of Chicago Press.

Egan, K. 1997. The arts as the basics for education. *Childhood Education* 73:341–5.

Fines, J., and R. Verrior. 1974. *The drama of history—An experiment in cooperative teaching.* Aberdeen, AK: Central Press.

Gagne, R., L. J. Briggs, and W. W. Wager. 1988. *Principles of instructional design.* New York: Holt, Rinehart, and Winston.

Gardner, H. 1983. *Frames of mind.* New York: Basic Books.

Gardner, H. 1991. *The unschooled mind: How children think and how schools should teach.* New York: HarperCollins.

Grimmestad, B., and E. DeChiara. 1982. Dramatic plays: A vehicle for prejudice reduction in the elementary school. *Journal of Educational Research* 76:45–9.

Goodlad, J. 1984. *A place called school: Prospects for the future.* New York: McGraw-Hill.

Graves, D. 1983. *Writing: Teachers and children at work.* Portsmouth, NH: Heinemann.

Heathcote, D., and P. Herbert. 1985. A drams of learning: Mantle of the expert. *Theory into Practice* 24:173–80.

Heide, A., and Stilborne, L. 1996. *The teacher's complete and easy guide to the Internet.* Toronto, Ontario: Trifolium Books.

Huck, C. S., S. Hepler, and J. Hickman. 1996. *Children's literature in the elementary school.* Orlando, FL: Harcourt Brace.

Johnson, D. 1983. Natural language learning by design: A classroom experiment in social interaction and secondary language acquisition. *TESOL Quarterly* 17:55–68.

Johnson, D., and R. T. Johnson. 1992. Approaches to implementing cooperative learning in the social studies classroom. In *Cooperative learning in the social studies classroom,* ed. R. J. Stahl and R. L. Van Sickle, 44–51. Washington, DC: National Council of Social Studies.

Johnson, L., and C. O'Neill, eds. 1985. *Dorothy Heathcote: Collected writings on education and drama.* London: Hutchinson.

Knight, P. 1989. A study of children's understanding of people in the past. *Educational Review* 4:207–19.

Kohlberg, L. 1976. Moral stages and moralization. In *Moral development and behavior,* ed. T. Lickona. New York: Holt, Rinehart.

Lee, P. J. 1983. History teaching and philosophy of history. *History and Theory* 22:19–49.

Lehr, F. 1983. Developing language and thought through creative drama. *Language Arts* 60:385–8.

Leigh, A., and Reynolds, T. 1997. Little windows to the past. *Social Education* 61:45–47.

Levstik, L. S. 1986. The relationship between historical responses and narrative in a sixth-grade classroom. *Theory and Research in Social Education* 14:1–19.

Levstik, L. S. 1990. The research base for curriculum choice: A response. *Social Education* 54:442–4.

Levstik, L. S, and Barton, K. 1996. "They still use some of their past": Historical salience in elementary children's chronological thinking. *Journal of Curriculum Studies* 28:531–76.

Maxim, G. W. 1998. *Social studies and the elementary school child.* 6th ed. Columbus, OH: Merrill.

Morgan, N., and Saxton, J. 1987. *Teaching drama: A mind of many wonders.* Portsmouth, NH: Heinemann.

Myers, J., and Philbin, S. 1990. *Classroom drama: discourse as a mode of inquiry.* ERIC #ED323144.

National Council for the Social Studies (NCSS). 1984. In search of a scope and sequence for social studies: Reports the National Council for the Social Studies Task Force on Scope and Sequence, November 1, 1983: Preliminary position statement of the board of directors. *Social Education* 48:249–62.

National Council for the Social Studies (NCSS). 1989a. In search of a scope and sequence for social studies: Report of the National Council for the Social Studies Task Force on Scope and Sequence, July 1, 1989. *Social Education* 53:375–87.

National Council for the Social Studies (NCSS). 1989b. Social studies for early childhood and elementary school children preparing for the 21st century: A report from NCSS task force on early childhood/elementary social studies. *Social Education* 53:14–23.

National Council for the Social Studies (NCSS). 1994. *Curriculum standards for social studies: Expectations of excellence.* Bulletin No. 89. Washington, DC: National Council for Social Studies.

Nelson, P. 1992. *Stories, memorials, and games: Fourth graders respond to history in classroom and museum contexts.* Unpublished Ed.D. diss., Northern Illinois University, DeKalb.

O'Neill, C. 1985. Imagined worlds in theater and drama. *Theory into Practice* 24:158–65.

Putnam, L. 1991. Dramatizing non-fiction with emerging readers. *Language Arts* 68:463–69.

Ravitch, D., and C. Finn. 1987. *What do our 17-year-olds-know? A report on the first national assessment of history and literature.* New York: Harper and Row.

Ritchie, G. 1991. How to use drama for cross cultural understanding. *Guidance Counselor* 7: 33–5.

Rosenblatt, L. 1982. The literacy transaction: Evocation and response. *Theory into Practice* 231:268–77.

Rosenblatt, L. 1983. *Literature as exploration.* New York: Modern Language Association of America.

Rosenblatt, L. 1985. Viewpoints: Transactions versus interaction—A terminological rescue operation. *Research in the Teaching of English* 19:96–107.

Routman, R. 1994. *Invitations: Changing as teachers and learners K–12.* Portsmouth, NH: Heinemann.

Selman, R. 1971. The relation of role taking to the development of moral judgment in children. *Child Development* 45:803–6.

Sewall, G. T. 1988. American history textbooks: Where do we go from here? *Phi Delta Kappan* 69:553–8.

Shand, G. D. May, and R. Linnell. 1990. History as ethnography: A psychological evaluation of a theater in education project. *Teaching History* 65:27–32.

Slavin, R. 1983. *Cooperative learning.* New York: Longman.

Stahl, R. J. 1992. From "academic strangers" to successful members of a cooperative learning group: An inside-the-learner perspective. In *Cooperative learning in the social studies classroom,* ed. R. J. Stahl and R. L. Van Sickle, 8–15. Washington, DC: National Council for the Social Studies.

Swartz, L. 1988. *Drama themes: A practical guide for the classroom teachers.* Portsmouth, NH: Heinemann.

Taba, H. 1955. *With perspective on human relations: A study of peer group dynamics in an eighth grade.* Washington, DC: American Council on Education.

Thornton, S. 1990. Should we be teaching more history? *Theory and Research in Social Education* 18:53–60.

Vacca, R., and Vacca, J. 1999. *Content area reading: Literacy and learning across the curriculum.* 6th ed. New York: Longman.

VanSledright, B., and Brophy 1992. Storytelling, imagination, and fanciful elaboration in children's historical reconstructions. *American Educational Research Journal* 29: 837–59.

Vass, P. 1992. Overwhelming evidence: Written sources and primary history. *Teaching History* 66:21–6.

Chapter 12

Illustration of the famous knight, El Cid, drawn by Greg Merema, Sixth grade. Used by permission.

Social Studies and the Arts

From Inner Journeys to Faraway Lands

Martha Brady
Northern Arizona University

Art is a human activity having for its purpose the transmission to others of the highest and best feelings to which man has rise.

—Leo Tolstoi

In order to preserve the genius and developmental potential of childhood, one must quite simply give the universe back to the child in as rich and dramatic form as possible.

—Jean Houston
The Possible Human: A Course in Extending Your Physical, Mental, and Creative Abilities

Objectives

—————————————————⌁—————————————————

Readers will

- appreciate the need to integrate the arts and social studies instruction;
- understand that the love of the arts is best established in elementary school; and
- be able to apply art activities in the teaching of social studies.

Introduction

The fifth-grade class sat huddled around two large posters, Andrew Wyeth's *Christina's World* and Diego Rivera's *The Tortilla Maker,* both of which lay in the middle of the classroom floor. Surrounding the prints were dozens of small bits of paper, each containing a handwritten sentence, or phrase, or word. Some students were in the midst of writing more sentences and phrases, tossing two or three tiny strips of paper near one or both of the posters. Many of the children merely looked at the paintings in silence, absorbing their beauty. A few students conversed with one another about what they were observing. After some time had passed, the teacher gathered the boys and girls back and continued the lesson. "Now," she said, "let's talk about the thoughts you wrote down on the slips of paper. By looking at the clues the paintings gave us, what are the cultures of the people we see in the paintings? How are the cultures similar? How are they different? And, this is a hard one, what might these people be thinking about themselves and their lives at this moment?"

Thus began a lesson that touched the perimeters of language arts and math while encompassing art and social studies. The lesson offered, for both teacher and pupils, an example of the value of the arts as a vehicle for making many aspects of certain lessons understandable. In addition, the arts can make lessons authentic, touchable, and engaging for all students in the classroom.

The discussions were rich and connected. Using the paintings as focal points with the bits of information on the slips of papers as resources and guides for dialogue, the students were able to make connections to clothing and culture, terrain and culture, faces and culture, occupations and culture, and, finally, actions and culture. The teacher then went a step further by having the students engage in reflection when she asked, what were the people in the paintings thinking about themselves and their lives at that moment? This allowed students opportunities to sympathize, empathize, and relive personal moments, and then make connections to their own places, their own families, their own environments.

Time was then devoted to facts and figures of the paintings and the artists themselves. Maps of Mexico and Maine, the locations of the two settings of the paintings, were shared. Biographies of Rivera and Wyeth were presented and discussed. Other works by the two artists were introduced and compared. Children used rulers on blank paper to draw the dimensions of the paintings in an attempt for them to grasp the sense of size. Examples of the media used by the artists, tempera and oil paints, were shown. Last, the class focused on a geography bulletin board that featured a map of major art museums throughout the world. Using pushpins and labels, students identified the locations of the Museum of Modern Art in New York City, where Wyeth's *Christina's World* is displayed, and the University of California School Museum in San Francisco, where Rivera's *The Tortilla Maker* is exhibited. This powerful and intriguing lesson was an excellent example of the integration of the arts and social studies.

Integrating Social Studies and Art

As children begin to create definitions of themselves for themselves, we as educators spend very little time watching this phenomenon occur. We are too busy attempting to fill their heads with cold coins of information. Rather, we might quite simply stop and watch these incredible young boys and girls as they move in between tasks that we ask them to do in school. Do we notice that they skip to recess in rhythmic steps, or play an original melody on the tabletop with their fingers. Do we catch them shaping a form out of a crumpled piece of paper before it dive-bombs into the trash can? Or see them follow the path of a raindrop all the way down the windowpane until it slowly disappears into their imagination? Do we notice that they can name, sing, and give a biographic sketch of the entire body of a popular rock group? Do we ask them to wash away the chalk drawing of the Alamo on the sidewalk before they head home from school? Do we constantly require them to stop doodling, or humming, or tapping their pencil? Perhaps there is a way of channeling those idiosyncratic moments that tend to drive some of us crazy. Integrating the social studies curriculum with the arts can be a proving ground for discovering who our children are, what potentials hide within them, and whose voices may well create the "choir of the millennium."

Social studies is the perfect curriculum for integration of the arts, as it can be vast, deep, mysterious, linear, global, minute, explosive, sweeping, methodical, intricate, intimate, and celebratory. Whatever social studies is, it too is life. The arts can be pulsating, swelling, complicated, intriguing, beguiling, fluid, fast, delicious, consuming, breathless, bountiful, and mirroring. Like social studies, whatever the arts are, they too are life. Hence social studies and arts can make a wonderful and exciting combination for children.

This chapter describes a variety of methods and strategies for bringing together specific social studies disciplines and the various arts disciplines (music, dance/movement, drama, and the visual and media arts). In addition, this chapter offers suggestions and examples for applying Howard Gardner's eight Multiple Intelligences (MI) (1983) to these integrated lessons with attention being given to the elements of research, creative writing, personal exploration and connections, fact finding, and creative expression.

Last, this chapter presents schematas that can be used to assist teachers in fulfilling their desire to implement social studies lessons with strong and varied arts components. These are outlined in the Multiple Intelligences (MI) Grids found throughout the chapter and a Theme Outline Tree (Brady 1998) found at the end of the chapter, which is a visual organizational formula for presenting specific social studies topics. These MI Grids and the Theme Outline Tree offer mapping strategies for the integration of the arts into all aspects of social studies whether it be the social sciences or the ten National Council for the Social Studies (NCSS) adopted themes of study.

Picasso defined art as "that which washes from the soul the dust of everyday life" (quoted in Brady 1998, 1). A student in a fourth grade in a classroom in Arizona defined social studies as "finding your way." Combining these two definitions may, at last, give us a glimpse of what the content of social studies can be for children.

The Golden Years for the Arts

Ages nine through eleven are considered the golden years for the arts (Coulter 1989) for it is during this age span that the left and right hemispheres are linked completely

Hudson explored for the English and the Dutch!

Russia

Spitsbergen

New Netherland

1607

1611

HENRY W. HUDSON

Hudson Sailed farther North than any previous sailor!

© Kurtis R. Fluck

and auditory pathways undergo growth spurts. It is a time when the arts make the most sense to children and when they are most apt to take risks with the arts. After age eleven or twelve, children rarely advance much further in art, music, athletics, grace of movement, or creative writing flair. Only a few that are referred to as being talented continue to grow in the arts beyond this point (Coulter 1989).

For younger children, ages five through eight years old, information that comes in a sensory way must come out in a motor way. In other words, if they don't move, they don't learn (Coulter 1989). This is clearly one more reason to include arts activities into our daily lesson planning to ensure that our classrooms are filled with meaningful opportunities for children to move forward and build strong connections to, and talents in, the arts. Embellishing our curricular areas, especially social studies, with arts experiences is a natural way for this to happen.

One of the first arts that children come to love and enjoy is music. Music played during the prenatal period can have a soothing impact on the yet unborn infant. When the same music is played again after the baby has been born, that soothing feeling still exists. Music exists in all cultures throughout the world. Thus, it is natural for us to begin with music.

❧ Music Is the Universal Language of Mankind

So wrote Henry Wadsworth Longfellow, the famous American poet. If his words ring true, then teaching social studies through music has limitless possibilities. For music gives us not only the capacity to make connections to information, but to place events, both personal and historical, into emotional arenas. Music massages our unconscious more than any other intelligence (Gardner 1983). It places us "here" and "there." It sets us down into the moment. Music gives us a more complete understanding of time and place by how the music of that time and place correctly defines that specific time and place. An example of that is the book *The Boy Who Loved Music* (Levene 1993), a story about the period in which Joseph Haydn lived and the circumstances surrounding some of his compositions.

For the early childhood student in the primary grades, music creates connections to holidays as well as special ceremonies and traditions that cannot be duplicated in other ways (Mayesky 1995). Additionally, integrating music into the social studies also brings different points of view to students. Boys and girls can use music as a means of understanding the panorama of all the elements that make up the human existence. A clear example of a first-person point of view is Ntozake Shange's (1994) powerful poem, "I Live in Music." Music is used by Shange as a metaphor for her life. In this piece, Shange introduces children not only to the "aura" of music through sensory application, but to her African American cultural background as well. This poem, like other arts-based poetry, lends itself to social studies lessons whereby students research global music and create cultural snapshots from these musical pieces.

To go a bit further, the following line in Shange's poem can be an interesting beginning point in which to direct children to reflect upon their own lives and how they see themselves: ". . . sound falls round me like rain on other folks." This line can be used to encourage intermediate-age boys and girls to create personal music metaphors and then compare those metaphors with the music metaphor pieces they have written about people from other cultures.

Jazz is another musical entry into the people, places, and environments of our world. The only music form that is inherently American, jazz music is a rich and fertile ground for learning about the sociology of the musicians who play jazz and about the communities like New Orleans, Memphis, and St. Louis that are considered birthplaces for this kind of music. In the Newbery Award Winner, *Bud, Not Buddy* (Curtis 1999), students learn about life as the son of a jazz musician during the Great Depression.

By studying about the jazz artists themselves, pupils gain a better understanding of the history of certain decades, the evolution of the music industry itself, and the culture that is jazz. In the liner notes of a CD performed by jazz singer Ann Callaway (1996), Miss Callaway writes, "In every century there are great musical artists who help us to know ourselves, forgive ourselves, and celebrate ourselves." Perhaps her words, too, are a definition of social studies. At the very least, they suggest the kinds of lessons we might bring to children.

The following Multiple Intelligence Grids are designed to give ideas with which to integrate music as a means of broadening the social studies curriculum, enlivening specific information, and generating renewed interest in the social sciences.

Key to Grids

V/L	Verbal Linguistic
L/M	Logical/Mathematical
V/S	Visual/Spatial
M/R	Musical/Rhythmic
B/K	Bodily/ Kinesthetic
Inter	Interpersonal
Intra	Intrapersonal
Nat	Naturalistic

Music and Social Studies				
Early Grades				
V/L	Keep an ongoing list of how music affects your own culture and other cultures.	Read about particular musical instruments and their relation to specific cultures.	Write a community song about unity.	Discuss lyrics to songs that relate to historical folk figures: D. Boone, Abe Lincoln, etc.	With your family, write a song about your family. Use the tune, *Old McDonald.*
L/M	Make a chart of well-known songs of cultures in your classroom.	Use specific social studies vocabulary words to create a chant.	Create different categories for cowboy songs.	Create fact/fiction cards about cowboys from information obtained in songs.	Make comparisons between your family song and the original, *Old McDonald.*
V/S	Design and draw an ABC Cowboy Book to accompany the songs.	Draw geographic pictures which represent what the music describes.	Create a mural which defines *America the Beautiful.*	Use background music for imagery purposes.	Create your own illustrations for them.
M/R	Listen to musical excerpts.	Sing songs with your family. Teach the class your favorite.	Collect and learn songs that deal with "work." Ex: *John Henry, I've Been Working on the Railroad.*	Write your own song about working in class and/or home.	Listen to common TV music jingles.
B/K	Use "junk" or paper rolls to make an invention that creates music.	Find, on the map, the regions to which the songs relate.	Learn songs from around the world. Create motions to accompany them.	Act out the songs.	Act out scenes from patriotic songs.
Inter	Teach the class a song your grandparents taught you.	With a partner, explore musical customs from another country.	Listen to music of other countries. Debate your likes/dislikes.	Teach the class a "holiday" song in another language.	Research the origination of the song.
Intra	"How/when does music make you feel better?"	"What kind of music could stop all conflict? Why?"	"When you think of the state you live in, what kind of music comes to mind? Why?"	Create an individual project from this information.	Write an individual report of the relationship between certain musical instruments and the "feeling" of certain music. Ex: Native American.
Nat	Collect environmental sound effects. Categorize them.	Research musical instruments of the rain forests. Collect rain forest music.	Write your own environmental song. Make percussion instruments.	Explore why some of these songs were "survivor" songs.	Show how nature plays a role.

		Music and Social Studies Middle Grades		
V/L	Research and discuss lyrics of songs that defined "turning points" in history.	Write original lyrics from point of view of: early Roman, soldier, president, and so on.	Write a community song about class rules.	Write a song that "sells" your state.	Write a report about "The Most Important Song Ever Written." Connect to social studies.
L/M	Compare several "pro" oriented songs written during a specific global conflict.	Compare several protest songs written during that same conflict.	Create a time line of songs that were important during a specific historical era.	Talk "Economics" in regard to the music industry.	Pose questions about music and regions and how they relate.
V/S	Create a mural illustrating one of the songs.	Use information from the lyrics to create a brochure.	Listen to national anthems of other countries. Draw a picture from that information.	Design a diorama for this song.	Create an album cover for some aspect of social studies.
M/R	Sing and learn the significance of campaign songs throughout history.	Research musical instruments of early history such as lutes, harpsichords, etc.	Collect and listen to music of early historical periods.	Listen to soundtracks of period movies. Use song titles as basis for discussion.	Use an existing melody to write an original song about one consumer good.
B/K	Use the Internet to find information about economics of music industry.	Global Music Industry. Ex: The Beatles	Create a musical social studies board game.	Put together collection of short music examples to be used in the game.	Put together a Cost Analysis/PR Packet for an original album.
Inter	Groups will select a 5/10-year period and explore that period through its music.	Present an oral report on one contemporary musical artist and his/her affect on "the times."	Present a musical collection whose lyrics define "human dignity."	With a partner, write a song about a "cause."	Use a synthesizer to create a sound effect/techno rock song.
Intra	"Think about how music might have changed history."	Set a goal which involves broadening your musical tastes.	Select one country a month. Listen to music of that region and area.	Reflect upon those experiences.	"Why is music such a significant part of many cultures and customs?"
Nat	Explore oceans and seas and the sea chanties that were written about them.	Use 10 facts about a particular ocean to compose an original sea chanty.	Explore the technology of the music industry in the last 50 years.	Research Woody Guthrie and other early songwriters whose songs spoke of "survival."	Compare the songs of today whose thrust is the environment.

Visual Arts—The Illustrated Dictionary of Our Time

The arts, in general, are about connections to ourselves and others. The visual arts, in particular, give shape and form to those connections. In so doing, they help us better understand our world and the cultures that make up that world.

Michael Day, president of the Art Education Association, points out that art teaches students to make judgments, to think metaphorically, and to provide multiple solutions to problems (Rasmussen 1998). Art does even more. It teaches students how to respond critically. It also transfers the art of articulation from verbal to visual (Rasmussen 1998). Art elicits comparisons and teaches students about quality and personal selections. In the area of social studies, visual arts are the illustrated dictionary of our time. The visual arts are the observable chronology of the world's five W's—who, what, when, where, and why.

If children use the visual arts as a tool for understanding the world around them, they become eyewitnesses to the genius of humans and to all the accomplishments, risks, dreams, conflicts, goals, and ethics that have emerged from all those who have come before. Thus, these visual observations can be guidance systems to our students' own perceptions of what embodies good citizenship, values, and contributions.

All aspects of the visual arts—drawing, illustration, painting, sculpture, printmaking, photography, architecture, graphic design, and landscape design—play easily into a social studies curriculum. How might children make connections between sculpture and people in leadership roles in history? What elements of printmaking define how written communcation has advanced through the ages? What imprints do the designs of buildings, tunnels, and bridges have on students and their grasp of a certain historical era? How can we use photographs to document our own personal history and compare that documentation with how the American cowboy was chronicled? How do cars, ships, machines, furniture, golf courses, city parks, sports complexes, and other designs created by people impact how students view and understand economics and technology, and what are the implications of these worldly necessities to their own lives?

There are as many ideas for using visual arts to create a climate of learning in social studies as there are children who love color, form, shape, and design. Build a scale model of an American colonial village, a 1900 city, or futuristic space colony. Create a visual display of Brazil's exports (Haslinger, Kelly, and O'Lare 1996). Create a relief map of Hannibal's journey from Carthage across the Alps to fight the Romans. Create masks or a piece of art unique to one culture such as an Egyptian sarcophagus to learn more about rituals, traditions, and ceremonies (Greenwald 2000). Draw a mural representing global currency systems, or bartering systems of ancient civilizations. Simulate cave drawings in a darkened classroom with brown butcher paper, flashlights covered with colored cellophane, plant dyes, and twigs (Brady 1994). Compare Greek and Roman history by comparing their architecture (Sporre 1987).

Bringing works of art into the classroom, as suggested in the following grids, not only helps students continue to make connections to other times and other lives, but also reinforces some of the skills and attitudes that nurture self-identity and growth. These skills include making choices, thinking critically, and understanding the art of compromise. In addition, there are other skills, attitudes, and knowledge to cover.

© Elizabeth Crews

Comparing Van Gogh's *The Starry Night* with the lyrics to Don McLean's "Vincent" offers children opportunities to see different points of view as demonstrated through different creative arts forms. Discussing Georges Seurat's *Sunday Afternoon on the Island of La Grande Jatte* can lead to conversations about the sociology of recreation. Studying kinetic art, that is, art that moves, and comparing moving works, such as Rodin's *Flying Figure C* to the *Imunu* figures from the tribes of New Guinea, give students alternative ways in which to learn the importance of, and make connections to, art and the look of dance and movement in all cultures, past and present.

Arts consultant Charles Fowler (1994) suggests that a strong school arts program impacts education in the following ways: (1) the arts make education more comprehensive; (2) the arts bring about a more engaging way to learn; (3) the arts make the curriculum more cohesive; (4) the arts create bridges to a broader culture; (5) the inclusion of the arts creates a more humanistic curriculum; and (6) the arts are our best definition of humanity.

How then, do we create meaning in the social studies by following Fowler's suggestions? Perhaps we become less verbal and more visual. When we study about World War II and neutrality, we show the film *Casablanca*. When we teach about global waterways, we bring in artwork that puts particular rivers, canals, lakes, and oceans into some visual, geographical, and historical perspective. When we research our nation's founding fathers, we bring in portraits to show how different artists "saw" them. When we teach about dignity, we look at black-and-white photographs that capture history's indignities—from Matthew Brady's photographs of Civil War casualties to depression-era pictures of soup lines to Holocaust victims to current-day photos of starving children in third world countries. When we study different native tribes, both in North America and abroad, we include works of art and icons as well as illustrations in children's literature. Such resources give us a clearer understanding of indigenous peoples.

Integrating art into any curriculum requires three basic things: materials, time to explore them, and validation (Clemens 1991). If children are to benefit from connections that come with the integration of the visual arts with social studies, students must be exposed to different art disciplines on a regular basis. They must be given time to make those connections between content and art. Last, they must get from their teacher a sense of encouragement for what they are doing, which helps validate art itself.

Sydney Clemens (1991, 4) wrote that "art has the role in education of helping children become more themselves instead of more like everyone else." That, perhaps, is our true mission as teachers.

✍ Children Are Drama

Clearly and simply, children *are* drama. Each and every school day, boys and girls bring to the classroom conflict, mystery, nuance, celebration, and resolution. Each and every day they bring emotions of fear and joy, anxiety and elation, sadness and happiness. Every Monday morning they walk through the classroom door covered in stories and dreams. They soar with pretending. They spin on life's stage. Alternately, they open up like summer's first rosebuds and droop like canopies drenched with rain. They use their imaginations to build bridges to places they have seen and places that beckon them. They are truly ripe for expressing the dramatic arts. Although drama was discussed earlier in Chapter 11, we will briefly elaborate on this topic here as it lends itself so readily to social studies.

What does drama bring to children? It is suggested that drama offers a creative and psychological balance to more academic instruction. Drama presents magical experiences that embrace play as a means of looking at reality. Drama showcases childhood through pretending and wonder. In addition, drama encourages better thinking in children (Cecil and Lauretzen 1994). Drama also brings a child's sense of being, empathy, and the ability to see life from another's perspective, to feel with that person (Heinig 1987). Drama brings to children creative arenas in which boys and girls can place themselves and stay a while, as they generate their own feelings and attitudes about the feelings and attitudes of others.

Social studies lends itself to the use of all facets of drama whether it be formal scripted plays, informal skits or scenes, pantomime, puppet shows, shadow plays, tableaux, circle stories, improvisation, musical theater and opera, reader's theatre, and choral reading.

In a scripted play format, students of all ages can select one aspect of social studies, for instance, right or wrong. Then by choosing a children's book as a focus for interpretation, such as *Riding Freedom* (Munoz 1998), based on the true adventures of Charlotte "Charley" Parkhurst. Disguised as a boy, Charlotte escaped from an orphanage to later become a legendary stagecoach driver and the first woman to vote in California, and probably in the United States. By writing an original script, youngsters can deliver their own formal performance of this important part of good citizenship.

Art and Social Studies				
Early Grades				
V/L	Look at design of several food packagings. Discuss "draw" to consumers. Relate to economics.	Look at pictures of people of different cultures. Write about stereotypes.	Look at well-known works of art. Discuss occupations.	Listen to story about an artist's life. Discuss similarities to yours.	Show environmental pictures. Discuss industries appropriate to the areas.
L/M	Make predictions regarding pollution, weather, population, etc.	Create pro/con chart for each package.	Create pro/con chart for selected TV advertisements.	Look at art work that represents "long ago" and "now." Make comparisons.	Use city and state maps to assist students in drawing and labeling personal maps from home to school.
V/S	Use sandtrays to create and design different landforms.	Use pictoral magazines to create culture montages.	Assemble portfolio of famous art in relation to one aspect of social studies.	Draw your family. Find well-known works of art that represent your family.	Create a strip cartoon of your physical growth from birth to now.
M/R	Look at and discuss the "art" and design of musical instruments.	Look at cultural art work. Play music appropriate to that culture. Make connections.	Use pictures as a stimulus for creating a sound poem that defines "working."	Create a vocabulary list from geography slides. Create a rhythmic chant using the words.	Find appropriate music to accompany the montages.
B/K	Take a walking field trip around your community. Look for artwork. Talk civic pride.	Use clay to recreate parts of the community you saw on your field trip.	Build your community out of boxes.	Construct an interactive bulletin board with original art work entitled *Tools*.	Using paper rolls, groups build a sculpture entitled *Conflict*.
Inter	With a partner look for pictures that represent wants and needs.	Turn to a partner and draw what they will look like when they are old.	Use the computer to draw a machine of the future. Teach the class about it.	Interview family members about their favorite foods.	Brainstorm a design for a class logo to be put on T-shirts.
Intra	Think about and illustrate a book on "good deeds."	Reflect on one good deed. Draw a cartoon to depict it.	Use pipe cleaners to show the definition of *Hands Across America*.	Draw what you value the most.	Find a painting that represents you the most. Write about the similarities.
Nat	Bring photos of your animals to class. Talk about pet care and responsibility.	Create a filmstrip of objects in your house that make you safe.	Pick one food, and create a sequential drawing from "field to table."	Look at pictures of global dwellings. Compare to the house you live in.	Draw the perfect house for your family.

Art and Social Studies Middle Grades				
V/L	Research an artist's life from three different historical periods.	Write and illustrate your autobiography.	Use selected works of art in *The Art Book* (1994) to discuss global geographic locations.	Use other works of art to discuss cultural differences as seen by different artists.	Write a story about family traditions. Ask family members to illustrate.
L/M	Create a pictoral time line of a decade in the 20th century.	Laminate and cut into puzzle pieces.	Compare components of the original ad campaign to an existing one.	Use pictures to categorize architectural styles from different historical periods.	Collect postcards from around the world. Categorize appropriately.
V/S	Use Matthew Brady's photographs to study the Civil War.	Create a visual ad campaign for an original consumer product.	On paper, design a futuristic colony.	Look for abstract art examples which may be similar to structures.	Construct a mobile of presidential facts.
M/R	Create a rap that describes each structure.	Create ostanatos (repetitive rhythm patterns) with art history facts.	Write a song from a patriotic poster of the 40s.	Use dustbowl photos and Woody Guthrie songs to write impressions of the period.	Add appropriate music to each year in the decade.
B/K	Use stacked chairs to construct structures defining: war, hunger, skyscrapers, etc.	Use boxes to construct the colony.	Select a visual artist. Create a board game about his work and life.	Take a trip to an art museum.	Go on an "art scavenger hunt" while there, looking for specific social studies facts.
Inter	Bring photos of yourself, birth to now. Teach a lesson about YOU.	In groups, present a report on a "group" in history such as cowboys. Use pictures.	In groups, select a public issue. Represent it through geometric designs on the overhead.	With a partner create a portfolio of print ads which define cultural stereotypes.	Lead a discussion on technology using ads as your resources.
Intra	Keep a reflective sketch journal for social studies.	Using a painting, write a first-person account of "being there."	Create an independent project using art work to study important battles in our nation's history.	Create a diarama of a historical event. Put yourself in the event. Reflect.	Write a report on one Norman Rockwell painting. Compare the painting to your life.
Nat	Through art, show different architectural styles through the ages.	Discuss the design of Frank L. Wright's *Falling Water* residence in relation to environment.	Use other works of art/buildings to learn about geographic regions/ environments.	Build global human habitats to describe survival and environment.	Draw a topographical map of your yard, block, street, etc.

In an informal activity, students use the art of improvisation to bring clarity to a social studies issue, a historic fact, or even a point of view. Pantomime works extremely well in a classroom setting as this dramatic discipline is less threatening to some. Pantomime also works successfully as an alternative review technique. Tableaux bring together students who create a "still life" of an event with dramatic interactions among players of a scene. For example, students may freeze-frame a scene from the Holocaust and then interact verbally with each member who is in the freeze-frame.

Puppet shows, reader's theatre, and choral reading are all dramatic events that present students with opportunities to interact with each other for the "common good" while learning the life skills of patience, effort, tolerance, compromise, confidence, and responsibility. In the early grades, puppet shows can be used to learn more about family, neighborhood, and community structure. In the upper grades, puppet shows can be a stage for understanding and comparing global conflicts. Reader's theatre, a form of oral presentation with an emphasis on reading aloud rather than on memorization

Creative dramatics includes using puppets to present a play.

© Elizabeth Crews

(Bauer 1987), can lead students to improved reading skills while at the same time bringing cultural folktales to life. Choral reading, another form of oral presentation that uses vocal tones as a method of verbally orchestrating a text, can bring a fullness to the meaning and reading of the Gettysburg Address or a deeper understanding of the lyrics to "America the Beautiful."

If one could teach a social studies lesson that includes imaginative thinking, creative problem solving, movement, spatial awareness, sensory awareness and recall, verbalization, structure, characterization, aesthetic development, and intrapersonal and interpersonal development (Cottrell 1987), then one would also be a drama teacher.

The Multiple Intelligence Grids for drama that follow give lesson plan ideas for incorporating the preceding elements as well as other methods of engaging children in a social studies curriculum.

Drama and Social Studies
Early Grades

V/L	Select a culture-based children's story. Teacher reads, students perform narrative pantomime.	Research similar global folktales. Create finger puppets to act them out.	Create improvised actions about an experience with your grandparents.	Vocabulary Drama. Call out a vocabulary word. Students act out definition.	Write and act out a folktale from another country.
L/M	Use math skills to "block" the play.	Create a time line of events along the Oregon Trail. Act out the events.	Create a state historical events calendar. Enact events through improvisation.	Gather and categorize hats to be used in drama situations.	Use inductive/deductive reasoning to create "before/after" scenes.
V/S	Use pictures and photos to stimulate drama experiences.	Create global, culture masks to distinguish different characters.	Make paper hats to define different characters.	Create "props." Ex: lightbulb. Students act out what happened before and after invention of lightbulb.	Design and draw the program for the holiday play.
M/R	Create "circles of sound" that define different community workers.	With an older class create a social studies music video.	Present a melodrama of facts about the Old West.	Sing holiday songs with sounds and actions.	Write and perform a holiday play with music and dancing.
B/K	Present a concept about "home." Students create add-on-pantomimes to original idea.	Play the game *Spectator*. Students act out "watching something."	Take a field trip to a holiday play.	Create Past, Present, Future scenes about your family.	Students write and present choral reading using the same book.
Inter	In groups, students create simple debates about historical facts or events.	Create pair debate scenarios such as: Parent/Child, Policeman/Speeder, etc.	Select a culture poem. Organize class in choral reading of the poem.	Partners conduct telephone conversations with two different people in history.	Create point of view scenes in groups.
Intra	Create a first-person character monologue of a community helper. Use tape player.	Create a first-person monologue for one of these animals.	Think about how it feels to get up in front of the class and act.	In a circle, students pantomime "Who Am I."	Create a book-on-tape voice characterization of your family members.
Nat	Role-play two ways to survive in outer space.	Act out "day-in-the-life" of certain animals.	Create frozen sculptures of landforms such as mountains. Create sound/actions.	Act out the water cycle.	Students play "Human Machines." (Brady, 1994).

Drama and Social Studies Middle Grades				
V/L	Research the history of the American Theater and how it mirrored events taking place in history.	Write a 3-part choral reading piece about one event in history such as Hindenburg disaster.	Poll community members about how they support their local theater.	Discuss cultural stereotypes as depicted in movies.	Write a puppet show script about Transportation. Be factual.
L/M	Chart the economic differences in Broadway Theater and movies.	Use math skills to create sets for the documentary.	Compare theater during Greek, Roman Medieval, Turn of the Century times.	Critique it for factual or nonfactual interpretation.	Create a "shooting schedule" for the documentary.
V/S	Use boxes to design background sets for informal drama scenes.	Watch a movie that has significance to some aspect of social studies. Ex. *Grapes of Wrath.*	Use colored cellophane to create overhead puppetry skits about social studies.	Document a first-person event in history using the video camera.	Create puppets as modes of transportation.
M/R	Rewrite a chapter book with a historical premise into a children's musical.	Act out lyrics from World War II songs.	Explain how certain music sets the mood for dramatic experiences.	Find music or sound effects to accompany commercials dealing with goods and services.	Find sound effects to accompany the puppet show.
B/K	Create verbal scenarios representing American presidents and their moments of greatness.	Select one social studies issue. Act out Yesterday, Today, and Tomorrow skits.	Dramatize points of view from famous women in history.	Act out original commercials appropriate to different historical periods.	Pantomime the Bill of Rights.
Inter	Use the internet to research "drama success stories" of people of different cultures.	Report the information to the class.	In groups, create a monologue for one significant historical "turning point."	Brainstorm products that are appropriate to certain historical periods.	With a partner act out one significant event in your state's history.
Intra	Independently, research an actor who is a political spokesperson.	Think of the most dramatic moment in American history. Create a video. Play all parts.	Think of one global problem. Create and videotape a request for aid to help solve the problem.	"How do movies influence you?" Be specific.	Research current events in which tragedies occurred because of a movie's influence.
Nat	Be an environmentalist who will "guide" someone across your state.	Act out nature's cycles.	Create a two-voice poem about some aspect of global weather.	Assume inanimate roles as the guide tours your state.	Create a monologue as a "survivor" of a historical indignity.

❧ *Everyone Has the Right to Dance*

In the poignant picture book *The Last Dance* (Deedy 1995), Ninny, one of the main characters in the book, tells her friend Bessie, "that every human being has to right to do three things. To sing, even if you sing off-key. The crow has as much right as the nightingale. To tell stories. Those we love are never really gone as long as their stories are told. To dance. The great thing in life is not so much to dance well, but whether one is willing to dance at all."

Dance is the arts discipline that classroom teachers shy away from the most, yet it is the clearest creative forum in which children can recognize and understand that human response is an emotional reaction not restricted to either sex (Boorman 1971). Teaching children to accept dance and movement for what it is, an emotional reaction, must be the first step before we can begin to teach them to accept and risk learning about dance and movement as a viable component in all cultures everywhere.

Like music, drama, and art, dance takes us from the known to the unknown. Dance forces us away from the facts, figures, and words we use to create an understanding of what people are like, to the nonverbal essence of what people really are. Our memories come from the celebrations, rituals, and traditions of our lives rather than from the dates, the sequence of events, or the continuity of those events. What we remember in school is not the information, but what we used to glue that information to us permanently.

Many ideas come to mind when making attempts to forge the discipline of dance with social studies. Current events are excellent beginning points for integrating dance and social studies. Devote a couple of weeks to collecting data from newspapers in which local, regional, national, or global events are described or explained through dance, movement experiences, or performances. These experiences may include dance troupes from other countries touring within your state or regional ethnic groups performing in your own city or county. These experiences may also include something as simple as an ad in the newspaper highlighting a showing of dance artifacts from a particular historical period.

Use dance to foster originality. Ask students to define the Bill of Rights through movement. With the class, research colonial life. Create original dances that students think describe that time in history, then have them research authentic dances of the period and compare the two for similarities. When studying America's westward expansion, research various celebrations that occurred as settlers headed toward the Pacific Ocean. Create a unit of study on immigrants. Focus on the dance celebrations of these diverse groups as a way of chronicling their early history in this country. Chronicle, too, the decades of the 1940s, 1950s, 1960s, and so on, simply through the dances that defined the mood of each of those decades.

Explore the history, development, and practices of certain religions through various dance rituals that are attributed to these different religions. Research two diverse twentieth-century dance artists such as Rudolph Nureyev and Bill Robinson. Compare their styles, their rise to celebrity, and the cultural components that fostered their need and desire to find a voice through the discipline of dance.

| Dance and Social Studies | | | | |
Early Grades				
V/L	Research folk dances that are common to your region or state.	Write down directions on chart paper in sequential order.	Interview parents and family about family dances.	Read *Song and Dance Man* by K. Ackerman, interview grandparents about dancing.	Read various children's books that relate to dances as a family or cultural tradition.
L/M	Learn the steps to one cultural dance, sequentially.	Create a dance map. (Brady, 1994)	Chart similarities and differences in dances from 3 cultures or countries.	Use dance steps to review counting.	Categorize according to types of dance, culture, and so on.
V/S	Watch a video of ethnic dancing.	Lead students in a dance imagery.	Look at yourself in the mirror dancing.	Research ethnic dances (Native American, Island, Mexican). Draw clothing.	Draw a picture of why some ethnic groups include dance in their celebrations.
M/R	Explain the lyrics to a certain square dance.	Accompany the dance with homemade percussion instruments.	Sing social studies age-appropriate songs. Accompany with dance steps/hand motions.	Review information with original hand jives and foot jives.	Pick appropriate music for the dances. Discuss why music is appropriate.
B/K	Define social studies vocabulary words through movement.	Perform the improvisational dance at conclusion of imagery.	Learn a square dance.	Create a puppet play about holidays and incorporate the dances in the play.	Include kinesthetic experiences in the imagery.
Inter	Brainstorm with a partner questions to ask about this performance.	Use the Internet to find information about holiday festivals that include dances.	In groups, create a dance for your favorite holiday.	Ask the PE teacher to talk to your class about dances.	Teach one of the family dances to the class.
Intra	Reflect through drawing on why people dance.	Choose an emotion. Make up a dance to define that emotion.	"What is a barn dance?"	"Write about your feelings."	"I like to see members of my family dance because_."
Nat	Dance the seasons, different climates, and weather patterns.	Dance various cycles in nature.	Research dances that "bring in" seasons or define months.	Make connections to health and dances.	Research tribal dances that focus on healing.

Dance and Social Studies Middle Grades				
V/L	Research dances to one global culture.	Write a report about the significance of that dance to the culture.	Report on one famous dance artist of the 20th century.	Read about the history of square dances, and other regional American dances.	Create a myth about how the "Whirling Dervish" got his name.
L/M	Chart the information.	Create a time line of American dances from the turn of the century.	Collect and categorize data regarding dances during ancient civilizations.	Interpret the major differences.	Give reasons why dance is an integral part of certain rituals and ceremonies.
V/S	Use *National Geographic* magazines to create a montage of this culture's dance.	Preview several biblical movies. Look for instances when dances were used.	Collect photos of global ceremonies in which dance is a part.	Create a cluster that incorporates the economics of dance industry today.	Watch a video of *Riverdance*. Research People, Places, Environment associated with it.
M/R	Listen to music examples of: waltzes, minuets, hip/hop, big band, jazz, Native American, and so on.	Look for examples of these on TV, in movies, documentaries, and so on.	Listen to techno/synthesizer music. Create robot dance to accompany this music.	Select music that creates certain moods.	Research Celtic music that is similar to music used in the video.
B/K	Create your own dance that defines a period in history.	Learn a folk dance from a European country.	Attend a dance performance presented in your community or local university.	Research one significant event per decade in the last 100 years. Pantomime the events.	Use music and improvisational dance to define: *Poverty, Gangs, Pride, War,* and so on.
Inter	With a partner investigate popular dances during World War I and II.	Individually, research the exclusion of dances in certain religions.	With a partner, create *Jeopardy*-type cards to accompany these photos.	Debate its negative/positive impacts on today's youth.	In groups, discuss dances that define a part of present American culture.
Intra	Explain why dances could be the "universal languages" as well as music.	How does dance relate to celebration in some cultures?	"Why do football players often enroll in ballet classes?"	How does the music direct the dance steps? How does the music define the times?	Write about how, in your opinion, dance reflects a certain historical period.
Nat	Investigate "rain dances."	Investigate the significance of dance in the "coming of age" rituals of some tribes.	Use the Internet to investigate the "funeral marches" held in the French Quarter of New Orleans.	Research the connection between dancing and fitness.	Research "how and why certain animals or insects 'dance'."

The list of ideas for integrating dance into social studies lessons is endless. Teach children dances from around the world. Teach them dances specific to regions of the United States such as Cajun dances and clogging. Create pictorial montages from photographic magazines to coincide with the dances. Brainstorm futuristic cultures and original dances that help celebrate such cultures. Research a ballet dancer and an NFL quarterback or NBA player. Look for comparisons in grace, endurance, physical conditioning, salary, work ethic, social acceptance, longevity, and drawing power.

Some of us dance. Some of us observe others dance. The arts gives us the opportunities to do both, as do the dance-oriented activities for students included earlier in this section.

∂. *Putting It All Together in Interdisciplinary Instruction*

Even though Studs Terkel defined the world as a "human salad," teaching social studies in a loose, eclectic manner is not effective with children, particularly younger students. Teachers who use "a little bit of this and a little bit of that" often have lessons and units that constitute chaos of mind and body in the classroom. When a mishmash occurs, there is no sense of connection to the other elements of social studies or to personal meanings. Rather, interdisciplinary lessons should come to students with foundational components and experiences. Thus, children are presented with a starting reference that ultimately takes them where you, and they eventually, want and need to go. Whether you use the expanding environment approach to teaching social studies, the spiral curriculum approach, or even the NCSS social studies program (Welton and Mallan 1996), connections must be made from one element of social studies to another. For example, when working with primary-grade students as they learn more about Native Americans, an umbrella of lessons that include all of the social sciences along with the ten themes of study should be presented. Too often we spend the majority of our lessons on the names of tribes, location of tribes, headbands, dances, and houses. Children are capable of much more. We must give them appropriate learning experiences that create an entire picture of the Native American. The same is true for older students. When studying about the Vikings, it is imperative that we bring to class a menu of experiences that lead to a more complete understanding of this culture other than the long ships, Valhalla, or valor.

Often visual organizational tools assist teachers in creating units and lessons that are not watered down or unbalanced. They can also be used as guides for where to place arts experiences in the curriculum. Grids, outlines, or webs work wonders in this regard. Creating a social studies visual formula such as the social studies unit tree can be used to remind teachers of the areas to which they devote too much time and the areas they lightly touch or omit altogether.

Unit Tree

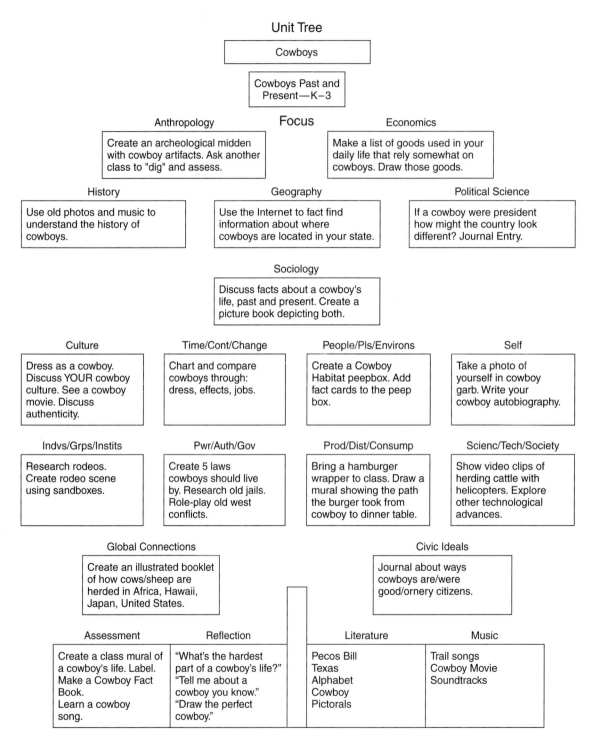

Cowboys	
Cowboys Past and Present—K–3	

Focus

Anthropology
Create an archeological midden with cowboy artifacts. Ask another class to "dig" and assess.

Economics
Make a list of goods used in your daily life that rely somewhat on cowboys. Draw those goods.

History
Use old photos and music to understand the history of cowboys.

Geography
Use the Internet to fact find information about where cowboys are located in your state.

Political Science
If a cowboy were president how might the country look different? Journal Entry.

Sociology
Discuss facts about a cowboy's life, past and present. Create a picture book depicting both.

Culture
Dress as a cowboy. Discuss YOUR cowboy culture. See a cowboy movie. Discuss authenticity.

Time/Cont/Change
Chart and compare cowboys through: dress, effects, jobs.

People/Pls/Environs
Create a Cowboy Habitat peepbox. Add fact cards to the peep box.

Self
Take a photo of yourself in cowboy garb. Write your cowboy autobiography.

Indvs/Grps/Instits
Research rodeos. Create rodeo scene using sandboxes.

Pwr/Auth/Gov
Create 5 laws cowboys should live by. Research old jails. Role-play old west conflicts.

Prod/Dist/Consump
Bring a hamburger wrapper to class. Draw a mural showing the path the burger took from cowboy to dinner table.

Scienc/Tech/Society
Show video clips of herding cattle with helicopters. Explore other technological advances.

Global Connections
Create an illustrated booklet of how cows/sheep are herded in Africa, Hawaii, Japan, United States.

Civic Ideals
Journal about ways cowboys are/were good/ornery citizens.

Assessment
Create a class mural of a cowboy's life. Label. Make a Cowboy Fact Book. Learn a cowboy song.

Reflection
"What's the hardest part of a cowboy's life?"
"Tell me about a cowboy you know."
"Draw the perfect cowboy."

Literature
Pecos Bill
Texas
Alphabet
Cowboy
Pictorals

Music
Trail songs
Cowboy Movie
Soundtracks

Unit Tree

Cowboys

Cowboys 'Round the World—4–6

Focus

Anthropology

Create an archeological midden with cowboy artifacts. Ask another class to "dig" and assess.

Economics

Use Internet to collect data on the Beef Industry. Categorize using visual montages, webs, spirals, graphs, charts.

History

Write report on differences/ similarities of North American and South American cowboys.

Geography

Use map skills to locate global areas that depend on cowboys for herding, ranching, etc.

Political Science

"Why would you trust/not trust a cowboy who runs for office?" Journal.

Sociology

Use creative writing skills and illustrations to describe: Rodeo culture, Cowboy culture, Gaucho culture, etc.

Culture

Create facts/fiction cards. Research 5 basic global cowboy cultures for: food, clothing, recreation, job, dances, music.

Time/Cont/Change

Use any areas of visual arts to create a Then/ Now Report on cowboys.

People/Pls/Environs

Interview real cowboys. Connect local environment to cowboys. Dramatize information.

Self

What about YOU, could you do the job of a cowboy? What couldn't you do? Reflect.

Indvs/Grps/Instits

Create a graph comparing social class cowboys are placed in around the globe.

Pwr/Auth/Gov

Research Old West laws vs. Modern Day Laws. Create a Cowboy Code.

Prod/Dist/Consump

Bring a hamburger wrapper to class. Draw a mural showing the path the burger took from cowboy to dinner table.

Science/Tech/Society

Using magazine pictures, create a montage of technological advances that have influenced cowboy life.

Global Connections

Write a song about the day in the life of a cowboy from another country. From this country.

Civic Ideals

"Why do you think cowboys are viewed as honest, hardworking, individuals?" Write a report.

Assessment

Class mural
Cowboy Diary
Test of Facts
Map Test
Biography
Interview

Reflection

Why are cowboys almost obsolete? Cowboys in other countries seem _. Cowboys get to_.

Literature

Biographies
Pictorals

Music

Tex Ritter songs
Trail Songs
Movie
Soundtracks

Chapter Summary

Teaching social studies with a rich smattering of drama, music, visual art, dance, or other arts disciplines gives students front row center access to who they are and what they may become. It forces them to take internal journeys as they navigate among the external highways of facts, figures, and hard information. Arts make the trip a much more meaningful and authentic experience.

Integrating arts and social studies in this way touches base with every kind of learner, with every multiple intelligence, with group dynamics of every configuration. It shifts the focus from vertical to horizonal, from linear to arches, from black and white to the entire spectrum of colors. It emphasizes the nuances of life instead of the products of life. It specializes in emotion. But more than anything, teaching social studies in an arts-integrated fashion is about valuing: valuing that which makes us human, that which makes us continue to go forward, and that which gives the world, past and present, some sense of believability and hope. It is also about valuing our students enough to give them all the options required to grow. Perhaps Perry Glasser (1997, 4) summed up teaching best when he wrote: "When the classroom door is closed and it's just you and them, give your students who you are and what you know. All of it. Not half. Not some. Everything. The rest is bunk." In social studies, the arts touch everything. For many students, they are everything.

Children's Books

Curtis, C. P. 1999. *Bud, not Buddy.* New York: Delacorte. A boy searches for his father who plays in an ever moving jazz band during the 1930s.

Deedy, C. 1995. *The last dance.* Illus. D. Santini. Atlanta: Peachtree Publishers. A story about young friends, one of whom wants to dance. (Gr. K–5)

Munoz, P. 1998. *Riding freedom.* Illus. R. Selznick. New York: Scholastic. A biography of Charlotte "Charley" Parkhurst who was a top-notch horse rider, stagecoach driver, and probably the first woman to vote in the United States.

Shange, N. 1994. *I live in music.* Illus. R. Bearden. New York: Stewart, Tabori, and Chang. Asian poetry is shared in this book.

References

Bauer, C. 1987. *Presenting reader's theater.* New York: H. W. Wilson.

Boorman, J. 1971. *Creative dance in grades 4–6.* Don Mills, Ontario: Academic Press Canada Limited.

Brady, M. 1994. *Artstarts.* Englewood, CO: Teacher Ideas Press.

Brady, M. 1998. *Social studies and the multiple intelligences: Bringing the world home to children.* Sedona, AZ: Pandy Music.

Callaway, A. 1996. *To Ella, with love.* CD. New York: After 9 Records.

Cecil, N. and P. Lauretzen. 1994. *Literacy and the arts for the integrated classroom.* New York: Longman.

Clemens, S. 1991. Art in the classroom: Making every day special. *Young Children* 52 (2): 4–11.

Cottrell, J. 1987. *Creative drama in the classroom 4–6.* Lincolnwood, IL: National Textbook Company.

Coulter, D. 1989. The brain's timetable for developing musical skill. *General Music Journal* 13 (1): 3–10.

Fowler, C. 1994. Strong arts, strong schools. *Educational Leadership* 52 (30): 4–9.

Gardner, H. 1983. *Frames of mind: The theory of multiple intelligences.* New York: HarperCollins Publishers.

Glasser, P. 1997. Not half; not some. *Educational Leadership* 78 (7): 504–5.

Greenwald, A. W. 2000. Team Egypt! Integrating the disciplines. *Middle Level Learning,* 7:M2–M4.

Haslinger, J., P. Kelly, and L. O'Lare. 1996. Countering absenteeism, anonymity, and apathy. *Educational Leadership* 54 (1): 47–9.

Heinig, R. 1987. *Creative drama resource book (K–3).* Englewood Cliffs, NJ: Prentice-Hall.

Levene, D. 1993. *Music through children's literature.* Englewood, CO: Teacher Ideas Press.

Mayesky, M. 1995. *Creative activities for young children.* New York: Delmar.

Rasmussen, K. 1998, June. Visual arts for all students. *Education Update,* 1–6.

Sporre, D. 1987. *The creative impulse: An introduction to the arts.* Englewood Cliffs, NJ: Prentice-Hall.

Welton, D., and J. Mallan. 1996. *Children and their world: Strategies for teaching social studies.* Boston: Houghton Mifflin.

Chapter 13

© Elizabeth Crews

Social Studies for All Learners

Carol J. Fuhler
Iowa State University

Child, teacher, and parent should celebrate each new learning by focusing on what is known rather than what is lacking.

—Dorothy S. Strickland
"Emergent Literacy: How Young Children Learn to Read and Write"

Objectives

———————————————————— ⟋⟍ ————————————————————

Readers will

- apply a variety of interdisciplinary strategies to enhance the learning of social studies content for all students;
- examine and explain the similarities and differences of students in the learning community labeled as gifted and/or learning disabled;
- summarize why social studies content can be thought-provoking and engaging to all learners; and
- design quality, appealing learning opportunities for students at various stages of the learning spectrum.

Introduction

The world within today's classroom is a reflection of the world outside its doors. Each year teachers will be confronted with greater ethnic diversity among students, an ever present range of socioeconomic backgrounds, and a widening range of intellectual abilities. Children labeled as gifted, learning disabled, attention deficit disorder (ADD), or slow learner will be thrown into the mix of eager faces looking toward the teacher. One reason for these challenging changes is the current inclusion

13.1 Focus Box

Successful Teaching Premises for All Learners

1. Each learner is unique. Therefore, all learning experiences must take into account the abilities, interests, and learning styles of the individual.
2. Learning is more effective when students enjoy what they're doing. Therefore, learning experiences should be designed and assessed with as much concern for enjoyment as for other goals.
3. Learning is more meaningful and enjoyable when content (e.g., knowledge) and process (e.g., thinking skills) have a real problem as their context. Therefore, students should have some choice in problem selection and teachers should consider the relevance of the problem for individual students as well as authentic strategies for addressing the problem.
4. Enrichment learning and teaching focus on enhancing knowledge and acquiring thinking skills. Therefore, applications of knowledge and skills must supplement formal instruction (Levstik and Barton 1997; Renzulli 1994–1995, 77).

movement. Although there is far from a consensus on the subject, advocates for inclusion strongly believe that students with learning disabilities increasingly benefit, both academically and socially, from placement in the regular classroom (Dugger 1994; O'Neil 1994–1995). In numerous schools, these often segregated learners will return to the regular classroom from either the self-contained or the resource classrooms where many currently receive all or part of their education. Proponents have put forth the convincing rationale that the regular classroom can bolster academic performance because students will now be held to higher expectations, exposed to more challenging content, and motivated by classroom peers; their social growth can also be strengthened (Dugger 1994; Willis 1994). Although some educators and members of the media argue against inclusion, these changes are already occurring in classrooms across America.

Depending on the school district, inclusion may extend to those students identified as gifted. This change is impelled by a spreading philosophy that encourages mixed-ability grouping and is facilitated by decreasing funding for separate programs for these bright learners (Renzulli and Reis 1993; Willis 1995). Such a move raises the ire of some educators and is strongly supported by others. On one hand, concerned educators worry that "detracking" (Sapon-Shevin 1994–1995, 64) will dilute the quality of education, will force students to learn the pallid fare of a dumbed-down curriculum, and will deny the existence of individual differences. On the other hand, advocates claim these bright young students should learn in a classroom reflective of the community they will eventually work in. Thus, gifted students may once again be an integral part of the classroom, no longer served by pull-out programs or by completely separate programs. The burden of meeting all these learners' needs ought not to rest entirely on the classroom teacher. Renzulli, a noted authority in the field of gifted education, suggests that in addition to classroom instruction, extremely bright children might benefit from mentor programs, special study groups, and classes outside their grade level (Silverman 1993; Willis 1995).

Reaching and teaching students along an extensive continuum of skills and abilities within the realm of social studies is the focus of this chapter. Based on the firm belief that all students can learn, suggestions are offered here that will perhaps "raise the floor and raise the ceiling" (Wheelock 1992, 6) of learning for students described as slow learners or learning disabled, students struggling with attention deficit difficulties, or exceptionally bright students. Despite their labels, all children deserve the opportunity to be tuned in and turned on to social studies. The challenge facing the teacher is just how to accomplish such an exciting but seemingly overwhelming task. The first step is to understand a little about some of the different students within the class.

❧ A Look at the Gifted Learner

According to Joseph Renzulli, there is no single criterion that determines who is gifted and who is not. Instead, giftedness consists of behaviors that indicate interaction among three clusters of human traits:

1. Above average (not necessarily superior) general and/or specific abilities, which means performance—or the potential for performance—representative of the top 15 or 20 percent of any given area of human behavior.
2. High levels of task commitment, which is the perseverance, hard work, and self-confident energy applied to a particular problem or performance area.
3. High levels of creativity, including fluency, flexibility, originality of thought, openness to experiences, curiosity, and sensitivity to detail (Siegel 1990).

These are simple guidelines, however. Some children may display these characteristics while others don't fit into any gifted mold. Brian, a primary-age gifted child, explains the term as meaning, "you have lots and lots of ideas in your head that are bumping into each other all trying to get out" (Siegel 1990, 8). At present we have no definitive description of what gifted children are like. New ideas of what the term means are constantly being developed; in the meantime, these learners will distinguish themselves in the social studies classroom in one way or another.

Suggested Classroom Strategies

The suggestions for teaching the brightest children in a classroom are exciting because they are strategies that can be adapted to challenge every learner. For example, in an effort to teach all the children in the classroom, strategies such as flexible grouping or tiered assignments can be implemented. In tiered assignments, all students explore the same topic but the level of questioning or the expected product varies, depending on ability levels. Ability-based reading and discussion groups could be formed for some projects. Learning centers could be filled with a wide range of materials for reading and research. Individual student contracts could be tied to specific research projects based on personal interest. Finally, mentorships with adults outside the classroom or the school could be carefully worked into the social studies curriculum (Silverman 1993; Willis 1995).

Another effective suggestion for bright students is curriculum compacting (Reis and Renzulli 1992). In this process, the teacher tests students on upcoming units to ascertain what they already know. While a specific unit is being taught to

Children can locate information on the Internet and share with classmates.

© Elizabeth Crews

the rest of the class, students who have mastered the content can pursue enrichment activities. That is, the teacher defines goals and outcomes of a unit and determines which students have already mastered the learning outcomes and which students can master outcomes in less time than their classmates. Then, in place of mastered material, more challenging and productive activities are provided, including content acceleration, peer teaching, and involvement in outside-the-class activities. Another important step for the teacher is to analyze the textbook, deciding which material is necessary for review, what else is necessary to cover quickly, and what should be covered in an in-depth manner (Renzulli 1994–1995).

An additional strategy is to allow students of varying abilities to work together on topics in which they are mutually interested. The major criteria for group effectiveness are commonality of purpose, mutual respect between students, harmony, specific interests, complementary skills, or even friendships. Group work based occasionally on friendships can help promote self-concepts and self-efficacy in students with high abilities as well as in students who struggle with academic demands. This type of grouping enables each child to stretch as a project is completed. To help children grow as learners, teachers need to tap outside sources when developing thematic units. Gifted children might develop a mentorship with an authority outside the classroom, but all children should be exposed to quality speakers, interesting field trips, or other projects that connect the outside world with the classroom world in real ways.

In a social studies classroom that reflects a wide range of abilities, another critical step for the teacher is to change focus. Rather than focus on skill development and the memorization of facts, teachers should refocus on interdisciplinary teaching and theme-based units, student portfolios, and cross-grade grouping whenever possible while continually keeping the individual child in mind. (Renzulli 1994–1995; Siegel 1990). The new focus of all students' work should be an inquiry-based curriculum that develops higher-level thinking skills (Silverman 1993; Wheelock 1992). In the process, students pursue topics as firsthand investigators rather than as traditional passive learners. A further strength of interdisciplinary teaching is that it broadens the arena for learning for all players, opens large blocks of time for in-depth study of a topic, and allows for more opportunities for student choice, a boon to every learner. Using this approach, students are actively "doing history" rather than being stuck in the traditional roll of chapter by chapter review of the year's social studies curriculum (Levstik and Barton 1997). If you are worried that some learners might falter using the preceding strategies, consider this advice. Teaching to the top helps meet the needs of the brightest in the class while the teacher strives to bring the others along; this tactic is much more efficient than teaching to the middle (Willis 1995).

☙ *A Look at the Student with Learning Disabilities*

A teacher entering an elementary school or junior high social studies classroom probably cannot at first glance single out a mainstreamed student with a learning disability. For the most part, these unique learners do not display an observable collection of symptoms. Because no two students labeled as learning disabled are alike, a straightforward, accurate definition remains elusive. More than fifty attempts to pigeonhole this group of learners are currently on the books. It is no wonder that numerous children have been misidentified, swelling the ranks of this catchall category to include a large number of underachievers or slow learners as well ("Learning Disabilities" 1990). Briefly, these children have a disorder in the basic psychological processes involved in understanding or using spoken or written language such that it hampers that student's ability to think, speak, read, or make mathematical calculations. If a severe discrepancy between ability and achievement is found based on the use of a discrepancy formula, the student is considered to be learning disabled.

In creating an appealing educational setting for these learners, teachers must consider the issue of motivation. After years of failure in and out of self-contained classrooms, many students with learning disabilities are reluctant to risk any more. Their battered, fragile egos are buried under a thick, protective covering of feigned indifference and negative or cocky attitudes. Their discouragement can be traced by backtracking along a lengthy trail of incomplete assignments. At a time when conformity and peer approval are a top priority, these students spend much time and energy proving they are not different from their agemates. This potent social-emotional overlap to basic cognitive deficits presents teachers and learners with a formidable challenge.

Here, too, working across the curriculum, making a serious effort to connect thinking content areas, is a sound educational strategy for learners identified as learning disabled or ADD with an individualized education plan, or to slow learners who have slipped through the cracks of the identification system. For instruction to be most beneficial, teachers must consider a learner's identified strengths and weaknesses. Isn't this just highlighting the fact that learning is an intensely personal endeavor? At first glance, integrating instruction while still individualizing teaching to meet student's needs might seem incompatible, but that is not the case. They mesh with a complementary, syncopated beat. When the class as a whole moves forward with a basic rhythm of its own, the educational accent shifts to a different beat, acknowledging specific individual needs that can be met with direct instruction. To maintain a toe-tapping tempo, then, teachers directly teach individual students what they need, when they need it, within the context of their own reading and writing (Hansen 1987; Routman 1991). These teachers maintain a catchy educational rhythm because they have learned to take advantage of those individual and collective teachable moments.

To get a better picture of a student with learning difficulties, let's look at the area of reading. Middle school and junior high students with learning difficulties are commonly reading three to four years below grade level, plateauing at the fifth- or sixth-grade level late in high school (Whyte 1983). Compare this to their gifted counterparts, who may be reading two years or more above grade level. In addition, these students may have short attention spans or auditory memory problems that hamper the development of proficient listening abilities. Some of these learners have difficulty forming thoughts well enough to speak smoothly in front of class, while others are lacking useful study strategies. The often-segregated skills of reading, writing, listening, and speaking, inherent in the successful navigation of the social studies curriculum, need to be addressed in a different way to meet this population's needs. An integrated teaching approach taught by enthusiastic, well-versed educators offers hope to students with learning difficulties.

Specific Teaching Strategies

The old adage practice makes perfect ought to be elevated to an interdisciplinary educational golden rule. Its application can improve all students' skills and should be kept in mind as learners read, write, think, and integrate knowledge across the curriculum. Teachers addressing the needs of students who have learning disabilities, who are considered slow learners, or who display symptoms of ADD should remember the following premises:

1. Allocate time for practice in reading and writing across the curriculum. Continue to teach critical skills and thinking strategies within the context of the students' reading and writing (Graham and Harris 1988; Routman 1991).
2. Whenever new concepts or learning strategies are taught, model, model, model.
3. Expose students to a broad range of reading and writing tasks. Replace contrived writing assignments with more natural writing activities (Hansen 1987; Negron and Ricklin 1996).
4. Create a supportive learning climate. Students will need to reestablish confidence so that they can risk without ridicule.
5. Integrate a writers' workshop format into social studies, breaking writing projects into less overwhelming stages.
6. Individual conferences can be used for a quick assessment of progress. They may be as short as forty-five seconds or as long as necessary. It is that concerned, personal touch that counts.
7. Small group work promotes constructive peer interaction. Combined efforts with everyone doing his or her share yield rewarding results.
8. Hold mini workshops—skills still need to be taught directly and reinforced frequently to promote academic success. Take a few minutes to highlight a skill that a number of students need to review before starting a new project.
   a. Present new information both orally and in writing, modeling procedures on the chalkboard or an overhead transparency.
   b. Repeat important information several times to ensure learning. Begin each day's reading or lecture with a review of previous materials to aid connections with social studies content.

    c. Continue to teach skills—such as previewing, questioning, and making predictions—within the context of literature books and the social studies text. Urge students to use what they know about language to continually construct meaning from text.

9. Allow for personal choices. Students have a greater vested interest in reading a book or poem or pursuing a project that they have personally selected than one that is assigned by the teacher. That critical element of choice facilitates the development of independence so important for the academic and social growth of students with learning difficulties.

ℛ *A Case for Children's Literature*

In an effort to stretch across the curriculum and integrate subject matter, teachers should infuse their courses with children's literature rather than unappealing textbook fare. A multitude of fiction and nonfiction offerings are available to stimulate a student's personal involvement with history. A judicious match between literature book and learner, whatever his or her abilities, can fill in the gaps left by a social studies textbook's factual approach, providing an opportunity to study a "frozen" slice of history at whatever pace or depth is desired (Cline and Taylor 1987). Within the pages of a narrative children's book are new worlds, thought-provoking experiences, and interesting people to widen a student's horizons and deepen understanding as he or she steps across the years (McGowan, Erickson, and Neufeld 1996). In addition, nonfiction children's literature provides an "interesting, lively way to share up-to-date information" (Young and Vardell 1993, 405). Such books push back the walls erected by the traditional remedial curriculum with impediments to learning so familiar to the student and make room in every learner's mind for fascinating historical worlds yet unexperienced.

Such enticing tools of the trade can also extend a teacher's capacity to reach every student in the class. Students' varying reading levels can be accommodated along with their individual interests when a large number of historically related children's literature books and magazines are available to complement the current textbook unit. The more adept reader can travel back in time to the siege of Petersburg during the Civil War, suffering the realities of the war with William, a plantation owner's son in *Across the Lines* (Reeder 1997). This book affords the reader a different perspective as well, as Simon, a slave, recounts the siege from amidst Union lines. The less able reader can gather information from *Cecil's Story,* as a young boy awaits his father's return from the war realizing how it may tragically change his life (Lyon 1991). Titles such as these enable the teacher to start where the learner is, progress from there, and create a richer, more diverse educational environment for the entire class.

To overcome flagging motivation often attributed to the student with learning disabilities, to challenge the gifted readers, and to hook the child with ADD, lively children's literature books are the answer (Hansen and Schmidt 1989; McGowen et al., 1996; Moir 1992; Tunnell and Ammon 1993). Making an assortment of literature available in both reading and social studies increases the possibility that reluctant learners and inquisitive students alike will become captivated by ideas and events in history. Ducking flying bullets with Tillie in *Thunder at Gettysburg*

(Gauch 1990), reacting in horror after shooting a man as Charley does in *Charley Skedaddle* (Beatty 1987), or cringing under the crack of the whip as it impacts bare skin in *True North* (Lasky 1996) makes history live within the mind of the reader. The magic of reader response is at work here. Readers and listeners are busy people. They reflect on what they hear, interpret it in their own unique way, make connections to an accumulation of previous knowledge, and often predict what might happen next. This process is the basis of the popular premise that response to a book is a transaction between reader and writer, a personal exploration of meaning (Rosenblatt 1983, 1991).

The teacher should capitalize on this premise by encouraging memorable connections between reader, writer, book, and history. The teacher can facilitate those personal transactions by presenting students with choices from numerous reading materials beyond the textbook. In addition to fiction and nonfiction books, poetry, song lyrics, recipes, maps, and old letters can be included. Their use can heighten enthusiasm, increase time spent in contact with social studies content, and invite a variety of written responses. It is highly probable that these efforts will have a positive impact on learning within the classroom (Cox and Many 1992; Tunnell and Ammon 1993). Levstik (1989, 183) reminds us of the value of historical fiction:

> It can lead to a richer, fuller, and more empathetic understanding of history.
> Through historical fiction children learn that people in all times have faced change
> and crisis, that people in all times have basic needs in common, and that these
> needs remain in our time. Children can discover some of the myriad ways in which
> humans depend on each other, and of the consequences of success and failure in
> relationships, both personal and historical.

To pique students' interest in a new area of study, the teacher can read an appropriate children's literature book aloud. Reading aloud daily, even briefly, should be a comfortable niche in the social studies regimen. There is nothing like a book well read to entice listeners and to tantalize children's imaginations (Evans 1992; Fuhler 1990; Gambrel 1998). Listening to a book provides an opportunity for readers with disabilities to "taste the delicacy" of well-written books regardless of the reading level (Fountas and Hannigan 1989). As listeners, students are exposed to rich vocabulary and complex sentence structure that would frustrate them if they tackled it on their own.

Students can read coordinated titles independently during reading class or as extra reading in social studies. The teacher then encourages readers to share their reactions and connections to the read-aloud sessions or to text lectures during both large- and small-group discussions. It is not too much to hope that students will carry their reading right out of the classroom when they walk side by side with a main character, caught up in the tale unraveling within the covers of their books.

Caught in their quest for knowledge, every learner is empowered with the responsibility for his or her own reading, writing, speaking, listening, and thinking in the process of getting an education. Working in small groups or paired with a partner, each child has more opportunities to be a successful learner despite the complexities of being categorized—either as gifted or with academic underachievement, inefficient learning strategies, cognitive processing deficits, personality problems, or inhibiting emotional reactions to their deficiencies. Thus, working across the curriculum, impelled by captivating literature, is a giant step in the right direction as students acquire skills in how to become independent learners across the curriculum.

✍ *Travels Back Through Time*

Teachers can invigorate the social studies curriculum by mixing and matching the activities suggested in this section to inspire and ignite learners of varying abilities. The thematic units on the Civil War and Native Americans that are presented here encourage interdisciplinary learning. With an eye to district curriculum guidelines, adjust or adapt the following ideas.

The Civil War

Introduce the Civil War with an appropriate read-aloud like *Pink and Say* (Polacco 1994) or *Bull Run* (Fleischman 1993), two fascinating books that will quickly capture the students' interest. Invite students to choose companion books from those listed at the end of this chapter or others that are readily available at the public library or school learning center. Choice should be based on personal interests and appropriate reading levels. In addition, you may want to refer students to the following issues of *Cobblestone Magazine:* April 1981 (on highlights of the Civil War), January 1985 (on the making of a newspaper), May 1987 (on Reconstruction), July 1988 (on Gettysburg), January 1989 (on children who influenced history), February 1989 (on Frederick Douglass). February 1993 (on the Antislavery Movement), April 1997 (on Stonewall Jackson), October 1997 (on the Battle of Antietam), and December 1998 (on the Battle of Vicksburg). These issues are relatively easy reading and might spark some intriguing group projects.

1. As the read-aloud unfolds, ask the students how events in the book mesh with information in the social studies textbook, the book they are reading, or research being conducted for group projects. Have students discuss and then list in their personal journals similarities and differences that they discover (Negron and Ricklin 1996). Encourage learners to continue observations on their own. Check progress periodically.

2. Have students keep track of colorful vocabulary words from the read-aloud, along with words from literature books they are reading in social studies or reading class. Students can record in their journals words and meanings as well as sentences in which each word is used correctly. Share words with the class on a weekly basis, adding the words, along with a pertinent illustration, to a class dictionary. Dedicate the finished dictionary to future social studies classes.

3. Choose a political figure from the period. Divide students into pairs to do research on the person, on his or her views of the war, and on the dress of the times. Students can present a vignette or play capturing a day of debates in Congress over issues underlying the war. Students could also take the roles of citizens of the time, displaying thoughts and emotions through conversation in the general store or a chance meeting on the street. Students could play two individuals representing opposing views who meet on a train. This

Newspapers and periodicals are superb social studies resources. These seventh graders are working on current events in a core English-social studies class.

© Elizabeth Crews

information could also be presented in a town forum. In the process, students will feel like a part of history.

4. Have students compare and contrast the kinds of information they can learn about the Civil War from literature books versus nonfiction selections and the textbook. Make a large chart with a catchy title for the classroom wall, listing information acquired from various literature books. Add to it as new information emerges. Ask students to examine their books for prologues, epilogues, or author's notes to glean the historical facts on which their books might be based. Invite the readers to discover if the information is accurate.

5. Involve the class in a discussion of the key issues involved in the Civil War. Groups are formed as students select which side of an issue they support. After students research the issue thoroughly, they present their findings to the class in the form of a presentation with visual aids, a play, interviews with prominent thinkers of the time, or other student suggestions. This is one way to demonstrate how students are able to produce rather than reproduce knowledge as they build on what they knew initially, reflect on what they have learned, and then share the results (Levstik and Barton 1997).

6. As students complete self-selected literature titles, divide the class into groups based on the setting of their stories, the time period covered, or issues such as slavery or the running of the Underground Railroad. Assign a recorder to each group. Ask students to share information that was similar or different in their individual books as you monitor group work. Encourage students to discuss their personal reactions, the feelings of their characters, or

the resolution of war-related conflicts within each story. Have each group write a summary of its findings to be shared with the class. Invite the groups to compare and contrast their findings to information from the textbook, class lectures, or both.

7. Work across the curriculum to create an edition of a Civil War newspaper. Provide actual models for the students to study. Perhaps students would like to compare separate issues reflecting the views of the North and of the South. Students can study and write editorials, want ads, ads for runaway slaves, or upcoming slave auctions. They may write reports of the battles between the Ironclads or of major battles in the field. After studying styles of clothing or menus of the times, they should intersperse that information along with daily news and war correspondence. A review of the use of sketches and photography to capture battle scenes might prompt artistic renditions along with articles by correspondents from different parts of the United States. Publish the final editions by displaying them in the learning center.

8. Have a Civil War reenactor come to class in uniform and discuss the segment of the Civil War with which he is most familiar. Women often followed the troops. A female participant in the reenactment group could also shed light on the reality of life on the battlefield. Students can integrate this information with what they have learned from other resources.

9. If possible, visit a museum that has displays covering the Civil War. Students could research answers to questions they are personally interested in as they study the museum artifacts. Notes taken during the trip can become references for individual research or group projects.

10. Students can be assessed on their research and group work based on conditions set up in individual contracts at the beginning of the thematic unit. Select three or four students a day to meet with briefly, noting progress via anecdotal comments. In that way all students in the class can be monitored during the course of a week. A final conference with each student at the end of the unit that includes the student's written self-evaluation will indicate his or her progress and grasp of knowledge.

Native Americans

The study of Native Americans traditionally falls into the elementary social studies curriculum. The following readings and activities are appropriate for younger students but have strong appeal to the older students as well. It is imperative that students of all ages develop a better understanding of different cultures. One place to begin is right here in America. By meeting Native Americans in another time or in another way, students may begin to better appreciate the rich heritage that Native Americans have bequeathed to all Americans. In addition, knowledge gained provides a firm base on which to later study the contemporary life of Native Americans.

Although the study of Native Americans can take many directions, a good place to start is with their myths and legends. Beautifully illustrated, wonderfully written picture books are available that will appeal to readers of all ages and abilities. You may want to choose a sampling of tales from tribes spanning the country or

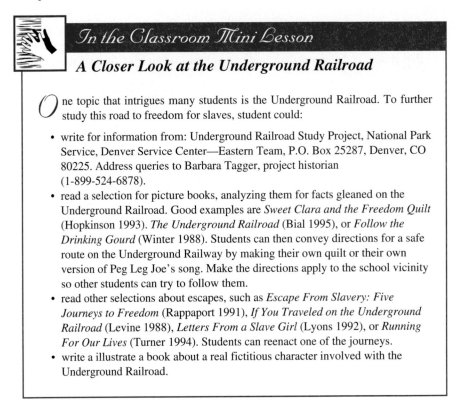

In the Classroom Mini Lesson

A Closer Look at the Underground Railroad

*O*ne topic that intrigues many students is the Underground Railroad. To further study this road to freedom for slaves, student could:

- write for information from: Underground Railroad Study Project, National Park Service, Denver Service Center—Eastern Team, P.O. Box 25287, Denver, CO 80225. Address queries to Barbara Tagger, project historian (1-899-524-6878).
- read a selection for picture books, analyzing them for facts gleaned on the Underground Railroad. Good examples are *Sweet Clara and the Freedom Quilt* (Hopkinson 1993). *The Underground Railroad* (Bial 1995), or *Follow the Drinking Gourd* (Winter 1988). Students can then convey directions for a safe route on the Underground Railway by making their own quilt or their own version of Peg Leg Joe's song. Make the directions apply to the school vicinity so other students can try to follow them.
- read other selections about escapes, such as *Escape From Slavery: Five Journeys to Freedom* (Rappaport 1991), *If You Traveled on the Underground Railroad* (Levine 1988), *Letters From a Slave Girl* (Lyons 1992), or *Running For Our Lives* (Turner 1994). Students can reenact one of the journeys.
- write a illustrate a book about a real fictitious character involved with the Underground Railroad.

decide to concentrate on one section of the country, highlighting the Plains tribes, for example. As each tribe is discussed, locate it on a map of the United States.

Begin the thematic unit with a K-W-H-L chart to be posted on a bulletin board or chalkboard throughout the unit. Activate prior knowledge by asking children what they already *know* about Native Americans. This is a critical step for every learner and is rooted in cognitive learning theory, more specifically in schema theory. This theory explains how people attach new information to previously existing information, or schemata, which are described as collections of related ideas. Learning occurs, then, as new ideas are integrated into a learner's current knowledge. Translating this information into classroom teaching practices suggests that in order for all students to learn most advantageously, it is imperative that new knowledge be built on what students already know. Therefore, being aware of just how much existing knowledge a student has before beginning a new unit of study is the first step in ensuring that every student, regardless of abilities, has the best opportunity to learn (Duis 1996; Levstik and Barton 1997). Schemata theory makes the Know segment of the K-W-H-L chart particularly important. Furthermore, judicious use of this chart or similar graphic organizers can facilitate thinking skills and offer time for reflecting on what has been learned, valuable skills needed long after students leave the classroom.

Then move to the column on what they might *want* to know and fill that in. The column headed by an H asks the students *how* they might find the information they are interested in. Finally, at the conclusion of the unit, ask the students to explain what they have *learned,* the final column on the chart. The responses that fill this column are one way to assess growth in understanding of the group as a whole.

1. Explain the value of storytelling and its critical role in many cultures since the earliest times in human society (Max 1997; Moir 1992). It is probably an activity that elementary students are already quite familiar with. Tell them that stories were the way Native American heritage was passed on to the present generation. Help listeners consider the value of the spoken word in a different light. To the Native Americans, the spoken word was sacred because they used it to pass stories, songs, and chants on to the younger generation. Respectful children who revered their elders retained these messages, regarding them as invaluable (Sneve 1989). As those children transmitted the words of their elders to their children, a body of knowledge gradually formed, one that future generations would be able to study and to enjoy.

2. Read a selection of chants or poems to the students and discuss their underlying meaning to the Native Americans: Invite students to browse through a collection of wonderful poetry books. Have them select a favorite and read it aloud to the class in a poetry session. Students might use *Dancing Moons* (Wood 1995), *Spirit Walker* (Wood 1993), *Songs of Our Ancestors* (Turcotte, 1995), *Earth Always Endures. Native American Poems* (Philip 1996), *Dancing Tepees: Poems of American Indian Youth* (Sneve 1989) or *The Sacred Path: Spells, Prayers, and Power Songs of the American Indian* (Bierhorst 1983). Tie in information on masks by using *They Put on Masks* (Baylor 1974), a poetic description of the importance of ceremonial masks.

3. A natural art activity extending from Baylor's book is to create pictures or papier-mâché masks to be displayed in the room or learning center. Children can write a brief explanation of what their mask represents if it is an original work of art. If it is a reproduction, they can write a short paragraph explaining its origins.

4. After more exposure to the Native American culture, students may want to write their own chants or poetry as they reflect on their own cultures. Older students might illustrate their writing with appropriate designs used as a border.

5. Demonstrate the power of the oral tradition by telling a Native American legend that is a personal favorite. Encourage students to discuss why the story might have been passed along over the years. Follow up by reading a selection such as the amusing *Iktomi and the Boulder* (Goble 1988), the beautifully illustrated *Beardance* (Hobbs 1997), the pleasing *Sunpainters: Eclipse of the Navajo Sun* (Whitethorne 1994), or a selection from *Earthmaker's Tales* (Mayo 1989). These easily read books will be picked up and reread by young readers as soon as you put them down. Bring storytelling into contemporary times by reading and discussing *Pueblo Storyteller* (Hoyt-Goldsmith 1991). If possible, invite a Native American speaker into class to tell several favorite stories.

6. Older students can research their family background for a story to share with the class. Invite parents or younger students to come to class for a Family Story Sharing Day. While the parent tells the story, the child might hold up an illustration he or she created. The oral tradition is a strong influence in many cultures and is a fine lesson for children to learn.

7. Provide a large selection of books of myths and legends for the students to read independently. Give brief book talks on several titles to entice readers to sample the fare. *Where the Buffaloes Begin* (Baker 1981), *The Star Maiden* (Esbensen 1988a), *Snail Girl Brings Water* (Keams 1998) or *Peboan and Seegwum* (Larry 1993) are a few suggestions. *Big Trouble for Tricky Rabbit!* (Mayo 1994) is an appealing collection of trickster tales that will delight readers and listeners from first through sixth grades. Consult the school librarian or visit the public library in search of other appropriate titles. The students should keep a record of the books they read, write a sentence or two in reaction to the book, and rate it on a class rating scale. Use this information to assess progress, interest level, and comprehension.

8. Discuss the structure of myths and legends, noting the simple plot that usually relates just one incident. Explain that if several events occur in a story, they are usually "chained together" in sequential order rather than having one event building on another to create a more complex plot. For example, read *Iktomi and the Buzzard* (Goble 1994) through from beginning to end. Then reread the story, having students pick out each incident. Work as a class to start an original Native American tale. After the first few incidents are recorded, let the students break into small groups to finish the story. Read the polished, illustrated versions in class or share them with another class.

9. Investigate the lives of Native American children and their families today. Hobbs's (1989) *Bearstone* is a fictional account of Cloyd Atcitty's struggle to find a place for himself, thought-provoking reading for older elementary students. Ashabranner's nonfiction account *To Live in Two Worlds* (1984) is also a catalyst for further reading that will begin to tie the past and the present together as readers deepen their understanding of Native Americans.

10. Visit a local museum to study a display depicting the daily lives of Native Americans in the past. Have an informed adult explain the display. Ask students to write about what they learned or what they want to know more about after returning to the classroom.

11. Invite Native Americans to share their music and their dances with the class. The symbolism behind the dances and the costumes can be explained in simple terms to the listeners.

12. As a culminating activity, children can act out their favorite myth or legend, or the one they created in class. Parents can help with simple costumes, and background music can be provided by a tape of authentic Native American music. Parents, another class, or both can be the delighted audience (Negron and Ricklin 1996).

Chapter Summary

Social studies becomes more relevant when teachers nurture all dimensions of intelligence rather than define and measure fixed ability as so often happens in a labeling process. Such nurturing is facilitated when students are given a choice of materials they can readily read, write about, and discuss. Pertinent integrated instructional activities can assist the classroom teacher in facilitating social studies instruction by treating students as citizens of a learning community rather than as products of an assembly line.

The wide range of narrative and nonfiction children's books currently available makes it easier to develop interdisciplinary thematic units for social studies. This chapter provided examples of children's literature and activities for the Civil War and an introduction to Native Americans. In actuality, most all the social studies can be taught through thematic units because of the vast variety and number of children's literature books and the activities that teachers and students can develop to accompany them. Wrapped up in history, literature, and choice, all learners can discover that "persistent effort is the precursor to success in life and is the basis for life-long learning" as future productive citizens in our democracy (Wheelock 1992, 8).

Children's Books

The Civil War

Ackerman, K. 1990. *The tin heart.* Illus. M. Hays. New York: Atheneum. (Ages 8+)
   Mahaley and Flora are best friends who live on different sides of the Ohio River. Traveling back and forth on her father's ferryboat, Mahaley is able to visit Flora frequently. Each wearing one-half of a tin heart, they pledge their friendship forever. As the Civil War erupts, more than the river threatens that pledge.

Armstrong, J. 1996. *The dreams of Mairhe Mehan: A novel of the Civil War.* New York: Alfred A. Knopf. Life in the Irish slum in Washington, D.C., in the 1860s is a struggle made worse when Mairhe's brother goes off to fight in the Civil War.

Altman, S., and S. Lechner. 1993. *Followers of the north star.* Chicago: Children's Press. Vivid poetry captures African Americans and their various accomplishments.

Beatty, P. 1984. *Turn homeward, Hannalee.* New York: Morrow. (Ages 10–14) Twelve-year-old Hannalee and her brother Jem are branded as traitors for making cloth and rope for the Confederacy. When they are sent north to work, Hannalee must serve a harsh employer while Jem is sent to a farm. Disguised as a boy, Hannalee runs away, finds Jem, and they return to devastated Roswell, Georgia.

Beatty, P. 1987. *Charley Skedaddle.* New York: Morrow. (Ages 10–14) A tough New York street kid and member of the Bowery Boys, Charley finds himself a drummer boy in the Union Army. Underneath the tough exterior is a young man who is lonely on the troop ship, horrified in battle, repulsed when he shoots a Rebel, and filled with guilt when he "skedaddles" from battle. An old mountain woman teaches him to believe in himself again.

Beatty, P. 1988. *Be ever hopeful, Hannalee.* New York: Morrow. (Ages 11–15)
   This sequel begins where *Turn homeward, Hannalee* ended. Davey returns from the war without an arm, intent on moving the family to Atlanta to begin a new life. Hannalee's strength of character and optimism still prevail as she works to help her family in this fast-paced historical novel that chronicles the post-Civil War period.

Bial, R. 1995. *The Underground Railroad.* Boston: Houghton Mifflin. Photos of artifacts and actual places make this an informative and appealing book.

Bunting, E. 1996. *The blue and the gray.* Illus. Ned Bittinger. New York: Scholastic.
   A young African American boy and his friend watch the construction of a house that will make them neighbors. Images of a Civil War battle vividly connect the past and the present as the boys reflect on the roots of their friendship.

Chang, I. 1991. *A separate battle: Women and the Civil War.* New York: Dutton. (Ages 10–14) Vivid stories of slave women, abolitionists, women's rights leaders, northern teachers, and southern refugees that relate how women influenced the Civil War.

Clapp, P. 1986. *The tamarack tree.* New York: Lothrop, Lee, and Shephard. (Ages 12–14) An eighteen-year-old English girl finds her loyalties divided as she and her friends experience the hardships imposed on them during the forty-seven-day siege of Vicksburg in the spring of 1863.

Climo, S. 1987. *A month of seven days.* New York: Crowell. (Ages 9–12) Twelve-year-old Zoe Snyder's father is fighting with the Confederates. The family farm is taken over by a Yankee army contingent during their march through Georgia. Frantic to get them away before her father returns, Zoe spends the longest week of her life concocting an elaborate plan to frighten the soldiers off.

Crane, S. 1981. *The red badge of courage.* New York: Watermill Press. (Ages 12–15) Young Henry Fleming is skeptical as he and his fellow U.S. Army men prepare to fight Confederate soldiers during the Civil War. Henry thinks of soldiers as heroes one moment and as cowards the next. As a result of his own cowardice, he must face his own worth both as a U.S. soldier and as a human being.

Davis, P. 1980. *Three days.* Illus R. Rosenblum. New York: Atheneum. (Ages 11–14) The Battle of Gettysburg is presented through the eyes of Robert E. Lee. The story follows the general from the time he enters Pennsylvania to the disastrous conclusion of the battle. Intertwined with Lee's account is the story of an anonymous Confederate soldier.

Fleischman, P. 1993. *Bull Run.* Illus. D. Frampton. New York: HarperCollins. (Ages 10–14) The first engagement of the Civil War is described through the vignettes of sixteen memorable characters. Each distinctive voice contributes to a picture of the life-shattering tragedy for anyone involved in this war.

Freedman, R. 1987. *Lincoln: A photobiography.* New York: Clarion Books. (Ages 10+) The author shapes a vivid portrait of the sixteenth president from historical photographs, magazine prints, and other pertinent documents. The facts of Lincoln's life, from the growing-up years to the turmoil of his presidency, are presented in informative, straightforward text.

Fritz, J. 1987 *Brady.* Illus. L. Ward. New York: Coward, McCann. (Ages 10–13) Brady cannot keep a secret, a fact that worries his parents when he discovers their activities with the Underground Railroad. Brady's resourcefulness in time of need saves the life of a runaway slave and proves he can do a man's work.

Fritz, J. 1993. *Just a few words, Mr. Lincoln: The story of the Gettysburg Address.* Illus. Charles Robinson. New York: Putnam. This relates the story of the Gettysburg Address at an easy reading level.

Gauch, P. L. 1990. *Thunder at Gettysburg.* New York: Coward, McCann. (Ages 9–12) Young Tillie is excited as she watches the beginning of the battle from an upper window of her home. Before the battle is over, she has experienced the pain and horror of war as she ducks flying shells and tries to comfort the wounded.

Hansen, J. 1993. *Between two fires: Black soldiers in the Civil War.* New York: Franklin Watts. (Ages 11–14) This book relates the often neglected story of 180,000 African Americans who served in the Union Army. They faced both the enemy fire and racial prejudice as they fought to gain freedom for themselves and their children.

Hopkinson, D. 1993. *Sweet Clara and the freedom quilt.* Illus. J. Ransome. New York: Alfred A. Knopf. (Ages 8–14) Sweet Clara applies her needlework skills to the scraps she collects in an effort to make a quilt showing the way to freedom.

Hunt, I. 1964. *Across five Aprils.* Chicago: Follett. (Ages 12–14) The hardship, suffering, and courage of a young farm boy living near Newton, Illinois, are related as nine-year-old Jethro Creighton gradually takes full responsibility for the farmwork as a result of tragic home situations caused by brothers and cousins who fight on opposite sides in the war.

Johnston, T. 1996. *The wagon.* Illus. James E. Ransome. New York: Tambourine Books. Born into slavery and supported by his caring family, a twelve-year-old boy relates the anger he feels as a slave and the sorrow he carries when he gains his freedom and Lincoln loses his life.

Kearns, 1998. *Snail Girl brings water.* Illus. R. Ziehler-Martin. Flagstaff, AZ: Rising Moon. The story of how the Navaho people got water.

Lasky, K. 1996. *True north.* New York: Blue Sky Press. This story unfolds through alternating voices. Fourteen-year-old Lucy lives a life of comfort in Boston while Africka, a young slave girl works her way alone along the Underground Railroad. The girls become bound together when Lucy follows her abolitionist grandfather's beliefs and helps Afrika complete her journey.

Lester, J. 1968. *To be a slave.* Illus. T. Feelings. New York: Dial. (Ages 12+) In this Newbery Honor book, the author combines the actual testimony of former slaves with his own commentary in an effort to bring the reality of the institution of slavery to the reader.

Levine, E. 1988. *If you traveled on the Underground Railroad.* Illus. R. Williams. New York: Scholastic. (Ages 8–12) A well-concealed railroad helped thousands of slaves escape from owners in the South to freedom in the North. How it worked, what the dangers were, and who helped along the way are explained in this fascinating, easy-to-understand book.

Lincoln, A. 1995. *The Gettysburg Address.* Illus. Michael McCurdy. Boston: Houghton Mifflin. Lincoln's powerful words penned in 1863 carry their strong impact to today's reader as well.

Lindstrom, A. J. 1980. *Sojourner Truth, slave, abolitionist, fighter for women's rights.* Illus. P. Frame. New York: Julian Messner. (Ages 9–12) This biography of a former slave who became one of the best-known abolitionists of her time tells her story from the harsh days of slavery to a meeting with President Lincoln. The text points out that newfound freedom for Sojourner's people was closer to a nightmare for the majority than it was the long-sought fulfillment of a dream.

Lunn, J. 1983. *The root cellar.* New York: Scribner's. (Ages 11–14) When her grandmother dies, shy Rose is sent to the northern shores of Lake Ontario to live with her Aunt Nan's lively family. The discovery of a vine-covered root cellar door draws her into a world of more than 100 years ago, where she is eventually pulled into the tragedies of the Civil War.

Lyon, G. E. 1991. *Cecil's story.* Illus. P. Catalanotto. New York: Orchard. (Ages 7–14) When his father goes off to war, a young boy takes on his father's chores while worrying and waiting for news about his safety.

Lyons, M. E. 1992. *Letters from a slave girl: The story of Harriet Jacobs.* New York: Scribner's. (Ages 11+) Harriet Jacobs escaped from slavery in the 1840s and went on to become an author and noted abolitionist.

Marston, H. I. 1995. *Isaac Johnson: From slave to stonecutter.* Illus. Maria Magdalena Brown. New York: Cobblehill. Based upon extensive research, this book details Isaac's life from the time he was sold into slavery as a seven-year-old to his escape to a better life in Canada.

Meltzer, M. 1989. *Voices from the Civil War.* New York: Crowell. (Ages 12–15) The author depicts life during the Civil War through the words of people who were there, using such primary sources as letters, diaries, ballads, newspapers, interviews, speeches, and memoirs. The text is highlighted with engrossing photographs.

Murphy, J. 1990. *The boys' war—Confederate and Union soldiers talk about the Civil War.* New York: Clarion. (Ages 9–14) This book presents a riveting picture of the Civil

War through the eyes of boys involved in it. More than fifty archival photographs are included.

Murphy, J. 1992. *The long road to Gettysburg.* New York: Clarion. (Ages 11+) Firsthand impressions of two teenage soldiers, one a seventeen-year-old corporal in the Union Army and the other a nineteen-year-old Confederate lieutenant, of the Battle of Gettysburg.

Polacco, P. 1994. *Pink and Say.* New York: Philomet. Two young Union boys from different backgrounds try to recover from wounds in Confederate territory.

Rappaport, D. 1991. *Escape from slavery: Five journeys to freedom.* Illus. C. Lilly. New York: HarperCollins. (Ages 10–15) The five stories relate how slaves gained their freedom with help from both black and white people.

Reeder, C. 1989. *Shades of gray.* New York: Macmillan. (Ages 9–12) Twelve-year-old Will Page regards the Yankees as the enemy because all his family lost their lives as a result of the war. He works the land and hunts the fields in the Virginia Piedmont beside his Uncle Jed, who has offered him a home. Will eventually comes to accept the fact that good people have different but still acceptable ideas and that all people suffer from war.

Reeder, C. 1996. *Across the lines.* New York: Atheneum. Readers get an understanding of the siege of Petersburg through the eyes of the son of a plantation owner and a slave serving in the Union army.

Reit, S. 1988. *Behind enemy lines: The incredible story of Emma Edmonds, Civil War spy.* San Diego: Harcourt Brace Jovanovich. (Ages 13–16) Sarah Edmonds was a feminist long before the word gained popularity. Disguised as a boy, she enlists in the Union Army, frequently acting as a spy for the North. Sarah is a shrewd and courageous heroine.

Rinaldi, A. 1988. *The last silk dress.* New York: Holiday House. (Ages 12–14) Determined Susan Chilmark longs to do something for the "Cause" during the Civil War, despite being hampered by her emotionally unstable mother and the scandalous reputation of her banished older brother. Love, death, and despair stalk her every move as she grows from a naive girl into a wise young woman.

Ruby, L. 1994. *Steal away home.* New York: Macmillan. Fascinating reading as history and mystery are woven into two integrated stories, one of the Underground Railroad and the other of a curious girl in Kansas in the 1990s.

Shore, L. J. 1986. *The sacred moon tree.* New York: Bradbury. (Ages 11–13) With her father fighting in the North and her mother living with her family in Richmond, twelve-year-old Phoebe is left to live on her grandfather's farm in Pennsylvania. She fills her days with wild imaginings until she and her friend Jotham set out on a wild adventure of their own to rescue Jotham's brother from a Southern prison.

Tappert, A., ed. 1988. *The brothers war: Civil War letters to their loved ones from the blue and the gray.* New York: Times Books. (Ages 12+) This collection of memorable letters written by both Union and Confederate soldiers and illustrated with photographs gives readers insight into what the war was like for the soldiers.

Turner, A. 1987. *Nettie's trip south.* Illus. R. Himler. New York: Macmillan. (Ages 7–11) The realities of slavery are portrayed in a sensitive manner as seen by a young girl of the North. Nettie writes her impressions of a trip in the pre-Civil War South to a friend. Her comments center on the institution of slavery as it includes the maid at the inn and those at a slave auction.

Turner, G.T. 1994. *Running for our lives.* Illus. S. Byrd. New York: Dutton. (Ages 8–13) Written from the viewpoint of eleven-year-old Luther, this book recounts how a slave family in Missouri tries to escape to Canada.

Winter, J. 1988. *Follow the drinking gourd.* New York: Knopf. This book describes how
songs were used to direct slaves to freedom via the Underground Railroad.

Wisler, G. C. 1995. *Mr. Lincoln's drummer.* New York: Lodestar. (Ages 10–14) Based on a
true story, this historic novel tells of Willie Johnston, a skinny boy from Vermont who
enlisted in the Union Army along with his father. Willie was awarded the
Congressional Medal of Honor for his heroics by President Abraham Lincoln.

Native American Literature: Myths, Legends, and Poetry

Ashabranner, B. 1984. *To live in two worlds: American Indian youth today.* New York:
Dodd, Mead. Describes the lifestyle of contemporary Native Americans and their
struggle to maintain their identity.

Baker, O. 1981. *Where the buffaloes begin.* Illus. S. Gammell. New York: Viking. (Ages 6+)
A Caldecott picture book that describes Native American life on the plains.

Baylor, B. 1974. *They put on masks.* Illus. J. Ingram. New York: Scribner's. (Ages 6+) A
poetic description of Native American dances.

Begay, S. 1992. *Ma'ii and Cousin Horned Toad.* Illus. S. Begay. New York: Scholastic.
(Ages 6+) A traditional Navajo story about the way Cousin Horned Toad outsmarts
tricky Ma'ii, the coyote.

Bierhorst, J. 1983. *The sacred path: Spells, prayers, and power songs of the American
Indian.* New York: Morrow. (Ages 10+) This book presents a variety of Native
American religious traditions.

Ellison, S. 1998. *Best of enemies.* Flagstaff, AZ: Rising Moon Press. Racial prejudice, unlikely
friendships, and a fight for survival test the courage and honor of a slave girl, a Native
American, and a ranch owner's son during the Civil War in New Mexico.

Esbensen, B. J. 1988a. *The star maiden.* Illus. H. K. Davie. Boston: Little, Brown. (Ages 7+)
The retelling of a Native American legend.

Esbensen, B. J. 1988b. *Ladder to the sky.* Illus. H. K. Davie. Boston: Little, Brown.
(Ages 7+) A Native American legend about climbing a ladder to reach the sky.

Goble, P. 1988. *Iktomi and the boulder: A Plains Indian story.* New York: Orchard Books.
(Ages 7+) A picture book about a humorous Plains Native American legend.

Goble, P. 1994. *Iktomi and the buzzard: A Plains Indian story.* New York: Orchard/Jackson.
The trickster is at work again in a humorous tale.

Hobbs, W. 1989. *Bearstone.* New York: Atheneum. As he works for an elderly rancher
during the summer, Cloyd searches for his identity in a world where he feels he
doesn't belong.

Hobbs, W. 1997. *Beardance.* Illus. Jill Kastner. New York: Atheneum. In a tale that explains
how the Ute Bear Dance began, a young boy seeks out an elderly bear who hasn't
appeared with the coming of spring.

Hoyt-Goldsmith, D. 1991. *Pueblo storyteller.* Photog. L. Midgale. New York: Holiday
House. (Ages 7+) A book about a young girl who is the storyteller of her village.

Larry, C. 1993. *Peboan and Seegwun.* Illus. C. Larry. New York: HarperCollins. (Ages 6+)
An Ojibwa tale that relates why the seasons change.

Martin, R. 1993. *The boy who lived with the seals.* Illus. David Shannon. New York:
Putnam. A Chinook tale about a boy who disappears while playing in the river only to
return years later after living with the seals. Unable to adapt to his former life, he
returns to the sea.

Max, J., ed. 1997. *Spider spins a story: Fourteen legends from Native America.* Flagstaff, AZ:
Rising Moon Press. In a book endorsed by tribal authorities, the power of myths and
legends is revealed through spider, a character common to many Native American tales.

Mayo, G. W. 1989. *Earthmaker's tales: North American Indian stories about earth happenings.* New York: Walker. (Ages 5–14) Depicts how the earth was created and how it should be cared for by its people.

Mayo, G. W. 1994. *Big trouble for tricky Rabbit!* New York: Walker. A collection of trickster tales that will delight many a reader.

Miles, M. 1971. *Annie and the old one.* Illus. P. Parnell. Boston: Little, Brown. (Ages 6–9) A young girl befriends an elderly Native American woman.

Normandin, C., ed. 1997. *Echoes of the elders: The stories and paintings of Chief Lelooska.* New York: DK Publishing. A collection of five tales that were long a part of the oral tradition of the Northwest Coast Indians are recorded for the first time. They teach the importance of revering the natural world and all of its creatures.

O'Dell, S., and E. Hall. 1992. *Thunder rolling in the mountains.* Boston: Houghton Mifflin. (Ages 10+) This book tells of the desperate flight for freedom by the Nez Percé. It describes the wisdom and courage of their leader, Chief Joseph.

Philip, N. 1996. *Earth always endures: Native American poems.* Illus. Edward S. Curtis. New York: Viking. Photographs complement this collection of poetry illuminating a number of facets of the Native American cultures.

Rodanas, K. 1995. *The Eagle's Song.* Boston: Little, Brown. When Ermine's brothers disappear, it is up to him to save them with the help of the eagle-man in this tale from the Pacific Northwest.

Sneve, V. D. H. 1989. *Dancing tepees: Poems of American Indian youth.* New York: Holiday House. (Ages 4–14) Poetry written by Native American children.

Turcotte, M. 1995. *Songs of our ancestors: Poems about Native Americans.* Illus. Kathleen S. Presnell. Chicago: Children's Press. This collection of poems focuses on famous Native Americans and events in their history.

Whitethorne, B. 1994. *Sunpainters: Eclipse of the Navajo sun.* Illus. B. Whitethorne. Flagstaff, AZ: Northland Publishers. A grandfather explains the solar eclipse to his grandson.

Wisniewski, D. 1994. *The wave of the Sea Wolf.* New York: Clarion. A Tlingit tale about princess Kchokeen who receives gifts in a vision that help her change the destiny of her people.

Wood, N. 1993. *Spirit Walker.* Illus. Frank Howell. New York: Doubleday. Beautiful poetry that reflects the determination, courage, and powerful spiritual faith of her friends, the Taos Indians of New Mexico.

Wood, N. 1995. *Dancing Moons.* Illus. Frank Howell. New York: Doubleday. A beautifully written collection of poems reflecting the spirituality and teachings of the Taos Indians of New Mexico.

Yolen, J. 1992. *Encounter.* Illus. D. Shannon. San Diego: Harcourt Brace. (Ages 7+) A Taino boy tells of Christopher Columbus's landing on San Salvador in 1492. Later, Spanish colonization alters the lifestyle, language, and religion of his tribe.

Web Sites

General Social Studies Sites

http://www. ncss.org

National Council of Social Studies presents an award-winning Web site packed with information for the professional social studies educator that includes numerous resources, professional development programs, and a section devoted to student use.

http://www.education-world.com/db/subjects.shtml
Best Educational Sites Today provides a wealth of materials for the social studies teacher and for other subject areas as well.

http://www.nationalgeographic.com
With a reputation long established, you know this site just has to be good.

http://www.xs4all.nl/~swanson/history
K–12 History on the Internet: A resource guide is found at the address.

http://www.csun.edu/~hcedu013/
Social studies lesson plans and resources from the Internet can be found here.

http://execpc.com/~dboals/k-12.html
Part of the History/Social Web Site for Teachers. Look for separate links for K–6 grades with specific lesson plans for social studies, educational resources for parents, and information about professional development.

Civil War Sites

http://funnelweb.utcc.utk.edu/~hoemann/cwarhp.html
This is the site of a Civil War home page.

http://cobweb.utcc.utk.edu/~hoemann/cwarhp.html
An award-winning site that is one of the most valuable resources on the Civil War.

http://www.cwc.lsu.edu/index.htm
This site focuses on the role of African Americans, Native Americans, and other minority groups during the Civil War era.

http://lcweb.loc.gov/exhibits/G.Address/ga.html
This site allows students a close-up of the two versions of the Gettysburg Address.

Native American Sites

http://hanksville.phast.umass.edu/misc/NAresources.html
Index of Native American Resources on the Internet.

http://falcon.jmu.edu/~ramseyil/mulnativ.htm
A resource for multicultural titles.

http//www1.pitt.edu/~lmitten/indians.html
Native American Sites home pages.

http://indy4.fdl.cc.mn.us/~ish'/books/bookmenu.html
Native American Indian art, culture, education, history, and science.

http://www.si.edu/cgi-bin/nav.cgi
Smithsonian Institute National Museum of the American Indian.

References

Cline, R. K. J., and B. L. Taylor. 1987. Integrating literature and "free reading" into the social studies program. *Social Education* 42:27–31.

Cox, C., and J. E. Many. 1992. Toward understanding of the aesthetic response to literature. *Language Arts* 69 (1): 28–33.

Dugger, J. M. 1994. Perceptions and attitudes of teachers toward inclusion of handicapped students. *Illinois School Research & Development* 30 (2) :5–7.

Duis, M. 1996. Using schema theory to teach American history. *Social Education* 60 (3): 144–6.

Evans, K.M. 1992. Reading aloud: A bridge to independence. *New Advocate* 5 (1): 47–57.

Fountas, I. C., and I. L. Hannigan. 1989. Making sense of whole language: The pursuit of informed teaching. *Childhood Education* 65 (3): 133–7.

Fuhler, C.J. 1990. Let's move toward literature-based reading instruction. *The Reading Teacher* 43: 312–5.

Gambrel, L. B. 1998. Creating classroom cultures that foster reading motivation. In *Teaching Struggling Readers,* ed. L. Allington. Newark, DE: International Reading Association.

Graham, S., and K. Harris. 1988. Instructional recommendations for teaching writing to exceptional students. *Exceptional Children* 54 (6): 506–12.

Hansen, J. 1987. *When writers read.* Portsmouth, NH: Heinemann.

Hansen, M. B., and K. S. Schmidt. 1989. Promoting global awareness through trade books. *Middle School Journal* 21 (1): 34–7.

Learning disabilities: A definitional problem. 1990. *Education of the Handicapped* 16 (21): 5–6.

Levstik, L. 1989. A gift of time: Children's historical fiction. In *Children's literature in the classroom: Weaving Charlotte's Web,* ed. J. Hickman and B. Cullinan. Portsmouth, NH: Heinemann.

Levstik, L. S., and K. C. Barton. 1997. *Doing history: Investigation with children in elementary and middle schools.* Mahwah, NJ: Lawrence Erlbaum.

McGowan, T. M., L. Erickson, and J. A. Neufeld. 1996. With reason and rhetoric: Building the case for the literature-social studies connection. *Social Education* 60 (4): 203–7.

Moir, H., ed. 1992. *Collected perspectives: Choosing and using books for the classroom.* 2d ed. Boston: Christopher Gordon.

Negron, E., and L. P. Ricklin. 1996. Meeting the needs of diverse learners in the social studies classroom through collaborative methods of instruction. *Social Studies and the Young Learner* 9 (2): 27–9.

O'Neil, J. 1994–1995. Can inclusion work? A conversation with Jim Kauffman and Mara Sapon-Shevin. *Educational Leadership* 52 (4): 7–11.

Reis, S., and J. Renzulli. 1992. Using curriculum compacting to challenge the above average. *Educational Leadership* 50 (2): 51–7.

Renzulli, J. 1994–1995. Teachers as talent scouts. *Educational Leadership* 52 (4): 75–81.

Renzulli, J., and S. Reis. 1993. The reform movement and the quiet crisis in gifted education. *Oregon English Journal* 15:9–17.

Rosenblatt, L. M. 1983. *Literature as exploration.* New York: Modern Language Association of America.

Rosenblatt, L. M. 1991. Literature—S.O.S.! *Language Arts* 68:444–8.

Routman, R. 1991. *Invitations: Changing as teachers and learners.* Portsmouth, NH: Heinemann.

Sapon-Shevin, M. 1994–1995. Why gifted students belong in inclusive schools. *Educational Leadership* 52 (4): 64–70.

Siegel, D. 1990. *Educating the gifted is a community affair: An educator handbook.* Helena, MT: The Montana Association of Gifted and Talented Educators.

Silverman, L. K. 1993. Instructional strategies for the gifted. *Oregon English Journal* 15:18–20.

Strickland, D. S. 1990. Emergent literacy: How young children learn to read and write. *Educational Leadership* 47:18–23.

Tunnell, M. O., and R. Ammon, eds. 1993. *The story of ourselves: Teaching history through children's literature.* Portsmouth, NH: Heinemann.

Wells, G., and G. L. Chang-Wells. 1992. *Construction knowledge together: Classrooms as centers of inquiry and literacy.* Portsmouth, NH: Heinemann.

Wheelock, A. 1992. The case for untracking. *Educational Leadership* 50:6–10.

Whyte, L. A. 1983. The learning disabled adolescent: A review of the research on learning disabled adolescents and its implications for the education of this population. *Mental Retardation and Learning Disability Bulletin* 11:134–41.

Willis, S. 1994. Making schools more inclusive. *Curriculum Update,* October, 1–8.

Willis, S. 1995. Mainstreaming the gifted. *Curriculum Update* 37 (2): 1, 4–5.

Young, T. A., and G. Vardell. 1993. Weaving readers' theatre and nonfiction into the curriculum. *The Reading Teacher* 46:396–405.

Chapter 14

© Photo by Jean-Claude
LeJeune

Automation, Innovation, Participation

Infusing Technology into Social Studies

Kenneth King
Northern Illinois University

The concept that we live on a round planet with large land masses interrupted by vast oceans is a primary geography learning which is part of any elementary social studies program. At a more sophisticated level of learning, we want elementary students to appreciate the unity and diversity of our world and use technology as a basis for communicating with students in other places.

—Joseph A. Braun
Connecting the Globe: From Cardboard to Telecommunications

Objectives

———————————————— ✺ ————————————————

Readers will

- recognize that technology provides a means of helping students to achieve National Council for the Social Studies (NCSS) learning goals;
- identify examples of presentation hardware commonly found in elementary and middle school classrooms;
- apply the appropriate technology to achieve a desired learning outcome in social studies;
- strive to use technology in such a way as to emancipate student learning, rather than to simply automate it; and
- evaluate and implement the use of educational software and web sites based on educational value.

Introduction

"I believe that the motion picture is destined to revolutionize our educational system and that in a few years it will supplant largely, if not entirely, the use of textbooks. I should say that on the average, we get about two percent efficiency out of schoolbooks as they are written today. The education of the future, as I see it, will be conducted through the medium of the motion picture . . . where it should be possible to achieve one hundred percent efficiency." (Thomas Edison, 1922, quoted in Cuban 1986, 9)

The imperative to use technology in the classroom comes from many sources. Decades ago, Thomas Edison agitated for an increased use of motion picture technology as a means of making instruction more efficient, more engaging, and more effective. That hew and cry continues today, with the computer and the Internet offered as the means of improving classroom practices for teachers and students alike.

Technology can serve as an important tool, as it serves to both innovate and automate tasks for teachers and students alike. Teacher utilities such as grading programs and bar coding software can assist the teacher in managing large amounts of information. Presentation software and Internet access can offer students the means to explore the world and share their findings with other students. Technology-based reference materials abound (Freiwald 1997). Unfortunately, the potential use for technology in the social studies has been limited. A survey of college-bound seniors reported only 8 percent of them having used computer technology to assist in learning about social studies problems (Copley, Cradler, and Engel, 1997). Thus, the challenge lies with teachers to make these rich resources available to their students in meaningful ways.

Technology can also serve as an effective means of connecting classroom instruction with the larger goals of social studies education as described in the *Curriculum Standards for Social Studies: Expectations for Excellence* (NCSS, 1994). Goal 8, Science-Technology and Society, and Goal 9, Global Connections, are but two of the themes that benefit from the infusion of instructional technology.

When considering the use of technology in the classroom, it is of critical importance that the instructional goals be identified first. This allows technology to serve a purpose in support of the curriculum and instruction rather than as an end in itself. The greatest benefits of using technology are derived from infusing technology into content area instruction. Thus, using technological tools to help foster learning within social studies provides such an integrated approach. The remainder of this chapter investigates various means of using technology in classroom instruction.

Teaching with Technology

Most teachers, if asked, would prefer that each student have access to his or her own computer at the same time. However, that is not a circumstance in which most teachers find themselves. Most opportunities to use the computer take place in classroom with a either a single machine or with a small handful of machines. Therefore, some suggestions for using the computer in the one-computer classroom are in order.

As a Presentation Tool

One means of using the computer in classroom instruction is as a presentation tool. This approach works for both students and teachers. Much like a chalkboard, the computer allows various types of information to be presented for large groups to see. The computer, however, moves beyond simple text and includes both moving images and audio information. *Video projection* and *LCD projector* units are simple means of presenting information on the computer to the entire class.

The video projector allows the image that would normally be visible on the monitor to be projected onto a screen. This allows for the entire class to see the information on the computer. The LCD projector panel does the same thing, but by laying a panel on top of an overhead projector. The overhead projector shines through the LCD panel, which then projects the computer's information in the front of the room.

A lower-cost alternative makes use of a technology that is probably already available in the classroom: a television monitor. Through the use of a device called a *scan converter,* a cable from the back of the computer can be connected to the scan converter, which in turn is connected to the television monitor. This allows the computer's information to be seen on the larger screen, meeting the needs of the entire class.

Using Four to Six Computers in a Classroom

Many school districts have provided four to six computers in each classroom. This offers the teacher an advantage in that individual assignments or cooperative learning groups can be carried out more efficiently than with a single classroom computer. An example would be a cooperative learning activity involving the historical study of the Mid-Atlantic states by fifth graders. Each group of students may take a state (New Jersey, New York, Delaware, Pennsylvania, or Maryland). For each state, students would generate questions such as the following:

- Why was the colony or state founded?
- Were political or religious beliefs a factor?
- Who is considered the founder of the state or colony?
- What were the strengths or weaknesses of the geographic location?
- What were the economic strengths or weaknesses of the location?

Students in their cooperative groups can assign or take a specific question to answer using their textbook, a computer CD-ROM encyclopedia, and by then searching the Internet using key words from the questions they generated. Each student would contribute to a larger group report, saving it on disk, revising and modifying as the final product was developed.

As a Learning Center Station

Some schools with a less generous technology infrastructure may have only a single computer in the classroom. The suggestions made for the four-to-six-computers

Laptop computers are being used increasingly in classrooms.
© Nubar Alexanian/Stock Boston

option can be adapted to make use of a single machine. One successful approach is to use the computer as one of several learning center stations. This requires that instruction be organized in such a way as to make use of multiple small groups of students. Students carrying out a computer-based simulation or an Internet search can use the computer while other students are engaged in related tasks, such as traditional text book research, writing, or interacting with other students. Other excellent suggestions for teaching in a one-computer classroom are offered by Dockterman (1997) as noted in the sources for this chapter.

ꙮ Technology in the Social Studies Curriculum

An appropriate way to consider the use of technology in the classroom is through the work of Tinker (1987). He proposed that teachers first consider the purpose for using the technology in the classroom, rather than initially focusing on individual software applications. This allows for a more thoughtful and productive use for technology in the classroom, rather than seeking uses after the fact for a collection of miscellaneous software.

Though Tinker's classification scheme was conceived with a focus on computers, the use of all classroom technologies fits into his scheme, thereby testifying to its versatility. Tinker (1987) saw this scheme as describing a transition from knowledge acquisition to knowledge generation. The first of Tinker's categories represents the use of the computer as an instrument of information acquisition. The others are data analysis, creativity, and communications.

Information Acquisition

The ability to gain and use information provides an essential purpose for technology. As a reference tool, technology offers many advantages. Technology has served to both automate and innovate our access to information. Using technologically enhanced research tools offers students a broad skill with applications across the curriculum. Technology allows students to rapidly locate and use information, with additional advantages of sorting information and using hypertext links to move on to related information. Textual information, graphics, audio, video, and databases provide a more comprehensive set of data for students to make use of in the classroom. Students in the upper-elementary and middle school grades find much success in the use of computer software such as Microsoft's *Encarta* and Grolier's *New Multimedia Encyclopedia.* Current events can be accessed via the Internet from multiple sources of information and opinion (Larson 1999).

Videodisc Technology

The videodisc offers an excellent tool for teacher presentation of information in the classroom. The ability to select and program images in sequence provides the teacher with a very powerful—and labor-saving—tool. While videotape is a helpful means of bring prerecorded information to class, accessing the information rapidly can often be difficult. Given that the prescribed order of presentation on the videotape may not match the instructional goals of the teacher, the videodisc allows for a means of selecting precise video images and presenting them in an order to better meet the needs of the lesson. Focus Box 14.1 provides and example of how software can be used to create bar codes for presentation purposes.

CD-ROM Databases and CD-ROM Encyclopedias

Numerous software applications have been made available by commercial vendors in recent years. As the use of this sort of software is conceptually similar to an encyclopedia or dictionary, the change in teacher behaviors required to use the software is minimal. It becomes a matter of sending a student to a computer to retrieve information rather than sending a student to the library. It could be infused into classroom practice with a minimum of changes in instructional strategies. Popular and engaging software products such as Microsoft *Encarta* conceptually resembled the standard bound set of encyclopedias, but with the addition of audio and moving images, and searching and hypertext-accessible information, all contained within a single CD-ROM. Students can click on a topic, read the information presented, and then follow another hypertext link to pursue their research needs.

In recent years, the Internet has provided an important means of accessing information. With the advent of the graphical browser, through software such as *Netscape* and Microsoft *Internet Explorer* the information available on the World Wide Web has become available to millions of individuals. As the challenges associated with locating and accessing has become simpler, the explosion of information on the Web has made having a critical eye toward the quality of the information more important than previously. Therefore, although the Internet provides many useful sources of information for students and teachers, some cautions are in order regarding its use.

14.1 Focus Box

Accessing Information on a Videodisc

The videodisc offers a number of advantages over a videotape. Beyond the simple issue of consistent quality over years of use, the ability to select precise images and present them in a desired order provides the advantage of instructional flexibility. A simple application such as Bar-n-koder allows the teacher to select images for instruction at the touch of a scanner.

A videodisc contains 55,000 separate images. The bar coding software allows for the teacher to select either a single frame or a series of frames for creating motion.

The remote control for the videodisc player gives the teacher the ability to display each individual frame. From this display mode, the teacher simply notes the frame number for the starting point and the ending point in the series of video images. These numbers are entered into the bar code software and the software produces a bar code that allows for immediate access to the video images.

The bar code can be inserted into a textual document, and descriptive language describing the contents of the images can be included. Finally, the teacher need only print out the document that includes the bar code and description. A bar code scanner will allow the teacher to scan the bar code and play the images for the class to use.

As in a library-oriented search, the teacher's role in identifying information in advance is critical. Just as identifying and marking books for student use focuses students on the task of using the information, the teacher's role in the use of the Internet is similar.

Telecommunications

The use of the Internet as an information resource has provided an important resource for students and educators. Many teachers find the use of the Internet to be among the more engaging and useful infusions of technology into their teaching practices (Harris and Bruce 1997). Among the recent reform efforts in the social studies, attempts have been made to better engage the student in the learning process. Among the techniques used are games, role-playing activities, and other sorts of simulations. Technology offers a means of developing those approaches to teaching. A "Virtual Field Trip" offers one example of this approach (Wilson 1997). In one example described by Wilson (1997), students take a virtual tour of historic Philadelphia. Starting with the use of a K-W-L chart to activate prior knowledge about the city during the time of the Revolutionary War, students navigate among a series of historic "sites" that are organized as part of the Web site. Following the Historic Mile (access first from URL: http://www.ushistory.org/), students can answer the questions they developed earlier.

Telecommunications offers numerous other sources of information for the teacher and student. The National Archives, http://www.nara.gov/nara/nail.html, for instance, can provide students with much in the way of original source material.

Entering the search terms "Vietnam" and "Nixon" provided a number of documents in response, including photographic images of the former president engaging in activities related to the Vietnam conflict.

C-Span (http://www.c-span.org/) offers teachers and students more current information. For instance, during the impeachment trial of President Bill Clinton in 1999, C-Span offered classroom resource materials on the topic of presidential impeachment and analyzing the process with the actions of the 105th Congress as a model of the practice. These on-line materials were usable in concert with the cable broadcasts taking place on a daily basis during that time.

Information Analysis

The use of the computer as an analytical tool represented the second of the applications of technology identified by Tinker (1987). This set of applications moved the computer-student experience further in the direction of increased student autonomy in that the student was engaged as an active participant in the activity. The use of the computer allowed for students to analyze data, rather than to simply collect it, or to use the technology as a simple source of content information. Among the experiences he listed in this category were the computer as a means of analyzing "database/spreadsheet [applications and] graphing/statistical [tools]" (Tinker 1987, 468).

As a tool to organize information, the computer has some natural advantages. It can manipulate large quantities of information. It removes drudgery from some operations. Thus, both teachers and students find it to be a means of being more efficient.

Simulations

Simulations, along with drill-and-practice programs, provided some of the earliest applications of the computer within education. In a simulation, the software allowed the user to engage in an activity that resembles a "real-life" event. Simulations were helpful in learning to detect patterns and in examining the effect of changing a variable on the overall outcome of the activity. The software program *The Oregon Trail* is an example of an exemplary simulation that allows students to re-create at their computer some of the elements of crossing the United States during the nineteenth century.

Information Creation

The ability to use technology as a means of creating information offers another means of providing engaged learning opportunities. Bazeli (1997) noted that students who were able to create presentations using slides, video, and narration were at a significant advantage in terms of creating and presenting ideas. As these presentations are typically organized as group projects, planning, cooperative grouping, and effective communications skills add to the social studies content knowledge being developed. Among the tools that can help achieve these goals are authoring tools, videotapes, and cameras.

Key pals may be from schools across the state, country, or world. Sharing everyday experiences with a key pal can be an enriching social studies experience.

© Elizabeth Crews

Authoring Programs

An *authoring program* is a software application that allows students and teachers to organize and present information in any way they care to. The software allows them to link text, audio, or graphics in any way they elect. Once created, their project can be used to present their information to others (Heinich, et al. 1996). Numerous studies have demonstrated the efficacy of such applications in a school learning setting. In addition to the learning advantages, Heidenreich (1997) noted an increase in the students' regard for learning social studies, his or her partner, and group work in general. Programs such as *Hyperstudio, Hypercard,* and *PowerPoint* are examples of authoring and presentation programs. *PowerPoint* generally requires a more linear movement through the information assembled, whereas *Hyperstudio* and *Hypercard* allow for a higher degree of flexibility in terms of the learner's path through the information.

An excellent example is that of classroom teacher Sharon Lewis's class social studies project. Sharon's students created a multimedia presentation offering a "virtual tour" of a museum. Using word-processing software, video cameras, videotape cameras, *Sound Machine* (software to create audio files), *Graphic Converter* (software to manipulate graphic images), and *Netscape Navigator* (to provide access to the World Wide Web), students designed exhibitions and presented their projects to their parents on two special evenings (Rose and Fernlund 1997).

Digital Images

Inserting appropriate images into a presentation is a simple matter with the use of digital images. *Digital cameras* and *scanners* provide an excellent means of introducing images of your choosing into your presentations. Composing a family history with photographic images included as part of the presentation is one example of the power associated with including digital images. Digital cameras operate in a manner similar to a standard camera, except that the photographic image is stored not on film, but as a computer file. This file can be imported into word-processing documents and placed in presentations for others to observe. Scanning software and scanners allow information to be imported into documents as well. *Optical Character Reading (OCR)* software allows text documents to be scanned and then imported into word-processing documents so that the text can be edited. This simple tool allows the teacher to scan text documents in the public domain and insert them into new documents developed for class. This saves teachers the burden of retyping existing textual information.

✆ Communication

The use of technology as a means of sharing information among students and teachers has been one of the most exciting and widely used applications of telecommunications technology. With an abundance of both commercial service providers and even communications services provided through the networks operated by local school districts, nearly all students have at least some ability to communicate beyond traditional classroom boundaries.

The two key tools to communicate using the computer are a web browser, discussed previously, and electronic mail. E-mail is conceptually identical to regular hand-delivered mail, but with the additional ability to send with the message sounds, photographic images, and computer files.

Numerous opportunities exist already for students to make use of e-mail as a means of corresponding with pen pals. Finegan-Stoll (1998) cited a number of advantages of using key pals as an opportunity, for example, allowing teachers to interact with other teachers and students to meet and share with students of other countries, cultures, and peoples. Further advantages of the electronic approach to correspondence is that the time between sending and receiving messages is measured in minutes and seconds, rather than weeks and days. The opportunity for students to discuss current events as they happen lends an important immediacy to this means of communication. Other important resources that may be drawn from electronic mail are called *listservs*. A listserv is a kind of community mailbox. Subscribers with a common interest send messages to a common address. The messages in turn are distributed to all members of the listserv for their edification and/or feedback to the individual who initiated the question. The response can be directed either to the individual who posed the question or to the entire list, for the benefit of all subscribers.

The key parts of an electronic mail message are as follows: the address, the subject line, the body of the message, and an attachment function. The *address* is constructed in the format *name@company.com, name@organization.org* or

14.2   Focus Box

Key Pals

*P*en pals can often be a frustratingly slow process, but key pals can help to speed up the process significantly. Several sources of key pals are available through the resources of the World Wide Web:

http://www.mightymedia.com/keypals/
http://www.epals.com/
http://www.xplore.com/xplore500/medium/kids.html
http://www.siec.K12.in.us/~west/proj/mail/index.html

These Web sites offer sources for students and teachers to connect with other students and teachers for correspondence. For instructional purposes, students may interact with each other, communicate by groups, or compose a letter as a class to share with another class.

Key pal–related activities serve to promote NCSS Standard 1, Culture and Cultural Diversity, and Standard 9, Global Connections.

---

name@school.edu. Many schools and school districts have made e-mail accounts available to their teaching staff; private service providers can do the same for a modest fee. The *subject line* informs the receiver of the message as to the message's topic. The *body* of the message is the space that contains the textual information to be passed on from one person to another. Allowing for an *attachment* makes it possible for entire documents, sounds, database files, photographs, or any other computer file to be sent from one person to another. This allows for an outstanding opportunity to share information from one class to another.

The Internet

In its simplest form, the Internet represents a network in which millions of computers are connected. Software allows the user to visit any computer for which he or she has the address and collect information from these computers. But the use of the Internet serves more than simply as a means of gathering information. The ability to share information beyond the walls of a classroom represents an important aspect of the net. Stated succinctly: "The integration of the Internet into the curriculum gives power to students and teachers, enabling them to construct meaning from current information and incorporate it into their growing body of knowledge" (Sunal et al. 1998, 14). By the middle 1990s, the first generation of teachers to use the Internet as part of their classroom practice had discovered the following several things. First, students can participate in projects that involve researching information electronically, and second, they may collaborate with each other and with experts available through electronic mail connections (Serim and Koch 1996). According to Dawson and Harris (1999) there are three genres of online activity: 1) interpersonal exchanges; 2) information collection and analysis; and 3) problem solving and critical thinking.

As the use of the Internet has entered more and more classrooms, the usefulness of the technology has become more apparent. A lesson described by Butler,

14.3 Focus Box

Student- and Teacher-Created Web Pages

*W*eb pages are more than simple sources of information. When the potential of the World Wide Web is truly exploited, it becomes a means of sharing and communicating information among a large number of individuals. Profiled here is a sample set of Web pages from a group of teachers in Illinois, examining the Civil War. The project began with second-grade students scanning photographic images of Civil War participants into an electronic format. The students then produced character descriptions for each of the individuals whose images had been scanned.

Seventh-grade language arts students created a dialog, plot line, and a description of the conflict between the Civil War participants, based on the character sketches provided by the second-grade students.

Finally, high school students created short stories from the materials generated by the second- and seventh-grade students. Their stories, along with the plot lines and character descriptions, were linked to the Civil War photographs.

© Steven Wallace

Continued

14.3 *Focus Box*   Continued

Goals 2000: School Improvement Planning - Netscape

File Edit View Go Communicator Help

Back Forward Reload Home Search Guide Print Security Stop

Bookmarks   Netsite: http://coe.cedu.niu.edu/~wallace/goals2000/civilwar/index.html

Instant Message   Internet   Lookup   New&Cool

Phase I

Margo Sickele's 2nd-grade classroom at Littlejohn Elementary School developed character descriptions and brief setting sketches for approximately 25 civil war-era individuals. The character descriptions were based on civil war photographs housed on a web page designed by the project team members. The work of each student was scanned into electronic format and linked to their respective civil war character (photograph). Please note that the work of each student is a "work in progress." Editing is continuous process. The works you see here are at various stages of the editing process.

The following page links to the work of the 2nd-grade students at Littlejohn Elementary School in DeKalb, IL.

Phase II

Melanie Smith's 7th-grade Language Arts class at Huntley Middle School in DeKalb, IL created a section of dialogue, a thumbnail plot line, and a detailed conflict scenario based on the work of Margo's 2nd-grade classroom. Students in Melanie's classroom worked in pairs to develop their dialogue, plot line, and conflict scenario. The work of each student was entered in electronic format (by the student) and linked to their respective civil war character. Please note that the work of each student is a "work in progress." Editing is continuous process. The works you see here are at various stages of the editing process.

The following page links to the work of the 7th-grade students at Huntley Middle School in DeKalb, IL.

Phase III

In the final phase of the project, Sue Nagle's high school social studies class will write a story woven out of the material provided by the 2nd-grade students from Littlejohn Elementary School and the 7th-grade students from Huntley Middle

Document: Done

Start   GroupWi...   Day   Eudora ...   Goals ...   Microsof...   CD Player   Paint Sh...

Flynn, Becker, and Zane (1996) is fairly typical of the use of the Internet as both a means of communication and as a rich data resource. In a series of lessons developed to support their school's earth science and geography curricula, the data analysis opportunities afforded by the Internet provided the essential content. To this end, a number of Web sites with current and active earthquake information were identified, and students used this information to develop inferences regarding plate tectonics, economics, industry, and related issues. The principles advocated in the NCSS standards were also present. Students used information acquired through the World Wide Web as a means of testing hypotheses and constructing models and testing inferences, as well as gaining deeper understandings of people, places, and their environment.

Journey North is a program developed and implemented during the middle 1990s as a means of exploiting the Internet as a tool to develop communications skills and content knowledge appropriate for a number of disciplines. The announcement for the 1996 project stated the objectives of the project:

> The Annenberg/CPB Math and Science Project is pleased to present Journey North, an annual Internet-based learning adventure that engages students in a global study of wildlife migration and seasonal change. Beginning on Groundhog's Day (February 2nd) students will travel northward with spring as it sweeps across the continent of North America. With global classmates and state-of-the-art computer technology, they'll predict the arrival of spring from half a world away. (Educational Research Service 1996, 32)

Teachers find the Internet invaluable in researching lesson plans, units, and Web sites for social studies instruction.

© Elizabeth Crews

Students use the Internet as a tool to share, record and examine data in a number of ways. In particular, the focus is on creating an inquiry-based model of scientific investigation. In all ways, the presence of NCSS standards are evident in each of the *Journey North* projects. Different activities occur each school year, but the intellectual activities remain similar from project to project. Data verification and testing, recognizing the value of primary source information, and communicating information serve as some of the key intellectual skills developed throughout the set of *Journey North* experiences (*Journey North* 1998).

ᕫ *Teacher Utilities and Information Evaluation*

A final mention needs to be offered with regard to teacher utilities. A popular tool among many teachers are grading programs, which allow grades to be calculated at

In the Classroom Mini Lesson

Project Storm Front—Examining the Influence of Climate on Lives and Livelihoods (Adapted from Project Storm Front by Kenneth King and Thomas Thompson 1998. Used by permission)

Unit Overview

In studying climates, students need to understand how different weather patterns, landforms, and overall climatic differences influence how different people live and their livelihoods. This unit will engage students in hands-on activities to collect and analyze weather data, develop a recognition of how different climates impact how people live, and use technology as a means of facilitating the development of this knowledge. This interdisciplinary unit will help students to integrate an understanding of science, mathematics, language arts, and exploratory arts as part of an upper-elementary social studies curriculum. This project will involve students in two other sites located around the country (or internationally) to collect and compare weather data and cultural data for the purpose of examining how weather and climate influence peoples' lives.

Unit Goals

To increase the student's knowledge of the impact of climate on communities and occupations (social studies)

To develop effective communications skills (language arts)

To develop weather content knowledge, data analysis skills and hypothesis-testing skills (science)

To develop measuring and recording skills (math)

To use technology to record, exchange, manipulate, and communicate information

Interdisciplinary Overview

Social Studies Students will compare and contrast cultures, occupations, and lifestyles of people in the three data collection sites. They will use this information in conjunction with the weather data collected to develop an understanding of how climate impacts cultures, lifestyles, and employment.

Language Arts Students will communicate electronically using electronic mail. They will compose letters individually and in small groups to compare local conditions with the conditions students are experiencing in the two other data collection sites.

Science Students will collect weather data over a six-week period. They will relate the weather data collected to the differences in the lives, customs, and employment of people living in the three different locations.

Math Students will collect and record weather data. Using graphing software, they will seek out existing patterns in the weather and compare the weather information between and among the data collection sites.

Lesson Plans

Social Studies

Objectives

1. Students will investigate the relationship between climate and culture.
2. Students will investigate the relationship between climate and forms of employment.
3. Students will compare and contrast the workings of two or more communities based on the impact of climate and geography on each community.

Materials

- Student-created survey highlighting culture, entertainment, employment, and other characteristics of a community
- Results of survey as completed by electronic key pals
- Weather data collected daily for six weeks by students on each of the investigation teams

Class Activity

After class discussion, students will develop a questionnaire to use in learning the characteristics (culture, work, and so on) of their partner groups. Students collect and organize information when a survey is returned from other students. Using the information collected during science to develop a profile of the community's climate, the different climates are compared with the results of the survey. Information related to climate is correlated with the findings from the survey, to determine the extent to which climate, geography, and weather influence the way people live.

Evaluation/Assessment

Students will be evaluated according to the reasonableness of their findings.

Language Arts

Objectives

1. Students will communicate effectively with students on each investigation team.
2. Students will develop a questionnaire and administer the questionnaire to students on other teams.
3. Students will conduct library research to learn about the climate and culture the students on the other teams experience.

Materials

- Word-processing software and computer
- Electronic mail software and computer
- Library and electronic database.

Class Activity

Students will develop a questionnaire designed to help learn about the lifestyles of other students on each of the investigation teams.

Evaluation/Assessment

Students will be evaluated in terms of (1) completing the assignments and (2) the quality of the written work. Students need to complete a questionnaire, compose letters to inquire as to the answers to the questionnaire, and then compose summary essays describing what patterns emerged from the questionnaire.

Science

Objectives

1. Students will collect weather data regularly over a six-week period.
2. Students will develop a hypothesis regarding what their prior knowledge suggests will be the typical weather conditions in each of the participating sites.
3. Students will examine the weather data to seek patterns present in each site.
4. Students will test their hypothesis and evaluate it according to support or nonsupport for the hypothesis.

Continued

In the Classroom Mini Lesson Continued

Project Storm Front—Examining the Influence of Climate on Lives and Livelihoods (Adapted from Project Storm Front by Kenneth King and Thomas Thompson 1998. Used by permission)

Materials
- Computer with Web browser
- Web site updated regularly by instructor with data from each of the test sites.
- Weather collection equipment: anemometer, barometer, thermometer, rain gauge.

Class Activity
Students will collect weather data daily over a six-week period. Weather readings will be collected and then posted to a Web site by electronic mail submission. The emerging data set will be used to examine existing or hypothesized patterns in the weather at each site.

Evaluation/Assessment
Students will be evaluated on the accuracy of their observations, the quality of their efforts in collecting the data, and the reasonableness of their conclusions, based on the data they collected.

Math

Objectives
1. Students will measure weather readings accurately.
2. Students will correctly compile data into a graph of the proper format.
3. Students will use simple descriptive statistics to describe each of the data collection sites.

Materials
- Weather collection software
- Data analysis software (e.g., the *Graph Club*)

Class Activity
Students will use the data collected over the duration of the project to develop graphs and summarize the data with simple descriptive statistics.

Evaluation/Assessment
Students will be assessed on the accuracy of their measurements, the accuracy of their statistical calculations (mean, median, and modal calculations), and the accuracy and appropriateness of their graphs.

the touch of a keystroke. The ability to produce individual reports for students is one advantage that many teachers appreciate. Reflective teaching practice may be data-driven when teachers are able to compare student performances not only within a single class, but also among different classes. A wide variety of these teacher utilities are available. Some school districts offer discounts or require the use of a standard software package.

One of the key points for us to keep in mind regarding the use of technology is using it appropriately in social studies instruction. Technology allows for the rapid and efficient dissemination of knowledge; it does not, however, evaluate the quality of the information being distributed. The critical and thoughtful evaluation of information is a more essential skill than ever. Web pages can be published by virtually anyone. Simply because information has a Web-based presence does not mean that the information is valid or reliable. Critical consideration of information can be one of the most important skills a teacher brings to his or her students.

Finding software that is both useful and engaging is important as well. Braun (1986, 81–2) offered some suggestions a decade ago that are still relevant today:

1. Execute the program as a good student would. Mimic the behavior of a student of this type to test the sophistication of the program.
2. Execute the program as an unsuccessful student might. How does the program respond to incorrect answers? What happens when a typing error occurs or the student doesn't follow directions?
3. Use an evaluation instrument that you are comfortable with to evaluate the software. Compare your findings with the claims of the publisher.
4. Is the supporting documentation of good quality?

These steps can assist in avoiding the purchase of software of marginal quality, and enhance the potential to automate and innovate instruction that technology brings to the social studies classroom.

Chapter Summary

This chapter provided an overview of various uses of technology in the curriculum. Technology was examined as a means of gathering information, analyzing information, creating information, and, finally, communicating information. Various technological tools and software applications are examined as a means of helping students to achieve NCSS goals.

Web Sites

Web Browsing Software
Microsoft Internet Explorer
   http://www.microsoft.com/
Netscape Navigator
   http://home.netscape.com/

Electronic Mail
Eudora
   http://www.eudora.com/
National Council for the Social Studies
   http://www.ncss.org/

Search Engines
Yahoo!
   http://www.yahoo.com/

Webcrawler
http://webcrawler.com/
Ask Jeeves
http://www.aj.com/
Lycos
http://www.lycos.com/
Excite
http://www.excite.com/
Hot Bot
http://www.hotbot.com/
Alta Vista
http://www.altavista.com/
Infoseek
http://guide-p.infoseek.com/
Deja News
http://www.dejanews.com/

Sites Supporting NCSS standards (Johnson and Rector 1997)
Time, Continuity, and Change—Sites That Support Historical Inquiry

Library of Congress
http://lcweb.loc.gov/
Rutgers University Library
http://info.rutgers.edu/
Rice University
http://riceinfo.rice.edu/
University of Maryland
http://inform.umd.edu/

People, Places, and Environments—Maps, Geography, and Cartography

2000 Census
http://www.census.gov/
CIA World Book
http://www.odci.gov/cia
U.S. Geologic Survey
http://www.usgs.gov
Geographic Information Retrieval Services
http://wings.buffalo.edu/geoweb/services.html
National Weather Service
http://www.noaa.gov/

Individual Development and Identity

Mayaquest
http://www.mecc.com/mayaquest.html

Power, Authority, and Governance

U.S. House of Representatives
http://www.house.gov/
U.S. Senate
http://www.senate.gov/

White House
http://www.whitehouse.gov/
Many government agencies
http://www.doc.gov/services/index.html
Many states and cities
http://banzai.nesosoft.com
Vote Smart
http://www.vote-smart.org/

Global Connections

Clean water home page
http://www.voyagepub.com/publish/stories/wat.htm

Civic Ideals and Practices

U.S. Department of State
http://dosfan.lib.uic.edu/
United Nations
http://www.un.org/
Amnesty International
http://www.io.org/amnesty/
American Red Cross
http://www.red-cross.org/
International Red Cross
http://www.icrc.ch/
National Budget Simulation
http://garnet.berkeley.edu/budget/budget.html

Web Publishing for Teachers

American School Directory
http://www.asd.com/
LION: Creating Web pages for K–12 Schools and Libraries
http://www.libertynet.org/lion/school.html
Cyber Bee Web Construction
http://www.cyberbee.com/schoolpage/school.html
Homestead
http://www.homestead.com

References

Bazeli, M. 1997. *Visual productions and student learning.* Selected readings from the Annual Conference of the International Visual Literacy Association. (ERIC Document Reproduction Service No. ED 408 969).

Braun, J. A., Jr. 1986. *Microcomputers and the social studies.* New York: Garland.

Butler, G., L. Flynn, D. Becker, and J. Zane. 1996, December. Earthquakes online. *The Science Teacher* 63 (9): 31–3.

Copley, R., J. Cradler, and P. K. Engel. 1997. *Computers and classrooms: The status of technology in U.S. schools.* Princeton, NJ: Policy Information Center-Educational Testing Service. (ERIC Document Reproduction Service No. ED 412 893).

Cuban, L. 1986. *Teachers and machines: The classroom use of technology since 1920.* New York: Teachers College Press.

Dawson, K., and J. Harris. 1999. Reaching out: Telecollaboration and social studies. *Social Studies and the Young Learner,* 12 (1): p1–p4.

Dockterman, D. A. 1997. *Great teaching in the one computer classroom.* Watertown, MA: Tom Snyder Productions.

Educational Research Service. 1996. *The internet roadmap for educators.* Arlington, VA: Educational Research Service.

Finegan-Stoll, Colleen. 1998. Key pals for young children. *Social Studies and the Young Learner* 11 (1): 28–9.

Friewald, W. D. 1997. *Computer use in elementary social studies.* (ERIC Document Reproduction Service No. ED 418 024).

Harris, G. H., and B. Bruce. 1997. *Adopting telecommunications: A teacher's personal quest toward implementation.* (ERIC Document Reproduction Service No. ED 409 889).

Heidenreich, B. 1997. *The effects of Hyperstudio on the achievement of seventh grade social studies students.* (ERIC Document Reproduction Service No. ED 412 895).

Heinich, R., M. Molenda, J. D. Russell, and S. E. Smaldino. 1996. *Instructional media and technologies for learning.* Englewood Cliffs, NJ: Merrill.

Johnson, C., and J. Rector. 1997. The Internet ten: Using the Internet to meet social studies curriculum standards. *Social Education* 61 (3): 167–9.

Journey North. 1998. *Teachers' manual.* [On-line]. Available: http://www.learner.org/jnorth/tm/.

King, K., and T. Thompson. 1998. Project Storm Front. *Science Scope* 21 (8): 46.

Larson, B. E. 1999. Current events and the Internet: Connecting "Headline News" to perennial issues. *Social Studies and the Young Learner* 12 (1):25–27.

National Council for the Social Studies. 1994. *Curriculum standards for social studies: Expectations for excellence.* Washington, DC: National Council for the Social Studies.

Rose, S. A., and P. M. Fernlund. 1997. Using technology for powerful social studies learning. *Social Education* 61 (3): 160–6.

Serim, F., and M. Koch. 1996. *Netlearning: Why teachers use the Internet.* Sebastopol, CA: O'Reilly.

Sunal, C. S., C., Smith, D., Sunal, and J. Britt. 1998. Using the Internet to create meaningful instruction. *The Social Studies* 89 (1): 13–7.

Tinker, R. F. 1987. Educational technology and the future of science education. *School Science and Mathematics* 87 (6): 466–76.

Wilson, E. K. 1997. A trip to historic Philadelphia on the web. *Social Education* 61 (3): 170–2.

Chapter 15

© James L. Shaffer

It All Depends on Your Point of View

Multicultural Education in the Social Studies

Carla Cooper Shaw
Northern Illinois University

One of the most significant and visible features of the contemporary United States is its multiethnic and culturally pluralistic character.

—National Council for the Social Studies
"The Columbia Quincentenary Position Statement"

Objectives

⌇

Readers will

- acquire techniques for teaching about diversity;
- appreciate and understand the need to help students develop positive attitudes toward different cultural, racial, and ethnic groups; and
- understand how to extend acceptance of others from the classroom to the multicultural community beyond.

Introduction

"Daddy, why did the Indians attack the settlers?"
"Because they were a wild and savage people."
"Who—the Indians or the settlers?"
"The Indians, of course. The settlers were just like you and me."

Children are not born prejudiced, but by the time they enter kindergarten, they may possess misconceptions and negative attitudes about cultural groups different from their own (Banks and Banks 1997; Byrnes 1988). Among the causes of prejudice in children are two natural tendencies: to evaluate and categorize people and to adopt the attitude of respected adults and other children. The relationship between personal identity and the need for group membership also plays a role in the formation of prejudice. In their quest for belonging, children may express group loyalty by denigrating people belonging to cultures unlike their own (Byrnes 1988). Elementary and middle school teachers must "help children express, share, and take pride in their family cultures, and so to teach about the contributions of all the people who have helped build the United States. . . . [In addition, the teacher needs to create] a response to the increasing hostility in the United States toward new immigrant groups" or people with lifestyles unlike their own culture (Singer and Harbour-Ridley 1998, 415).

Regardless of the causes of prejudice, its pernicious effects are legendary. World history and current events, as they affect whole nations and races of people, are replete with the harmful results of prejudice. On a more individual level, prejudice limits the opportunities of both those who are prejudiced and their victims, who often internalize society's negative stereotypes, leading to weakened self-esteem and ability to achieve. In a prejudiced society, the potential for various cultural groups to live together peacefully and to work together productively is greatly diminished.

This last effect assumes special significance in light of the large-scale demographic changes under way in the United States. If current trends continue, it is projected that by the year 2020, almost one out of two schoolchildren will be nonwhite. Diversity is rapidly becoming a fact of everyday life. If it is to be a cause for celebration rather than a cause of contention, the prevention and reduction of prejudice are imperative.

A major goal of multicultural education is to help all students—regardless of their culture affiliations—develop more positive attitudes toward different cultural, racial, and ethnic groups (Banks and Banks 1997). A primary reason for developing positive attitudes toward people from different groups is that "being an active participant in American society requires individuals to assume many different roles and often requires the ability to interact with people from diverse backgrounds" (Sunal and Haas 1997, 378). Our task is no simple matter—because, as Sleeter and Grant (1988, 208) put it, "People tend to live in small, rather insulated worlds with others who share their advantages or disadvantages." For children, this insulation is heightened. Teachers need to consider multiculturalism as they plan for instruction (Weil, Calhoun, and Joyce 2000).

It would seem that learning about different ethnic groups, perhaps by researching and preparing reports on the contributions of diverse cultural groups, would lead to positive attitudes. But such is not necessarily the case, for knowledge or cognition alone does not lead to enlightenment. Prejudice is a complex phenomenon consisting of at least three related components—the cognitive, the affective, and the behavioral—and so it demands a multidimensional attack (Pate 1988).

Children who are low in prejudice show "more sensitivity and openness to other points of view" (Byrnes 1988, 269) and are able to think critically. Among the attitudes necessary for the growth of critical thinking are open-mindedness, flexibility, and respect for other viewpoints (Walsh 1988). Research suggests that activities and materials with a strong affective component that invite children to enter vicariously into the lives of people of different ethnic groups are effective in the development of this flexibility of perspective (Byrnes 1988). Once students begin to feel empathy, they are well on their way toward respecting diverse points of view and thus becoming less prejudiced.

The overarching goal of this chapter is to outline an instructional unit that represents the meshing of an important affective goal of multicultural education with social studies content. The goal is the development of the ability to understand perspectives different from one's own and the content is knowledge of diverse cultural groups. The unit begins in Phase One with student participation in a variety of ethnic experiences. It proceeds to help students focus on a particular cultural group in Phase Two, and to develop an understanding of point of view and empathy in Phase Three. The unit culminates in Phase Four with students creating characters from different cultural groups, writing from their characters' points of view, and sharing their products. An optional extension provides students with an opportunity to envision a multicultural community.

The unit engages students in most of the elements of the whole language approach as outlined by Robbins (1990). It uses children's books that invite vicarious experience with characters from a variety of cultural groups. These books, when taken together, represent a multicultural perspective. Research suggests that reading such multiethnic literature can lead to increased awareness and decreased negative stereotyping of people from other cultures (Walker-Dalhouse 1993). Following the unit is a bibliography of pertinent children's literature categorized by cultural group.

The unit's first three phases serve as rehearsal for subsequent stages of the writing process—revision, editing, and sharing—contained in the final phase. As the unit progresses, it also guides students through important aspects of the creative process: sensory stimulation, focusing, and incubation.

Phase One: Bombardment of Experiences

In Phase One, students participate in a variety of ethnic experiences, both print and nonprint. The emphasis here is on exposure to diversity, on immersion without discrimination in the lives of people from a wide variety of cultural backgrounds. The teacher begins the unit by reading aloud a number of books that focus on the lives of children from various American cultures. The bombardment of experiences continues with whatever resources are available: guest speakers from the community; field trips to ethnic neighborhoods, restaurants, and museums with relevant exhibits; events for children such as might occur during Black History Month; recordings of ethnic music, such as salsa, African American spirituals, rap, and reggae; videotapes and films.

It is important in this phase for both print and nonprint experiences to be as primary and authentic as possible. That is, speakers should relate their own personal experiences in the spirit of storytelling rather than provide histories of their cultural

Children need to be in a supportive classroom environment where they learn to help one another.
© Elizabeth Crews

groups. In selecting stories to read aloud, the teacher should try to choose those that reflect accurate patterns of language use, such as folktales and stories with realistic dialogue. In reading aloud, the teacher should remain true to those patterns and inflections to the best of his or her dramatic ability. Films and videos should be stories of lifelike, sympathetic characters rather than documentaries. When visiting ethnic neighborhoods, children should be encouraged to interact with residents and shopkeepers instead of communicating through the teacher or an interpreter.

The keys to continuity throughout this initial bombardment of experiences are quiet times, occurring at regular intervals, in which the teacher reads stories selected with an eye toward reinforcing and clarifying experiences students have recently had or whetting their appetites for experiences yet to come. Younger students may benefit from the shared book experience as created by Holdaway (1979). Through a series of seven steps, the entire class becomes involved in reading a single book. Typically, a "big book" is shared because the illustrations and print are large enough for children to see as they sit on the floor, gathered together around the teacher. The seven steps outlined by Holdaway are these:

1. The teacher selects a book and briefly introduces it to the students.
2. The teacher asks the students to make predictions about what they think will happen in the story.
3. The teacher reads aloud to the class, pointing to the words as they are read.
4. At preselected points, the teacher asks students to validate or invalidate their predictions and to make new ones.

5. The book is reread, with the students joining in the oral reading with the teacher.
6. Students, singly or in pairs, volunteer to read the book or portions of it to the class.
7. The book is read either by the teacher or students to the entire class every day of the week.

Later, both students and teacher engage in sustained silent reading.

Primary-level students can engage in choral speaking or the reading of simple poetry. They can select a scene from a picture or a chapter from a book and act it out. They can make overhead transparencies to illustrate a story they have written about a specific culture and share them with the class.

Within the body of materials set aside for this phase of the unit, students should be encouraged to read whatever appeals to their interests of the moment. Time might be provided for students to respond actively and creatively to their reading. Hoyt (1992) suggests that students give expression to their reading by dramatizing and illustrating stories and interpreting them through readers' theatre. Students might also translate poetry into song and dance and write rap lyrics and perform them.

❧ *Phase Two: Focusing through Guided and Individualized Reading*

After their immersion in a potpourri of diversity, students will probably be interested in particular cultural groups. Once students have deemed which group they would like to focus on for further study, the teacher divides the students into learning teams according to their stated preferences and assigns one or two books to each team. Each student reads silently and individually and engages in periodic conferences with the teacher or aide for the purpose of monitoring comprehension.

When a team finishes a book, the teacher conducts reading conferences with that team. Discussions are shaped by a sequence of questions designed to move students gradually from viewing the character from the outside in to viewing the world from the inside out—or getting inside the character's skin to achieve empathy. In Stage One, *viewing the character from the outside,* the teacher asks students to describe the character in terms of such characteristics as physical attributes, home life, family, school, food, feelings, beliefs, and religion. In Stage Two, *comparing oneself to the character,* the teacher prompts students to select the most important aspects of the character's life. To facilitate comparison, the teacher lists these aspects on a chart and instructs students to do the same. Students individually complete their charts, and the ensuing discussion focuses on comparing themselves with the character.

Still using the charts, in Stage Three, *identifying with the character,* students discuss the ways in which their lives are similar to the character's life. Finally, in Stage Four, *developing empathy,* the teacher asks students to predict their own and the character's responses to hypothetical situations.

The following is a sequence of questions that might be used with "You Rap, I'll Reap," one of eleven poignant short stories about African Americans in *Guests in the Promised Land* by Kristin Hunter (1973), which is appropriate for upper-elementary students. "You Rap, I'll Reap" is a story about Gloria, who lives in an urban housing project where the residents on one's floor function as an extended family, and money, possessions, and living space are freely shared.

Phase Two, Stage One: Viewing the Character from the Outside

- Gloria says her skin is like "Yuban Coffee in the jar." What color is coffee?
- Gloria says Sheilah's skin is like Gulden's Spicy Brown Mustard. What color is that?
- Who has darker skin—Gloria or Sheilah?
- In what sort of a home does Gloria live—a house or an apartment building? How do you know?
- Some children live in families with a mother and a father and sisters and brothers. Some children live in a family with just a mother. Sometimes the people in a neighborhood are like a family. What kind of family does Gloria have?
- How old do you think Gloria and her friend Lola are? What makes you think that?
- How far does Gloria live from school?
- What is Gloria's job?
- Gloria says of Mrs. Stevens, the woman for whom she works: "There's a lot she *don't* know, because she's white, and I ain't about to tell her." What do you think Mrs. Stevens doesn't know? Why isn't Gloria going to tell her these things? Why do you think Gloria doesn't tell Mrs. Stevens about lending clothes to Sheilah and money to Mrs. Dawkins?
- Why can't both Gloria and Lola have roast beef sandwiches for lunch?
- What does Gloria like to do in her free time alone? What does she like to do with her friends?

Phase Two, Stage Two: Comparing Oneself to the Character

With the teacher's help, students develop charts such as the one shown in Figure 15.1, with the first two columns completed while the third and fourth columns vary from individual to individual. The following questions might be used with a predominantly white class in a middle-class suburban school.

- How is your family different from Gloria's?
- How is your home different from Gloria's?
- Gloria and her family and friends are poor: How is her life different from yours?
- How do you get to school? How far away is your school from your house? Why doesn't Gloria's mother drive her to school?
- How do you feel about your possessions and money? Do you share them the way Gloria shares hers? Why do you think Gloria has such a sharing attitude? Gloria bought lunch for Sheilah even though she works for her money and Sheilah doesn't. Do you think you would have done the same thing?
- How is the way Gloria talks different from the way you talk?
- Gloria says of Mrs. Stevens: "And now she really pulls her whiteness on me." What do you think she means?

Aspect	Gloria	Me	Same/Different?
Family	everyone on her floor		
Home	project- a very large apartment building		
Mother	strict- "won't let me leave the house unless I'm neat and clean"		
Economic background	poor		
Attitude toward possessions	sharing		
Free time alone	reading, watching TV		

FIGURE 15.1   Sample comparison chart.

- When Sheilah talks about the brothers and sisters, who is she talking about? When you talk about brothers and sisters, who are you talking about? Why do you think Sheilah refers to other African Americans as brothers and sisters?

Phase Two, Stage Three: Identifying with the Character

- Think about your grandparents and aunts and uncles and cousins. How is your family like Gloria's?
- How is Gloria's mother like your mother?
- What TV show do you think you and Gloria would both like?
- What are some of Gloria's special words, and what do they mean? (Students might construct a chart with Gloria's words in the left column and students' corresponding words in the right—e.g., *rap-talk.*) What are some of your

special words, and what do they mean? Do you think that all children and teenagers have their own slang?
- Think of all the ways that you and Gloria are alike.

Phase Two, Stage Four: Developing Empathy

- Suppose you spent a Saturday in the project with Gloria. What would you see and hear and smell? What would you and Gloria do?
- What would you like about living in Gloria's project? What would you dislike?
- How would you feel if you transferred to Gloria's school?
- How would Gloria feel if she joined our class?
- What would you and Gloria do if you had her over to your house to spend the night?
- Suppose you had to go without lunch because you didn't have enough money. How would you feel? How would you feel during the afternoon at school? Would you do well in your schoolwork? Do you think Gloria ever had to go without lunch?
- Do your sisters or brothers or friends ever borrow things from you and forget to return them? What do you do when that happens? If you were Gloria and your friend borrowed a Nintendo game and didn't return it, what would you do?
- Suppose you are Gloria and you really want Madame James down the hall to tell your fortune with her cards. She charges $3, but you have only $1. What would happen?
- Gloria is returning home after spending the night with you. How would she describe you and your home and your family to her friend Lola?

Sequence Flexibility

The progression suggested by this questioning sequence leads students in a gradual manner from viewing the character from an external, observer point of view to developing empathy, or viewing the world from the character's perspective. However, if students appear to be ready to empathize upon completing their books, this sequence need not be followed in a lockstep manner. Depending on students' states of readiness, stages of the sequence might be omitted; the boundaries between the stages should remain flexible.

Similarly, at the conclusion of this phase of the unit, students should have a strong intuitive grasp of the concept "point of view" and may be ready to move immediately into the fourth phase of the unit, that of creating a character through language experience. However, the teacher may wish to use some or all of the activities in the third phase to provide students with additional practice in empathizing.

✎ *Phase Three: Point of View*

The purpose of the third phase of the unit is to facilitate a deeper understanding of point of view and to discuss the concept with students in an explicit manner. Like the sequence of questions in the previous phase, the sequence of activities here moves students in a gradual progression—this time from their own physical points of view regarding an object to viewing life from the perspectives of people different from themselves.

Activity 1. The teacher places a globe in the center of the room, positions students around it in various locations, and asks them to draw it. The teacher then guides the students in comparing their finished pictures with questions such as these:

- You have all drawn the same thing. Why are all the pictures different?
- Tiffany and Jonathan were in almost the same place, but their pictures are still different. Why?
- Is one point of view right and the others wrong? Why or why not?

Activity 2. The teacher states that the students have learned that everyone has his or her own point of view or own way of seeing things and that no two points of view are ever exactly the same. Now the teacher asks the students to think about the globe's point of view with such questions as the following:

- If the globe had eyes, how do you think our room would look to it? What is the globe's point of view on our room?
- Is the globe a male or a female or neither? Why?
- How does the globe feel being looked at by us? Do you think it feels popular? Or do you think it would like a little privacy?
- How does the globe feel when we spin it around?

Activity 3. As a variation on activities described by Walsh (1988) and Weil, Calhoun and Joyce (2000) the teacher asks students to take pennies from their pockets and *become* those pennies.

- How do you feel jangling around in somebody's pocket with lots of other coins that are worth more than you?
- How does a human's hand feel to you?
- How do you feel when someone sees you on the sidewalk and doesn't bother to pick you up?
- Suppose someone sees you and says, "Aha! I've found a penny. Now I'll have good luck!" How do you feel?
- Describe a day in your life as a penny.

Activity 4. Students simulate the experience of being visually or hearing impaired by wearing blindfolds or earplugs. Once they are sighted and hearing again, the teacher encourages them to discuss their experiences.

Visually Impaired

- How did you get around? Which senses did you use?
- Did you depend on other people to help you get around? How did you feel about having to depend on other people?
- Since you couldn't see the faces of people talking to you, how could you tell what they were feeling?
- Describe our classroom from your point of view as a person who is blind.

Hearing Impaired

- How did you communicate? How did you know whether you were talking loudly enough? Which senses did you use to understand other people?
- How did it feel to see people playing and talking and having a good time and not being able to hear them?
- Since you couldn't hear people's voices when they were talking to you, how did you know what they were feeling?
- Describe our classroom from your point of view as a person who is deaf.

Up until Activity 2, when the teacher provides the meaning of point of view, the class has been "sneaking up" on a definition. When the teacher is sure that students grasp the meaning of the concept, she or he should reinforce it at every opportunity by relating point of view back to the characters in the books read in the second phase of the unit. For example, after asking students to describe a day in the life of a penny, the teacher might ask them to do the same for a particular character. For "You Rap, I'll Reap," the teacher might ask, "What would Gloria's point of view be on our classroom?"

✍ *Phase Four: Creating a Character through Language Experience*

At this point, students have been steeped in a wide array of ethnic experiences, and they have delved deeply and vicariously into the lives of one or more characters belonging to the cultural group in which they are the most interested. Students also possess a firm cognitive and affective understanding of point of view. They are now ready to create characters and write their own stories.

The fourth phase of the unit begins with a questioning sequence designed to help students imagine characters of their own creation, visualize settings for these characters, and as professional fiction writers do, view the world from the characters' perspectives. After informing students of the purpose of the upcoming activity, the teacher asks students individually to imagine people from the cultural groups they have explored in depth. The teacher leads them through the process with questions, separated by pauses for reflection, such as the following:

- Is your person male or female?
- Is he or she a child or an adult?
- Is your person fat or thin or in between?
- What are the colors of your person's skin, hair, and eyes?
- What language does he or she speak?
- How does your person's voice sound? Is it soft or harsh, high or low?
- What is his or her name?
- Where does your person live? Does he or she live in the country with trees and rivers? Or in the desert? Or in the ice and snow? Does he or she live in the city?
- In what sort of dwelling does your person live—a house, an apartment, a tent, a cabin, or something else?
- What makes your person happy and sad?

Even in a classroom environment where the student population does not have a wide range of diversity, students can learn about cultural differences.

© Photo by Jean-Claude LeJeune

The teacher then asks students to add flesh and bones to their characters by compiling portfolios consisting of completed character data sheets, such as the one shown in Figure 15.2, and drawings of the character, his or her family, home, and other important aspects of his or her life. To help students get started, the teacher may wish to model the process with a character she or he has created. It is crucial that students begin work on their own portfolios as soon as possible before images fade.

When the portfolios are complete, students convene in teams representing their characters' cultural groups and are instructed to introduce each of their characters in such a way that all team members can "see each one in their mind's eye" and imagine each as a living person. After each introduction, students should be encouraged to ask each other questions similar to the questions from Stage Four in Phase Two. For example:

- How would your character feel in our classroom?
- What is your character's point of view on McDonald's? Would it seem like a strange place to him or her?
- If your character had a whole free day, what would he or she do?

In answering these and similar questions, students round out aspects and visualize details of their characters that had not previously occurred to them. Before concluding this stage of character development, the teacher informs students that soon they will write stories from their characters' points of view.

Students engage in language experience as they dictate their stories. When the written versions are ready, students enter the writing process, as outlined by

---

Character Data Sheet

Name _____   Age _____

Birthday _____   Ethnic group _____

Height_____   Weight _____   Hair color _____   Eye color _____

Address _____

_____

Place of birth _____

Describe your family_____

_____

_____

_____

What do you do during the day? _____

_____

What do you do for fun? _____

_____

If you go to school, what is you favorite subject?_____

What do people like most about you? _____

_____

FIGURE 15.2   A Character Data Sheet such as this one is designed to help students flesh out their story characters.

Robbins (1990), at the revision stage and proceed on to editing, either individually or in cooperative groups. The teacher works on her or his own story when not working with students.

Finally, students share their stories with the rest of the class and compile them in final form into a book. Students decide how they would like to present their creative efforts to parents and other students and teachers—perhaps via a program in which they dramatize their stories or read them in fireside storytelling sessions.

✍ Extension: The Multicultural Community

This unit began with a wide-angle, multicultural view as students were immersed in a plethora of ethnic experiences. Starting with Phase Two, the focus narrowed, with students selecting particular cultural groups they wished to explore. The focus narrowed further as students articulated their visions of single characters. As the unit progressed, its focus became still finer and more specific.

If student interest remains strong, the teacher may consider widening the focus again to help students develop a fresh multicultural perspective. Implement-

Field trips require much preplanning and preparation by the teacher and students as well. The knowledge gained and aesthetic appreciation from such experiences often last into adulthood.

© Tony Freeman/PhotoEdit

ing this extension, in which students create multiethnic communities and write stories about them, will bring the unit full cycle.

As a whole group, students decide which characters might live in the same community, with the only stipulation being that a variety of cultural groups must be represented. Arranged in community groups, students engage in discussions with a purpose similar to that of the previous character-creation questioning sequence. They travel together on a collective imaginative journey, hitchhiking off each other's ideas, to visualize a community: its physical setting, its name, the characters' relationships to one another, and the ways they interact. Materials in the group portfolio might include such items as maps of the community and town phone books.

Keeping in mind the physical and interactive communities they have created, students engage in group language experiences as they discuss possible story lines, with their ideas being recorded. Students review these ideas and select the ones to be included in the story. Each group dictates its story, perhaps in "chain" fashion. When the initial version of the story is complete, students begin revising and editing, both of which promise to be more involved and time-consuming than they were earlier because students are now working cooperatively. Finally, students decide on the means for sharing their work and receiving feedback.

To reinforce the theme of this unit's extension, the teacher should conduct debriefing sessions both in groups and with the whole class. Questions conducive to reflection on living together in multicultural communities include the following:

- As you were thinking of your story, did it matter that your characters came from different cultural groups? Why or why not?
- Were some people more powerful and important than others? Why or why not?
- You probably did not write down any rules or laws your community had for living together. If you had, what would these rules and laws be?

In the Classroom Mini Lesson

Thematic Unit

Unit: Prejudice Reduction Through Perspective Taking
Grade Levels: 5, 6, 7

Social Studies

- Research various cultures. Use new knowledge in the writing of language experience, point-of-view stories.
- Debate current issues. Encourage learners to assume different points of view from their own.
- Learn about the history of a variety of cultural groups—including those of students—in the United States.
- Engage in simulations such as "Bafa Bafa" and "Brown Eyes, Blue Eyes."

Math

- Write word problems using demographic data (see, e.g., Shaw 1993). Discuss implications of the data from the points of view of the cultural groups involved.

Science

- Explore the ways in which people are physiologically similar.

Art

- Learn about the use of perspective in drawing. Discuss the similarity between perspective in art and the ways in which our perspectives influence the ways we view people and events.

Physical Education/Health

- Learn and play games and dances popular in various cultural groups.
- Explore other cultures' views on wellness—for example, the holistic approach taken by many American Indians. Discuss how our views of health care could benefit from consideration of alternate views.

All Subjects

- Engage in activities that *require* the cooperation of all members of the group.

15.1 *Focus Box*

Teaching about Culture

Culture can be defined as the values, beliefs, perspectives, and ways of interacting that distinguish one group of people from another. Another way of defining culture is its program for survival in and adaptation to particular environments. We can see an example of both definitions of culture in groups of people who have experienced discrimination in their environments, clinging tightly to their cultures and sometimes, to the language of their communities.

It is important for students to realize that we all have at least one culture—even if we are in the majority and are not aware of having a distinct culture. Culture often influences us at a subconscious level, and sometimes it is easier to see the cultural influences in other people than in ourselves.

It is also important for students to understand that there are many different kinds of culture: ethnic, gender, socioeconomic, religious, and geographic region, to name a few. Just because people come from one culture does not mean they cannot be part of another. For example, a person might grow up in the South but live as an adult in the Midwest, or a student might be African American but attend school with mostly European American classmates. Sometimes there may be more than one culture present in a person's home. For instance, a student's mother may be Christian and father Jewish.

Finally, it is important for students to understand that no culture is superior to another: *every* culture makes significant contributions to society. In order to feel comfortable with people whose cultures are different from ours, we must first feel comfortable with our own cultural background. Next, we should learn about other cultures—and the easiest and most effective way to do that is to make friends with people who are different from ourselves.

- How did the people in your community deal with conflicts?
- Do you think people in your community live together the way people *should* live together? Is your community a good model for us to follow in the real world?
- Let's think about our own country as a great big community with many, many different cultural groups. How should we treat each other if we are going to live and go to school and work together peacefully?

This extension takes an inductive approach as students derive codes of conduct from the ways their individual characters interact in a multicultural setting. To place special emphasis from the beginning on the means by which people live together in diverse communities, the teacher may wish to take an opposite, deductive approach in which students first formulate rules and laws for peaceful coexistence and the resolution of conflicts. Story lines then unfold in accordance with these predetermined codes of conduct. The ensuing debriefing explores with students the extent to which their characters abided by the community's rules and whether these rules should be modified.

In the Classroom Mini Lesson

Using Literature and Technology to Teach about the Middle East

by John W. Logan, Ph.D., Assistant Superintendent
Northbrook School District 27, Northbrook, IL

My life changed dramatically when I moved from Chicago to Saudi Arabia to accept a one-year sabbatical assignment as a curriculum director in an international school district. In this new role, I visited many classrooms and school libraries. After just a few visits to classrooms, I realized quickly that children from the international community share a keen, natural interest in learning about their transplanted home and its rich cultural heritage. To promote a better understanding of the Middle East, teachers use extensive literature collections and technology (especially videotapes and CD-ROMS) to teach about all areas including the fine arts, politics, language, geography, science, cooking, religion, architecture, and history. This article presents information about narrative and expository literature useful in teaching students about the Middle East. Also, it provides several videotape and CD-ROM resources to support the suggested reading literature. Finally, the article provides classroom literacy activities to help teachers introduce students to the wonderful and mysterious world of the Middle East.

Exploring Middle Eastern Literature

In *The Day of Ahmed's Secret* by Florence Parry Heide and Judith Heide Gilliland (1990), readers share in a day of the life of a young Middle Eastern boy. The colorful illustrations reflect a realistic view of the sights and sounds of a Middle East town. The story is told from the main character's point of view and is especially appropriate for young readers.

A timeless, heartfelt book for children of all ages and written more than fifty years ago is Sue Alexander's *Nadia the Willful* (1983). The story is about a Bedouin family (Arab desert people) whose favorite son disappears forever and how his sister, Nadia, keeps his memory alive despite her father's proclamation that no one speak about the brother ever again.

Ali Baba and the Forty Thieves (Early 1989) retells the most popular story from the classic tales in *The Thousand and One Nights*. This retelling features the exquisite and highly detailed illustrations of Aus-

tralian artist Margaret Early. The illustrations are designed to represent authentic Persian miniatures of the tenth century. In addition to reading the classic tale of Ali Baba and his encounter with robbers, teachers can use the illustrations to teach children about various components of art.

A most fascinating translation of a 3,000-year-old Egyptian fairy tale, written directly from an original papyrus manuscript (British Museum, London), is entitled *The Prince Who Knew His Fate* (Manniche 1981). In this book, Lise Manniche creates illustrations about one of the world's oldest known fairy tales. She copies Egyptian artwork done during the time the story was written on the original, ancient scroll. At the end of the book, she includes a narrative about how she came to write the book and provides her own perspective as an author about the historical value of ancient writing.

Informational Books, Videotapes, and CD-ROMs That Teach about the Middle East

Beginning readers will enjoy learning how to count in Arabic (from 1 to 10) in Jim Haskin's *Count Your Way Through the Arab World* (1991). In this book, Arabic numbers are written phonetically to help the reader pronounce them. The numbers are written in both English and Arabic languages. Also, the book provides a brief overview of the Arab world and Islamic beliefs using language young children can understand. The book is an excellent resource for teachers who want to teach young children how to count in another language.

Informational book series generally contain descriptive chapters and colorful photography about specific countries in the Middle East. Series books explore a country's special geography, people, history, government, industry, culture and other topics. Intermediate and middle grade level students will find the following series selections of interest. In *Enchantment of the World: Iran* (1991), Mary V. Fox provides accounts of where and how Iranians live; the rich cultural heritage of Iran; and a photographic tour of Iran. *Iraq . . . In Pictures* (Lerner Publications 1992) is another example of a well-documented, yet highly readable chapter book from an informational books series that uses a variety of photographs to support the book's thorough content.

Ali, Child of the Desert (London 1997) is a picture book which portrays the modern life of an Arabian child. The story goes through a day for young Ali.

Young adult readers will find *The Gulf War Reader,* edited by Micah L. Sifry and Christopher Cerf (1991), a rich resource to learn the historical background and causes of Desert Storm. Several contributors are world leaders such as former Presidents George Bush and Jimmy Carter. Even Saddam Hussein provides a perspective of the war.

Desert Storm, The War in the Persian Gulf (Time-Warner New Media 1991), is a compelling interactive. CD-ROM that chronicles the events of Desert Storm. This CD-ROM was assembled by the editorial staff of *Time* and provides a compilation of reports, eyewitness accounts, photographs, audio recordings, and research about Desert Storm.

The British-made videotape series *ARABIA: Sand, Sea, & Sky* (FF & McKinnon 1990) provides three perspectives of the unique natural history of the Arabian Peninsula. The first videotape in the series, *The Mountain Barrier,* explores Arabia's wildlife in the high Sarawat mountains of western Arabia. In this video, exotic birds, snakes, lizards and the barren landscape are featured, including a look at the volcanic moonscape land and rugged mountains. In *Red Sea Rift,* the second videotape of the series, thousands of miles of the Red Sea off the coast of Arabia are visited, all teeming with spectacular sealife. This videotape also explains the feeding behaviors and life-cycles of various sealife. Characteristics of marine behavior of each zone are examined. The third videotape in the series is entitled *Eye of the Camel.* Filmed as a journey with a Bedouin family on their winter migration through the country's Empty Quarter, viewers also learn of the many survival strategies used by desert wildlife including camels, gazelle, oryz, plants, and insects. A visit to al-Hasa Oasis bridges modern life with the heritage of ancient traditions.

Classroom Literacy Activities That Promote Middle East Awareness

The following are literacy-based classroom activities that teachers can use to help children understand and learn about the Middle East.

- Read aloud and discuss Arabic folktales to your students from Iner Bushnaq's *Arab Folktales* (1986). Compare the literary elements of Arabic folktales with those found in folktales from other countries.
- Introduce children to Arabic food by reading to determine a recipe to prepare in class from Christine Osborne's *Middle Eastern Food and Drink* (1988).
- Arrange for your class to visit a mosque and request a guided tour with a question and answer time built in. Encourage children to write about the experience and share their writing with others.
- Write a letter to a Middle Eastern Embassy in Washington, D.C., or to a consulate near your part of the country. Develop questions to ask the ambassador or consulate general about that country. Request a reply.
- Use *Butterflies of Saudi Arabia and Its Neighbors* by Torben B. Larsen (1984) to examine similarities and differences between Middle East butterflies with those of other continents.
- Form cooperative groups to research and report a topic about a Middle Eastern country. Examples for report writing can include dress, food, music, art, geography, climate, history, religion, architecture, and literature.
- Invite a speaker or author to your classroom who can discuss a topic relevant to Middle East studies. Create a panel of children to discuss what was presented and have the speaker interact with the panel and the whole class.
- If you live near a university, invite a professor of Arabic or Middle East studies to visit your class and talk with your students. Prepare and send a list of student-generated questions to the visitor prior to the class visit. Ask the professor to provide a bibliography for you and your students so you can learn more about the Middle East.

Continued

In the Classroom Mini Lesson   *Continued*

The collective use of literature and technology can help teachers create more realistic experiences for their students to teach them about the Middle East. Reading literature provides a rich blend of informational and narrative genres to explore about all aspects of life in the Middle East, while the use of technology helps teachers make real connections between and among diverse cultures. Literature and technology can be used to cultivate awareness and understanding while helping children learn that in most ways, peoples of the world are more alike than they are different.

References

Alexander, S. 1983. *Nadia the willful.* New York: Random House.

Bushnaq, I. 1986. *Arab folktales.* New York: Pantheon.

Early, M. 1989. *Ali Baba and the forty thieves.* Sydney: Abrams Books.

FF & McKinnon. 1990. *ARABIA: Sand, Sea, and Sky.* London: FF & McKinnon. Videotape series.

Fox, M. V. 1991. *Enchantment of the world: Iran.* Chicago: Children's Press.

Haskins, J. 1991. *Count your way through the Arab world.* Minneapolis: Carolrhoda.

Heide, F. P., and J. H. Gilliland. 1990. *The day of Ahmed's secret.* New York: Lothrop, Lee, & Shepard.

Larsen, T. B. 1984. *Butterflies of Saudi Arabia and its neighbors.* New York: Stacey.

Lerner Publications. 1992. *Iraq . . . in pictures.* Forth Worth: Lerner.

London, J. 1997. *Ali, child of the desert.* Illus. T. Lewin. New York: Lothrop, Lee, & Shepard.

Manniche, L. 1981. *The prince who knew his fate.* New York: Philomel.

Osborne, C. 1988. *Middle Eastern food and drink.* Los Angeles: Wayland.

Sifry M. L., and C. Cerf. 1991. *The Gulf War reader.* New York: Random House.

Time-Warner New Media. 1991. *Desert Storm, the war in the Persian Gulf.* New York: Time Warner, CD-ROM.

Chapter Summary

The goal of the unit described in this chapter is to facilitate the development of the ability to view life from cultural perspectives different from one's own. After immersing students in a variety of ethnic experiences in Phase One, the unit's scope is progressively refined. In Phase Two, students focus on particular cultural groups for further exploration; in Phase Three, they develop an understanding of point of view; and finally, in Phase Four, students become creative writers as they write from the points of view of characters of their own creation. At the beginning of the unit, students view ethnic groups through their own cultural lenses. By the unit's conclusion, students add new cultural lenses to their repertoire of perspectives. In short, they achieve a flexibility of perspective.

Implementation of the unit's extension leads to the development of a fresh multicultural perspective in two ways. Students create a diverse community and in the process, they engage in the same kinds of cooperative interactions as their characters. Further, if students in the learning groups are themselves from different cultural groups, prejudice will probably diminish in the process of working together toward a common goal (Slavin 1989–1990).

In addition to aiding both the reduction of prejudice and the growth of critical thinking in all subject areas, the skill of perspective taking, together with the knowledge gained about diverse cultural groups, provides students with an intuitive grasp of a number of issues related to living in a multicultural society. This deep understanding, which is at once cognitive and affective, can serve as a foundation for dealing with these issues in more complex ways later in life.

Children's Books

Criteria for Selecting Multicultural Literature

Selecting multicultural literature for children is not an easy task for teachers. For some ethnic groups, such as African Americans, there is a multitude of children's literature available from which to choose. However, for other cultures, such as Latvian, there are few titles available. The areas of Asian American and Latino children's literature can be confusing to teachers because these are conglomerates of many cultural groups. For instance, Asian American children's literature includes not only Chinese and Japanese children's books but also Cambodian, Indonesian, Korean, Laotian, Malaysian, Thai, and Vietnamese, among others. Likewise, Hispanic includes Cuban, Dominican, Mexican, Nicaraguan, and Puerto Rican, as well as the South American countries—all very different cultural groups.

Cullinan and Galda (1999, 351) suggest that teachers look for books representing culturally diverse groups that

1. avoid stereotypes,
2. portray the cultural groups and their values in an authentic way,
3. use language that reflects standards set by local usage,
4. validate children's experience,
5. broaden our vision, and
6. invite reflection.

Through discussing and sharing multicultural literature with other teachers, teachers can become more familiar with appropriate titles to relate to students.

There should be enough books available to give students different perspectives on issues and historical events, such as the Native American view on the European settlement of North America, both on the eastern seaboard and in the Southwest. In addition, books should be available that correct distortions of information (Bishop 1992), such as the fact that many Native Americans died, not at the hands of pioneers and soldiers, but from illnesses such as smallpox, a disease brought to North America by Europeans.

Following is a list of African American, Asian American, Hispanic, and Native American multicultural books.

African American

Bryan, A. 1991. *All night, all day: A child's first book of African-American spirituals.* New York: Macmillan/Atheneum. (3–8)
Burchard, P. 1995. *Charlotte Forten: A black teacher in the Civil War.* New York: Crown. (4–7)

Collier, J., and Collier, C. 1981. *Jump ship to freedom.* New York: Delacorte. (5–8)

Cox, C. 1993. *The forgotten heroes: The story of the Buffalo Soldiers.* New York: Scholastic. (5–8)

Farris, P. J. 1996. *Young mouse and elephant: An East African folktale.* Illus. V. Gorbachev. Boston: Houghton Mifflin. (K–3)

Golenbeck, P. 1990. *Teammates.* Illus. P. Bacon. Orlando, FL: Gulliver. (3–8)

Hamilton, V. 1985. *The people could fly: American black folktales.* Illus. L. Dillon and D. Dillon. New York: Knopf. (3–8)

Hamilton, V. 1991. *The all Jahdu storybook.* Illus. B. Moser. San Diego: Harcourt Brace. (3–8)

Hamilton, V. 1992. *Drylongso.* Illus. J. Pinkney. San Diego: Harcourt Brace. (3–6)

Hansen, J. 1986. *Which way freedom?* New York: Walker. (5–8)

Harris, J. C. 1986. *Jump! The adventures of Brier Rabbit.* Orlando, FL: Harcourt Brace Jovanovich. (K–8)

Haskins, J. 1993. *Get on board: The story of the Underground Railroad.* New York: Scholastic. (5–8)

Hoffman, M. 1991. *Amazing Grace.* Illus. C. Birch. New York: Dial. (K–3)

Hopkinson, D. 1993. *Sweet Clara and the freedom quilt.* Illus. J. Ransome. New York: Knopf. (2–5)

Hoyt-Goldsmith, D. 1993. *Celebrating Kwanzaa.* Illus. L. Midgale. New York: Holiday. (K–8)

Isadora, R. 1991. *At the crossroads.* New York: Greenwillow. (3–5)

Kimmel, E. A. 1994. *Anansi and the talking melon.* Illus. J. Stevens. New York: Holiday. (K–3)

Knutson, B. 1990 *How the guinea fowl got her spots: A Swahili tale of friendship.* New York: Carolrhoda. (K–2)

Lawrence, J. 1993. *The great migration: An American story.* New York: HarperCollins. (3–6)

Mettger, Z. 1994. *Till victory is won: Black soldiers in the Civil War.* New York: Lodestar. (5–9)

Mollei, T. M. 1995. *Big boy.* Illus. E. B. Lewis. New York: Clarion. (K–3)

Myers, W. D. 1988. *Scorpions.* New York: Harper & Row. (5–8)

Myers, W. D. 1991. *Now is your time!: The African American struggle for freedom.* New York: HarperCollins. (4–8)

Pinkney, A. D. 1993. *Seven candles for Kwanzaa.* Illus. B. Pinkney. New York: Dial. (K-up)

Ringgold, F. 1991. *Tar beach.* New York: Crown. (1–3)

Ringgold, F. 1992. *Aunt Harriet's Underground Railroad in the sky.* New York: Crown. (1–4)

Asian American

Cassedy, S., and Suetake, K. (Trans.). 1992. *Red dragonfly on my shoulder.* Illus. M. Bang. New York: HarperCollins. (K–3)

Choi, N. S. 1991. *Year of impossible goodbyes.* Boston: Houghton Mifflin. (4–8)

Coerr, E. 1993. *Sadako.* Illus. E. Young. New York: Putnam. (3–8)

Compton, P. A. 1991. *The terrible eek.* Illus. S. Hamanaka. New York: Simon & Schuster. (1–3)

Conger, D. 1987. *Many lands, many stories: Asian folktales for children.* New York: Tuttle. (3–5)

Dunn, M., and Ardath, M. 1983. *The absolutely perfect horse.* New York: Harper & Row. (3–6)

Hamanaka, S. 1990. *The journey: Japanese Americans, racism, and renewal.* New York: Orchard. (4–7)

Haugaard, E. C. 1995. *The revenge of the forty-seven samurai.* Boston: Houghton Mifflin. (6–8)

Hong, L. T. 1991. *How the ox star fell from heaven.* New York: Albert Whitman. (4–6)

Jiang, J. L. 1998. *The red scarf.* New York: Harper Trophy. (6–8)

Johnson, R. 1992. *Kenji and the magic geese.* Illus. J. Tseng and M. Tseng. New York: Simon & Schuster. (K–2)

Lord, B. B. 1984. *In the year of the boar and Jackie Robinson.* New York: Harper & Row. (4–6)

Morris, W. 1992. *The future of Yen-Tzu.* Illus. F. Henstra. New York: Atheneum. (1–4)

Nhuong, H. Q. 1982. *The land I lost: Adventures of a boy in Vietnam.* New York: Harper & Row. (4–8)

Salisbury, G. 1994. *Under the blood-red sun.* New York: Delacorte. (6–8)

Say, A. 1990. *El chino.* Boston: Houghton Mifflin. (4–8)

Say, A. 1993. *Grandfather's journey.* Boston: Houghton Mifflin. (K–3)

Shea, P. D. 1995. *The whispering cloth.* Illus. A. Riggio and Y. Yang. Honesdale, PA: Boyds Mills. (K–2)

Siberell, A. 1990. *A journey to paradise.* New York: Henry Holt. (4–6)

Surat, M. M. 1983. *Angel child, dragon child.* Racine, WI: Carnival/Raintree. (3–5)

Uchida, Y. 1993. *The bracelet.* Illus. J. Yardley. New York: Philomel. (K–2)

Wallace, I. 1984. *Chin Chiang and the dragon's dance.* New York: Atheneum. (3–7)

Yacowitz, C. 1992. *The jade stone.* Illus. J. H. Chen. New York: Holiday. (1–3)

Yee, P. 1990. *Tales from gold mountain: Stories of the Chinese in the new world.* Illus. N. Ng. New York: Harper & Row. (4–8)

Yee, P. 1991. *Roses sing on new snow.* Illus. H. Chan. New York: Macmillan. (3–6)

Yep, L. 1989. *The rainbow people.* Illus. D. Wiesner. New York: HarperCollins. (4–8)

Yep, L. 1993. *Dragon's gate.* New York: HarperCollins. (5–8)

Hispanic

Aardema, V. 1991. *Borreguita and the coyote: Tale from Ayutia, Mexico.* New York: Knopf. (K–3)

Ada, A. F. 1998. *Under the royal palms: A childhood in Cuba.* New York: Atheneum. (6–8)

Ancona, G. 1994. *The piñata maker/El piñatero.* San Diego: Harcourt. (K–8)

Anzaldua, G. 1993. *Friends from the other side/Amigos del otro lado.* Chicago: Children's Book Press, (1–7)

Bunting, E. 1990. *The wall.* Illus. R. Himler. New York: Clarion. (3–8)

Charles, F., and R. Arenson. 1996. *A Caribbean counting book.* Boston: Houghton Mifflin. (K–1)

Cisñeros, S. 1994. *Hairs/Pelitos.* New York: Apple Soup/Knopf. (K–3)

Clark, A. N. 1980. *Secret of the Andes.* New York: Viking. (4–8)

De Gerez, T. 1981. *My song is a piece of jade: Poems of ancient Mexico in English and Spanish.* Boston: Little, Brown. (3–8)

de Paola, T. 1980. *The lady of Guadalupe.* New York: Holiday. (3–6)

Dorros, A. 1991. *Abuela.* New York: Dutton. (4–8)

Gershator, P., and D. Gershator. 1998. *Greetings, sun.* New York: Richard Jackson Books. (K–2)

Gonzalez, L. M. 1996. *The bossy gallito (rooster): A traditional Cuban folktale.* New York: Scholastic. (Available in both English and Spanish). (K–3)

Hausman, G., and A. Wolff. 1998. *Doctor bird: Three lookin' up tales from Jamaica.* New York: Philomel. (2–3)

Isadora, R. 1998. *Caribbean dream.* New York: Putnam. (1–3)

Mohr, N. 1993. *All for the better: The story of El Barrio.* Dallas: Steck-Vaughn. (2–5)

Mora, P. 1995. *The desert is my mother/El desierto es mi madre.* Illus. D. Leshon. Houston: Piñata. (3–6)

Mora, P. 1998 *Delicious hulabaloo/Pachanga deliciosa.* Illus. F. Mora. Los Angeles: Arte Publico. (3–5)

Myers, W. D. 1996. *Toussaint L'Ouverture: The fight for Haiti's freedom.* New York: Simon & Schuster. (6–8)

O'Dell, S. 1981. *Carlota.* Boston: Houghton Mifflin. (5–8)

Palacios, A. 1993. *¡Viva Mexico!: The story of Benito Juarez and Cinco de Mayo.* Cleveland, OH: Modern Curriculum Press. (2–5)

Pitre, F. 1993. *Juan Bobo and the pig: A Puerto Rican folktale.* Illus. C. Hale. New York: Lodestar. (1–3)

Rodriguez, G. M. (1994). *Green corn tamales/Tamales de elote*. Illus. G. Shepard. Tucson, AZ: Hispanic. (2–4)

Roe, E. 1991. *Con mi hermano—With my brother*. New York: Bradbury. (5–8)

Shute, L. 1995. *Rabbit wishes*. New York: Lothrop, Lee, & Shepard. (2–4)

Soto, G. 1990. *Baseball in April and other stories*. San Diego: Harcourt. (3–6)

Soto, G. 1992. *Neighborhood odes*. Illus. D. Diaz. San Diego: Harcourt. (5–8)

Soto, G. 1993. *Too many tamales*. Illus. E. Martinez. New York: Putnam. (K–3)

Tamar, E. 1996. *American City Ballet*. New York: Harper Trophy. (5–8)

Villaseñor, V. 1994. *Walking stars: Stories of magic and power*. Houston: Piñata. (3–6)

Winter, J. 1991. *Diego*. New York: Knopf. (5–8)

Native American

Baylor, B. 1975. *A god on every mountain top: Stories of southwest Indian mountains*. New York: Scribner's. (3–6)

Baylor, B. 1978. *The other way to listen*. New York: Scribner's. (K–8)

Bierhorst, J. 1979. *A cry from the earth: Music of the North American Indians*. New York: Four Winds. (K–8)

Bierhorst, J. 1983. *The sacred path: Spells, prayers, and power songs of the American Indians*. New York: Four Winds. (K–8)

Bierhorst, J. 1995. *The white deer*. New York: Morrow. (2-up)

Bierhorst, J. 1997. *The dancing fox*. Illus. M. K. Okheeng. New York: William Morrow. (2–5)

Bierhorst, J. 1998. *The deetkatoo*. Illus. R. H. Co. New York: William Morrow. (4–6)

Bruchac, J. 1993. *Fox song*. Illus. P. Morin. New York: Philomel. (K)

Bruchac, J. 1995. *Gluskabe and the four wishes*. Illus. C. Nyburg. New York: Cobblehill. (1–3)

Bruchac, J. 1988. *The arrow over the door*. Illus. J. Watling. New York: Dial. (1–4)

Bruchac, J., and London, J. 1992. *Thirteen moons on turtle's back*. Illus. T. Locker. New York: Philomel. (1–4)

Carey, V. S. 1990. *Quail song: A Pueblo Indian tale*. Illus. I. Barnett. New York: Putnam. (K–4)

Cherry, L. 1991. *A river ran wild*. Orlando: Harcourt Brace Jovanovich. (K–8)

Cohen, C. L. 1988. *The mud pony: A Traditional Skidi Pawnee tale*. Illus. S. Begay. New York: Scholastic. (3–7)

De Felice, C. 1990. *Weasel*. New York: Macmillan. (5–8)

Dorris, M. 1992. *Morning girl*. New York: Hyperion. (3–5)

Ekoomiak, N. 1990. *Arctic memories*. New York: Holt, Rinehart & Winston. (4–6)

Freedman, R. 1988. *Buffalo hunt*. New York: Holiday. (3–8)

Freedman, R. 1992. *Indian winter*. Photo. K. Bodmer. New York: Holiday. (5-up)

Fritz, J. 1983. *The double life of Pocahontas*. New York: Putnam. (3–7)

George, J. C. 1983. *The talking earth*. New York: Harper & Row. (4–8)

Goble, P. 1988. *Iktomi and the boulder: A Plains Indian story*. New York: Orchard. (K–4)

Goble, P. 1990. *Dream wolf*. New York: Bradbury. (1–3)

Goble, P. 1992. *Crowchief*. New York: Orchard. (K–2)

Gregory, K. 1990. *The legend of Jimmy Spoon*. Orlando, FL: Harcourt Brace Jovanovich. (4–8)

Grossman, V. 1991. *Ten little rabbits*. Illus. S. Long. San Francisco: Chronicle. (K–2)

Hoyt-Goldsmith, D. 1991. *Pueblo storyteller*. Photo. L. Migdale. New York: Holiday. (1–4)

Kesey, K. 1991. *The sea lion*. Illus. N. Waldman. New York: Viking. (5–8)

Larrabee, L. 1993. *Grandmother Five Baskets*. Illus. L. Sawyer. Tucson, AZ: Harbinger. (3–8)

Larry, C. 1993. *Peboan and Seegwun*. New York: Farrar, Straus, & Giroux. (K–3)

Marrin, A. 1984. *War clouds in the west: Indians and cavalrymen, 1860–1890*. New York: Atheneum. (5–8)

Martin, R. 1992. *The rough-face girl*. Illus. D. Shannon. New York: Scholastic. (K–4)

Moore, R. 1990. *Maggie among the Seneca*. New York: HarperCollins. (5–6)

O'Dell, S. 1988 *Black star, bright dawn.* Boston: Houghton Mifflin. (5–8)

Paulsen. G. 1988. *Dogsong.* New York: Bradbury. (5–8)

Rodanos, K. 1992. *Dragonfly's tale.* New York: Clarion. (5–8)

Rodanos, K. 1994. *Dance of the sacred circle.* New York: Little, Brown. (4–8)

Roessell, M. 1993. *Kinaalia:A Navaho girl grows up.* Minneapolis, MN: Lerner. (3–6)

Sewall, M. 1990. *People of the breaking day.* New York: Atheneum. (5–7)

Seymour, T. V. N. 1993. *The gift of changing woman.* New York: Henry Holt. (3–5)

Sneve, V. 1989. *Dancing teepees: Poems of American Indian youth.* New York: Holiday. (4–8)

Sneve, V. 1994. *The Nez Perce: A first Americans book.* New York: Holiday. (2–6)

Strete, D. K. 1990. *Big thunder magic.* Illus. G. Brown. New York: Greenwillow. (K–4)

Thomson, P. 1995. *Katie Henio: Navaho sheepherder.* Photo. P. Conklin. New York: Cobblehill. (2–4)

Van Laan, N. 1993. *Buffalo dance: A Blackfoot legend.* Illus. B. Vidal. Boston: Little, Brown. (1–8)

White Deer of Autumn. 1983. *Ceremony—In the circle of life.* Racine, WI: Raintree. (4–8)

Wisniewski, D. 1991. *Rain player.* New York: Clarion. (K–3)

Yolen, J. 1992. *Encounter.* Illus. D. Shannon. San Diego: Harcourt Brace. (3–8)

Other Multicultural Works

Aamundsen, N. R. 1990. *Two short and one long.* Boston: Houghton Mifflin. (4–8)

Ashabranner, B. 1991. *An ancient heritage: The Arab-American minority.* Photo. P. S. Conklin. New York: HarperCollins. (5–8)

Heide, F. P., & Gilliland, J. H. 1990. *The day of Ahmed's secret.* Illus. T. Lewin. New York: Lothrop, Lee, & Shepard. (K–3)

Langton, J. 1985. *The hedgehog boy: A Latvian folktale.* Illus. I. Plume. New York: HarperCollins. (2–4)

Lankford, M. D. 1992. *Hopscotch around the world.* Illus. K. Milone. New York: Morrow. (1–2)

Mayers, F. 1992. *A Russian ABC.* New York: Abrams. (K–4)

Philip, N. 1991. *Fairy tales of Eastern Europe.* Illus. L. Wilkes. New York: Clarion. (K–8)

Reed, D. C. 1995. *The Kraken.* Honesdale, PA: Boyds Mills. (3–6)

Taken from P. J. Farris *Language Arts: Process, Product, and Assessment.* 3rd ed. Boston: McGraw-Hill, 2001. Used by permission.

Teaching Resources

Barrett, K., L. Bergman, and G. Dornfest, 1996. *Investigating artifacts: Making masks, creating myths, exploring middens—Teacher's guide.* Berkeley, CA: University of California.

Bigelow, B., and B. Peterson. 1998. *Rethinking Columbus: The next 500 years.* Minneapolis, MN: Rethinking Schools.

Lee, E., D. Menkart, and M. Okazawa-Rey, 1998. *Beyond heroes and holidays: A practical guide to K–12 anti-racist, multicultural education and staff development.* Berkeley, CA: NECA.

Videos

"The World Through Kids' Eyes." 1997. 67 minutes. Maryknoll World Productions. Available from *www.americas.org* for $29.95 plus tax and shipping.

Six short segments of children at risk from six different countries (Philippines, Peru, Brazil, United States, India, and South Africa).

References

Banks, J. A., and C. A. M. Banks. 1997. *Multicultural education: Issues and perspectives.* 3rd ed. New York: John Wiley.

Bishop, R. S. 1992. Multicultural literature for children: Making informed choices. In V. Harris (Ed.). *Teaching Multicultural Literacy* (pp. 37–54). Norwood, MA: Christopher Gordon.

Byrnes, D. A. 1988. Children and prejudice. *Social Education* 52:267–71.

Cullinan, B. and L. Galda. 1999. *Literature and the child,* 4th ed. San Diego: Harcourt Brace.

Holdaway, D. 1979. *The foundations of literacy.* Urbana, IL: National Council of Teachers of English.

Hoyt, L. 1992. Many ways of knowing: Using drama, oral interactions, and the visual arts to enhance reading comprehension. *The Reading Teacher* 45:580–4.

Hunter, K. 1973. *Guests in the promised land.* New York: Scribner's.

National Council for the Social Studies. 1992. The Columbia Quincentenary Position Statement. *Social Studies and the Young Learner* 4: n.p.

Pate, G. S. 1988. Research on reducing prejudice. *Social Education* 52:287–9.

Robbins, P. A. 1990. Implementing whole language: Bridging children and books. *Educational Leadership* 47 (6): 50–4.

Shaw, C. C. 1993. Taking multicultural math seriously. *Social Studies and the Young Learner* 6 (1): 31–2.

Singer, J.Y., and T. Harbour-Ridley. 1998. Young children learn about immigrants to the United States. *Social Education* 62:415–416.

Slavin. R. E. 1989–1990. Research on cooperative learning: Consensus and controversy. *Educational Leadership* 47 (4): 52–4.

Sleeter, C. E., and C. A. Grant. 1988. *Making choices for multicultural education: Five approaches to race, class and gender.* Columbus, OH: Merrill.

Sunal, C. S., and M. E. Haas. 1997. *Social studies and the elementary/middle school student.* Orlando, Fl: Harcourt Brace Jovanovich.

Walker-Dalhouse, D. 1993. Using African-American literature to increase ethnic understanding. *The Reading Teacher* 45:416–22.

Walsh, D. 1988. Critical thinking to reduce prejudice. *Social Education* 52:280–2.

Weil, M., E. Calhoun, and B. Joyce. 2000. *Models of teaching.* 6th ed. Englewood Cliffs, NJ: Prentice-Hall.

Chapter 16

© Skjold Photographs

Social Studies, Bilingualism, Respect, and Understanding

Making the Connections

Mary Louise Ginejko
*Jr./Sr. High Hispanic Drop Out Prevention Program Teacher and Titled
Resource Specialist, Gompers Junior High, Joliet, IL.*

*Scholars describe the United States as one of history's first universal or world
nations—its people are a microcosm of humanity with biological, cultural, and
social ties to all other parts of the earth.*

**—National Council for the Social Studies
"The Columbia Quincentenary Position Statement"**

Objectives

————————————————————✎————————————————————

Readers will

- develop a greater awareness of the different cultures as well as their own;
- understand the need to learn the traditions and mores of the different cultural
  groups represented in their own school and community.
- understand that diversity occurs even within peoples from seemingly the
  same geographical area; and
- understand the need to develop personal relationships in the classroom, both
  student to student and teacher to student.

Introduction

While there is an increasing awareness of the diversity of students, there is also
great controversy over the placement of bilingual students. Rosalie Pedalino Porter
(1990) has questioned whether placement decisions are based on the children's

needs or on the needs of politicians and bureaucrats. She condemns transitional bilingual education (TBE), which demands native-language instruction. She purports that this is an unjust form of segregation, thereby sending a message that these students are remedial or less than acceptable in general education classes. The editors of *When They Don't All Speak English,* Pat Rigg and Virginia G. Allen (1989, ix) agree: "[S]econd-language students need to be with first-language students. If they are isolated from active-English-speaking students, they cannot learn English from them, nor can they share any of the riches they have to offer." According to Lim and Watson (1993, 393).

> Combining authentic and natural language experiences with content-rich classroom practices leads to optimal language learning and optimal subject matter learning. When the instructional focus moves away from language as an object and away from content as facts to a content-rich, usable language, second-language learners will gain confidence in themselves, and their knowledge of both language and content will flourish. Effective language learning, either native or second language, depends not on the direct teaching of identified skills, but rather on a sound philosophy of learning and teaching, underlying a meaning-filled curriculum.

Many educators disagree with this argument.

One of the boldest conclusions Porter offers is a rejection of the concept that first language and cognitive abilities must be learned in the native language before these skills can be transferred into the second language. Much research to the contrary indicates that it takes more than five years for ESL (English as a Second Language) students to become proficient enough to compete with their general education peers (Cummins 1981, 1984). Although this is worthy of detailed examination, the focus of this chapter is on the challenges of the general education classroom teacher.

This chapter addresses the concerns of the general education teacher, who is becoming increasingly aware of the large number of students in the classroom who speak English only as a second language. According to the 1990 census figures, 31.8 million people in the United States communicate in 329 different foreign languages. Spanish is the most common foreign language. It is spoken by more than 17 million people of whom 54 percent do not speak English at home, according to M. L. Vsdansky in an article titled "Census Language Not Foreign at Home," published in *USA Today,* 28 April 1993.

Statistics in 1994–1995 indicated 7 percent of all children in America's school system to be designated as LEP (Limited English Proficient.). By the school year 1995–1996, the percentage of children having difficulty speaking English increased to 13.9 percent. Of school-age children living at home, 6.3 million with a language other than English entered our schools. Of these, 5 million spoke Spanish at home. Ruben Rumbaut, who presented the paper "Transformations: The Post-Immigrant Generation in an Age of Diversity," at the annual meeting of the Easter Sociological Society, Philadelphia, PA, on March 21, 1998, reveals that based on March 1997 census data, 20 percent of our students are foreign-born (3 million children) or living with at least one foreign-born parent (10 million children).

Many of these children are Mexican American students. They are part of a group referred to as people of color. Membership in this group is exclusively reserved for nonwhite minority individuals. James A. Banks (Banks and Banks 1997, XVIII) defines *people of color* as follows:

In most instances, the phrase *people of color* rather than *ethnic minority* is used to refer to groups such as Mexican Americans, African Americans, Puerto Ricans, and Native Americans. *People of color* is used to reflect new demographic realities: These groups are majorities rather than minorities in a growing number of schools and school districts.

Of the three major Hispanic groups, Mexican Americans are increasing in the U.S. population at a much faster rate than Puerto Ricans and Cubans. In 1988, Mexican Americans accounted for approximately 62 percent of all Hispanics in this country.

When considering statistics, one should keep in mind that the population figures given by the U.S. Bureau of the Census are invalid in terms of the Mexican American population in the United States because a substantial number of undocumented Mexican aliens are continually entering the United States. Moreover, the birthrate in the Hispanic communities is high.

Because of this unknown number of illegal aliens and the large number of legal immigrants coming from Mexico to the United States, teachers in this country have more Hispanic students to teach each year. Few general education teachers have had any specialized training in ESL. However, this has not prevented teachers from encountering each student with predisposed expectations about the student and themselves. Although xenophobia (fear of foreigners) is still an intricate part of American society, teachers must be sensitive to the needs of all children. General education teachers can gain confidence in themselves and their professional abilities by becoming more knowledgeable about Mexican American culture and by examining teaching strategies that promote rather than impede learning in both first-language and second-language classrooms. The next section offers insights into respect and understanding of culture. Educators have the responsibility to assist their students in reconceptualizing American society.

✎ *Cultural Awareness*

Cultural awareness means more than the designated multicultural month of February celebrated in most American schools. It means more than speeches, reports, bulletin boards, displays, and school assemblies to acknowledge that—at least for one month of the year—everyone has a culture. Cultural awareness does not mean presenting the contributions of each culture in isolation. It does mean understanding the interaction of the contributions of various cultures. It means making cultural connections.

Cultural awareness means understanding that each of us has a culture that is part of our very being. Together, we all make up the tapestry called America. We each bring threads of cultural values, historical pride, experiences, and aspirations to this fabric. Understanding and respecting cultural differences and similarities perpetuate an environment conducive to an appreciation of life.

In the nineteenth and twentieth centuries, our society viewed the perfect solution to cultural differences as a melting pot. It expected each person to begin the process of acculturation, acquiring the culture from a geographic area rather than maintaining and nourishing his or her own unique language and customs, in essence, his or her own consciousness. This ideological assumption fostered a nation where people of diverse backgrounds would blend into one. Ethnic groups would assimilate to form one culture identity. It resulted in no identification of individual culture appreciation, no

16.1　Focus Box

Multiethnicity

*A*s the minorities become the majority in most U.S. schools, teachers recognize the need to develop appropriate curricula that will foster our country's democratic philosophy. It becomes necessary for the classroom environment and teaching strategies in those environments to change in order to meet the needs of the new majority. Pang (1994) emphasizes the need for the teacher's understanding of self and other cultures before attempting to create a multicultural classroom environment.

Although current thought is caught between the clash of two paradigms, assimilationism and ethnic pluralism, the focus will be on the latter. A sensitivity to all students predisposes their academic success. All children should learn and take pride in their own ethnicity. They should learn and respect the ethnicity of others. In this chapter, two ethnic groups are explored: Asian and Pacific Americans (APAs) and Mexican Americans. An appreciation of diversity and unity must be developed. Multiple perspectives should be encouraged. James Banks (Banks and Banks 1997) reminds us that the "west" in our "U.S. western movement" is, for the Mexicans, the "north," for the Chinese, the "east," and for the Sioux, the center of the universe. An important part of all of this is a willingness to make decisions through compromise. Students must learn to accept alternate perspectives regarding the same phenomenon. Cook and Gonzales (1994) offer the multiethnic classroom as the place for this to happen.

To reduce prejudice and foster tolerance, we must teach people history, not as dates but as popular movements. Time lines and events must translate to the history of common people. Each historic figure should be portrayed, as not a hero, but as a human being with both good and bad characteristics. George Washington and Thomas Jefferson were great men; however, they also owned slaves. Teach the whole story. Don't rewrite history to present a balanced picture. Focus on major ideas of history and all the ethnic groups that are part of history. Don't focus on any one single cultural group for Cultural Awareness Month.

---

existence of ethnicity. If all the cultures in the United States could be melted together, they would only produce a tasteless homogenized pretense of humanity.

After society recognized the folly of the melting pot idea, the metaphor of a stew or salad began appearing to capture society's view of its cultural self. However, this allowed individuals to dictate which culture qualities should or should not be chosen to be part of an American stew or salad. Such elitism promotes the destruction of cultural pride and esteem, encouraging discrimination and prejudice. It does not recognize the need for society's pluralism or the individual's need of enculturation, the process of absorbing one's own culture. The variations in culture patterns are the strength of a multigroup society with an emphasis on diversity. It is not necessary to give up the first language/culture to learn a second. Biliteracy development not only is possible but also should be encouraged.

The image of a national fabric or tapestry precludes a respect and acceptance of all humankind's diversities. It makes all of us a part of this nation and allows for the appreciation and interaction of cultures. No social intimidation threatens the loss of

Variations in culture patterns are the strength of a multigroup society.
© Richard Hutchings/PhotoEdit

any individual culture. While allowing for cultural assimilation, it does not rob the individual of his or her culture. This view is by no means universally accepted. Janzen (1994) offers an explanation of the ethnic pluralism/assimilationism (melting pot) debate, a debate that will be played out in the schools. The following abbreviations used by educators recognize the diversity of our population in the area of language.

APA	Asian and Pacific Americans
BICS	Basic Interpersonal Conversation Skills (Survival Language)
CALP	Cognitive Academic Language Proficiency
EFL	English as a Foreign Language
ELL	English language learners
ESL	English as a second language
ESOL	English for Speakers of Other Languages
LCD	Linguistically and Culturally Diverse
LEA	Language experience approach
LEP	Limited English proficiency
LEPS	Limited English proficiency speakers
LPL	Language proficiency level
MEP	Migrant Education Program
NABE	National Association of Bilingual Education
NCBE	National Clearinghouse for Bilingual Education

PEP	Potential English proficiency (new term now being used to replace LEP)
REAL	Readers and writers of English and another language
SAE	Students Acquiring English
SOL	Speakers of Other Languages
TBE	Transitional bilingual education
TESOL	Teachers of English to speakers of other languages
TPI	Transition Program of Instruction
TPR	Total physical response

❧ The Complex Diversity within the Asian and Pacific American Communities

Based on 1990 census data, the fastest growing minority group in the United States is the Asian and Pacific Americans (APAs). By the year 2040, it is projected that the APA population will increase from the current 7.3 million to more than 34 million. But confusion blankets the term APA. Ethnic ties include Chinese, Japanese, Filipino, Korean, Hmong, Vietnamese, Cambodian, Laotian, Thais, Malaysians, East Indians, and Pakistanis. Each of these groups of people maintains a separate thread of identity and history.

The first Asian immigrants were attracted to the California gold rush in 1848. They arrived from the district of Toishan, in the South China province of Kwangtung. Ninety-five percent of this population was male. Large numbers of females did not arrive until after 1945. The first Japanese immigrants arrived in Hawaii in 1868. Their history in this country includes their 1942 removal from the West Coast and internment to relocation camps in various states. They differed greatly from the first Chinese in that they had the advantage of a strong family life with their wives and children.

The third major Asian group in America were the Filipino Americans. Their numbers grew in Hawaii and they eventually migrated to California. Like their predecessors, they too met with anti-Asian attitudes. The Korean Americans followed in the early 1900s.

The end of the war in Vietnam in 1975 resulted in a large number of educated Vietnamese entering the United States. This was followed in 1979 by the second large wave of mainly less educated "boat people." Both groups have met with mixed reactions and success. Many of these refugees spent time in camps waiting to enter the United States. The Cambodians were next to follow. The formally educated Cambodians spoke their own language and French (the language of the educated and the government). They suffered many atrocities before arriving in the United States.

I spent several years in an elementary school at this time receiving many Asian immigrants. Our problems were unique. It was difficult to find anyone who could translate. In Laos, Cambodia, and Vietnam, at least twenty languages are spoken. Communication was difficult. Neither the APA children nor the adults could speak English. However, before arriving in this country, some children learned "military French" from the camps. This proved to be a problem, especially to those who understood the language.

The immigrants' first Halloween in the United States was traumatic. They believe strongly in the spirit world and were shocked, frightened, and confused by children wearing masks and roaming the neighborhood in the dark. I learned this from the Hmong when we started making masks in class. The families had no support groups or other family waiting here in this country to help explain American customs.

Many of the APAs had never been in a school; their parents had never been in a school. Many were farmers and this was their first contact with formal education in any form. We discovered a need to help parents adjust to our country. I remember trying to explain a water bill to a family who spoke no English and had no concept of "bill." We were fortunate to have church groups sponsor families. They played a big part in educating the families.

As teachers, we learned early that not all Asian groups were friendly with each other. It was not uncommon to see two children begin fighting for no apparent reason until you realized one was Vietnamese and the other Cambodian. It was a learning experience for children and teachers alike.

The APA children were eager to communicate. Teachers and children volunteered for English classes held before school began each morning. As more APA immigrants came into our school, they had the support of the first group.

✍ *Personal Observation of the Mexican American Community*

The Mexican American enters the U.S. educational system with a rich literary, political, economic, and historical background. Acuña (1988), Kanellos (1990), and Keefe and Padilla (1987) provide an extensive account of the Mexican American experience in the United States. For our purposes, we will briefly examine the cultural values of Mexican Americans and how they influence teaching styles.

While recognizing the diversity within the Mexican American culture, one can make the following observations about the traditional Mexican American value system. This culture promotes a strong emotion of identity with its loyalty to family, community, and ethnic group. Achievement for children means achievement of the family, not necessarily individual achievement as is encouraged in many Anglo-American children. It is important to the education of Mexican American students to include parent involvement as part of the educational process. Parents provide a positive support system. Every possible attempt should be made to keep parents informed of their child's progress. Sending work home or accepting items from the home for display strengthens the necessary home-school relationship.

Competition in school can be confusing when one's culture dictates cooperation for mutual rewards. Mexican American students function better in cooperative learning situations. Motivation is found in the group activity rather than in the personal gain of achievement or grade.

Another strong value to be considered is sensitivity to the needs and feelings of other people. Relationships become personalized and interpersonal. Teachers should encourage children to help each other. Mexican American children are attuned to verbal and nonverbal calls for help. They are also the recipients of such help in their culture. This may in part explain their reluctance to ask the teacher a question; their request for help may be nonverbal.

The Mexican American humanistic orientation extends beyond the immediate family into the community. Extended families include: *primos* (cousins), those with the same last name but no blood relation; *tocayos* (namesakes), those with the same first name; *concuños* (brothers-in-law), two or more men married into the same family; *cuñadas* (sisters-in-law); and very important *padrinos* (godparents), *ahijados* (godchildren), and *compadres,* natural parents of godparents. Children acquire two godparents at baptism, one godparent when they receive the Sacrament of the Eucharist, and one godparent when they make their confirmation in the Catholic Church. Female children may also choose to have a *quinceñiera* when they become fifteen years old. It is possible at this ceremony for a girl to receive an additional ten to fifteen godparents. *Damas* (bridesmaids) and *chamberlans* (grooms) also become participants. In this ceremony, as throughout their life, the *abuelos* (blood grandparents) play a major role.

Mexican American children learn security through interpersonal relationships rather than institutional assistance. In school, students also expect a close and personalized relationship with the teacher. They view their teacher as a mother or father in a classroom environment. They expect to see personal family pictures or even visits from the teacher's family members. Mexican American students function better in a humanized curriculum. Traditionally, a more personalized curriculum offers more meaning. Their culture is child-centered rather than task-centered.

In such an extended family, the status and role of the individual is precisely defined. These are usually dictated by sex and age. Older children have more responsibilities than younger children. This should be a consideration when assigning homework. Mexican American parents may find it difficult to understand why teachers feel that schoolwork is more important than home responsibilities. Parents may feel that staying home for a family commitment is as important as going to school for the day. Respect for parents is expected of all individuals regardless of age. Sexual roles are clearly defined. Females are responsible for the condition of the home, preparation of food, health care, child rearing, and religious obligations. Males have a higher status. They are the wage earners. Teachers should be aware of this when assigning duties.

A powerful factor in the lives of Mexican Americans is their identification with Mexican Catholic ideology. This forceful power reinforces their value system. Lack of respect for parents or customs is sinful. Any interpretation of failure to meet family responsibilities is a serious infraction. Guilt becomes a serious consequence. A cycle of failure begins. This is evident in the psychological and physical school dropout rate. Teachers must intervene by making students aware of the educational continuum and long-range goals rather than let them become discouraged by immediate setbacks.

✌ Cultural Sensitivity through Interdisciplinary Teaching Strategies

Being sensitive to the educational needs of children means listening to all cultural voices and promoting the skills necessary to become a successful member of society. (Parker and Jarolimek 1997). Integrated instruction provides a reason to learn a language. Students become active learners.

Bilingual students experience specific academic difficulties that teachers should consider. Factors that influence the success of a bilingual student are past life experience, personal/family educational experiences, self-image, learning styles, multiple intelligence, classroom organization and management, perceived teacher/student roles, body language, proxemics, gestures, and facial expressions. Approaches to language acquisition require sensitivity to sociocultural interrelations. Teaching strategies can make a significant difference in academic achievement (Feinberg and Morencia 1998). This section suggests ways in which teachers can use integrated instruction strategies to promote the language development of these students.

Initially, bilingual students are placed in a bilingual or an ESL classroom. In a bilingual classroom, the students usually receive ESL instruction for part of the day and instruction in their native language during the rest of the day. This is justified by the premise that it is more important not to interrupt the learning process than it is to teach English. The ESL program differs. Students attend ESL classes for part of the day and are mainstreamed into general education classes for the remaining portion of the day. Exit from either program is accomplished by passing an LPL (language proficiency level) test.

Placing bilingual students in general education classrooms emphasizes the fact that there is a difference between the skills needed to communicate in English and the skills necessary to comprehend content material.

It may take five to seven years for students with limited English-speaking abilities to acquire the command of English they need to perform successfully in academic areas (Cummins 1984). Barriers to their effective communication, comprehension, and understanding exist, especially in tasks that involve reading and writing. Sometimes such barriers are disguised by the students' relatively quicker acquisition of conversational language and mastery of decoding skills in reading. Thus those students who appear to have command of English may in actuality be struggling to communicate and discover meaning when they are faced with academic settings and tasks that are decontextualized and cognitively demanding (Sutton 1989).

This problem can be compounded by the age of the student. Academic content is much more difficult at the middle or high school level, where students may be more inclined to drop out of the school system completely. If they have been isolated from content subjects because of time spent learning English, there will be gaps of knowledge in their schema. Teachers must consider this fact when establishing a foundation of prior knowledge before assigning an activity.

Vocabulary development also becomes an essential part of a bilingual student's learning development. Strategies to elicit meaning from words must be taught. Vocabulary development is essential in language learning, language processing, communication, reading comprehension, and understanding concepts that are content specific. Teachers should be aware that vocabulary is learned most successfully through personal experiences and interaction with the environment. Using this knowledge, teachers can provide an environment rich in language experiences. They can emphasize a hands-on environment where a love for learning is nurtured through concrete experiences. Word webs and word walls help clarify concepts.

Journal writing provides a vehicle for a true communicative situation while allowing the teacher to become more aware of a student's development. A journal

Working in a center, such as this art and writing center, can provide quiet time for a second language learner like this student.

© Photo by Jean-Claude LeJeune

kept by a bilingual student, explaining strategies used to elicit meaning from content material, can provide the teacher with valuable insights into the student and the learning process. Such insights can then be used as a basis for future instruction to aid other students. An excellent example of this is provided by the RESPONSE method as conceived by Jacobson (1989) and further tested by Farris, Fuhler, and Ginejko (1991).

Journals allow the teacher to learn what students already know (prior knowledge), how well they understood the concepts that have been discussed, and what misconceptions they may hold. Through journals, the teacher learns what students view as teaching approach strengths and weaknesses that the students believe affected their learning, how aware students are of themselves as learners, and whether they perceive any problems with the material. Journals provide a personal glimpse of each student's feelings and emotions and are a window to each student's progress.

Because learning is a social process, cooperative learning is a viable strategy to foster the development of pragmatic skills. The learner interacts with people of diverse backgrounds, and a sharing of ideas and self results in better understanding.

Interdisciplinary instruction means interaction with the printed word, with people, and with learning. It allows the development of skills necessary to lead a fulfilling life. It includes an exposure to language through model reading, book sharing, LEA (language experience approach), SSR (sustained silent reading) storytelling, student-authored books, literacy portfolios, brainstorming, choral reading, partner fluency reading, using visuals and manipulatives, and all the culturally sensitive strategies listed thus far in this chapter.

In the Classroom Mini Lesson

Thematic Unit Activities: Immigration (Grade 6)

1. Draw your family tree: use pictures, write down any anecdotes you know about any family members, write about which member had the greatest influence on you.
2. When and how did your family arrive? How did historical events affect your family (Gold Rush, Irish Potato Famine, Industrial Revolution, Great Depression, war)? What language did they speak? Create a profile of the year your family arrived in this country.
3. Describe your favorite family holiday. Does your family eat certain traditional food? Does your family have any sentimental treasures? Have you ever been to a family reunion? How would you plan one? Interview family members.
4. Make a welcome booklet for students arriving from different cultures. Share information they will need at school and in the neighborhood. Don't forget to include idioms (e.g., "Don't dis me, man"), phone numbers (e.g., doctors), stores (e.g., grocery store), and so on. Plan a one-day tour around your town: list places/times.
5. Make an ancestor doll; identify the doll by name, country, and interesting information.
6. Create a Venn diagram: Slavery/Indentured Servitude. Write three paragraphs: (1) Same, (2) Different, (3) Best.
7. Make a chart: Bread Basket listing country/name of bread/description (e.g., Mexico/tortilla); Fairy Tale listing title/country/hero/villain/magic/lesson (e.g., Sleeping Beauty); Folk Art listing country/name/ materials/directions (e.g., Polish/wycinaki); Science, Spices listing country/spice/plant/use (can be accompanied by a display of spices in small jars with holes in the lids for sampling); Math, Population listing who/when/how many/why; Art, Population (e.g., pictorial time line showing waves of immigration).
8. Put on an International Festival: organize each classroom into cooperative groups with each group representing a different country. Students make themselves passports (including a self-portrait) that can be stamped at each country visited. Culmination includes a dinner and entertainment representing a variety of countries. Remember to invite parents and guest speakers. Participants may receive an international cookbook compiled by the students.
9. Assemble a bulletin board: Flag display, e.g., world flag quilt; Hall of Fame, e.g., famous immigrants; Word display, e.g., words borrowed from other countries; Welcome, e.g., foreign words.
10. Take a field trip to an ethnic restaurant.

It also includes the addition of technology as a classroom tool to promote language, academic, and cognitive development for meaningful communication. Computers with microphones, laser discs, digital cameras, scanners, projectors, printers and tape recorders become part of the natural approach to acquiring English. Multimedia software and the Internet offer effective learning opportunities to acquire content. As in all classes, technology and the experiences it provides can motivate while engaging students in meaningful learning activities.

❧ *Social Studies for Bilingual Students*

This section provides examples of activities designed to encourage language and content learning. The activities are instructionally organized into a thematic unit. The purpose of including such a large number of activities is twofold. First, they offer variety to students and teachers; engaged learning incorporates choice. Second, even though not all the activities presented here could be used in any one thematic unit, they may, with minor changes, be applied to other thematic units.

The thematic unit selected is entitled "Pioneers." An extensive variety of published teacher-directed materials provide a wealth of ideas. A thematic unit on Mexican Americans was not selected because "culturally sensitive" does not mean one thematic unit a year per culture. Each thematic unit should contain opportunities for students to be proud of their own culture while respecting other cultures.

A. Prereading Activities/Cooperative Groups/Discussion
1. A *T* chart can be made by drawing one vertical line down the middle of a sheet of paper and one horizontal line across the top, leaving room above this for column headings only. In column 1, list all the items that are necessary for your life in this country. In column 2, list reasons why each item is necessary. This is a *T* chart.
2. Make a *T* chart. In column 1, list all the items you would take with you if you moved to another country. In column 2, list reasons why you would take each item. First list 12 items. Then eliminate 2 items. Now eliminate 5 items. Finally, choose the one item you would most want to take with you.
3. Make a *T* chart. In column 1, list all the dangers you encounter in a day. In column 2, list the solution to each danger. Make another *T* chart. In column 1, again list all the dangers you encounter in a day in this country. In column 2, list all the dangers you might encounter in a day in another country. Highlight dangers that are the same in both countries.
4. Make a *T* chart. In column 1, list all the forms of entertainment you enjoy. In column 2, list all the forms of entertainment your grandparents enjoyed at your age. Make another *T* chart. In column 1, again list all the forms of entertainment you enjoy in this country. In column 2, list all the forms of entertainment you might enjoy in another country. Highlight items that are the same in both columns.
5. Using a map of your choice, make a matrix of the regions (desert, mountains, plains, seacoast) to compare and contrast their geographic elements. Write a paragraph for each comparison or contrast point, explaining what life would be like in each region.
6. Using an appropriate map, locate where you live and a place you have visited or would like to visit. Make a *T* chart comparing and contrasting the two locations.
7. A K-W-L (what you know, what you want to know, what you learned) chart is made by dividing a sheet of paper into thirds by drawing two vertical lines and then drawing one horizontal line

across the top of the paper, leaving room only for the column headings (*K, W,* and *L*). Create a K-W-L chart entitled "Pioneer Life on the Prairie." Cite the sources of your information.

8. Create a K-W-L chart for Native Americans or Mexicans in southwestern regions before those regions became part of the United States. Cite the sources of your information.

9. Create a semantic map or web entitled "Types of Pioneers" (e.g., in space, in medicine, in westward movement, immigrants).

10. Create a semantic map about pioneers' schools, clothing, food, travel, homes, dangers, hardships.

11. Show the class an artifact such as a hand tool or piece of harness. Identify the item. Explain its use. Has the item been replaced? If so, what has replaced it?

12. Read "Western Wagons," a poem by Rosemary and Stephen Benét. As a class, give a choral reading of the poem.

13. Listen to *Where the Buffaloes Begin,* an award-winning picture book by Olaf Baker (1981). Then write about the book in your literature response journal or draw a picture about the book.

14. Search for evidence to validate or invalidate the right of Native Americans to receive compensation for the land that was taken from them. Debate the issue. (After the research is completed, students should draw slips from a hat to determine which side of the issue they are to defend. Emphasis should be placed on the difference between facts and opinions. The teacher may find it beneficial to videotape the debate and show the video at the end of the unit.)

15. Listen to a recording of "Polly-Wolly-Doodle" or a Native American musical recording. Do a square dance. Compare the types of instruments originally used to play these selections with instruments commonly used today.

16. After explaining historical fiction, the teacher writes down a class list of historical fiction titles that students have read.

17. Write what you think life was like for a Native American before the United States became a country.

18. Write what you think life was like for a pioneer on the prairie.

19. The teacher presents a book talk, introducing each literature book of the unit and including information about the author. Then the teacher asks students to predict how the cover or title might relate to the book.

20. Form small groups and with other members of your group, choose a book to read for the unit.

B. Postreading Activities/Discussion

1. Choose a pioneer (Daniel Boone, Davy Crockett, Buffalo Bill Cody, Jim Beckwourth, Kit Carson, Mary Ellen Lease, Carry Nation, Susan B. Anthony, Kate Shelby, or someone else of your choice). Research and then trace the route of the pioneer on a map with yarn or cutout covered wagons.

2. Research and write articles about why some cities grew more rapidly than others.

3. Write an essay comparing frontier prairie life to your own life. What aspects are similar? Which are different?

4. Make a diorama of a pioneer scene or a scene with characters from the literature book you read for this unit.

5. Would you like to have lived in the mid-1800s? Explain your answer.

6. Using reference materials, find out why the pioneers referred to warm days in autumn as Indian summer.

7. Put on a skit about going to school on the prairie.

8. Make soap and candles the way the pioneers did.

9. Follow prairie recipes for foods such as soda bread, johnnycake, and dried apple pie. Make butter by putting whipping cream in a jar and taking turns shaking it until it turns to butter. Invite visitors to a prairie lunch. Include both Native American and pioneer food.

10. Construct a model of a covered wagon, a pioneer home (cave, hut, log cabin, dugout home, sod house), or a pioneer or Native American village.

11. Using reference materials, find out what Illinois is often called. (Answer: the prairie state.)

12. Watch a movie about pioneer life *(Sarah, Plain and Tall; Son of the Morning Star; Dances with Wolves)*.

13. Many pioneer clothes were made from calico. The teacher brings in some calico material to show the class.

14. The teacher invites someone to demonstrate whittling for the class.

15. Reproduce a toy used on the prairie (button/string, rag doll), or demonstrate a pioneer game in the gym or outside if possible.

16. Take a field trip to such places as a historical museum, a farm, or an antique shop.

17. One representative from each group reading a Laura Ingalls Wilder book meet together to construct a time line of Laura's life based on the events depicted in the books the various groups have read.

18. Make a Venn diagram (overlapping circles) identifying the jobs girls and boys did on the prairie or do today in this country or another country.

19. Play the computer game *Oregon Trail Deluxe.*

20. Gather wild flowers and grasses. Take them home and hang them up to dry. Use them to make a winter decoration. Discuss their uses as sickness remedies.

21. Start a seashell collection *(Sarah, Plain and Tall)*.

22. Pretend you are placing an ad in the newspaper for a wife and mother or a husband and father. Write down what you would say. As a class, create an entire newspaper that could have been published in the 1800s.

23. Make a list of some things that are often found where you live but are rare in other parts of the country. Choose one of the items and write a descriptive paragraph about it.

24. Pretend you are a travel agent. Write a travel brochure about the prairie, state, or country you have visited.

25. The teacher invites an artist to come to class to demonstrate how to make Native American or Mexican pottery. Then the teacher arranges to have a pottery wheel and clay in the classroom so that the students can experiment with them.

26. The teacher brings in collections of poetry by Mexican American and Native American poets and shares their poetry through themes such as nature, people, and so on.

27. The teacher assigns a different Native American tribe to each group. Members of each group construct a bulletin board display about aspects of their particular tribe, highlighting famous battles, specific cultural differences, shelter, food, and religious beliefs.

28. Pretend your literature group is an advertising department. Your job is to devise an advertising campaign to promote your book. Present your campaign to other classes. Ask students to choose anonymously which groups' books they would buy on the basis of the campaigns presented to them.

29. Produce a book jacket for the next printing of the book you read for this unit.

30. Make a poster, mural, collage, mobile, TV screen with rolled paper pictures, or bulletin board advertisement for the literature book you read for this unit.

31. The teacher explains to students that many Native American tribes depended on the buffalo for their survival and that the Native Americans prided themselves on using all of the animal. Then the teacher asks students to research how the Native Americans used the buffalo and instructs each group to make a drawing of the animal, label the parts, and indicate the use(s) of each part.

32. Make a family tree of the characters in the literature book you read for this unit. How does it compare to your family tree?

33. Make a nine-patch quilt.

34. Make puppets and act out your favorite part of the literature book you read for this unit.

35. Choose your favorite part of the literature book you read for this unit and make it into a "big book." Then share it with another class.

36. Complete your K-W-L chart.

37. Make a sociogram (web of interacting feelings showing arrows from each character to the main character and returning arrows and identifying each arrow with an emotion) for Laura Ingalls or any other main character in the book you read for this unit.

38. Conduct a trial for Custer. Students volunteer for the roles of judge, prosecuting attorney, defense attorney, jury members, witnesses, and the defendant. Attorneys prepare evidence and interview witnesses before the trial begins. Witnesses might view the movie *Son of the Morning Star* or rely on research for data.

39. Write an epilogue to the book you read.

40. Make a "realia" box or time capsule. Collect real items important to the literature book you read for this unit.

41. Write several diary entries that might have been written by the main character of the literature book you read for this unit.
42. Make a crossword puzzle or word search using the vocabulary of the literature book you read for this unit.
43. Create a cassette of poems to accompany this unit. Make an illustrated book to be viewed while listening to the cassette.
44. Create and illustrate a poem.
45. Write a letter to your favorite author.

Chapter Summary

Integrated instruction can reflect the effective inclusion of culture in educational instruction. It is a bridge that connects the students and their individual cultures to an understanding of a cross-cultural society. Our national identity is dependent on successful learning by a culturally diverse population. Good teachers facilitate learning by providing opportunities for active learning by both monolingual and bilingual children. Teachers who appreciate the unique abilities of each student also recognize the importance of culture in self-development.

Children's Books

Baker, O. 1981. *Where the buffaloes begin.* Illus. S. Gammell. New York: Penguin-Viking.
MacLachlan, P. 1985. *Sarah, plain and tall.* New York: HarperCollins.

Web Sites

http://www.ncbe.gwu.edu/
The National Clearinghouse for Bilingual Education
http://www.ncbe.gwu.edu/miscpubs/jeilms/vol14/index.htm
The Journal of Educational Issues of Language Minority Students Winter 1994, Volume 14, published by The Bilingual Education Teacher Preparation Program, Boise State University, Boise, Idaho 83725, (208) 385-1194
http://www.cal.org/
Center for Applied Linguistics
http://www.inform.umd.edu/CampusInfo/Committees/Assoc/NAME/
The National Association For Multicultural Education
http://www.ed.gov/offices/OBEMLA/
Office of Bilingual Education and Minority Language Affairs
http://www.tesol.edu/
Teachers of English to Speakers of Other Languages
http://nces.ed.gov/
The National Center for Education Statistics (NCES)
http://www.ets.org/research/
Educational Testing Service

http://www.redmundial.com/ben/k_12.html
  Bilingual ESL network links to K-12 resources
http://www.eslcafe.com/
  Dave Sperling's ESL Care on the Web for teachers and students
http://www.elfs.com/
  English Learning Funsite
http://www.kids-space.org/
  International Kids Space
http://www.estrellita.com/bil.html
  Bilingual Education Resources on the Net
http://curry.edschool.Virginia.EDU/go/multicultural/
  Multicultural Pavilion at the University of Virginia

References

Acuña, R. 1988. *Occupied America: A history of Chicanos.* New York: Harper and Row.

Banks, J. A. and C. A. Banks, 1997. *Teaching strategies for ethnic studies.* 6th Ed. Boston: Allyn and Bacon.

Cook, L., and P. C. Gonzales. 1994. Helping ESL students in English-only classes. *Reading Today* 12 (2): 25.

Cummins, J. 1981. *Bilingualism and minority language children.* Toronto: Ontario Institute for Studies in Education.

Cummins, J. 1984. *Bilingual and special education: Issues in assessment and pedagogy.* Clevedon, England: Multicultural Matters.

Farris, P. J., C. Fuhler, and M. L. Ginejko. 1991. Reading, writing, discussing: An interactive approach to content areas. *Reading Horizons* 31 (4): 261–71.

Feinberg, R. C., and C. C. Morencia. 1998. Bilingual Education an overview. *Social Education* 62 (7): 427–31.

Jacobson, J. M. 1989. Response: An interactive study technique. *Reading Horizons* 29 (2): 86–92.

Janzen, R. 1994. Melting pot or mosaic? *Educational Leadership* 51 (8): 9–11.

Kanellos, N. 1990. *A history of Hispanic theatre in the United States: Origins to 1940.* Austin: University of Texas Press.

Keefe, S. E., and A. M. Padilla. 1987. *Chicano ethnicity.* Albuquerque: University of New Mexico Press.

Lim, H. L., and D. J. Watson. 1993. Whole language content classes for second-language learners. The *Reading Teacher* 46:384–93.

National Council for the Social Studies. 1992. The Columbia Quincentenary Position Statement. *Social Studies and the Young Learner* 4, n.p.

Pang, V. O. 1994. Why do we need this class? Multicultural education for teachers. *Phi Delta Kappan* 76 (4): 289–92.

Parker, W. C., and Jarolimek, J. 1997. *A sampler of curriculum standards for social studies: Expectations of excellence.* Englewood Cliffs, NJ: Merrill/Prentice-Hall.

Porter, R. P. 1990. *Forked tongue: The politics of bilingual education.* New York: Basic Books.

Rigg, P., and V. G. Allen, eds. 1989. *When they don't all speak English.* Urbana, IL: National Council of Teachers of English.

Sutton, C. 1989. Helping the non-native English speaker with reading. *The Reading Teacher* 49 (9): 684.

Name—Title Index

Subject Index